Kiel○
Eutin○
Lubeck○
○Hamburg

○Oldenburg
○Bremen

POLAND

○Hannover
○Brunswick
Hildesheim○

●BERLIN

E R M A N Y

Göttingen○
Cassel○
Sondershausen ○Halle
Leipzig
○Oschatz
Dresden
Breslau

Erfurt
Eisenach○ ○Weimar
Gotha ○Freiberg
Chemnitz

sen ○
○Meiningen
Frankfurt am M. ○Hildburgshausen

Hanau
Offenbach Zeil Bayreuth ○Eger
dt ○Aschaffenburg Marienbad
○PRAGUE

Würzburg Bamberg
nheim ○Erlangen CZECHOSLOVAKIA
delberg ○Amorbach ○Amberg
Nuremberg ○Taus
sruhe Ansbach

○Ludwigsburg
en ○Stuttgart
en

○Augsburg
○Munich VIENNA
●
ausen ○Baden
Constanz
ich Lindau Salzburg
Winterthür

D A U S T R I A
wald ITALY
H.J.B.

CARL MARIA
VON
WEBER

By the same Author

SIX GREAT COMPOSERS
CONCISE OXFORD DICTIONARY OF OPERA
(*in collaboration with Harold Rosenthal*)

CARL MARIA VON WEBER

A portrait by Ferdinand Schimon

CARL MARIA

VON

WEBER

BY

JOHN WARRACK, *1928–*

THE MACMILLAN COMPANY

NEW YORK

Printed in Great Britain

TO CATKIN

She is the clernesse and the verray lyght
That in this derke world me wynt and ledeth.

CHAUCER: *The Legend of Good Women*

CONTENTS

ILLUSTRATIONS

PREFACE

ON THE afternoon of 15th December 1844, Richard Wagner addressed the group of mourners gathered in Dresden for the reinterment of Weber's remains. It was a deeply affecting occasion, the return to Germany after eighteen years of the composer whose life had been so closely bound up with the movement towards national independence; and Wagner knew how to play upon his hearers' sympathies. 'There never lived a more German composer than you,' he declared, going on in much quoted words to assert that while the Englishman might honour Weber and the Frenchman might admire him, only the German could truly love him. Certainly in Germany Weber has always been held in an affection of almost personal intensity, touching as he does on so much in the common experience of his countrymen; but his appeal to musicians and music-lovers all over the world has not lessened with the years, nor has his influence on composers of succeeding generations been confined to his own country. Berlioz, Liszt and Debussy were among his greatest admirers and beneficiaries.

Yet while his life and work have been documented with great thoroughness in Germany, comparatively little has appeared elsewhere. England, the country which approached him with the invitation that led to *Oberon* and in whose capital he was to die, has produced fewer studies than his accepted significance would warrant. Apart from the inadequate version of Max Maria von Weber's life of his father and Julius Benedict's charming little memoir, all that has appeared in book form has been William Saunders's brief survey in the 'Master Musicians' series. An American work by Richard and Lucy Poate Stebbins, *Enchanted Wanderer*, is based on more thorough, professional research than its title and style might suggest, but is not intended to do more than recount for the general reader the colourful story of Weber's life without reference to his music. None of these books is currently in print.

In attempting a fuller study of Weber's life and work, I have tried not only to discuss the music in some depth but also to suggest how important it is to an understanding of what went into the later achievements of Romanticism.

I have also hoped to show how the most representative musician of his age responded to a Europe struggling to be reborn in the chaotic aftermath of the French Revolution and the turmoil of the Napoleonic Wars. It was a time when, perhaps more than at any other phase of European history, the arts spoke for a broad mass of people; and it was one when a significant proportion of poets, writers and painters looked to music as the ideal art. Weber at once took an essential part of his character from the period and helped to give it a distinctive artistic colour. If he lacked a Wagnerian force of personality to compel everything around him to his own use, his gentleness, his sharp wit, his acute perception of the world as a colourful tragi-comic drama make him a particularly human and diverse composer; and his genius for dramatizing experience of almost any kind into music ensured that he became an exceptionally lucid mirror of an age. Consequently it has been essential to deal with the music as part of Weber's life, as he came to write each work, and not to try and discuss it as if it were some activity totally divorced from the man he was and the world he lived in. I have made major breaks in the narrative only in the case of the most important operas, over each of which I have taken a chapter so as to examine how, from their literary origins, they were shaped into a vehicle for Weber's particular kind of dramatic music. To facilitate reference to individual sections, I have sometimes repeated or re-emphasized facts; but each work is intended to be viewed in the context of a continuously developed theme.

In referring to Weber's works, I have made use of the numbers allotted in chronological order of composition by F. W. Jähns in his monumental thematic catalogue, *Carl Maria von Weber in seinen Werken* (1871). Though subsequent research has filled in some gaps left by Jähns and corrected some errors, the book remains authoritative and provides a system of reference much more convenient than the opus numbers. These are incomplete, confused and contradictory, Weber and his various publishers having often taken different action over the numbering of a work or omitted to number it altogether. Since opus numbers are still often attached to a good many of the works, I have included those in conventional use; but there is a strong case for going over to general use of J. numbers.

I have incurred many debts of gratitude during the preparation of this book. The following libraries were generously forthcoming with facilities for working, with access to sources and with invaluable help and advice: the Music Department of the German State Library, Berlin; the Library of the Rudolfinum, Prague; the Music Department of the National Museum, Prague; the Leningrad Public Library; the Library of the Royal College of Music, London; the Department of Printed Books and Department of Manuscripts of the British Museum, London; the London Library; and the College of Arms. I am also grateful for help and advice on specific points to Mr. Peter Branscombe, Mr. Julian Bream, Dr. Wilfried Brennecke, Mr.

Oliver Davies, Dr. Karl-Heinz Köhler, the late Dr. Joseph Löwenbach, Mr. David Lloyd-Jones, Mr. Richard Macnutt, Dr. Jaroslav Mastalíř, Miss Joan Trimble, Frau Friederieke von Wedelstädt, Mr. Harold Rosenthal and Dr. Hans Schnoor; and for medical opinion on the course of Weber's illnesses to Dr. John Greenwood Gant. Mr. Andrew Porter read the entire typescript and contributed a wealth of perceptive and scholarly comment. My thanks are also due to the Editors of *The Musical Times*, *Opera* and *Opera Annual* for allowing me to use material that originally appeared in their pages; to *The Sunday Telegraph*, as music critic of which I was enabled to undertake essential journeys to Germany, Czechoslovakia and Russia; to the BBC and *The Gramophone* for the loan of scores and records; to Miss Tessa Trappes-Lomax for adding much useful comment to her work as typist; to Mr. F. T. Dunn for preparing the Index; and to my wife for helping with the catalogue and for enduring a time-consuming task.

Milton Abbas   JOHN WARRACK
October 1967

MONEY VALUES

The values given are only approximate and are stated for the purchasing power of American money in the early nineteenth century. To have an approximation of what these values would be today the American equivalents need to be multiplied by ten.

$$4 \text{ Pfennig} = 1 \text{ Kreuzer (about } \tfrac{1}{2} \text{ cent)}$$
$$3 \text{ Kreuzer} = 1 \text{ Groschen (about 2 cents)}$$
$$60 \text{ Kreuzer} = 1 \text{ Gulden (about 40 cents)}$$
$$90 \text{ Kreuzer} = 1 \text{ Reichsthaler (about 60 cents)}$$

Gold
$$4\tfrac{1}{2} \text{ Gulden} = 1 \text{ Ducat (about \$2.25)}$$
$$7\tfrac{1}{2} \text{ Gulden} = 1 \text{ Pistole (about \$4.00)}$$
$$8 \text{ Gulden} = 1 \text{ Friedrich d'or (about \$4.00)}$$
$$9 \text{ Gulden} = 1 \text{ Carolin (about \$5.00)}$$

The French Louis d'or was worth rather more than 2 Ducats, i.e. about \$5.00.

ABBREVIATIONS

AMZ	*Allgemeine Musikalische Zeitung.* Leipzig, 1798–1848.
BM	British Museum.
DM	*Die Musik.* Berlin and Leipzig, 1901–15; Stuttgart, 1922–43.
Grove	*Grove's Dictionary of Music and Musicians*, 5th edn, ed. by Eric Blom (1954).
Hirschberg	Leopold Hirschberg: *Reliquienschrein des Meisters Carl Maria von Weber* (1926).
J	F. W. Jähns: *Carl Maria von Weber in seinen Werken. Chronologisch-thematisches Verzeichniss seiner sämmtlichen Compositionen* (1871).
Kaiser	Georg Kaiser: *Sämtliche Schriften von Carl Maria von Weber* (1908).
M&L	*Music and Letters.* London, from 1920.
MMW	Max Maria von Weber: *Carl Maria von Weber. Ein Lebensbild* (3 vols., 1864–6).
MQ	*The Musical Quarterly.* New York, from 1915.
MT	*The Musical Times.* London, from 1844.
NZfM	*Neue Zeitschrift für Musik.* Leipzig, 1834–1902; Mainz, from 1951.
RCM	Royal College of Music.
Weberiana	F. W. Jähns: *Weberiana.* The comprehensive collection of MSS, documents, printed scores, books, pictures, mementoes and other relevant material catalogued and lodged with other books and MSS in the *Weber-Gedächtniszimmer* in the Music Department of the State Library, Berlin.
WG	*Carl Maria von Weber: Musikalische Werke. Erste Kritische Gesamtausgabe* (2 vols. only completed, 1926).
WoO	Werk ohne Opuszahl.

INTRODUCTION

> Men are governed by many things, climate, religion, laws, maxims of government, examples of things past, customs, manners; from all of which is derived a general spirit.
>
> MONTESQUIEU

ON 17TH AUGUST 1786, three months before Weber was born, Frederick the Great died in his armchair at Sanssouci. He left Prussia dominating the loose confederation of some three hundred independent sovereignties, ecclesiastical states and free cities that formed the notoriously ill-named Holy Roman Empire. Germany, as a single political unit, was still eighty-five years from realization, and a political concept of much complexity; for even when the term 'German Empire' officially came in with the Hohenzollerns in 1871, divisions remained as legacy of the ancient tribal separations. Most of the major issues in German history have always in some way been connected with unification; and at no time was this longing for unity deeper or more widespread than at the turn into the nineteenth century. The threat of Napoleon proceeded to bring to boiling point nationalist feelings that were already simmering under Prussia's domination; and no study of the Romantics and their most representative composer has proper meaning unless seen against the background of this aspiration. For with the body politic in a state of decay, it was to the poets, writers, philosophers and musicians of Germany that the initiative passed and from them that the age took its characteristic colour.

Frederick's last-minute creation of a *Fürstenbund*, an association of princes for mutual protection, was inadequate to confer strength on the Empire's ailing frame, which now, after almost a thousand years, was tottering to its grave. Its bodily parts remained, preserving their outward shape though scarred by disease and senility; it was still capable of a gesture in imitation of the old grandeur, as Mozart found when he visited Frankfurt for the Coronation of Leopold II as Holy Roman Emperor in 1790; but its authority was enfeebled, its energy spent. Prussia went rapidly to seed under Friedrich Wilhelm II; and the chaos of the other states was exemplified in South Germany, where Carl Friedrich of Baden lamented, 'My neighbour of Württemberg[1] does his best to ruin his land and I do my best to improve mine; but neither of us succeeds.' The Electorates were often in the hands of reactionary and corrupt bishops; the Free Cities, especially Bremen, Lübeck and above all Hamburg, fared a little better; while the Imperial

---

[1] King Friedrich: see Chapter 4.

Knights, an absurd, archaic survival, lorded it over diminutive territories that could not support themselves and indeed often became derelict. The Empire was based politically on an intricate and rusty set of anachronisms, economically on feudalist agriculture and a primitive industry still controlled by mediaeval guilds.

Yet if Germany was politically decrepit, her intellectual life was at fever pitch. The Empire could, it is true, boast a few famous institutions: Hanover supported the University of Göttingen, Saxony encouraged the book trade of Leipzig and in 1765 had founded Europe's first geological school in the Academy of Mines at Freiberg. But these few signs of grace gave no adequate representation of the tremendous throb of individual energy beneath. 'While political life was backward and anaemic,' writes G. P. Gooch, 'a vigorous intellectual activity held out the promise of better days. Wolff and Lessing, Moses Mendelssohn and Nicolai, the leaders of the *Aufklärung* . . . exhorted their countrymen to use their reason without fear; and deeper notes were struck by Kant and Herder, Hamann and Jacobi. The Augustan age of German literature opened with Klopstock. Lessing and Wieland, Kleist and Gleim, Goethe and Schiller, Lenz and Klinger, Bürger and Voss, Thummer and Salzmann, Kotzebue and Iffland poured forth a flood of poems, satires, novels and dramas, which created and delighted a reading public.'[1] The very lack of a centralized society favoured then, as now, the cultivation of scattered, mutually exclusive intellectual groups, as Mme. de Staël observed: 'Since there is no capital where the social life of Germany gathers, the spirit of Society has little effect; the empire of taste and the force of ridicule have no influence. Most writers and intellectuals work in solitude.'[2] New periodicals circulated among these groups, reflecting the growth of a fresh critical spirit which preferred the individual and his own judgement against the mentally inflexible state.

The first target of this new questioning was religious: after Lutheran dogmatism had yielded to the extravagances of Pietism, and Pietism to rationalism, it was now the turn of the human heart. But the political course it also, more significantly, took was noted by Goethe in 1790: 'Knights, robbers, an honest Tiers Etat and an infamous nobility—such are the ingredients of our novels and plays during the last ten years.' The theatre, as usual, gave warning of the attack to come; the aristocracy, as usual, either ignored it or hoped by tolerance and patronage to draw its teeth. The ferocity of the attacks on the social and political establishment makes surprising reading to those who fancy that theirs alone is the age of fresh, rebellious outspokenness.

Yet though there was a ferment of ideas, a solid tradition of political thinking to organize it was lacking. For all the brilliance of the opposition,

[1] G. P. Gooch: *Germany and the French Revolution*, p. 18 (1920).
[2] Mme. de Staël: *De l'Allemagne* (1810).

headed as it was by such as Schiller, Lessing and Wieland, with the voice of Kant in the background, it was left to a lawyer's son and a journalist to rally the attack. Friedrich Carl Moser's *Der Herr und der Diener* drew critical attention to the problem of rulership; but more effective still was the journal founded by a certain Schlözer which scourged the nobles so relentlessly that its editor had every need of the protection guaranteed him by the government of Hamburg. The longing for a new age of brotherhood also found expression in secret societies—principally the Freemasons, who numbered among them Goethe, Herder, Lessing, Wieland and Mozart, perhaps also Voltaire; and the Illuminati, an exceedingly quaint cult founded by an idealistic charlatan, Adam Weishaupt. Each was to varying degrees oppressed. A few conservative spirits hoped to revive the failing Empire by infusing fresh vigour into old customs; this right wing to the movement of unrest was headed by Herder, but the left could boast Goethe, Schiller and Lessing and, behind them, the general weight of feeling. The whole of German idealism is connected not to a false classicism but to the Romantic movement, and takes its theoretical origins from Kant, Fichte and Schlegel. Kant's great *Critiques* are of political significance only in their influence on those writers whose voices were rousing the nation; Fichte, on the other hand, provided a direct trumpet call. He is a founder of German nationalism, and if his exhortations have a distasteful ring in view of subsequent German history, they contain at least one sound observation (as Weber and many another artist was to demonstrate) in claiming that an essential part of the German spirit lay with her simple burghers. When we acknowledge Wagner's genius in cultivating the Romantic traits of subjective eroticism, heroic legend and religious quest, we should not forget *Die Meistersinger von Nürnberg*.

There were, further, three major outside influences on this intellectual ferment. One was Rousseau, whose writings caused him virtually to be deified in Germany. Equally important, as witness of theory put into heroic action, was the American War of Independence, in which France had taken an active part against England. But crowning everything was the marvellous example of the French Revolution. It is impossible to exaggerate the emotion with which the news of this was received in Germany. Not even the Terror could stem the tide of emotion. Some excused what was happening with the argument that only fire could cleanse a plague house; others retained faith in the drama of revolution while deploring the clumsiness of the performers; a group of conservatives, such as the poet Gleim and the famous traveller Carsten Niebuhr, mistrusted the whole thing and blamed the secret societies; few, in a Europe inexperienced in revolution, were percipient enough to see that what had happened in France (as well as the reactions to it) was to be an example for well over a century to come. On the whole, the aristocrats naturally feared the revolution, the burghers applauded and were then shocked by the turn of events, intellectuals managed to formulate arguments to justify their faith, and the peasants began wondering if they too might take matters into their own hands. In a few cases they actually did so briefly; but admiration did not generally inspire imitation. As a mere bundle of states, Germany could not easily take national action; feudalism, though incompetent, was seldom as oppressive as in France; and as Mme. de Staël observed, 'The Germans combine the greatest audacity of thought with the most obedient character.'[1] Respect for religious and civic traditions held good.

But the events following 1789 left Germany permanently changed. Her political decline was hastened: after the Congress of Rastadt ceded the left bank of the Rhine, Görres wrote his sarcastic obituary of the invalid who had lingered too long:

> On 30th December 1797, at three in the afternoon, the Holy Roman Empire, supported by the Sacraments, passed away peacefully at Regensburg at the age of 955, in consequence of senile debility and an apoplectic stroke. The deceased was born at Verdun in the year 842, and educated at the Court of Charles the Simple and his successors. The young prince was taught piety by the Popes, who canonized him in his lifetime. But his tendency to a sedentary life, combined with a zeal for religion, undermined his health. His head became visibly weaker, until at last he went mad in the Crusades. Frequent bleedings and careful diet restored him; but, reduced to a shadow, the invalid tottered on through the centuries till violent haemorrhage occurred in the Thirty Years' War. Hardly had he recovered when the French arrived, and a stroke put an end to his sufferings. He kept himself unstained by the *Aufklärung*, and bequeathed the left bank of the Rhine to the French Republic.

The way was open for an upsurge of national and individual emotion in which poets and musicians, now replacing Church and State, set about voicing the aspirations of an emergent middle class—a major part of the movement of feeling we call Romanticism. There could be no more exciting time into which might be born a composer with an inherited love of the theatre, a naturally acute sensibility, an instinct for his country's scenery, legends and hopes, and a distinct personal flamboyance. His failings, some of them purely of physique, were to prevent the realization of all the promise stored up in him: he was a slow developer, and all his music is early music. But his very weaknesses give Weber something of his essential virtues; and though he cannot, like Beethoven, transcend his age in solitary greatness, by being so intimately bound up with it he expresses it more completely, both helping to form it and taking his characteristic colour from it. Germany was rediscovering its essential spirit; like a well-tuned violin string, which has lain slack and has not yet tautened to hysterical pitch and finally snapped,

---

[1] Mme. de Staël: *op. cit.*

it was in a state of ideal tension, to the skilled musician giving forth its truest note.

✳

Weber's son Max Maria always believed that the family was descended from one Johann Baptist Weber, a Doctor of Jurisprudence born in about 1550 and heir to considerable estates in the Pisemberg and Krumbach districts of Austria. In 1622 he was given a barony by Ferdinand II, becoming a Lower Austrian government chancellor in 1642. His only direct descendant was a daughter, though his younger brothers probably left landed property outside Austria; one of these, Joseph Franz Weber, was supposedly the composer's ancestor. Traces of this line disappeared in the Thirty Years' War, to re-emerge in the Upper Rhineland in the War of the Austrian Succession.

These beliefs were repeated from Max Maria[1] in all Weber literature until 1913, when Arthur Schurig pointed out the unreliability of Max Maria's work.[2] The question was taken up by Rudolf Blume,[3] who cast doubts upon the descent from Johann Baptist and suggested that Weber's grandfather Fridolin had been superintendent of the Imperial armoury at Freiburg and later steward at Schönau, marrying first Katharina Baumgartner and then Eva Maria Schlar. There matters rested until what seems to be the final truth was established in a genealogical study by Friedrich Hefele.[4]

Hefele discovered that the background of the Weber family was considerably more humble than the composer and his son had been led to believe. Their earliest known ancestor seems to have been one Hans Georg Weber, originally a miller's boy at Stetten. In 1678 he married a widow, Kunigunde Has; she died in 1699 and he shortly married Maria von Stein (possibly his employer's *schöne Müllerin* daughter). Most of his fifteen children died early: of them three were named Anna, two Fridolin, three Maria, three Johann Jacob and two Joseph. Hans Georg is known to have been a godfather 23 times over, a sure sign of respect and popularity. He died in 1704, leaving, among his surviving children, a son Fridolin, born in 1691. Intended for the priesthood, Fridolin was sent at the age of 15 to study at the Ludovica Albertinus University in Freiburg; hence he graduated as *baccalaureus philosophiae*. His first position was as tutor to the son of the local baron of Stetten, Franz Ignaz von Schönau. It was a difficult post: the boy suffered from persistent ill-health, and despite every care from Fridolin, who sat with him day and night, he died in 1712. On top of this disaster the family

[1] MMW, Vol. I, pp. 4–6.
[2] Schurig: *Wolfgang Amadeus Mozart* (1913).
[3] Blume: *Freiburg im Breisgau, der Geburtsort der Gemahlin und des Vaters Carl Maria von Webers* (1917).
[4] Hefele: *Die Vorfahren Carl Maria von Webers* (1926).

fell seriously into debt, and Fridolin was compelled to look for a new post. This he found in 1721 as a steward in Zell, where he married a barber's daughter from Freiburg, the 27-year-old Maria Eva Schlar.

This marriage brought into the family some French blood, a fact which has been held responsible for the brilliant element in Weber's music. Maria Eva's father was one Lorenz Chelar from Gingham (probably either Guignen in the Dep. Ille-et-Vilaine in Lower Brittany or Guingamp in the Dep. Côtes du Nord). Freiburg contained at that time a considerable French minority: the scene of many battles in the Thirty Years' War, it had changed hands often, been the subject of a particularly strong migration in the years 1677 to 1697, and finally been relinquished by the French at the Peace of Aix-la-Chapelle in 1744. It was about the year 1695 that Lorenz Chelar had come to find work as a barber. He married Susanna Oxenriedin, whose family has been traced back to the last third of the 16th century and to Swiss stock from the French-speaking part of the Canton of Basel. Maria Eva, the youngest of his three children, was born on 6th April 1698, less than a month after her father's death. She was brought up by her mother, who by the end of the year had married another French barber, Michael Jullin.

When the War of the Polish Succession broke out in 1733, the Baron asked Fridolin to take the lease of his estate; and despite the difficulty of the times, this Fridolin agreed to do. The struggle between the great powers flowed over Fridolin's new estates, which suffered equally from the Imperial and the French troops. The people of Zell refused to pay their contribution to the French, who promptly arrested a number of hostages, among them Fridolin, whom they held prisoner for thirty-eight days until payment was made. But his freedom was bought hard: the difficulties arising from the debt caused friction with the Baron that developed into a series of legal wrangles not finally settled until 1750, ruining Fridolin in the process. In 1732 he requested citizenship of Freiburg, and here he lived until his death in 1754.

Fridolin's children were five in number—Maria Johanna Adelheid (1729?–1807), Fridolin II (1733?–1779), Franz Anton, father of the composer (1734?–1812), Maria Eva Magdalena (1739–1791), and Johann Nepomuk Fidel Felizian (1740– ?). There was a tradition in the family that Fridolin I had played the violin and the organ and was a gifted singer; certainly a musical strain revealed itself in Fridolin II, who also had a good voice and who played the violin well. His love of music led him to leave his steward-ship for a musical post in Mannheim, where he was pianist, perhaps had a job as bass player, and is known to have been especially busy as a copyist and choral répétiteur. His daughters Josepha, Aloisia and Sophie were singers—Aloisia was already famous at 15 and became prima donna at the Vienna Hofoper when 19—while the fourth sister, Mozart's future wife Constanze, was also a singer and a pianist. Nothing is known of Fridolin I's four other children, except Franz Anton. Not only the musical gifts but a strain of restlessness began to show in him: Hans Georg had been the miller's boy whose *Lust* was traditionally *das Wandern*; Fridolin I spent most of his life on the move; and in Franz Anton this, combined with a distinct instability of character, degenerated into a fecklessness in which the family intelligence became little more than sharpness of wit.[1]

There is, so far, no question of the prefix 'von'. Certainly Max Maria genuinely believed that his family was noble, and quotes a deed of 1738 whereby Carl VI bestowed on 'the brothers Fridolin and Xaver Weber' the 1622 barony conferred on Dr. Johann Baptist Weber. This has crept into at least two German heraldic books,[2] which claim that the brothers Weber took Dr. Weber's arms, a divided shield with on the left a silver moon on a gold ground, on the right a golden star on a blue ground. On the other hand there is no trace of this in other volumes. In any case, Fridolin I knew nothing of this. His son Fridolin II was, it is true, described as *nobilis* on his marriage in 1756; but *nobilis*, in an age replete with titles, was not at all the same thing as *adelig*. Councillors and professors were addressed as *hochedelgeboren*, upper class students as *wohledel und wohlgelehrt*, distinguished citizens as *edel* or *wohledel* and so forth—courtesy titles of the kind that still survive in the formal addressing of letters in various countries, as with our own 'Esq.' The deed of 1738 has not proved traceable. There are many noble Webers in lists of the Austrian nobility, but no deeds for these Webers; while as for the coat of arms—this was affected by many citizens.

But upon the usages concerning coats of arms a crucial point hangs. In 1743 Fridolin Weber I signed a receipt for 666 thalers, and in the following year a letter, using a seal. The helmet shown on this is the *Stechhelm*, the closed steel helmet (shown sideways) resembling the English squire's helm, and not the *Spangenhelm*, the barred helm reserved in England for the sovereign and princes of the royal blood. Originally a helmet was indeed a sign of nobility. But in the Holy Roman Empire, 'the pressure for the use of the helmet was great on the part of those burghers whose arms were unrecognized as having any nobiliary or patrician value at all . . . Owing to this pressure for the use of a helmet, a stage was reached in some realms when the non-nobles could not be denied the use of a helmet and so we find them being

[1] Carl Maria passed this wandering strain on to his son, and biographer, Max Maria (1822–1881), a gifted writer who joined the Rhine and Saxon Railways and rose to be a Ministry official. He visited North Africa, Vienna and Berlin, later travelling as foreign trade representative in England, France, Scandinavia and North America, whence he was recalled in 1880. He inherited none of his father's musical gifts, though he was enough of a Weber to produce a work on railways and nationalism (1876). Carl Maria's younger son, Alexander Heinrich Victor Maria (1825–1844) was a promising painter whose work includes a good drawing of Max Maria.

[2] *Knechtes Deutsches Adelslexicon* and *Stammbuch des blühenden und abgestorbenen Adels in Deutschland*.

allowed a closed helmet, while an open helmet was considered the prerogative of the noblesse.'[1] Since the sixteenth century, in fact, the *Spangenhelm* had been used by nobles and doctors, the *Stechhelm* by burghers; and with the decline of heraldry in the eighteenth century, even these distinctions were often ignored. It follows, then, that if the Webers had really been noble, they would never have used the lower-ranking *Stechhelm*, as Fridolin did on his seals. The Breisgau ancestors of Carl Maria knew nothing of any nobility in their family; nor did Fridolin II, who only a few months before his death, in 1779, signed himself Hofmusikus Fridolin Weber (without a 'von'). Everything, then, points to Franz Anton as the culprit; and certainly the pretence at nobility accords entirely with his character.

Franz Anton Weber was, as we have seen, Fridolin I's second son. He was born not in Freiburg, as is often declared, but in Zell.[2] He began his career as a Lieutenant in the Palatinate Army, fought in the Seven Years' War, and may have been wounded during Frederick the Great's famous lightning victory at Rossbach over superior Allied numbers on 5th November 1757; he is said to have carried his violin into battle with him. Max Maria, however, states that he was already at Hildesheim by then, engaged to be married to the daughter of his chief. Certainly in the same year, according to the State archives of Hanover, the Elector Clemens August of Cologne (who at that time occupied various sees including that of Hildesheim) gave by decree to Maria Anna Fumetti, the eldest daughter of the Court financial councillor, the stewardship of Steuerwald; this carried with it the understanding that she should marry someone of good report so that he might be appointed steward. Franz Anton married her in 1758; three months later he wrote to the Elector, thanking him for the appointment and requesting also the directorship of the establishment at Hildesheim. To this the Elector agreed, in the face of objections from Hildesheim itself that nothing was known of Franz Anton's capabilities; and later he intervened to insist on the appointment becoming effective forthwith. Franz Anton retained the post for ten years. He was eventually dismissed in 1768 by Clemens August's successor, Bishop Friedrich Wilhelm, with an annual pension of 200 Reichsthaler for the education of his children. The grounds for his dismissal are not known, though in a later decree the Bishop speaks of them as just; nor is there other evidence of his stewardship except that he quarrelled with his inferiors. But even Max Maria records Franz Anton's habit of playing his violin on long

[1] Robert Gayre: *The Nature of Arms*, p. 119 (1961).

[2] The Freiburg University register gives Franz Anton as having been born there; but there is no entry in any church register, and in any case Fridolin was steward in Zell from 1721 to 1738. Franz Anton's younger sister and brother (born in 1739 and 1740) are both entered in a Freiburg church register. The Zell church registers have been burnt, so that no exact date for his birth is available. Carl Maria never refers to his father's birthday nor mentions it, like others, in his diary, although he was a dutiful son. Max Maria presumed that the date was 1734.

walks when the papers on his desk lay in dust and confusion. His appeal to have the pension continued in 1784, after the death of his wife, was refused; it was transferred to his brother-in-law Fumetti von Winzenburg. But meanwhile Franz Anton was calling himself von Weber, even though named simply Weber in the Elector's decrees: the first mention of the 'von' is in his dismissal notice. From everything we know of him, it is typical that he should have assumed this false title. Max Maria describes him as 'conceited and ambitious, boastful and bragging, reckless and eccentric and untruthful.' It seems to have been no exaggeration. Though never more than a Lieutenant, he allowed himself to be addressed as Major in Salzburg in 1797; while in Stuttgart in 1809 and Mannheim in 1811 he described himself as Baron (*Freiherr*) and Chamberlain (*Kammerherr*). Clearly he encouraged everyone, even within his family circle, to regard him as a noble: Carl Maria inherited the belief in perfectly good faith, and his aunt Adelheid, Franz Anton's sister, styled herself Baroness. It is thus through usage, not inheritance, that the composer retains his 'von'.

From Steuerwald, Franz Anton went on to become music director in Lübeck in 1778, and in the following year he took up a post as *Kapellmeister* to the Prince Bishop of Lübeck in the little town of Eutin. On a visit to Vienna to hand his sons Fritz and Franz Edmund over to Haydn as pupils, he met Genovefa Brenner; and there he married her on 20th August 1785 with the composer Righini and the actor Lange—later Aloisia's husband— as witnesses. Genovefa had originally come from the region of Kaufbeuren in Swabia. Her father was Markus Brenner, a peasant turned cabinet-maker who eventually became chief cabinet-maker to the Bishops Joseph and Wenceslas of Augsburg, whose summer residence was the Castle of Oberdorf. In 1749, when 19, he was apprenticed to Leonhard Fischer (maker of the famous high altar at Oberdorf), and in the same year married Viktoria Hinterland. Genovefa was their fourth child, born at Markt-Oberdorf on 2nd January 1764. Her paternal grandfather was a peasant, Johann Brenner; her maternal grandfather was Georg Hinderlang, a 'distinguished hunter and an excellent man' according to the church register. Genovefa was 21 when she met Franz Anton, 'blonde, blue-eyed, pretty and calm' according to Max Maria, as melancholy and dreamy as her fellow Swabian, Kleist's Käthchen von Heilbronn. She was also a singer of some experience and talent (she had visited Naples, probably as a member of a musical troupe, when only 10), a fact which was made use of by Franz Anton, when, tiring of arranging music for consecrations and wedding receptions in his capacity as town musician of Eutin, he formed a theatrical troupe with his family as backbone and set out on his travels across Germany.

All the foregoing is more than documentary obligation in preparing the way for a study of the composer. In it we find several vital strands beginning to converge. That Weber was not of the aristocracy is itself of some importance. As we have seen, the lower and middle classes from which he really sprang were beginning to emerge as the dominant class of the new Europe, guardians of the spirit of liberty and the source of most of the Romantic artists. A little further back, Weber was of country stock—his four great-grandparents were miller, surgeon-barber, peasant and huntsman—and Romanticism is also largely the revolt of the country against the town, of the awe-inspiring and irrational qualities in Nature against the order and reason of society. Part of the change from the Enlightenment towards Romanticism is from moderation and intelligent scepticism to an enjoyment of violence and the irrational for its own sake as well as for the exciting new vistas of feeling it opened up. Weber was, by birth alone, very much a man of his time.

CHAPTER ONE

CHILDHOOD: 1786–1800

Fort! Du musst hinaus; fort ins Weite. Des Künstlers Wirkungskreis ist die
Welt . . . Fort!

WEBER: *Tonkünstlersleben*

EUTIN LIES some twenty miles north of Lübeck, in the district known to
the citizens of Hamburg who enjoy weekends among its lakes and
woods as the Switzerland of Holstein. It is still a charming, quiet town,
famous for its cultivation of roses, with woods lying between the house where
Weber was born (now a café) and the lake by which stands the old Prince
Bishop's palace, and on whose shores summer performances of *Der Freischütz* are given. Founded in 1143, the town first became more widely known
in the eighteenth century when its relaxing atmosphere began to attract a
number of writers and artists: these included the painter Tischbein and the
poet and translator of Homer, Johann Heinrich Voss, who became rector of a
school there in 1782. The circle which they and their friends formed earned
Eutin the nickname The Weimar of the North.

Here, '*im Spechtschen Haus an der Lübschen Strasse*' in 1786, was born
Carl Maria Friedrich Ernst von Weber. Over the actual date some confusion
has existed. It was long thought to be 18th December, according to a note in
Franz Anton's writing, at 10.30 p.m., with the baptism on 20th December,
but the baptismal date at the Landeskirche is registered as 20th November,
implying a birth of 18th November: this was the date Weber himself later
accepted. Prince Carl of Hesse stood as godfather. Otherwise, all we know of
his earliest months is that he was a weakly child, with a damaged right hip-
bone that was to give him a permanent limp.

By the time Weber was born, his father had already tired of the post of
town musician and was requesting the Prince Bishop for reinstatement as a
pensioner; this was reluctantly granted on 30th March of the following year.
Promptly selling his instruments, Franz Anton moved to Hamburg and,
staying with a Masonic Lodge, set about organizing the enterprise dearest to
his heart, the Weber Theatre Company. His Masonic credentials show that
he was in Vienna in 1788, with three sons by his first marriage; the following
year in Cassel, where Genovefa bore him another son that survived only a
month; in 1790 in Meiningen; in 1791 in Nuremberg. The little known of
the company comes from one of its former members, an actor named Carl
Ludwig Costenoble, who observed that, 'Franz Anton von Weber was a

friendly director, and his wife could be called a thoroughly good person. Carl Maria von Weber, the only fruit of his second marriage was then [1795] a weak, acutely lame little boy of 8 or 9.' Costenoble describes Fritz as a good buffo but a bad character, Genovefa as a safe actress though no virtuoso, 'so mannered we could hardly believe we heard aright.'[1] The company was typical of the hundreds of similar groups of strolling players upon whom the villages and even some of the larger towns of Germany depended for their theatrical entertainment, its repertory centring around the fashionable Iffland and Kotzebue, as well as certain musical pieces. Most of the family were pressed into service, among them Franz Anton's sister Adelheid, a remarkable and forceful character who had abandoned a distasteful marriage in order to join her brother. Carl Maria was included in the caravan, and is said to have first learned to play among the painted scenes and props of the company. Already his father was nursing dreams of a Mozartian *Wunderkind*: the boy had his first music lesson at the age of three from his father and his half-brother Fridolin—not a success, Weber later recalled, for the exasperated Fridolin had torn the bow from his hands exclaiming, 'Whatever else may be made of you, you'll never be a musician!' Nevertheless, instruction continued in Erlangen, Augsburg and Nuremburg, on the Bavarian circuit on which the Weber Theatre Company had settled; while in Nuremberg he was also given lessons in painting and engraving. The company's fortunes vacillated: once, after Salzburg, the actors had to be put on half pay.

This itinerant life was obviously bad for the steady development of the boy's talent, still more for the precarious health he had inherited from his mother. When in 1796 the company came to Hildburgshausen, on the River Werra some nineteen miles from Meiningen, Genovefa's health broke down and Weber was enabled to spend more than a few weeks in one place. Living in Hildburgshausen was the 23-year-old Johann Peter Heuschkel, an oboist, organist, conductor and composer, especially of songs; and in him Weber found his first real musical friend. Heuschkel, he later wrote, gave him 'the true, best foundation for strong, clear and characteristic playing on the pianoforte and the equal training of both hands.'[2] His rapid development dates from this moment. But by 1797 Genovefa was better, and in the autumn the family moved to Salzburg, from which Franz Anton intended a tour of Bavaria, Baden and the Palatinate.

He was forestalled by Napoleon. Though then campaigning in Italy with a success that was startling all Europe, the French armies were also making advances in Bavaria. Moreau was outside Munich; the Austrians had been driven back to the mountains before Napoleon's Italian advance and were glad to agree to the armistice signed at Leoben on 18th April 1797. Six months later, the Treaty of Campo Formio compelled them to agree to sur-

[1] Costenoble: *Tagebücher* (1818).
[2] *Autbiographische Skizze* (Kaiser 127).

render Belgium, the Rhine frontier and Lombardy in exchange for a share of Venice. Thus the French were brought to the Rhine, and despite the Treaty, anxieties ran high. Franz Anton decided it would be wiser to stay in Salzburg, although here Mozart's old enemy Count Colloredo was still installed, supporting an orchestra but showing no encouragement to the stage. Making the best of the situation, Franz Anton sent his intended *Wunderkind* to Michael Haydn for instruction. Now 60, dry in manner and unforthcoming, Haydn took considerable interest in the limping little 10-year-old and worked hard with him on the basic grammar of music; though Weber later wrote that they were remote from each other and that he had learned little and with difficulty.[1]

It was while under Haydn that Weber wrote his first work, a set of Six Fughettas (Op. 1: J.1–6) which he published in the following year at Salzburg. They are very short—the longest is only 13 bars—and were dedicated to his brother Edmund 'as connoisseur, as teacher, and finally as brother, these first fruits of his musical work from your deeply loving brother Karl Marie von Weber in the eleventh year of his age' (Franz Anton having quietly lopped one year off the true age). These were given a friendly reception in the *AMZ* by Johann Friedrich Rochlitz, the journal's founder and the leading critic of the day: 'That a young artist, like this composer, in his eleventh year can compose fugues, and such good ones, is an excellent and unusually promising rarity.' Rochlitz was being generous: even ignoring the consecutives (fifths in one and octaves in another), the fugues are artistically negligible. Nevertheless, three of the ideas were serviceable enough to be used again in later works—No. 1 appears complete in the quartet 'Fort, fort von hier' in *Peter Schmoll*, No. 2 is rewritten from 3/4 into 4/4 as the subject of the fugue at 'Cum sancto spiritu' in the Dresden E♭ Mass and No. 6 becomes the subject of the fugue at 'Et incarnatus est' in the same work. Otherwise, the only detectable legacy of Michael Haydn's teaching is in Weber's characteristic fondness for the staccato thirds and octaves he may have admired in Haydn's piano variations in C major.

Meanwhile, on 13th March 1798, Genovefa died of tuberculosis. By the end of the year Franz Anton was once more engaged—to a widow from Bamberg named Beer; but the marriage never took place, and Weber passed into the care of his Aunt Adelheid. When the Company went on to Munich at the end of the year, Adelheid, now 69, at last put her foot down and stayed behind. Weber had already apparently paid a brief visit with his father to Vienna, where he made friends with a young law student who played the flute in the orchestra and who was to become a kind of brother confessor and exemplar to him, Ignaz Susann. Now he travelled on to Munich with his father, who was at last showing anxiety about regular teaching. First they sought out Joseph Grätz, a musical theorist who had lived a life almost as chequered as Franz Anton's, but who refused the boy (Max Maria suspects

[1] *Autobiographische Skizze* (Kaiser 127).

because he guessed there would be difficulty about payment). So, on the grounds that 'no-one can write well for the voice or compose a good opera who can't sing decently himself', Franz Anton approached Johann Evangelist Wallishauser. Better known by the Italian name Valesi he had taken, Wallishauser (who was now 63) had recently been pensioned by the Elector of Bavaria. He had in his time trained over 200 singers, among them Mozart's Belmonte, Valentin Adamberger. Weber was also placed under Johann Nepomuk Kalcher, a 32-year-old ex-pupil of Grätz who had that year recommended him for his appointment as court organist. The outcome was Weber's first opera, written under Kalcher's eyes and now lost, *Die Macht der Liebe und des Weins*; and the first draft of the so-called *Jugendmesse* in E♭. Throughout 1799 he continued working—excessively hard, according to Max Maria—under Kalcher and Valesi, while another important influence came his way in Joseph Maria Babo. Born in 1756, Babo had been theatre secretary in Mannheim and made a name as the author of a series of comedies and knightly dramas before being summoned to Munich (where the *Ritterdrama* particularly flourished) by the Duke Carl Theodor and taking up his position as Director of the Munich Theatre in 1799. Here he revised the repertory to include a large number of *Singspiele* and (in spite of the times) French operas—both of them genres which were to feature prominently in Weber's Prague and Dresden repertories and are the chief ancestors of Romantic opera. The composers included Mozart, Winter, Haydn, Danzi, Dalayrac, Gaveaux, Paër, Salieri, Cannabich and Wenzel Müller; and though not all of these names were introduced during Weber's stay in Munich, he undoubtedly responded to the trend. Another theatre manager with whom a contact was made in Carlsbad in 1799 was Carl von Steinsberg, with whom the libretto of an opera for Weber may well have been discussed; but an association of more immediate importance was that with an old friend of Franz Anton's from Nuremberg days, Aloys Senefelder.

Senefelder was then nearly 28, another of the soldiers of fortune to whom Franz Anton regularly gravitated. Sent to study law, he found himself on his father's death obliged to earn a living and so reverted to the family trade of strolling player, also writing music and dramatic pieces for his company. Unable to get these published, he set about looking for a cheap method of reproduction, without at first any success. It was while experimenting one day that he was asked by his mother to write out her laundry list; this he did on the nearest surface to hand, which chanced to be a flat piece of stone, one of the blocks from the Kehlheim quarries near Munich used as flagstones for large houses. Struck with the idea of taking an impression by eroding the part of the stone not marked by his greasy ink with weak acid, he was thus led to the key process of his new invention, lithography. So thoroughly did he work the system out that few changes, and those only in detail, have since been necessary. The process was invented in 1798; in 1799 Senefelder received a 15 year concession for lithography in Bavaria. Franz Anton took to him immediately, not least since he saw here a means of publishing Weber's works, which had been fruitlessly going the publishers' rounds. Weber became Senefelder's apprentice, and is even said to have invented an improvement in the process—though Senefelder makes no mention of this, nor indeed of Weber in his treatise.[1] Meanwhile, a fire in a cupboard at Kalcher's house had destroyed much of the music Weber was writing at the time. Some canons and four-part songs, the opera *Die Macht der Liebe und des Weins* and a farce derived from it seem all to have been lost, though a print had already been made (inaccurately, but with beautiful calligraphy on the title page) of Six Variations on an Original Theme for piano (Op. 2: J. 7), fulsomely dedicated to Kalcher. Rochlitz was again friendly in his notice of the work, which indeed shows many more signs of character than the Fughettas. Though the first two variations are barely more than *études de vélocité* for alternate hands, the third shows a more individual liking for sudden dramatic contrasts, with in the second half a fierce 'orchestral' tremolo. The remaining variations revert to the keyboard study type of variation—Var. 5 is a nimble Toccata, the first of many—and though crude, especially harmonically, the work does show the pleasure in keyboard sounds and techniques that was to colour Weber's more mature works. There is also the first sign of his habit of approaching a harmony note in the melody by way of the semitone below. But according to Max Maria, the combination of Senefelder's jealousy and Weber's superstition that the fire expressed divine criticism of his composing caused father and son to move on in the hope of setting up on their own as lithographers. Weber himself put it rather differently: 'The youthful urge to give oneself to everything new and sensational awoke in me the idea of seizing supremacy in Senefelder's newly discovered process of lithography . . . The wish to try this out on a large scale impelled us to go to Freiberg, where all materials seemed most conveniently to hand.'[2]

The famous Bergakademie (Mining Academy) had been founded in Freiberg in 1765 as a learned adjunct to the neighbouring lead and silver mines, which had been in operation since 1163. Here Humboldt was established as a scholar, and its revelation of the wonders of natural science had prompted some of Novalis's prose work. The town was full of students and throbbing with life. One of the chief rendezvous, for theatre people as well as for the professors and students, was the inn owned by Vater Hene, the *Goldene Löwe*; and hither the Webers naturally gravitated. Franz Anton now announced in the *AMZ* that he was proposing to establish a lithography works; nevertheless, before long Weber found that 'the extensiveness and the mechanical, soul-destroying nature of the business soon made me give it up

[1] Aloys Senefelder: *Vollständiges Lehrbuch der Steindruckerey* (1818).
[2] *Autobiographische Skizze* (Kaiser 127).

2

and set myself with redoubled enthusiasm to composition.'[1] This decision coincided with the arrival in Freiberg of Steinsberg, at the head of his troupe. On Weber's return from a concert tour of Erfurt, Gotha and Leipzig in the summer of 1800, Steinsberg gave him a libretto, *Das Waldmädchen*, which posed the inexperienced young composer the problem of writing an opera with a dumb heroine; nevertheless, Weber immediately set to work on it and finished the second act in ten days (having been spurred on, he later admitted, by tales of other composers' feats of speed).

No playbill survives for the first performance of *Das Waldmädchen*, given in Freiberg[2] by Steinberg's company on 24th November 1800, but an announcement in the local paper, the resoundingly entitled *Gnädigst bewilligte Freyberger gemeinnützige Nachrichten für das chursächsische Erzgebirge*, promised a 'Romantic-comic opera in two acts by Ritter Karl von Steinsberg, set to music and dedicated by permission to her Electoral Highness, Maria Amalia Augusta, in deepest respect, by Carl Maria, B[aron] von Weber, 13 years old, a pupil of Haydn'—Franz Anton having prudently neglected to mention which Haydn. The opera was duly performed in the important Buttermarket Theatre, the concession to which Steinsberg had secured by winning the confidence of the town council; it was also toured by the company, some 30 strong, in the neighbourhood with a repertory that included the most popular pieces of Iffland and of Kotzebue, upon whose notoriously tawdry Romanticism Steinsberg seems to have modelled his style. Franz Anton had drummed up custom so vigorously (and no doubt so tactlessly) that opposition grew in the town, especially from the Cantor, I.G. Fischer; the supporters were chiefly the mining students, who enjoyed Franz Anton's company at the *Goldene Löwe*. The piece was not ungenerously reviewed by the local music critic, who observed that it was 'a mere blossom of genius, which promises better and riper fruit.' Taking this as a slight, the incensed Franz Anton replied with a violent article attacking the conducting of the Stadtmusikus, Siegert, who retorted blaming Weber's incompetence; and a controversy dragged on through January—to the credit of no-one except possibly the young composer himself, who is said to have made an approach to Siegert and been reconciled with him that November. In fact, Weber seems to have more or less agreed with his critic, later remembering the opera as 'a very immature piece, though perhaps here and there not a completely uninventive one.'[3] He adds that it was also produced in Prague (in Czech) and St. Petersburg, though no traces of these performances survive; certainly it was given in Chemnitz as *Das stumme Waldmädchen* on

---

[1] *Autobiographische Skizze* (Kaiser 127).
[2] Not in Chemnitz as according to MMW, Vol. I., p. 53, and others following him.
[3] *Autobiographische Skizze* (Kaiser 127). The whole controversy is reprinted in K. Knebel: 'Weber in Freiberg 1800–1801' in *Mitteilungen vom Freiberger Altertumsverein*, XXXVII, p. 72–89 (1900).

5th December 1800 and in Vienna as *Das Mädchen in Spessarter Wald* on 4th December 1804.[1] Later the text of *Das Waldmädchen* was taken by Hiemer for *Silvana* and Weber re-used some of the music, regarding the work as dead. At any rate, the score has disappeared apart from two fragments—an aria without a beginning and a terzett without an ending.[2] Perhaps Weber destroyed it himself; he once declared that 'Puppies and first operas should be drowned.'

It is doubtful whether the loss is serious. The surviving fragment of Mathilde's aria, declaring that she cannot leave her lover for Prince Sigismund, is evidently built on *da capo* principle with a new modulation during the reprise, and is no masterpiece: its rhythmic structure is haphazard, its harmony limited and with some clumsy progressions. It is ambitiously but inexpertly written for the voice with a tessitura that includes middle C and top E, in one instance consecutively. What remains of *Das Waldmädchen* suggests a fledgling talent that has outgrown orthodox teaching but cannot take flight on its own with much certainty. There are, however, signs of the direction it was to take. The aria's D-E♭ modulation in the middle section shows a well-placed dramatic instinct (though the return is crudely managed), and the melodic line in both pieces shows Weber's fondness for putting two fairly quick notes to a syllable, thus creating a flowing melodic line. The coloratura, however, is awkward. During the controversy Fischer wrote of the first piece, 'I recall the aria which Mme. Seiffert sang, passages in tasteless triplets all through, now high, now low. The good lady was so tormented that she didn't know how to get through the aria.' In the terzett—for Count Arbander, Prince Sigismund's squire Krips and Mathilde—she has been reproached by her angry father in a letter brought by Krips. She refuses to defy him, and is ready to offer her hand to Sigismund. This is much superior, a fresh and quite characteristic piece of writing. No more of Steinsberg's text survives, except in Hiemer's transformation as *Silvana*. The importance of *Das Waldmädchen* for Weber, as far as one can tell, is that even through the Kotzebue-fogged spectacles of Steinsberg, it gave him his first glimpse of Romantic opera.

---

[1] In records of these performances the work is sometimes attributed to Wenzel Müller (W. Krone: *Wenzel Müller* (1906), F. Hadamovsky: *Das Theater in der Wiener Leopoldstadt* (1934)). Possibly it was given with additional music by Müller, who was then conductor there.

[2] WG, Reihe 2, Bd. 1 (J. Anh. 1).

CHAPTER TWO

ADOLESCENCE AND AWAKENING: 1800–1803

Das sind die schöne Früchte der Revolution
JOSEPH TÜRK: *Peter Schmoll*

LITTLE IS known for certain of Weber's life and movements during the earliest years of the new century. Max Maria's imagination supplies various details: all that seems certain is that having offered his lithographic process to Artaria in Vienna,[1] he visited Chemnitz[2] and Munich, arriving in Salzburg by November 1801. Here confusion reigned in the wake of Moreau's departing French army. Nevertheless, Weber was able to write his third opera, *Peter Schmoll und seine Nachbarn* (J.8) under the eye of Michael Haydn, who declared that it was 'composed according to the true rules of counterpoint, with much fire and delicacy, and appropriately to the text.' He also revised, under Haydn, the Mass he had begun and probably mostly laid out during his study with Kalcher. Franz Anton's intention was that a dedication to the Prince Archbishop Colloredo would secure Weber a post; but Colloredo left hurriedly, and the fair copy, dated 3rd May 1802, was left at his residence, to disappear (presumed lost in the fire in Kalcher's cupboard) until found in the Salzburg Museum in 1925 and edited by Constantin Schneider. Possibly Weber retained his original draft, or at any rate sketches, for one or two passages recur in the better known Eb Mass of 1818 —notably the very opening (with chorus added) and first soprano entry.

By far the most original element in this so-called *Jugendmesse* is its symmetrical construction around a central Eb Credo cast as an almost operatic recitative for bass—an extended scena on the repeated word 'Credo', with chorus answering and finally taking over for a jubilant Et Resurrexit. It is an odd conception, if not completely successful certainly giving a remarkable foretaste of the ease with which Weber was to build extended musical paragraphs out of different materials and tempos in *Euryanthe*. On either side of the Credo lies a C major chorus ending fugally—before, the Quoniam; after, the Sanctus. Before the Quoniam comes the A minor Qui tollis, for tenor solo with oboe obbligato; after the Sanctus comes the G major Benedictus, for soprano solo with cello obbligato (as in the 1818 Eb Mass, though the present example is closer to the world of *Singspiel* in its three-part song form). Moving further away from the centre again, the second number of the Mass

---

[1] Letter of 9th October 1800—ignored by Artaria.
[2] There are letters from Chemnitz dated 24th April and 17th May 1801.

is a C major Gloria chorus, while the eighth and penultimate is a B♭ Agnus Dei set fascinatingly as a canon for four voices on a subject no less than sixteen bars long. The first and last numbers, Kyrie and Dona nobis pacem, use identical music, thus completing the arch in which this unusual piece is designed, with the dramatic declaration of faith in the Credo as its keystone. Whether or not Haydn or Kalcher suggested the scheme, it makes a satisfying musical design for Weber to fill out, a structural image of faith that could accommodate music not always notable for religious intensity of feeling. Unity may have been a major consideration (he also uses the theme of the Gloria for a fugue at 'Cum sancto spiritu'), but there is a pleasant diversity of invention that makes the Mass a good deal more than a student exercise.

At this time Weber also published his Six Petites Pièces Faciles for piano duet (Op. 3: J. 9–14), written either in Salzburg or during a journey on which he met the pianist and composer Paul Schulthesius, to whom they were dedicated; and, with Schulthesius's Augsburg publisher Gombart, his Twelve Allemandes for piano solo (Op. 4: J. 15–26). The Op. 3 pieces, though with a Secondo that plays little more than an accompanying role, are engaging trifles that should be better known to domestic pianists: one, the March (No. 5), was remembered by Weber at the end of his life when he used it for a wind piece and, in another version, for choir and orchestra—his last work apart from a single song, written just before his death in London.

Weber's own account of this period adds little: 'Taken to Salzburg by family affairs, I wrote there, according to my new plans, the opera *Peter Schmoll and his Neighbours* . . . It was given in Augsburg, naturally without any special success. I later revised the overture and had it engraved by Gombart.'[1] The choice of Augsburg was clearly dictated by the presence there of Weber's brother Edmund, who had left the family theatre company in 1798 and was conducting in the theatre and working in the employment of the Prince Bishop Clemens Wenzeslaus—a wealthy man, despite the losses of lands in Trier and Coblenz at the Peace of Lunéville, and a keen supporter of the arts. Weber seems to have gone there with his father in June 1802; but when hope of a production faded by the autumn, they left and apparently travelled through Meiningen, Eisenach, Sondershausen and Brunswick back to Eutin. Here Weber came into contact with Voss, who furnished him with various texts for songs (only two of them actually by himself)—for instance, Matthisson's *Die Kerze* (J.27), written that October in Hamburg,[2] and the anonymous *Umsonst* (Op. 71, No. 4: J.28). The latter is untypical of the songs Weber was to write in such profusion, suggesting as it does, not the easy

---

[1] *Autobiographische Skizze* (Kaiser 127)

[2] Costenoble: *op. cit.* describes the concert at which 'Old Weber, in some kind of uniform, booted and spurred, led Weber to the piano and turned the pages for him'. He records that the concert was not greatly appreciated, and that the Webers left Hamburg with hopes dashed.

folk-like lyricism of his maturity but a repressed operatic talent. The opening C minor section resembles a *recitativo stromentato*, with heavy chords repeated in quasi-orchestral effect, while the figuration in the major section is monotonous and curiously limp. From this time, too, date the Six Ecossaises (J. 29–34), a batch of brief, lively pieces whose chief indication of Weber's development is in the dedication 'To the fair sex of Hamburg'. But tiny as they are—each in two eight-bar sections, repeated—these Ecossaises are confidently handled. Wisely, Weber had not yet attempted any extended piece of abstract writing. Even some of the variations of this period show uncertainty in the development of the ideas he never lacked; the Ecossaises are simply idea and answer. Of them, No. 5 is perhaps the most interesting as Weber's first (and very successful) attempt at his characteristic kind of melody in racing semiquavers—more familiar from the *Abu Hassan* and *Oberon* overtures.

In December 1802, Weber returned to Augsburg, where he remained until the end of July. His minor works of these months include an excellent three-part vocal canon, *Mädchen, ach meide Männerschmeichelei'n* (Op. 13, No. 6: J.35) which Mahler was later perceptive enough to realize would serve admirably in his completion of *Die drei Pintos*; a three-part song *Ein Gärtchen* (J.36); a *Grablied, Leis wandeln wir* (J.37), for two tenors and bass, first written on the death of a Munich friend and later (in Breslau, 19th November 1804) orchestrated for the funeral of the wife of the theatre's co-director, Hayn; and the song *Entflieht schnell von mir* (J.38). But the majority of his time was taken up with preparations for the delayed production of *Peter Schmoll*. Max Maria guesses March as the most likely date for the première, and it is possible that there were also performances in Munich in 1807;[1] nothing of this is certain.

Alongside the popular *Ritterdrama*, the popular play of mediaeval derring-do into which the historical tragedy of the *Sturm und Drang* had degenerated, there flourished around the turn of the century another minor form that was to assume importance with the rise of Romanticism, the *Schauerroman*, or Tale of Terror. Among its most notable practitioners was Carl Gottlob Cramer, who was born in 1758 and in 1798–9 published in two parts his novel *Peter Schmoll und seine Nachbarn*. Though scarcely a *Schauerroman*, it makes use of certain features common to much of the lesser writing of the time—a feeling for Nature, a strong use of fateful coincidence, the intervention of a holy man to set the ways of erring folk to rights, and incidentally a tendency to allow the lesser, bourgeois characters to assume fuller prominence and life than the ostensible heroes and heroines. We shall meet these and other features of equal importance again in *Der Freischütz*, of course; they are far from unique to that work, though in it they assume their com-

---

[1] But there is no mention of them in Max Zeuger: *Geschichte der Münchener Oper* (1923) or Grandauer: *Chronik des Kgl. Hof- und Nationaltheater in München* (1878)

plete expression. Copies of *Peter Schmoll* are exceedingly rare: Jähns could not find one at the time he compiled his catalogue, though he was later more fortunate and left a copy in his Weber collection[1] as well as a full synopsis into which we can fit the arias in the score.[2] The novel opens in France.

Peter Schmoll, a very rich Dutch merchant, lives with his daughter Minette and two friends—his companion Helmers (who first appears in the opera in Act 2 as the Old Man) and the Abbé Saurin (who first appears in the opera at the end, but does not sing). He also has a steward, Hans Bast. The French Revolution breaks out. Helmers's presence in the interior of France becomes necessary; being a widower, he takes with him his twelve-year-old son Carl (in the opera, the Overseer). No word comes from the Helmers family. The Abbé undertakes to find them and regretfully leaves Schmoll. Hans Bast now begins to behave badly to his moody, blustering but goodhearted master; he grows worse the longer the Abbé is away. The Revolution bursts into full flame and Schmoll emigrates with his daughter and Hans Bast. From Michelsen, a horse dealer, he buys a deserted remote old castle, Bärenburg, on the German side of the frontier. Here he remains, embittered over the Revolution, in the deepest secrecy for fear of attack and devoted to all his old pursuits—keeping his books, fruitlessly reckoning up his old accounts with Minette, Bast and the others. [Here Weber's opera begins, and we encounter Schmoll with Minette and Bast in No. 1, Terzetto: 'Das sind die schöne Früchte'.] Soon Schmoll becomes ill from lack of exercise. At their suggestion he plays Blind-Man's Buff with Minette and Bast (No. 2, Terzetto: 'Spiele, alte Esel, du'). Minette is now sixteen and very bored with isolation; she longs for news and on her walks in the surrounding woods she takes to meeting Michelsen's overseer, a handsome young man named Carl. She falls in love with him and manages to win a confession that this love is returned (parted from him, she sings No. 3, Romanza: 'Im Rheinland eine Dirne'; parted from her, he sings No. 4, Aria: 'Der Wüstling verschwendet'). Hans Bast sings the introductory poem to Chapter 7 of the novel (No. 5, Arietta: 'Die Menschen sind schon so'). Michelsen now writes to Schmoll giving a number of plausible reasons why his overseer should be given a post in the castle. Hans Bast, who has seen the letter in the hands of Niklas, a farm hand, is against admitting a stranger. Minette and Niklas prevail on him to think again (No. 6, Terzetto: 'Wenn er nur Ruh'). So Carl comes secretly to the castle. Bast now perceives the state of affairs (No. 7, Aria: 'Hans Bast! gieb acht'). Carl reflects upon the nature of love (No. 8: Recitativo und Arie: 'O Hoffnung') and the two declare their love (No.9, Duetto: 'Dich an diess Herz'). In the following duet (No. 10, Duetto: 'Der edle, schöne, junge Mann') Minette confesses everything to Hans Bast. Carl, Minette and Bast are re-united (No. 11, Terzetto: 'Es ist das seeligste Vergnügen'). But Schmoll learns nothing of all this. Thus the first act closes. Shortly after the end of the first volume of the novel, Carl, on a horse trading expedition, comes upon a wretched old man, also an émigré, lying by the road and takes him to be tended by a neighbouring head ranger.

[1] *Weberiana*, Classe VII, No. 15–16.
[2] WG Reihe 2, Bd. 1.

Since then Carl has been thoughtful and melancholy. Minette tries to cheer him up (No. 12, Aria: 'Du fröhlicher Jüngling'). He leads her to the Old Man, who warmly greets him as his saviour. She gives Carl the money for the horse deal which he had charitably bestowed on the Old Man. (In the opera, this is No. 14, Terzetto: 'Empfanget hier'; when they have left, there follows the Old Man's Aria, (No. 15: 'Wie der bange Pilge zittert'), in which he thinks of his lost son). Meanwhile Schmoll has often observed Carl in the paddock through his telescope, and is beginning to take an interest in the handsome horse-tamer; at the same time he develops a longing for the outside world (No. 13, Aria: 'Ja, Gottes Erde ist doch schön'). Eventually he decides to go out for the first time, to visit a distant church. Carl is recommended by Bast to arrange personally with Schmoll that Michelsen, Carl's master, lend Schmoll a horse and cart, and so the young man knows he has won Schmoll's favour: on giving Schmoll this recommendation, Hans Bast's conscience pricks him (No. 16, Arietta: 'Ein Lügner ist ein grosser Mann'). But before Carl can properly conclude this very promising transaction, he is violently rejected since he has changed his clothes in order to make the request and thus is not recognized as the figure Schmoll has seen through his telescope. This rejection of Carl is the subject of No. 17, Quartetto: 'Fort, fort von hier'. Finally the journey to the church is undertaken; Bast stays at home, congratulating himself on his position (No. 18, Aria: 'Fürwahr, fürwahr'). On his way through the forest, Schmoll is suddenly taken seriously ill. A passing Hermit restores him to life with a holy drink, to the profound gratitude of Carl and Minette (No. 19, Duetto: 'O grosser Gott'). The Hermit reveals himself to Schmoll as the lost Abbé Saurin. Together with Helmers, soon after he had left Schmoll some years previously he became implicated in the French Revolution and was drawn into the fighting as a soldier. But he became separated from his son Carl, who was compelled by hardship to join some circus riders and so later came into Michelsen's service. Carl now hurries to his charge, the Old Man, to say that he is going away to seek his father, since Saurin is already found and reunited with Schmoll. The name of Schmoll causes the Old Man to recognize his son Carl. He is led to the others in the castle and received amid general rejoicing (No. 20, Finale: 'So hab' ich').

What possessed Weber to set this tale, with its cardboard characterization and, to say the least, contrived plot, we cannot tell. Presumably he was under pressure from Franz Anton, whose ever-open eye to the main chance had lit upon the novel's popularity (it quickly ran to several editions). Not only the incidental features already mentioned, but also the contemporary setting must have made the work seem a likely source for a modern opera—the problem of the émigrés who had fled the Revolution and were forming themselves into discontented groups on the German side of the frontier was a very present one, and the source of friction between the two countries.

The libretto was prepared in two acts by one Joseph Türk or Türke, an obscure figure possibly related to the pianist and composer of beginners' pieces, Daniel Gottlob Türk, but the dialogue is now lost. Each of Cramer's chapters begins with a poem, and Türk made five of these the basis of arias. The form is that of *Singspiel*, keeping nervously close to the original novel. With the encouragement of a lost text, various attempts have been made to reconstruct the work. A revival at Lübeck in December 1927 had new dialogue by K. Eggert; and a reconstruction by Hans Hasse that involved considerable reshaping of the work and rewriting of the sung text, though no tampering with the music, was staged at Freiberg by the Dresden State Opera on 18th May 1943, with scenery and costumes by Hugo Lange. The Dresden Opera repeated the work in a double-bill with *Abu Hassan* on 19th February 1944; and the distinguished Weber scholar Hans Schnoor, who had greatly admired the dramatic effectiveness of the work in Hasse's version, put on another production at Bielefeld in 1955. Yet another version, based on an idea of Rolf Lauckner by Willy Werner Göttig, was published by Litolff and Peters in 1963.

In spite of everything, the original does show considerable dramatic flair, and it is an extraordinary piece of work for a fifteen-year-old composer with such a chequered background of training. The construction is sound, with an expressive use of key-patterns that was to be developed to a high degree in *Der Freischütz*. The basic tonality of the work is E♭—the key of the overture, the introduction (Terzetto, No. 1), the two finales, and the principal love duet (No. 8). Three other numbers, including Schmoll's romantic apostrophe to Nature, are in B♭; and the duet of thanksgiving for Schmoll's restoration to life (No. 19) is in A♭. The only sharp keys to be used are D for the Blind Man's Buff Terzetto (No. 2) and for the Quartetto (No. 17) when Schmoll

Ex. 1

orders Carl away, E for Hans Bast's Arietta (No. 16) about liars, and—the remotest from E♭—A for the Terzetto (No. 6) that includes Niklas, the remotest from the action.

Where the young composer's inexperience naturally shows most is in the harmony, which is seldom more than merely correct. But even here we find instances of the dramatic idea firing Weber to an imaginative stroke that would never have come to him from an abstract effort of thought in music. When Schmoll, musing on Nature and Man, mentions the storms of Fate that are but shadows passing across the light, there is an effective sudden turn from B♭ to G♭ at the mention of Fate, resolving back via B♭ minor quavers on strings for the shadows to a fortissimo B♭ major chord at 'Light'. This perhaps no more than matches simple verbal image with simple musical equivalent; there is a more individual note as Schmoll contrasts the complaints of man with the Elysium in which he lives (Ex. 1, p. 41).

Ex. 2

It is, however, in his attempts to infuse a real sense of character into Cramer's near-puppets that the born opera composer's talent is revealed. There is one female role in the entire opera—Minette, described as a *lyrische Soubrette*, and hence, as her music soon reveals, an ancestress of Aennchen rather than of Agathe. With Carl, a lyric tenor, Weber does little: he is not the last composer, especially in Germany, to find difficulty in expressing upright, heroic sentiments without triteness, even though Carl is not in fact of heroic or noble stock. But the range of treatment accorded him, the baritone Schmoll, the *seriöser Bass* Helmers and the *Bassbuffo* Hans Bast springs from a real instinct for dramatic reality and variety and is expressed with not a little skill. To expect profound psychological penetration in a boy composer is absurd; we do not get it, but there is a sure instinct in the manner in which Hans Bast—in fact, the dominating role of the opera—is allotted music of a robustness arising from German folk music that expresses his bluff good nature well. His Arietta (No. 16) derives from the type of ballad that also lies behind Papageno's entrance aria, which Weber had rather too vividly in mind (Ex. 2, opposite page).

The somewhat blunt ending to this phrase is part of a tendency to allow his tunes to flag in their second strain which Weber never wholly shook off; but it does also fit with the musical character given to Bast. This is nowhere more entertainingly shown than in the Blind Man's Buff Terzetto (No. 2), where Bast, lumbering about in the dark, is cleverly set against the nimbler, more graceful flute representing Minette dancing around him; while the strings indicate his futile grabs at her. No stage directions survive for this number, but they are scarcely needed, so wittily and graphically has the composer done his job. Bast's final success in catching Minette is outlined by flute and cello coming closer together into the same two slowly arpeggiated chords—though in fact it turns out he has merely caught hold of her clothes. By now Bast is out of breath, and his simple progressions become more desperate and chromatic until the game is broken off, its purpose in cheering up Schmoll successful, and the three of them abandon the separation imposed by the game and become musically at one again.

In all, Bast appears in seven of the ten ensembles, and has four arias to himself—more than anyone else in the opera. His bluffness is well adapted to the jovial manner of his Arietta (No. 16) and to the more pathetically comic folk manner of his aria (No. 18) when, a mixture of Pooh-Bah and Figaro, he reassures himself of his versatility as a steward and his courageous devotion to his duty. It can also assume implacability in the Aria (No. 7) when he puts himself on guard, as it were, to watch Carl; and is shown at its most deft in the clever little Arietta (No. 5) where in the course of 36 bars his obsessive little unaccompanied phrase, 'People are like that', becomes the pivot on which three completely varied strains are hung. This is a brilliant piece of comic timing.

Ex. 3

For part of his characterization of Bast, still more with the others, Weber depended upon the wonderful ear for instrumental textures with which he seems to have been born. Minette, he indicates, is more than the bouncy little soubrette we shall also see: her Romanza (No. 3),[1] sung as she is parted from Carl, is a simple ballad tune in 6/8 set against dark chords on the lower strings—no violins, two-part violas, cello and bass—and a bassoon scale figure *Zwischenspiel* between the voice entries. The sense of melancholy is enhanced by the lonely sound of an unaccompanied flute to introduce the third verse, and (with magical effect) to drift into silence by itself echoing to the final phrase on solo cello. This is an Aennchen capable of introspection. Flute tone, indeed, plays a prominent part in the work. In three of the numbers the flutes are required to change to piccolos—used not with the sinister grotesquerie of Caspar's *Lied* 'Hier im ird'schen Jammertal' in *Der Freischütz*, but to nimbly comic effect in Bast's Aria (No. 18) and again as they race away in triplets in No. 7 while Bast reflects morosely on the general scarcity of luck with women and gambling. In the Aria (No. 15) they scamper in a panic-stricken unison over sombre trombone chords (the trombones' only appearance) as the Old Man describes the storm, sinking in chromatic thirds as it dies—a remarkable passage that Berlioz would have admired (Ex. 3, opposite page).

But the most striking of the twenty numbers from the point of view of orchestration is No. 14, the Terzetto sung by the Old Man, Carl and Minette, which makes use of a pair of recorders and a pair of basset horns. With no instruction to guide him, Weber boldly takes on instruments he can scarcely have heard in anything resembling the manner he was to use them. 'An article in a music paper',[2] he tells us, 'awoke in me the idea of writing in another manner, of bringing back into use old and forgotten instruments.'[3] Perhaps their 'archaic' quality suggested to Weber the ancient who turns out to be the lost Helmers; if so, he must have conveniently forgotten that the basset horn was a favourite of Mozart's (there is the important obbligato part in *La Clemenza di Tito*, which had appeared only ten years previously, in 1791), and that recorders had been a common instrument within the last fifty years. It is a small but telling indication of how remote the post-Revolution nineteenth century felt itself from the previous age. At all events the strangely hollow, luminous texture of the opening of this aria justifies the choice and the acuteness of the young composer's aural imagination (Ex. 4, p. 46).

[1] This number was later used, with modifications, in *Abu Hassan*. A shortened and slightly altered version of No. 9 was also used for insertion in the Haydn pasticcio *Der Freybrief* at Stuttgart in 1809; the finale provided material for the finale of *Oberon*; and other pieces were used for *L'Accoglienza*.

[2] *AMZ*

[3] *Autobiographische Skizze* (Kaiser 127).

The alternative scoring for ordinary flutes and clarinets (which Weber
allows) would be totally different and less suggestive in effect; not least
because of the predominance of the flute, already mentioned, and of Weber's
beloved clarinet, which appears in every number but one, and is put to full-
blooded romantic use in the Recitativo to No. 8.

Despite this maturely German Romantic use of clarinet, and later of horn
over throbbing strings, Carl's aria owes something to Italian example. Much
else in the work serves to remind us of what the emerging Romantic opera
owed to French opéra-comique. The picture of comfortable bourgeois
family life disturbed by Fate, the spiritedness, the sense of political fever in
the background, the raciness of some of the exchanges—these are a few of the
common denominators present in *Peter Schmoll*, many more of which were
to reveal themselves as Romantic opera developed. Of course in ostensible
form, the work is also directly in the line of German *Singspiel*. Weber was too
inexperienced, and probably too much influenced by Franz Anton's urging
that he should match popular forms, to impose his own more acute sense of
operatic structure on the plot; but though the historian can chart a *Singspiel*
family tree that includes the names of Dittersdorf, Wenzel Müller and
Schenk, examination of the music suggests a young talent cautiously evolving
away from the main line of succession. Not only are there ample indications
of an individual musical personality—few composers had shown such an
appreciation of the raw, fresh sound of solo wind instruments—but the
melodic line outside the strictly composed, ballad-type numbers and the
handling this imposes on the accompanying music, show a certain restless-

Ex. 4

ness with set forms and patterns. It would be absurd to claim anything approaching greatness for *Peter Schmoll*; but this is not a negligible work. It is filled with characteristic melody, both in the popular folk style and in the more elegant, reflective or brilliant manner Weber was to make his own; and there are more than hints in certain of the numbers that he would not long remain content with the fixed dramatic situation imposed by a number in totally predictable form. The Blind Man's Buff terzetto is one such; but here the dramatic action positively insists on variety of treatment. Carl's aria (No. 8) dispenses with much of its Italian framework and is turned into a dramatic scena of considerable confidence. It may have occasional need of crutches, but it does not rule out the possibility of Max's 'Durch die Wälder' or even the *unendliche Melodie* of which Wagner was to learn so much in *Euryanthe*.

If *Peter Schmoll* as a whole is unlikely to earn more than the rarest revivals, its overture at least has survived as a lively and effective concert piece in Weber's 1807 revision (originally entitled *Grande Ouverture à Plusieurs Instruments*). It follows Weber's lifelong principle of drawing its material from the opera—the second main theme of the Allegro from No. 8, the Largo passage from No. 14, possibly also elements from other arias, though one should be wary of assuming a melodic *tic* or one of the frequent harmonic clichés in the work to be evidence of cross-reference. It is notable that Weber's revision, and improvement, of the opening melody of the Vivace retains its striking three-bar phrase patterns.

CHAPTER THREE

VIENNA, BRESLAU, CARLSRUHE:
1803–1807

Süss lacht die Liebe den Jüngling an,
Sie streuet Rosen auf seine Bahn.
J. G. RHODE: Rübezahl

HISTORY has reserved for the Abbé Georg Joseph Vogler her unkindest cut of all—ridicule. Like that of a later and greater musical Abbé, his talent for the sensational dazzled his contemporaries while concealing something of a soul divided against itself; but lacking Liszt's fitful genius, he appears now no more than a stimulating charlatan, a grotesque footnote to the careers of his pupils Weber, Meyerbeer, Winter, Ritter, Danzi and the singer Aloysia Weber.

Vogler was born in Würzburg in 1749 and showed a very early love of music, rapidly teaching himself the violin and several other instruments as well as the organ, which he took up when only nine. That this facility was shallowly grounded was revealed when he came under Mozart's beloved old teacher Padre Martini; the slow discipline of a thorough course in counterpoint fretted Vogler, leading Martini to complain that his pupil showed neither aptitude nor perseverance. He appeared at Mannheim as a teacher, advocating a new system that would turn his pupils into composers more quickly, and spent probably five years here, from 1775 to 1780, before his restless energies drove him off on a series of travels that was to last twenty years and embrace Spain, Portugal, Greece, Africa, Armenia, England, Greenland and Scandinavia (where he was taken up by Gustavus III of Sweden). By 1800 he was back in Germany, reaching Vienna, after a brief period in Prague, by 1802 or 1803. Here he was promptly engaged for the theatre by Schikaneder, and set about conquering Viennese musical society.

A small, squat man, generally dressed in a broad-tailed frock coat with black satin trousers, red stockings and gold-buckled shoes, flaunting a large decoration on the left side of his chest beneath his flowing Abbé's cloak, Vogler was a figure to excite attention. His exuberant ego, together with his elaborate compositions and a long tale of monster concerts and personal successes in half the courts of Europe, succeeded in impressing a good many musicians, even though at least as many suspected him and were in turn amused and irritated by his antics. Experienced judges praised his playing; Carl Junker 'never failed to wonder at his astonishing execution' though he

FRANZ ANTON VON WEBER
Anonymous portrait

MICHAEL HAYDN
Copy by Sebastian Stief of an anonymous portrait

THE ABBÉ VOGLER
From the portrait by Anton Urlaub

FRANZ DANZI
From the drawing by H. E. von Winter

preferred Beethoven's clearer and more inventive style;[1] Vogler's pupil Gänsbacher wrote in similar terms, but upholding his teacher:

> Herr Sonnleithner gave a musical soirée in Vogler's honour, and among various artists invited Beethoven. In Vogler's quintet I played the viola. Then Vogler was invited to improvise at the piano; he willingly set himself at the keyboard and introduced a 4½-bar theme given him by Beethoven, first an Adagio and then fugued. It was a completely unified performance, but one using harmonic progressions and modulations so new to me that I was inflamed with amazement and with delight for Vogler . . . After Vogler, Beethoven improvised on a theme given him by Vogler, 3 bars long (the C major scale, *alla breve*). I was hearing both masters for the first time. Beethoven's excellent piano playing, together with an abundance of the most beautiful ideas, astonished me beyond measure, but could not arouse my feelings to the same pitch of enthusiasm for Vogler's learned playing, with its matchless harmonic and contrapuntal treatment.[2]

Vogler was a teacher who managed to fire his pupils with at least as much enthusiasm for himself as for his music. A child of the Enlightenment, he professed a passion for order and discipline, continuing to recommend his mysterious private System; yet he also gave himself the airs of a mystic, perhaps to lend profundity to his conversation and to paper over the factual cracks in his knowledge. His own compositions at least have facility. It is appropriate that Browning's poem using his name should take the form of a flamboyant, semi-mystical monologue with rather a slippery grasp of musical metaphor.

Having gained his experience of artistic human nature through such figures as Grätz and Senefelder, and above all his own father, Weber was only too ready to fall under Vogler's influence. He arrived in Vienna at the end of September 1803, intending to study under Joseph Haydn; it was the Abbé who became his master. By 8th October he was writing to Ignaz Susann in awed tones:

> I have had the joy of learning to know Abbé Vogler, who is my best friend and with whom I am now studying his magnificent system. Every day I am with him for four or five hours. Imagine my happiness when I was with him in the evening a few days ago (you are to understand that he is writing an opera for the Theater an der Wien of which *not a soul* has seen or heard anything because he composes entirely in the night) and all at once he runs out into the third room, locks the door, closes the shutters, and acts so busily that I haven't an idea what it all means. At last he produces a stack of music, sits down at the piano, and plays to me—after I take an oath of solemn silence—the overture and other pieces from his opera. It is really heavenly music and then—what do you suppose?—he gives me his own score of the overture written in his very

---

[1] Letter to Bossler's *Musikal. Correspondenz*, 23rd November 1791.

[2] Johann Gänsbacher: Autobiography, unpublished but quoted variously including in August Schmidt: *Denksteine*, p. 121–2 (1848).

own hand in order that little by little I can work out the piano version of the whole opera. Now I sit over it and study and rejoice like the very devil for happiness.

Clearly the impressionable Weber could give Vogler the necessary injections of admiration to keep him going; however, he probably paid fully for his lessons by making the vocal score (J.39) of the mysterious opera, *Samori*, for ten days later, 18th October, he is writing to tell Susann that 'preparing the vocal score of so large an opera is no small matter.' Admiration was further expressed in two sets of variations—Eight Variations for piano (Op. 5: J.40) on the Air de Ballet from Vogler's opera *Castore e Polluce* (a lasting success in Munich, where it was first produced on 12th January 1787); and Six Variations for piano, with optional violin and cello accompaniment (Op. 6: J.43) on Naga's aria 'Woher mag dies wohl kommen?' from *Samori* itself. The J.40 Variations represent little advance in Weber's idiom: there is no sign of any new 'system'[1] or influence of Vogler's somewhat dry piano style, nor scarcely any sign of musical enterprise beyond the wish to translate the theme into various forms of piano study. Imagination plays a rather stronger role in the finale of this set, when the theme suddenly turns into a lively mazurka; and still more so at the end of J. 43. The *Samori* theme, a simple affair of rocking thirds alternating with a scale, now suggests musical rather than merely pianistic invention, as when in Variation 6 it becomes a heavily figured, chromatically harmonized Funeral March in the minor. This evaporates, by way of the thematic thirds building up a seventh-chord, into a charming 6/8 version in the major. More than in J. 40, Weber is here taken with the musical rather than the virtuosic possibilities of the theme.

The relationship between the shrewd old charlatan and his somewhat starstruck young pupil was by no means one-sided. If Weber gave Vogler much, he also found his eyes opened to several important influences during the months in Vienna. It was Vogler who seems to have awakened Weber's Romantic interest in the exotic, by way of his own wide travels, and drawn his attention to the beauties of folk song, a growing force on the young Romantics and one that was given extra impetus in the emotion surrounding the death of Johann Friedrich Herder in Weimar that December. Fired by Hamann's dictum, 'Poetry is the mother tongue of the human race', Herder had published in 1778 and 1779 his collection of *Volkslieder*, at one stroke awakening the interest of his younger contemporaries in the art that had lain concealed all about them. At Herder's feet, Goethe had learned all about folk poetry;[2] and the notion of a new area of poetry, of a vast, unexplored artistic

---

[1] 'The variations are in Vogler's system.': Weber to Susann, 2nd April 1804.
[2] 'Herder taught us to conceive of poetry as the common gift of all mankind, not as the property of a few refined cultivated individuals'. Goethe: *Dichtung und Wahrheit*.

kingdom extending among simple country people unspoiled by the sophisticated rationalizations of the city-dweller's Enlightenment and awaiting the appreciation of poets and musicians with open hearts and unprejudiced minds—this was doctrine to be drunk up thirstily by the young Romantics of the new century.

It was certainly heady wine for the young Weber. With Franz Anton at a safe distance on business in Salzburg and Augsburg, he reacted to the long hours of hard work under Vogler by taking the guitar he had now mastered and his pleasant singing voice on the round of the Viennese taverns, where his cadaverous good looks ensured that the pleasures of wine and song were soon joined by that of women. Here he made an acquaintance with popular song that was to reflect itself in his own numerous songs, and to colour his entire way of melodic thinking. His companion on these excursions was a fellow pupil of Vogler who was to remain a friend for life, Johann Gänsbacher. Now a lively and worldly twenty-five, eight years older than Weber, Gänsbacher was a Tyrolean by birth. After studying organ, piano and violin, he entered Innsbruck University in 1795, but a year later sold his violin to buy military equipment and joined the Landsturm, subsequently being decorated with the gold *Tapferkeitsmedaille*. He was in Vienna by 1801. As well as undertaking Weber's emancipation, he introduced him to Schuppanzigh, Neukomm, Salieri, Gyrowetz and Anton Wranitzky (whose daughter Caroline was later to be the first Agathe, and whose elder brother Paul had written an Oberon opera). Gänsbacher was, by every account, a dashing and well-liked character; and his effect, coupled with the hard practical study under Vogler (and the absence of Franz Anton's watchful eye), was to give Weber a chance to find the confidence he needed in his own personality—in fact, to begin growing up.

Weber studied hard but composed little in Vienna. As he wrote to Susann, 'It was no small thing for a creative soul to sit in such productive surroundings for nine months and not write a note; but it was my firm intention to listen, learn and collect for a long while before I wrote anything again.'[1] He renewed his acquaintance with Joseph Haydn and met Hummel—not Beethoven, however, whom he only came to know and admire much later. Certainly he made a strong impression on Vogler with his knowledge of the stage, for when Johann Gottlieb Rhode, the Dramaturg at Breslau, wrote to Vogler asking him to put forward names for the post of *Kapellmeister*, it was Gänsbacher and Weber who were recommended. When Gänsbacher refused the nomination, Weber was accepted, though barely seventeen and a half, and the appointment was confirmed on 8th May 1804. He paused briefly in Salzburg in June to collect his father and here on the 4th he wrote the song *Wiedersehn* (Op.30, No. 1: J.42) inspired by a Viennese love affair, thinks Max Maria, though the dedication is to Amalie Beer, Meyerbeer's

[1] Letter of 2nd April 1804.

mother. By 8th June the Webers were in Augsburg, and on the 11th they arrived, by way of Carlsbad, in Breslau.

Weber's difficulties at Breslau began before his arrival. Under his predecessor Heinrich Ebell, the versatile and talented leader of the orchestra Joseph Schnabel had taken over the direction of performances, and naturally kept his own eye on the post. On hearing of the new appointment—he was then almost thirty-seven, nineteen years older than Weber—he promptly resigned and took over the organization of the Cathedral music and the control of several important musical societies, among them the influential 'Friends of the Muses.' One can sympathize with him for being passed over; but he was to show too violent a resentment, and, not least by allowing the rivalry to be discussed in the Press, he made matters unnecessarily difficult for a boy not yet eighteen struggling with his first job. There was also disapproval awaiting Weber from at least one key player, Janitzek, who remained to make difficulties, and from the Prussian nobility who filled Breslau. For the latter, artistic considerations weighed less heavily than the indignity of someone bearing the aristocratic 'von' lowering himself to work among a troupe of players; and despite all appeals, the officers from the garrison had formed the habit of going to the theatre chiefly in order to break up performances. Later, on 16th March 1805, vitriol was thrown on the stage from both sides of the house, possibly on the orders of an un-named Prince.[1]

All the same, Weber quickly made friends, especially with the young organist of St. Elisabeth's, Friedrich Wilhelm Berner, and the pianist Josef Wilhelm Klingohr. He was reasonably well paid, and without Franz Anton's business speculations and bad debts would have been quite comfortably off. Nevertheless, he seems to have continued his Viennese way of life, and he embarked upon a long series of love affairs (perhaps including one with his prima donna, Diezel) in the intervals of furious work at the theatre. Here he plunged into the business of opera with the enthusiasm of an old pro. He formed the habits of a lifetime by taking a hand in the production, the décor, and the stage machinery, learning his natural trade the hard way, and unforgettably.

Not surprisingly, he also managed to cause great offence. Ebell criticised his tempos; he annoyed the company by insisting on the novel idea of small group rehearsals; he upset the singers when they felt that he was paying greater attention to the orchestra than to them; and as later at Dresden, he irritated audiences with his rearrangement of the players' seating. By tradition, the plan was the reverse of modern practice: the wind sat in front, with the strings at the rear. Weber tried placing first violins, oboes, horns, one cello and one bass on the right; second violins, clarinets and bassoons on the left; the violas behind; and right at the back, the trumpets and drums.

[1] Maximilian Schlesinger: *Geschichte des Breslauer Theaters* (1898).

Evidently he was trying for greater homogeneity of tone, but the players complained that they could no longer hear themselves, and the Breslauers, who liked the sound of brass, complained that the balance was bad. They added that they could not hear the orchestra properly and that this made the overtures particularly ineffective.[1] As if this were not enough, he managed to upset the town corporation by insisting on the dismissal of artists who had outlived their talent or never possessed enough of it, and by dropping poor operas that were good box-office. The new works he prepared instead included *La Clemenza di Tito* (a performance well received by the critics and noted in his diary by the young Eichendorff, then studying locally), *Don Giovanni* and a version of *Così fan tutte* by Rhode entitled *Mädchenrache*, as well as Paisiello's *Schöne Müllerin*, Salieri's *Axur* (a new version of his *Tarare*), Winter's *Elise*, Weigl's *Corsar aus Liebe*, Paer's *Camille*, Reichardt's *Tamerlan*, Himmel's *Fanchon* and Süssmayr's *Gulnare*. But before long the directors placed a veto on extra expenditure. Weber was obviously too young to carry through reforms of this searching nature and no doubt he was tactless in his handling of people: he later confessed that he only knew vaguely what he wanted or what he had to do.

He had an important ally in Rhode, who loyally stood by his appointment. Perhaps part of the reason lay in Rhode's own dramatic ambitions: he was a journalist and a bad poet who had once been a friend of Lessing and may have hoped to raise his own reputation with the new lease of life he looked for in his theatre. He had already published in the local weekly, *Der Breslauer Erzähler*, a libretto, *Rübezahl*, based on an old Silesian folk tale written down, as the first of his collection of Rübezahl tales, by J. K. A. Musäus in his *Volksmärchen der Deutschen* (1782–1789). The central figure of the mountain spirit is transformed from a kind of magical Oberon-cum-Robin Hood, who aids the poor and oppressed but shows no mercy to the proud or wicked, into a subterranean sprite of questionable morals. In Rhode's libretto, Rübezahl first appears disguised as a handsome young man; he is in love with a princess who is out for a walk in the neighbourhood. Her attendants, Klärchen, Kunigunde and Elsbeth, are easily lured away by magic sights, sounds and scents, giving Rübezahl the chance to explain that he has often invisibly accompanied her on these walks ('Ich war's der oft im Walde, unsichtbar mit dir ging'). Startled and not at all attracted by this surprising figure, and in any case being herself in love with Prince Ratibor, she calls for help; Rübezahl takes her in his arms and they sink into the ground, much to the mystification of the three girls who have returned on finding all the pretty luring things turned into horrors. When they have fled, the old steward Kurt appears looking for the Princess. Gnomes offer to show him; but upon

---

[1] Carl Hoffmann: *Die Tonkünstler Schlesiens* (1830) records these complaints from an anonymous 'competent judge', who nevertheless praises the precision and confidence of Weber's conducting.

finding himself sinking into the ground he loses his resolve and climbs angrily out again. Meanwhile the Princess has revived in Rübezahl's palace garden. Offers of immortality if she will abandon Ratibor do not move her any more than a pantomime of shepherds and shepherdesses, and she faints. Rübezahl, seizing his opportunity, swiftly dismisses his spirits and takes her in his arms, at which she comes to, calls on Ratibor, and faints once more. The frustrated Rübezahl now leaves her to sleep. In any case, he has been reminded of his duty as ruler of the spirits, and pausing only to substitute a magnificent bedroom for the garden, he vanishes. She wakes and, like Gretchen, is tempted by some jewels he has left for her; but her guardian angel prudently appears to remind her of her duty. Her reaction, yet again, is to swoon. At this point the libretto breaks off. Later, in Musäus's original tale, the princess manages to secure her captor's magic sceptre and sends him into the garden to count turnips (hence the name Rübezahl) each of which turns into a person; while Rübezahl's attention is distracted, she summons a griffin who carries her home. Only three numbers of this farrago have survived in Weber's setting (J. 44–46), and it seems unlikely that he composed much more (he later catalogued the work as a fragment). His work at the theatre absorbed most of his energies, and he took seven months, from October to May, over these undistinguished pieces. No. 3, an off-stage chorus of spirits, is four-square and empty; Kurt's recitative and arietta (No. 7) is mildly attractive, with quite an original bassoon obbligato; the quintet, No. 10, includes a graceful theme for the Princess but at the mention of friendship and love relapses into the banality which has ensnared many German composers who have attempted the simple nobility of Sarastro's music. The whole enterprise seems doomed from the start; Rhode was thinking in terms of twenty-seven scenes in two acts (fifteen in Act 1, twelve in Act 2) with eleven solo roles (perhaps not all singing) and several choruses. Weber later gave No. 3 in a concert at the Mannheim Museum on 31st March 1810, and the quintet was praised in the *AMZ* as 'gay and theatrically effective', though Spohr was scornful of the whole affair. But the fact that Weber put the work firmly behind him is confirmed by appearances of parts of it in the *Jubel* overture, the cantata *L'Accoglienza* and *Oberon*. The most successful outcome was the overture. The original is lost, apart from eleven bars of the first violin part, but the piece has become well known in Weber's reworking of the material in 1811 as *The Ruler of the Spirits* (Op. 27: J.122). Even if Marschner did not know *Rübezahl*, he was pursuing a similar vein of the supernatural when he came to write *Hans Heiling*.

Little else was composed during the two years at Breslau. It must have been a period of great strain, even for one whose life had never been easy, and the only small sign of his unfolding talents is in the choice of subjects for the two others works of the period. For the merchant and amateur flautist C. J. Zahn, he wrote at Christmas 1805 a *Romanza Siciliana* with orchestral accompaniment (J. 47), allegedly based on 'original Saracen-Sicilian motives' (a feature ignored by the *AMZ* in its favourable notice); and an *Overtura Chinesa*, now lost, that was based on a theme from Rousseau's *Dictionnaire de Musique* and was the original of the later overture to Schiller's *Turandot* (it was performed in Breslau on 1st July 1806). They are an indication of how, spurred no doubt by Vogler's tales of his travels, Weber's imagination was moving along the Romantic lines of inspiration in the exotic.

The end of the Breslau period came abruptly. Weber had asked Berner one evening to come to his house after the theatre and go over the *Rübezahl* music with him. Berner was detained, but seeing the light still on when he arrived, knocked, and receiving no answer tried the door. A pungent smell met him, and taking a step he fell over Weber's prostrate body. At Berner's shout, Franz Anton ran in from the next room and they sent for a doctor. It was discovered that Weber had absentmindedly drunk from a wine-bottle which Franz Anton had filled with acid for engraving. He was ill for two months, and never recovered his singing voice. Moreover, when he was able to get back to his work, he found that his enemies had profited by his absence to undo all his reforms. The situation was impossible; he resigned.

The next step was not so easy. Franz Anton had failed to secure his son a new post, and was himself unwell and in need of care; Weber's resignation was the signal for the creditors to pounce. The only solution seemed to be the now classic Weberian one of travelling. But at that moment Aunt Adelheid turned up, adding yet another difficulty to the situation. Help came from one of the pupils which Berner had generously passed on to his friend in need, Fräulein von Belonde, maid of honour to the Duchess of Württemberg.

Duke Eugen Friedrich Heinrich von Württemberg-Öls had since 1793 been ruler of Carlsruhe in Upper Silesia and there had established a small cultural kingdom at his residence in the depths of the forest. In his youth a rake and a dabbler in occult sciences, including Mesmerism, he had turned to the arts and now saw himself as the patron of a new Weimar. His father, Carl Christian, had reclaimed the deep, swampy woods and built at the centre of a star of alleys a beautiful little hunting lodge. Temples, grottoes, hermitages and all the paraphernalia of the Romantic landscape garden surrounded it, while swans and gondolas plied along the ornamental canals. A theatre was begun on the accession in 1793 of Duke Eugen, a vigorous supporter of the arts and himself a keen amateur oboist.[1] Weber first approached him, making much of his own supposedly noble lineage, to grant a title that would smooth the next stage of his career; the Duke sensibly replied that he would do no such thing, offering instead the honorary office of Intendant, solely on account of his talent. This was of little practical help, as Fräulein von Belonde realized, and on her insistence the Duke asked Weber to visit him, generously including Franz Anton and Adelheid in the invitation. The

[1] Martin Klose: *Carlsruhe in Oberschlesien*, in *NZfM* Vol. 87.

absence of Weber's name from the Duke's payroll confirms that he was purely a visitor.

After the intense hard work and the difficulties of Breslau, this was to be the period Weber later called a 'golden dream'. The Duke's ménage seems to have been modelled in miniature on Versailles as much as on Weimar. With his relations lodged in the town and himself established in a house on the castle square, served breakfast by the Duke's footmen and dining at the Duke's own table, Weber had the material contentment to encourage composition once more. He wrote first a brief fanfare for twenty trumpets (J. 47a), a love song *Ich denke dein* (Op. 66, No. 3: J.48), then Six Variations for Viola (J.49) mentioned nowhere by Weber and subsequently discovered by Jähns in Stuttgart. It is based on an Austrian theme, 'A Schüsserl und a Reindrl ist', known in Swabia as 'Es gefallt mi nummen eini', and was presumably written for one of the two ducal violists, Ricordeau or Baretsky. Weber later used the theme in a canzonetta for bass and piano (J. 88: 1810).

The Duke himself is honoured in Weber's only two symphonies, the first (Op. 19: J.50) composed between 14th December and 2nd January, the second (J.51) between 22nd and 28th January. Their scoring reflects the composition of the Duke's band—one flute, two oboes (for whom prominent parts were written in respect of the Duke's special interest), two each of bassoons, trumpets and horns, timpani and strings. The absence of Weber's beloved clarinet[1] has the effect of leading him to darken the scoring so as to compensate for what he felt to be the loss of its mournful, introverted character. The symphonies have another negative merit in that they show Weber's talents to lie in a different sphere. By the beginning of 1807, Beethoven's *Eroica Symphony* was two years old: there is no trace of its influence or any sign that the symphony was to Weber a viable and interesting form. He recognized the works' formal deficiencies when he later wrote of the First Symphony to its dedicatee, Gottfried Weber, that its first movement was more in overture than symphony style,[2] and later to Rochlitz, 'I am not really very pleased with anything in it except the minuet and possibly the Adagio. The first Allegro is a wild fantasy movement, perhaps in overture style, in disjointed movements, and the last could have been better worked out.'[3] The finale is perhaps more effective than he thought: it has a lively theme, and a real sense of pace. The Scherzo does show some recognition of Beethoven, in realizing that he had taken the Haydn minuet into scherzo territory: it is a vehement piece that also carries some suggestions of Ländler which Mahler must have liked. The best movement, however, is the Andante, in which Weber, freed from the necessity of mustering symphonic energies,

[1] Regehly: *Geschichte und Beschreibung von Carlsruhe in Oberschlesien* (1799) records that one of the two clarinettists had to double on viola.

[2] Letter of 9th March 1813.

[3] Letter of 14th March 1815.

can indulge his fondness for novel and dark-hued instrumental textures. There is here a Schubertian note that returns with the opening movement of the Second Symphony, even to the use of one of Schubert's favourite modulations:

Ex. 5

The minuet is rather perfunctory, the finale once more a neat idea rather carelessly worked out: as before, the most imaginative movement is the Adagio, in which Weber's love of viola tone and feeling for the atmospheric darkness of wind instruments creates an extraordinary mood from barely half a dozen instruments (Ex. 6, p. 58).

The Duke can have had little opportunity to enjoy either his symphonies, the concerto written for his horn player Dautrevaux (later to be revised in 1815 as Op. 45: J.188), or the Seven Variations on Bianchi's air 'Vien quà, Dorina bella' (Op. 7: J.53), which are the most interesting set Weber had so far composed—he had learned that a simple, even banal, theme is often the best spur to originality, and the work's virtuoso elements do not dominate his enriching imagination. The French army was drawing nearer: General Vandamme's troops were close at hand, and only the chance that Eugen fought with the Allies, and his brother against them, kept his lands safe from either side's marauding. Nevertheless, he was forced to be away for much of Weber's time at Carlsruhe, leaving affairs in the hands of his Duchess. Most writers follow Max Maria in assuming that Weber's departure in February was as a result of the ensemble's closing: in fact it continued until 1809 (a musician named Weber, presumably Franz Anton, is recorded as receiving a lodging allowance in 1808), and the reasons for Weber's departure remain obscure. Nevertheless, armed with the promise of a post as private secretary to Eugen's brother Ludwig, he left his father and aunt in Carlsruhe on 23rd February 1807, and on 17th July he arrived in Stuttgart. The discrepancy of five months is accounted for by a series of characteristic adventures. Having gone to Breslau for his papers, he fell in with his old friends and spent a happy ten days enjoying himself until he was recognized by a creditor and had to leave town hurriedly. During an improvised concert tour in the Nuremberg area he visited Bayreuth, Erlangen, Ansbach and Amberg. He seems to have travelled with one Backofen (probably the clarinettist and harpist Johann Backofen) and to have met his brother Edmund once or twice. Enjoying the period of travel and liberation, he was no doubt postponing the moment when he would have to take up a new and probably uncongenial appointment.

Ex. 6

CHAPTER FOUR

STUTTGART: 1807–1810

Hier kann ich's nicht erstreben,
Es treibt mich von dem stillen Leben,
Von der Paläste todter Pracht.
TOLL: Silvana (revised version)

WÜRTTEMBERG, AS Weber found it, was in the later stages of its spectacular and squalid death-throes. Despite its organization into Estates, which led Fox to declare the only constitutional governments in Europe to be those of England and Württemberg, and although Swabian poetic dreaminess of mind had been to some extent galvanized by the *Aufklärung* and the French Revolution, the state suffered under a succession of despots whom neither brilliant criticism nor force of law could restrain. For twenty years the country had been ruled by the tyrannical Duke Eberhard Ludwig and his mistress Wilhemina von Grävenitz, whose memorial is the great palace of Ludwigsburg; but worse was to follow with Carl Eugen. In spite of his education at the court of Frederick the Great, who wrote the tract *Le Miroir des Princes* for him, he set about contesting the authority of the Estates and imprisoning his opponents; he ruined his little country with his extravagance, selling his subjects abroad and auctioning public offices to pay for his pleasures. Operas and ballets (Jommelli was his *Kapellmeister*, Noverre and Gaetano Vestris his *maîtres de ballet*), fêtes, balls and especially hunting dominated these—Max Maria records that he even had whole lakes warmed for the winter duck-shooting—and in this tiny, impoverished corner of Germany, the court was encouraged to fashion its manners and morals after those of Versailles. Bankruptcy forced upon him a gesture of repentance in 1768—read out in the churches on his fiftieth birthday—and a sharp reduction of expenses, but it took the influence of his latest mistress Franziska, soon to be his second wife, to put his good resolutions into effect. He founded the Carlschule in Stuttgart as token of his intellectual abilities, which were admired by Schiller; yet an outspoken critic such as the poet and journalist Schubart paid for his comments with ten years in a dungeon.[1]

In 1793 Carl Eugen was succeeded by his two sons: first, Ludwig Eugen, who promptly suppressed the Carlschule and caused riots in Stuttgart when

---

[1] For a scholarly and lively account of this period, see Alan Yorke-Long: *Music at Court*, Ch. 2 (1954).

he proposed to do the same for the French Revolution by force of arms; and on his death in 1795 by his much more enlightened brother Friedrich Eugen, another protégé of Frederick the Great and the possessor of his father's more admirable qualities. But Friedrich Eugen in turn died after only two years, bringing to the throne his son Friedrich.

This was the ruler whom Weber found in full despotic control on his arrival to serve as secretary to the younger Duke Ludwig. In 1780 Friedrich had married Augusta of Brunswick, sister of George II's Queen Caroline, who had borne him two sons and a daughter; but she subsequently refused to return home with him from Russia, where he spent some time as guest of his brother-in-law the Tsarevich Paul, and remained in Catherine the Great's favours until it was discovered that the two women were sharing a lover: for this indiscretion she is believed to have been buried alive when in the last stages of pregnancy. In 1797, the year of his accession, Friedrich married George III's daughter Charlotte.

Friedrich's early days held out a good deal of promise for the much-tortured state of Württemberg; he had taken an oath on his accession to respect the Constitution, he had restrained the nobles and improved the condition of the middle class, and in general given signs of recognizing the changing spirit of the age. But this supposed liberalism proved to be no more than a struggle for his own autocracy against the nobles' oligarchy, as Hegel made clear in a bitter pamphlet *On the Latest Events in Württemberg* (1798): 'The picture of better, juster times has flashed on the souls of men, and a longing for a purer, freer condition has set all minds in motion,' he declared, exhorting, 'It is time the people of Württemberg should cease to oscillate between fear and hope, between expectation and disappointment.' But Friedrich had hardly anything except disappointment to offer. The sense of princely duty which, like his predecessors, he had learned at the feet of Frederick the Great, soon gave way to total self-indulgence. By now so immensely fat that a semi-circle had to be cut out of his table to accommodate his paunch,[1] he had nevertheless inherited a passion for hunting: accordingly whole tracts of the country were laid waste while the game was driven into the open for him. He was homosexual, and surrounded himself with handsome stable-boys and forest rangers whom he appointed to prominent court positions: chief among these was Count Dillen, an ex-groom twenty-two years his junior whom he exalted to become the second most important man in the State, and who invented for him the system of selling to young men nominal appointments at court that would exempt them from conscription. Though he was able and witty, the Duke's interests were

---

[1] Spohr: *Selbstbiographie* Vol. I: 'The great size of the latter, and the little extent of the kingdom, gave rise as is well known to the smart caricature in which the King in his Coronation robes, with the map of his kingdom fastened to the button of his knee-breeches, is represented as uttering the words: "I cannot see over all my estates!"'

KING FRIEDRICH OF
WÜRTTEMBERG

*Engraving by P. W. Tomkins, after the
portrait by Schweppe*

KING FRIEDRICH OF
SAXONY

*Engraving by C. G. Rasp, after the portrait
by Anton Graff*

predominantly sensual, and to feed them he treated Württemberg like a private hoard: indeed, when the French advanced under Moreau and Vandamme in 1800, he promptly fled to Erlangen with the treasury, later ordering his people to raise the huge indemnity demanded. At first he opposed the French, but when their success seemed probable he played a waiting hand. With the so-called Princes' Revolution in 1803, Bavaria, Baden, Württemberg and Hesse set themselves up in a commanding position over the crumbling remains of the Empire, which were finally shattered at Austerlitz in 1805. Friedrich received Napoleon at Ludwigsburg, and was rewarded with recognition of his state as a monarchy, himself as King.

The surroundings in which the twenty-year-old Weber found himself were thus an extraordinary mixture of past and future, of ridiculous, doomed feudalism and intellectual ferment, of absorption in hunting, gambling and drinking, yet delight in music: Friedrich gave operas nightly at Stuttgart or Ludwigsburg and had amazed Napoleon with a performance of *Don Giovanni*, though Spohr caused a sensation when he insisted on quiet among the card-tables during his own playing.[1] It was not the *ambiance* into which to put a lively young man with a strain of weakness in his character; yet Weber's two and a half years in Stuttgart were to prove deeply formative. He was no Beethoven to answer the King's ludicrous oppressions with a gesture of defiance; he could see, however, that any hope of a new lead must lie with artists and intellectuals, and while frankly enjoying much of the feudal existence—to the point of fitting himself out with a horse and an unscrupulous groom named Huber, and riding with the ladies on their daily carriage trips to Cannstadt or Schwieberdingen—he found greater stimulus in the strong literary background to his life here. Friedrich's treatment of the arts as a princely adornment and his impoverishment of his state gave little encouragement to music or painting outside the court: 'It is certainly hard to find good things in Stuttgart,' Weber wrote when he was on the point of leaving, 'since there exists no public centre for the arts which the citizens can come to know.' The theatre, 'despite the praiseworthy industry of the director, for a thousand reasons is no longer the road to goodness and beauty but directed almost entirely towards filling the till . . .'[2] There had been a Museum (i.e. a club) which stimulated talent, but it had shrunk to a reading circle. Hence literature, the most private but most inflammatory of the arts, was the best off; and for all the nervy despotism that would send Dukes hurrying off to uproot Trees of Liberty planted by students, Württemberg was well-stocked with intellectuals and poets. Nor did Weber merely sink

[1] Spohr, *op. cit.* Vol. I. Spohr met Weber on this visit and listened to some of *Rübezahl*: he loftily declared it amateurish, 'being always accustomed to take Mozart as the type and rule by which to measure all dramatic works.'

[2] A description couched in rather pretentious style, ending up with a list of prominent local personalities (Kaiser 6).

himself in Swabian musings over past heroics: the court librarian, Dr. Lehr, encouraged him to read Kant, Wolff and Schelling, with enduring results on his capacity for clear thinking.

Weber's post as secretary to Friedrich's younger brother Ludwig soon revealed itself as complicated in its demands. Aged fifty-one in 1807, recently established in Stuttgart on the frustration of his hopes of becoming King of Poland, Ludwig was in a state of antagonism to his brother while totally dependent on him for funds. He had little interest in opera, Max Maria records, except for the sake of the prettier singers; Weber was primarily employed in trying to bring some order into the Duke's accounts and presenting the King with begging notes for further funds. These letters he was unwise enough to embellish with phrases he knew would irritate the King, to whom he lost no time in taking a strong dislike that was cordially returned. Sometimes after keeping Weber waiting for hours in the antechamber, the King would roughly turn him out unheard, and it was not long before Weber's wit got the better of his discretion. Meeting in the passage an old woman asking for the court washerwoman, he politely directed her into the King's private room. Friedrich furiously ordered Weber's arrest and imprisonment—though only for a day, and in a room with a piano, which Weber proceeded to tune with a door-key and so to compose the song 'Ein steter Kampf ist unser Leben' (Op. 15, No. 2: J.63). It is a song which suggests exasperation rather than penitence or gloom.

Sixteen songs and several minor vocal pieces, as well as the opera *Silvana* and the cantata *Der erste Ton*, date from Weber's Stuttgart years; indeed, only nine of the thirty one works of this period are purely instrumental. It will be time to examine his solo songs—about a hundred in number all told—when they can be considered in a more general context; but we may note that much encouragement for them came from the nature of his surroundings in Stuttgart and Ludwigsburg. Extended composition was not easy; there was the direct stimulus of another new friend, the singer Gretchen Lang; and the young nobles of the court were delighted to welcome to their nightly parties a newcomer with talent and charm—for though the acid had scarred his singing voice, he could make skilful use of what remained and could always improvise cleverly with piano or guitar on any theme set him. Chief among these companions was his employer's son, the fifteen-year-old Prince Adam, who nightly used to have food, drink and illumination sent up in generous quantities to Weber's room; he seems to have shared with Chaplin's millionaire patron in *City Lights* the habit of irritably forgetting next morning the generosities of the night before, and many careful explanations had to be made by Weber's companions.

Weber also joined enthusiastically in the more intellectual company of the various Stuttgart poets, playwrights and artists who formed themselves into a society known as *Faust's Höllenfahrt* in which each member had to answer to a nickname: Weber's was 'Krautsalat'. If these gatherings, with their emphasis on a narrow, loyal brotherhood of like spirits and their carefully cultivated air of mystery, now seem merely childish, we should remember that it was a time in which artists badly needed each other's support and encouragement, and that Central European artistic life has always tended to form itself into small, mutually exclusive groups. *Faust's Höllenfahrt* was one of hundreds such, a largely frivolous counterpart to the more serious secret societies, and no more harmful or significant than the *Stammtisch* of a German restaurant. Out of these and many similar gatherings came the male voice choruses which Weber based on the traditional songs he heard there (many of these songs are still not extinct). More important, he came to know poets who could offer him verses for his songs and stimulate his literary taste. As complement to his readings under Lehr's guidance and his discussions with Haug (the editor of *Das Morgenblatt*), Matthisson (poet of Beethoven's *Adelaide*), and Reinbeck, whose verses he was to set, he met the painters Hetsch and Müller and the sculptor Dannecker—figures now forgotten but considerable in the small artistic enclave they inhabited. A more influential friend still was the poet Franz Carl Hiemer. By turn officer, actor and painter, amusing and with a lively turn of mind, convivial and idle, Hiemer was clearly cast in the mould of Weber's earlier friends, from Senefelder to Gänsbacher. Weber set him to work on the discarded Steinsberg libretto of *Das Waldmädchen* in the November he arrived in Stuttgart; the opera *Silvana* which it became was not finished until February 1810, well over two years later, and then only under pressure for more of the text, in the form of repeated demands and cajoling verse letters from the composer.

Still more influential, and as 'Rapunzel' (rampion, a salad plant) his proposer for *Faust's Höllenfahrt*, was the composer Franz Danzi. Born in 1763, he had in his day also been a pupil of Vogler and had worked in the famous orchestra at Mannheim before coming to Stuttgart as *Hofkapellmeister*; but although he undoubtedly enlarged Weber's natural appreciation for orchestral virtuosity, he also played an important part simply in recalling the young composer to his sense of vocation. Even allowing for the difficult period of settling into strange surroundings and a new job, a single song and a revision of the *Peter Schmoll* overture make a poor tally for the five and a half months that remained of 1807, before Danzi arrived and made himself felt. It is difficult to assess his influence in concrete terms. Certainly Weber's references to him show nothing but respect and affection for the senior musical friend he so urgently needed; he addressed to Danzi comic letters in verse and in musical recitative, dedicated to him among several works the cantata *Der erste Ton*, and talked long and seriously on country walks with this 'plump little man with rounded head and sharp, clever eyes that always seemed good-humoured.'[1] Danzi's cheerful nature in turn seems to have

[1] MMW, Vol. I, p. 143.

found a kindred personality he could believe in and encourage with practical advice. Moreover, his success with at least two operas gave him much in common with the composer who was to take German opera into the new territory of Romanticism.

It was through Danzi and his connexion with the theatre that Weber had come to know one of the younger members of the company, the soprano Margarethe (Gretchen) Lang. She was about twenty, daughter of the Munich violinist Theobald Lang, the possessor of what Max Maria—whose account is torn between a wish to play up his father's romantic ardour and disapproval at such strayings—calls 'a plump, seductive little figure' and 'a fund of sprightly, charming humour'.[1] Constantly in her company, he began neglecting his somewhat scanty duties and even his friends; the affair actually came to the notice of the King and roused his displeasure. There was no question of marriage, which Weber could afford even less with the debts Gretchen rapidly began mounting up for him. The little we know of her suggests an Aennchen rather than the Agathe he was soon to meet in Caroline Brandt. The only letter extant between them is a facetious invitation to the rehearsal of a travesty called *Mark Antony* in which all Weber's friends took part—travesty in two senses, for Weber played Cleopatra, with Danzi as his nurse, Hiemer was Octavia, Lehr the asp, the singer Mme. Miedke was Octavius, while Gretchen Lang herself took the part of Antony.

No encouragement to piano composition existed in Stuttgart to match the combined song-writing stimulus of Gretchen Lang, the convivial musical parties and the society of poets—with a minor exception. When Faber, Ludwig's comptroller and bailiff, returned from an appointment in the commissariat of the army and was reinstated in his former post, Weber's duties were much reduced. An obvious task for him was giving music lessons to the Duke's family; and from this came the Six Pieces for Piano Duet (Op. 10: J.81–6)[2] dated 27th November and dedicated '*à Leurs Altesses Sérénissimes Mesdames les Princesses Marie et Amélie de Württemberg*'. They are charming little pieces, each based on a simple melodic idea with characteristic accompaniment, much more genuinely four-handed than the Op. 3 set, both accessible to schoolgirl fingers and forming a neat introduction to various melodic manners. The excellent Masurek (No. 4) is in Weber's most pleasant vein; though the subject of No. 3 may actually be Danzi's by origin (Ex. 7, opposite page). It appears in other works of the period, firstly in the course of an affectionate joke musical letter (J.60) where it appears setting the words 'Ach ! nur bei Dir allein, liebster Rapunzel [i.e. Danzi] kann ich nur schmunzeln weichet der Schmerz' (this continues with a request to greet all his

---

[1] MMW, Vol. I, p. 159.

[2] No. 2 was used by Hindemith for the third movement of his *Symphonischen Metamorphosen Carl Maria von Weber'scher Themen für grosses Orchester*, to give an entertaining piece its full cumbersome title.

friends, especially—in a tender mock *bel canto* phrase—'la mia cara Puzzicaca' (i.e. Gretchen) and after some sinister Faustian sevenths closes with Weber's *Faust's Höllenfahrt* signature, 'Krautsalat'). Whether it was Danzi's own phrase or merely had come, by this letter, to be associated with him, Weber liked it well enough to make it the subject of two groups of variations as well as the third of the easy piano pieces. It appears as the Andante subject for three variations in the course of a *Grand Pot-Pourri* for cello with orchestra (Op. 20: J.64), written for the cellist Graff and probably hastily rearranged from some other form. There are traces in the autograph to suggest as much, while the finale uses a theme identified as a song of Danzi's. The Variations for Cello (J.94), finished in Mannheim on 28th May 1810 for Weber's cellist friend Alexander von Dusch, make further use of the theme: indeed, the first two variations are the same as those in the *Pot-Pourri* and the third is the second in the piano duet piece; while Var. 5 is harmonically similar to the duet's Var. 3 and Var. 6 the same as the *Pot-Pourri*'s Var. 3. In fact, the only new music in the piece is the Introduction, Var. 4 and the Coda. The explanation lies in the different technical demands of the two pieces; Graff was a virtuoso, Dusch an enthusiastic amateur who needed a piece in a hurry for a Heidelberg concert on 30th May and could presumably not have managed the quite elaborate solo part of the *Pot-Pourri*.

There was, of course, another virtuoso in Stuttgart who might have acted as greater stimulus to piano composition—Weber himself. But only four works were produced, three of them in the early part of 1808. The Variations (Op. 9: J.55), the fifth of his sets of his piano variations, is of little account except as a nimble-minded demonstration of a virtuoso's technique, and the *AMZ* did it no service by making comparisons with Beethoven's greatest variations. The review also complains of the finger-stretch being too great: Weber had exceptionally large hands that could actually play twelfths, while repeated chords of tenths with other notes filling out the harmony (say, C-G-Bb-E, as in Var. 4) are common throughout his music. With the toccata-like Leggieramente of Var. 1, the contrasting smooth scales in thirds and tenths of Var. 2, the virtuoso left hand of Var. 3 and right of Var. 5 and the need to bring out the line from flowing triplets in Var. 7, the variations make an enjoyable practice piece. Not even the characteristic 'Spagnuolo

Ex. 7

3

moderato' of Var. 4 nor the operatically inclined Fantasia of Var. 6 give them enough strength to make a concert work except by way of modest light relief.

The *Grande Polonaise pour le Pianoforte* (Op. 21: J.59) is, as the title declares, a considerably more ambitious piece—indeed, it is formally by far the most elaborate structure Weber had attempted. A *Largo* introduction foreshadows the *alla polacca* theme, very characteristic with its cheerful rhythms and its somewhat lame dominant-seventh cadence to the second strain. This is the subject of a loosely constructed rondo with some sonata characteristics. An answering episode deriving from parts of the theme leads into a long development section where, for the first time, Weber experiments with an elaborate cycle of modulations; the theme passes from E♭ and is developed through E major, F♯ major, C♯ minor and hence back to E♭. The succeeding episode is more purely pianistic, though it culminates in a surprise chordal handling of a figure from the introduction.[1] Even after the final appearance of the theme with its first episode in full, the quavers of the second bar are extended to initiate the coda, which succinctly brings into one 24-bar section almost all the thematic elements that have been used. The piece, in fact, justified its serious pretensions: it never lapses into the improvisatory harmonies of Var. 2 of J.55 and successfully brings off its unusual and dangerously loose formal structure. The brilliance of the piano writing has at last a real structural purpose to serve, and takes on a correspondingly greater power. If it is long for its content, at least Weber was trying to feel his way into larger forms that need not rely on classical sonata. The brief *Momento Capriccioso* (Op. 12: J.56), on the other hand, is a scintillating little showpiece toccata based on pattering crotchets in alternating adjacent notes and on scales—a *prestissimo* tour de force on one main idea that comes off brilliantly. Staccato chords at such speed were an unheard of boldness for the time; despite a resemblance to the scherzo of the *Eroica Symphony,* the atmosphere is much nearer Mendelssohn.

Weber also brought with him to Stuttgart the Adagio of a Piano Quartet dated Carlsruhe, 15th October 1806; to this he added three more movements (unless, as is possible, the opening Allegro was composed at the same time as the Adagio), dating the finished work 25th September 1809 (J.76). Though largely a concertante work for piano, the piece is reduced to genuine chamber scale—a simple, imaginatively handled sonata movement, a characteristic Adagio whose dramatic outbursts are well handled though somewhat doubtfully motivated, a brief, pleasant minuet and trio and a really excellent finale, rapid of invention and very well developed.

The remaining instrumental work of Weber's Stuttgart period, Nine Variations on a Norwegian Air for piano and violin (Op. 22: J.61), is of less

---

[1] The connexions between Introduction and Polacca were coolly ignored by Liszt when he removed the Introduction and pasted it in front of the *Polacca brillante* (Op. 72: J.268) and gave the whole an orchestral accompaniment.

importance. Nevertheless Weber had an affection for it and used to play it
with friends—for instance, in later years at the Prague houses of his doctor,
Jungh, and of the banker, Kleinwächter, to whom it was dedicated. From
this time also dates the Andante and Rondo Ungarese for viola and orchestra
written for his brother Fridolin, the original version (J.79) of the work for
bassoon (Op. 35: J.158).

Despite their slender nature, the Variations were extravagantly praised by
Rochlitz, who had meanwhile associated himself still more closely with
Weber by writing for him the words of *Der erste Ton* (J.58). Half recitation
with orchestra, half cantata, this salutes in high-flown and turgid language
the creation of the world, from 'gloomy Chaos's infinite powers' to the
arrival on an otherwise gracious scene of the one missing element—sound;
whereat the chorus breaks in with a fugue Weber had already composed
under Vogler. Weber's models in this work were evidently Vogler's own
Lampedo (1779) and Danzi's *Kleopatra* (1780), recitations which had enjoyed
a fair measure of success in their day. Unhappily the naïveté of Rochlitz's
words lacks the charm of Van Swieten's comparable text for Haydn's
Creation, and this coloured Weber's response to it. The tiny musical interpolations, sometimes of a single bar, can do little more than mimic or strike a
posture; and in this manner the central narrative part of the work moves
from pictorial imitation of light, clouds, the earth flowering and the arrival of
birds and animals, to man himself (chord of C major) made in God's image
(another chord of C major): only Sound, *der erste Ton,* is lacking, and the
appearance of this sets the trees rustling, the rivers roaring, birds and animals
trilling and baying.

It would be difficult to perform *Der erste Ton* today. Nevertheless, the
piece is by no means without interest and there have been enthusiasts who
find the work a breakthrough for the Romantic fusion of words and music
using new illustrative means. But if there is little in this part of the work
that marks any advance on countless Nature-imitations in seventeenth and
eighteenth century concertos such as Vivaldi's *Seasons,* it did release something hitherto dormant in Weber. Sensing a need to bind so ramshackle a
conception together somehow, he takes the chord of the diminished seventh
—already something of a cliché in his harmony—and uses it not merely as a
colouration but both as *Leitmotiv* and as the basis for harmonic explorations

Ex. 8

without precedent in his language.[1] The representation of Chaos on which the work opens exposes the chord melodically (Ex. 8, p. 67).

This gives rise to the shape which implies the words 'der erste Ton', and is built up into a long introduction:

Ex. 9

It is possible to see Danzi's encouragement in this passage, which somewhat overbalances an already lopsided work with its extended use of chromatic harmony; but the insistence on the diminished seventh does serve as a genuine unifying force through the recitation, and leads to a striking anticipation of Wagner at the mention of man's longing for the company of woman:

Ex. 10

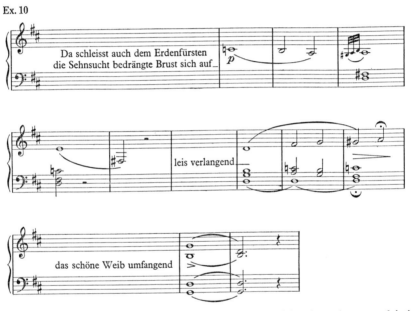

Da schleisst auch dem Erdenfürsten
die Sehnsucht bedrängte Brust sich auf

leis verlangend

das schöne Weib umfangen

Not only Sieglinde but Isolde herself are foretold in these bars; and it is sad to have to relate that thereafter the music collapses into banality. Whether or not Wagner ever heard *Der erste Ton*—and his knowledge of Weber was profound enough to make it perfectly likely—he certainly admired *Euryanthe*, towards which, more than any other work of Weber's early years, this music points.

[1] There is a curious echo of this fascination for the chord in Grillparzer's story *Der arme Spielmann*, where the old violinist describes it almost as a mystical entity, quite apart from any context.

With Danzi to encourage him, Weber might well have contributed more to the theatre during his Stuttgart years. But Hiemer's sluggishness with the *Silvana* libretto restricted him; and the only work he did for Danzi was the incidental music for a production of Schiller's five-act drama *Turandot* in September 1809 (Op. 37: J.75). The choice may seem odd, but we should remember that the fantastic and exotic elements in Gozzi's plays had excited all the Romantics, not only E. T. A. Hoffman but Schlegel and Tieck, even Goethe and Schiller themselves, to the point at which they could proclaim Gozzi 'the Father of Romanticism'. The first of his plays was translated into German as early as 1777; and when in 1790 Goethe and Schiller founded at Weimar a German National Theatre, Goethe's especial fascination for *Turnadotte*[1] placed it among their first choices. It was translated for production there in 1804 by Schiller, whose version (translated back into Italian by Maffei) later became the source of Puccini's opera.

For the music, Weber revised the *Overtura Chinesa* (now lost) which he had written in Breslau in 1804, adding six pieces by 12th September 1809. With the exception of No. 3, a March in Act 2, they are all based on the single theme of the overture: in Weber's own description, 'Drums and pipes introduce the strange, bizarre melody, which is taken up by the orchestra and presented in various forms.'[2] He had originally discovered the tune in Vol. 2 of Rousseau's *Dictionnaire de Musique* (1768), given as an 'air chinois' in the following form:

Ex. 11

The most striking characteristic of this simple tune is the F♮ in bar 3, which gives it the peculiar tinge that was later to appeal to Hindemith when he made it (in more chromatic and rhythmically attractive form) the subject of the second movement of his Weber Metamorphoses. Indeed, in a tune otherwise blamelessly pentatonic on the notes DEGAB, this note was

[1] Goethe described it as containing 'das Abenteuerliche verschlungener menschlicher Schiksal' ('human destinies fantastically interwoven').

[2] A note for a concert in 1816 (Kaiser 82).

odd enough to arouse the suspicions of Paul Listl,[1] who traced Rousseau's
source in a work by Jean Baptiste du Halde entitled *Description géographique,
historique, chronologique, politique et physique de l'empire de la Chine et de la
Tartarie Chinoise* (1735). Here the third bar is indeed given as follows:

Ex. 12

Regrettably, the overture is less interesting than its history;[2] and one may
doubt if a production of Schiller's play would be much enhanced by pieces
that have every air of being put together hastily (perhaps one may except the
final funeral march, in which flutes, oboes and clarinets sing a slow dirge over
the plodding rhythm of brass and percussion—a very Weberian piece of
scoring). But Weber clearly recognised something of himself in the subject,
and so did his contemporaries, as Mosco Carner has pointed out:

> Gozzi's influence on the German stage is best seen in those absurdly fantasti-
> cally spectacular scenes which began to find their way into the Viennese
> *Stegreifkomödie*, a local pendant to the Italian Comedy of Masks—low-class
> farces with a largely improvised dialogue. A Gozzian echo is clearly heard in
> *Die Zauberflöte*, as witness the fantastic plot in an oriental setting, the spec-
> tacular stage effects, and the two comic characters, Papageno and Monostatos
> —Viennese cousins of Truffaldino and the Moor of the Italian Masks.[3]

It was an influence that was to return in Weber's last stage work, *Oberon*;
and lived after him in countless German Romantic operas after Gozzi, among
them the first opera of the youthful Wagner, *Die Feen* (after Gozzi's *La
Donna Serpente*).

But by the time of *Turandot*, Weber's affairs in Stuttgart had begun to
approach crisis point at a speed that was accelerated by Franz Anton, who
arrived without warning in April 1809, in a carriage with a double bass
strapped on the top and, among his personal belongings, two large dogs.
Aunt Adelheid had died in Carlsruhe on 22nd August 1807, and eventually
the old man had no course but to seek out his son. Now past seventy-five,
feebler in wits but a touchingly proud father, Franz Anton lost no time in
meddling well-meaningly with his son's affairs. Little harm was done by his
pompous correspondence with Rochlitz,[4] to whom he sent the score of *Der*

[1] Paul Listl: *Weber als Overtürenkomponist*, p. 27 (1936). See also Wilfried Brennecke:
Die Metamorphosen-Werke von Richard Strauss und Paul Hindemith, in *Hans Albrecht In
Memoriam* (1962).

[2] A view not shared by Stravinsky, a great Weber admirer, who singles it out for praise;
a conversation quoted by Erwin Kroll: *Carl Maria von Weber* (1934).

[3] Carner: *Puccini: a Critical Biography*, p. 441 (1958).

[4] MMW, Vol. I, pp. 164–6.

erste Ton he found lying in their room; but unfortunately he did not confine his interference to musical matters. Towards the end of 1809, coming upon eight hundred gulden Duke Ludwig had passed to Weber for the purchase of horses in Silesia, Franz Anton promptly despatched the entire sum to settle his own Carlsruhe debts. Weber was thrown into a panic by the loss, the more so when he failed in his hopes of borrowing from an acquaintance named Höner, the keeper of a country inn at Schwieberdingen where he had been in the habit of spending freely. He had already confessed and promised restitution when Huber, his former groom, approached him with the news that Höner had changed his mind and sent a thousand gulden. Suspecting no ulterior motive in Höner's loan, Weber thankfully settled his obligations. He had forgotten the King's practice of selling posts at court to handsome young men, who were thereby saved from conscription into the army; and Höner, who doubtless overrated Weber's influence with the King, had a son of military age. Then in January 1810 the boy was called up. Höner promptly brought an action against Weber to recover his loan, and the King agreed to prosecute. *Silvana* was by now in rehearsal; and on 9th February Weber was at the theatre with Danzi when the police entered and arrested him. He was confined for sixteen days in a room in an inn, cut off from his father and his friends and ignorant of what charges were to be brought against him.

These proved to be three in number. Before his arrest there had been a minor scandal over the disappearance of some silver; the servants' quarters were searched, but Weber had refused to submit to this indignity. During his imprisonment his rooms were gone over and several articles, including a pair of silver candlesticks, were discovered. It is impossible to believe that Weber or even his father actually stole them; and hardly more probable that some enemy arranged a 'plant'. The most likely explanation seems to be that they were left behind by Prince Adam after one of the many parties in Weber's rooms and never formally returned. Franz Anton, put under considerable pressure, stood up well to questioning and defended his son hotly, adding that he himself was only a 'poor foolish man whose memory was gone'. Certainly no-one, not even the hostile King, seems to have believed in the charge.

The matter of the embezzlement of Duke Ludwig's eight hundred gulden was also easily dealt with, since the money had been repaid. But this had been done with the sum borrowed from Höner; and the third charge, of bribery and association with plots for military exemption might have proved less simple to dispose of. Weber was able to swear that he had no idea that the loan had any sinister purpose behind it; but matters must have looked bad for him until the King, realizing that it would be as well for the whole practice of buying appointments not to receive too much public scrutiny, allowed the matter to drop. Weber was about to be banished when forty-two other creditors got in first and had him rearrested on 17th February. He owed two thousand five hundred gulden, rather more than three times his assets; but when the King refused to press these charges officially, the matter was settled by Weber's agreeing to consolidate his debts and pay them off by degrees.

This made possible his release, but also his banishment by the King. On the morning of 26th February 1810, the Webers were awakened by a police officer, told to pack up their effects, and put into a carriage which was to take them to the nearest frontier point. They had between them forty gulden; but fortunately their escort, a police officer named Götz, had remained sympathetic to Weber throughout his troubles and now privately added twenty-five gulden of his own. He also passed on some letters of introduction to friends in Mannheim, given him by Danzi. So the Webers came, not to the fortress of Hohenasberg as their few remaining friends feared, but to the frontier post of Fürfeld, where they were officially informed that they were banished from Württemberg in perpetuity.

CHAPTER FIVE

SILVANA

Waldeinsamkeit,
Die mich erfreut,
So morgen wie heut'
In ew'ger Zeit;
O wie mich freut
Waldeinsamkeit.

TIECK: *Der blonde Eckbart*

THREE DAYS before he and his father were precipitately expelled from Württemberg, Weber finished the finale of *Silvana* (J. 87),[1] dating the orchestration 23rd February 1810. The first number to be written, the hunting chorus (No. 3) bore the date 18th July 1808; and the opera was, it will be remembered, a re-fashioning of Steinsberg's *Waldmädchen* libretto of 1800. How much actually survived into *Silvana* it is not now possible to say, since Weber may have destroyed his previous workings. There are three names in common, Silvana herself, Krips and Mechtilde (in the revised version, Mathilde), and certainly the overture is a re-working of *Waldmädchen*—it is also exceptional in Weber's output in not being based on themes from the opera.[2] A sentimental-romantic text by Steinsberg was re-fashioned, intermittently and under pressure from the composer, by the second-rate poet Hiemer; the whole was set to music that had first been conceived in 1800 and reassembled, revised and recomposed over a period of a year and a half filled with other distractions; it is surprising that the opera has any kind of coherence at all. But for all the work's unevenness, both in its proportions and in its style, it contains some striking music alongside patches where convention has the upper hand, and much to show an original talent developing along its natural course. It is indeed remarkable what Weber does with a plot, larded with very routine comic relief, that gives every opportunity for stock sentimental and heroic posturings.

After the overture, Act 1 opens on a wooded landscape: on the left is a cave, on the right undergrowth and wild berries. Horns herald a bear-hunt led by

---

[1] The score is in WG, Reihe 2, Vol. 2.

[2] There are three references to the opera, however: the first three bars recur in the Act 2 finale to introduce the Herald; bars 7–20 of the Andante are bars 10–23 of Silvana's awakening music in No. 12; and the second subject of the Allegro reappears in both versions of No. 4 (a and b).

Fust (bs.): they sing a chorus (No. 1, Introduction: 'Das Hifthorn schallt')
before continuing their chase. Silvana, dressed in furs and leaves, now emerges
timidly from the cave with a basket; she begins picking berries and dancing
between the bushes, but disappears again when the bear arrives, pursued by
the hunters who kill it in front of the cave and disperse. When Rudolf's squire
Krips (bs.) appears with food and wine, he is at first startled by the bear and his
relief at finding it dead is dispelled by a glimpse of the mysterious Silvana.
He revives sufficiently to sing to the returning hunters his first song (No. 2,
Aria: 'Liegt so ein Unthier ausgestreckt'), before leaving. Count Rudolf
von Helfenstein (ten.) now appears, to be greeted by a chorus in praise of the
freedom and comradeship of the woods (No. 3, Coro: 'Halloh, im Wald nur
lebt sich's froh!'). But Rudolf is melancholy, for he cannot return the love of
Mechtilde, betrothed to him by her father, Count Adelhart (No. 4a, Scena:
'So Soll Denn Dieses Herz'; or No. 4b, Scena: 'Arme Mathilde!') Both he and
Krips now catch a glimpse of Silvana, and having unsuccessfully ordered Krips
into the cave (No. 5, Duetto: 'So geh' '), he enters himself, leaving Krips voicing grave doubts (No. 6, Arietta: 'Ein Mädchen ohne Mängel'); eventually
Krips decides to climb a tree. Rudolf emerges with the reluctant Silvana, who
though dumb manages to answer his kindly questioning by signs and slowly
responds to his warmth. Rudolf is enchanted; the more so when she responds
to his declaration of love by laying her head on his breast. He sends Krips for
his retainers, and questions Silvana, whose refusal to leave with him he puts
down to a secret he cannot fathom (No. 7, Scena: 'Willst du nicht diesen Aufen-
thalt'). She in turn, frightened by the arrival of his men, tries to make him stay
with her in the cave; he is due at a tournament in Adelhart's castle, but first
calls for refreshment. In No. 8 (Finale: 'Geniesst, jedoch bescheiden'),
Rudolf takes Fust on one side while Silvana is dancing and tells him to drug
her wine; and during his drinking song 'Vater Rhein' she gradually falls
asleep in his arms. The company steals away, carrying Silvana with them.

Act 2. In a room of his castle, Adelhart (bs), is angrily trying to persuade
Mechtilde (sop.) to accept Rudolf, whom she does not love (No. 9, Duetto:
'Wag es, mir zu widerstreben.'): since the disappearance of her sister Ottilie,
stolen by Hanns von Cleeburg in revenge for his rejection by Adelhart's wife,
his fortunes depend on the marriage. Left alone, Mechtilde bemoans her
situation (No. 10a, Scena: 'Er geht!'; or No. 10b, Scena: 'Weh mir, es ist ges-
chehn'), but consents to follow her maid Clärchen (sop.) who arrives looking
oddly secretive. The scene changes to the garden, where Albert von Cleeburg
(ten.) son of Hanns, is waiting with his squire Kurt (bs.). The two couples
separately declare their love (No. 11, Quartetto: 'Mechtilde! Geliebter!').
Failing to persuade Mechtilde to disobey her father and flee, Albert leaves to
reason with Rudolf. Meanwhile, Silvana is lying asleep in Rudolf's room; a
large mirror hangs on the wall. In No. 12 (Scena: Pantomime), Rudolf regards
her tenderly but hides himself as she stirs. She wakes slowly and seems puzzled,
but catching sight of herself in the mirror she begins to respond to her reflection, then to dance before it, finishing up in Rudolf's arms. He begs her to stay
with him, and discovering that she has a father in the woods sends Krips to

fetch him; Silvana now embraces him, and he declares his love (No. 13, Aria: 'Ich liebe dich!') Krips interrupts to summon him to the tournament, giving him an anonymous letter revealing that Mechtilde loves another. Rudolf is naturally delighted, and departs leaving the bemused Krips to relieve his feelings in a drinking song (No. 14, Tempo d'un Tedesco: 'Sah ich sonst ein Mädchen'). In the finale (No. 15: 'Triumph! Triumph!'), Adelhart, Rudolf and Mechtilde enter the ceremonial hall and the Herald (ten.) announces the winner of the first three prizes in the tournament—an unknown knight who is eventually persuaded to reveal his name. It is Albert von Cleeburg; but when Adelhart orders his arrest, Rudolf, supported by Mechtilde, comes to his defence.

Act 3. In the forest, by Silvana's cave, a storm is raging (No. 16, Introduzione, Coro: 'Wie furchtbar'). Albert has escaped with his men, and is now brooding angrily on the insult shown him. The storm gradually abates, and Kurt is urging him to go further away when the voice of Ulrich (speaker) is heard calling for Silvana; presently, aged and dressed like a pilgrim, he appears in search of her. He reveals himself as Hanns von Cleeburg's former squire, and tells how he had been forced to take Adelhart's daughter away into the woods one stormy night and kill her. But taking pity, he brought her up instead as Silvana and would now like to restore her to her father. Lights are seen: Fust appears with his men looking for Silvana's 'father', shortly followed by Adelhart's servant, Hugo, who has them all seized and taken back to the castle. Meanwhile, Adelhart, furious at the turn of events (No. 17, Aria und Recitativo: 'Welch schrecklich Loos'), has Silvana brought in with an executioner. Resisting all pleas, he orders her death (No. 18, Terzetto: 'Nieder mit ihr!'); but Rudolf and Mechtilde interrupt and a violent quarrel ensues. Adelhart draws a dagger and seizes Silvana. Hugo now enters with his captives: Albert tells Adelhart he is about to kill his own daughter, and by a birthmark she is indeed identified as the lost Ottilie. She now recovers her voice, silenced at Ulrich's command; Adelhart joins her to Rudolf, Mechtilde to Albert, and all ends in feasting, rejoicing and dancing (No. 19, Coro, Finale: 'Mit dem Liebesgott im Bunde').

Silvana was originally described as a 'Romantic Opera in Three Acts'; in later scores 'Romantic' is sometimes altered to 'heroic' or 'heroic-comic'. Act 2 of the original MS is missing; the principal sources for the music are the MS of the copy Weber made for the première in Frankfurt on 16th September 1810, the revision for the Berlin production of 1812 (which included new versions of Nos. 4 and 10), and finally, most authoritatively, a score he made in Dresden. But the opera to some extent reflects its Stuttgart origin in its careful writing for the members of the royal company—Rudolf was composed for the tenor Krebs, Krips for Weberling, Silvana for Gollin and Mechtilde for Gretchen Lang, who wanted a sentimental-romantic part. Moreover, Danzi provided the direct incentive, as Weber acknowledges: 'Here, stimulated and encouraged by the friendly sympathy of the excellent

Danzi, I wrote an opera, *Silvana*'.[1] It was Danzi, too, who won from Count Winzingerode permission to stage the completed work—a plan that was frustrated by the Webers' abrupt departure. The importance of the cello part may well reflect Danzi's liking for the instrument; he was the son of a famous cellist.

Along with his own originality and instinct for the stage, Weber acquired from his surroundings a well-developed sense of what was merely effective. If a convention went across well, he was readily persuaded of his merits; and some of the numbers lean rather heavily on the primitive Romantic conventions suggested by Hiemer's archaic, platitudinous text. Weber had not yet developed the skill and confidence to trust to his own sense of effect. This note of caution extends to the comic relief; for though praised by most Weber biographers as in the spirit of Papageno or Osmin, Krips is a considerably more conventional retainer figure, bumbling and cowardly, speaking musically in the normal popular accent of German folksong without contributing much of his own. His Arietta (No. 6) draws its engaging character less from the simple melody than from the accompaniment, lightly scored strings with an obbligato flute and bassoon two octaves apart for the *Zwischenspiele*. His Tempo d'un Tedesco (No. 14) has a lively violin obbligato dancing round the cheerful tune: this drinking song, with its refrain 'Rumbidiwidibum', anticipated other Weber songs by becoming a popular beer-cellar number beyond his own immediate circle.

Adelhart is a more ambitious piece of character drawing. Though not yet developed as the villain type Weber was to characterize in Caspar and Lysiart, his lineage is clear from even a brief excerpt (see Music Example No. 50, p. 217–8). But he is more than a mere type, and though shaken by violent and not always convincing fits of coloratura in the middle of No. 17, he does show genuine affection for Mechtilde. She remains a somewhat shadowy figure; Weber does not seem to have had a very clear idea of how to portray an oppressed woman whose nature is sympathetic but who nevertheless stands in the way of the hero and heroine's happiness. It is significant that she flowers most in the Quartet (no. 11), when with *Tristan*-like cries of 'Mechtilde! Geliebter!' she and Albert fall into one another's arms and join their retainers Kurt and Clärchen in a declaration of love. Weber was wise not to give her and Albert a love duet, however, since such a luxury is obviously denied his principal lovers, Rudolf and Silvana. Rudolf himself is quite precisely characterized; indeed, though he foreshadows *Oberon's* hero, he is in many ways more vivid than the monotonously knightly Huon. His wooing of Silvana has real musical tenderness, the natural complement to his reluctance (in No. 4) to hurt Mechtilde and indeed the product of a more introspective nature than operatic knights generally permit themselves. His chief defect is one common to Weber's style at this period, and one he only over-

[1] *Autobiographische Skizze* (Kaiser 127).

came with difficulty—a tendency to think of melodic lines in instrumental rather than vocal terms.

The whole nature of the opera tends in this direction. As soon as the characters find themselves in the open air, new invention breathes into them; and this is through no great transformation of their vocal lines but by way of the natural scenery Weber was able to depict through his genius for instrumental sound. The very opening shows us the flair that was to be fully realized in *Der Freischütz*: a soft, slowly stirring string melody dissolves into a mysterious tremolo over which horns call from different quarters of the stage; and the arrival of the hunters is the signal for a chorus inferior in invention to, but no different in nature from, that of *Freischütz*. Again, the same scene in the forest at the start of Act 3 this time produces an impressive storm, all swirling strings, booming syncopated horns and flashing piccolo and flute; but with the effects made thematic and brilliantly built into the music of the apprehensive chorus of retainers and the outraged and desperate Albert. Weber is feeling his way towards the Romantic identification of personal mood and natural phenomena. This concept was meanwhile being expounded by one of the philosophers he was studying at the time, Schelling, in many ways the philosophic voice of the Romantics, for whom nature and spirit were each part of a so-called *Weltseele*: 'Die Natur soll der sichtbare Geist, der Geist, der unsichtbarer Natur seyn.' When Berlioz's Faust contemplates the *Nature immense* all around him, or Siegfried lies in the dappled forest by Fafner's cave, we cannot properly distinguish whether Nature produces the mood or whether man is projecting his mood upon his surroundings. So, tentatively, it is with Albert in Silvana's wood; and the graphic, instinctively well-controlled music shows how Weber's invention rose to recognize something of himself in the situation.

Silvana herself is, of course, an intensely Romantic conception. The hunters sing that only in the woods can they find contentment; but she actually embodies it, so much so that Krips's first reaction on catching sight of her is to believe her to be a wood-spirit. She is a child of nature, elusive and fascinating, a creature of the instinct and simplicity that had somewhere been lost in the Enlightenment, remote but (as Rudolf finds) accessible to man when he woos her with an open heart. Her dumbness can be conquered and her voice set free again; this also gives her an exciting oddity, and of course plays straight into the hands of a composer with a stronger instinct for instruments than voices. She is characterized mostly with the oboe and the cello, generally representing the skittish and the tender sides of her personality. After she has first stolen out of her cave, over cautiously moving string chords, it is to one of Weber's favourite polaccas on the oboe that she dances around picking berries; but when Rudolf questions her, it is the cello which graphically 'speaks' her reluctance to leave a place she has grown to love. His suggestion that a human love—for himself, in fact—might be substituted is met with a tender string phrase in which, as in *Der erste Ton*, we catch a foretaste of Sieglinde:

Ex. 13

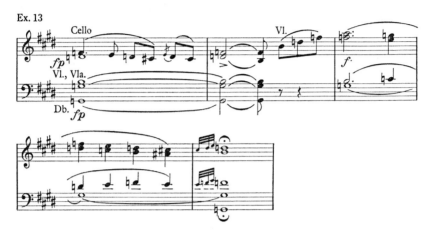

The rest of their conversation is carried on by way of pantomime cleverly illustrated in the cello, until Silvana breaks once more into a nimble dance to a tune played by oboe (later flute, then together) over the rustic, open-air sound of wind instruments—clarinets, bassoons and horns, in sturdy rhythms and harmonies—which only much later is 'humanized' with the addition of strings to prepare the way for Rudolf's drinking song.

This technique is more fully developed in the scene of Silvana's awakening in Rudolf's room. She stirs out of sleep (hushed strings as Rudolf steadily gazes at her) to a woodwind figure from the overture, tries the mirror out to brief, puzzled woodwind scraps, makes a nimble by-play to a gawky oboe phrase before going into another of her lively dances, this time on flute. With Rudolf's more passionate declaration, she comes her nearest to actual utterance. It is the 'oboe' side of her as well as the 'cello' side that Rudolf is wooing; and when he begs her to answer his avowal of love, if not with her voice then with her eyes, it is impossible not to see the feminine sparkle in them as the oboe keeps him in suspense for just a moment before summoning the resources of full woodwind to reply ardently with his own phrase (Ex. 14, opposite page).

Passionate scales on the strings are now united with the throb of the horns and bassoons, and though the oboe's more decorative answer to the repeated question is still reassuring, there is a cadenza of considerable independence before Rudolf is permitted to break into his rapturous 'Mein! Mein!'—at which the wit and charm of the music unfortunately dissolves into more matter-of-fact jubilation.

Silvana, then, is a mixture between simple, rather naïve folkiness and ambitious coloratura arias, between enchanting strokes of Weber's own

Ex. 14

imagination and the invasion of routine *Singspiel* convention. It foreshadows both the knightly world of *Euryanthe* and the simple open-air charm of *Freischütz*, attempting a marriage between the two basic Romantic concepts they represent—mediaeval chivalry and the pure life of the woods. Only Weber could have brought off a love duet between a tenor and an oboe; but a man more sure of his ground would have seen through the hollowness of most of the chorus work—the ensembles are rather more distinctive, though by virtue (or rather, deficiency) of his vocal style, he was unable to give definition to separate characters speaking contrasting points of view in the same situation.

These defects were plain to a number of Weber's colleagues, and with his usual candid self-criticism (at any rate, after the event), he paid more attention to them than to two reviews, one of which did little more than catalogue a list of virtues: 'Firm delineation and unity of character, truth of musical expression, lively inner feeling, original and not overloaded scoring...' etc, etc.[1] This was at the time when he conducted the Berlin première of 10th July 1812—an occasion made tense by the various cliques ranged against him, led chiefly by his rivals Righini and the regular conductor, B. A. Weber. It was principally after criticism by his namesake, and by his friend Friedrich von Drieburg (a composer and expert on Greek music), of the instrumental style of his vocal lines that, as well as making other minor revisions, he completely rewrote Nos. 4 and 10 to new texts by a Berlin lawyer named Toll.[2] They are undoubtedly superior in their second form; though similar material is sometimes drawn upon, the arias are shorter, formally sounder, better written from the singer's point of view and (especially with Rudolf's No. 4) more sharply characterized. Weber knew this, and even attributed the success of the Berlin performances partly to the new arias with which, he declared in his diary, he at last obtained 'real insight into aria form. The old ones were too long, and when corrected lost their real coherence and became too varied. I have also made a note that I must watch over my style so as not to become monotonous. In my melodic forms the holdings of notes are too many and too prominent. Also in respect of tempo and rhythm I must in future try for more variety.' He goes on to express pleasure at the success of the scoring and at the admission from his enemies that he possessed genius; but the passage shows that the most painful part of an earlier interview had sunk in. His diary for 13th May 1812 had recorded:

> Early to see Drieburg. He told me that everything would go well with my opera, and made various observations: I grasp at effects, the scoring is the most brilliant aspect, the voice parts are sometimes neglected, and one piece

---

[1] *AMZ* XIV, p. 532 and 572 ff.

[2] The tune of the Andantino of Mechtilde's original No. 10 was salvaged to make the subject of the variations of the fifth of the Violin Sonatas (Op. 10, No. 5: J. 103) and again as the theme of the Seven Variations for clarinet and piano (Op. 33: J. 128).

seems rather like another, so that a considerable monotony spreads over the whole . . . I find a good deal of truth in the first remark: my opera *Abu Hassan* is much clearer and sounder . . . The last remark made me very sad, since I cannot decide whether it is just or not. Have I no variety of ideas, so that I lack evident genius? . . . This uncertainty depressed me enormously: at no price will I be in the middle rank of thousands and thousands of composer-lings; if I cannot climb to a high and unique position, I would rather not live, or beg my bread as a pianist with lessons . . . so I make no secret of my motto: Perseverance leads to the goal. I shall watch closely over myself, and time will teach me and the world whether I have made good use of this very honest opinion.

Silvana was the first of Weber's operas to achieve a success, and the earliest to be translated (into English, by C. A. Somerset: London, Surrey Theatre, 2nd September 1828). In 1877 a version was made by Widor; and for production at Hamburg on 5th January 1885 Ernst Pasqué rearranged the piece into a Prologue, four acts and an Epilogue, conflating the four principal characters into two and giving Silvana words to sing in place of the oboe and cello solos. The music was revised by Ferdinand Langer to incorporate songs, the *Invitation to the Dance* and parts of the piano sonatas. It was given in this form in many German theatres, regardless of the removal of one of the main points, Silvana's dumbness, and of the butchery of the music. There is a case for reviving *Silvana* in a sympathetic production that does not try to make the work something it is not; the opposition to the Pasqué-Langer version was trenchantly put at the time by Hanslick: 'If this is not barbarism, to tear fragments out of separate sonata movements and other pieces to make cheap operatic effects the composer never dreamed of—then I don't know the meaning of the word. A genuinely pious feeling would leave the old *Silvana* undisturbed and the new one—unperformed.'[1]

[1] Eduard Hanslick: *Webers Hundertster Gebürtstag*, in *Musikalisches Skizzenbuch* (1888).

CHAPTER SIX

MANNHEIM AND DARMSTADT: 1810–1811

Zum zweiten Mal geboren . . .
Weber in his diary, 26th February 1810

MANNHEIM WAS the obvious destination of the two refugees. It lay a short journey along the Neckar valley from Stuttgart; it was the town in which Franz Anton had begun his career and in which he might hope to find old friends; his son had been armed with letters of introduction there from the faithful Danzi. Moreover, the musical lustre that Mannheim had possessed in Danzi's heyday there was by no means entirely dimmed. Under the Elector Carl Theodor, the famous orchestra had risen to heights of virtuosity that were to influence Mozart and indeed the whole course of symphonic music; but the opera, too, had won a name as among the best in Germany before the Elector had transferred his court to Munich in 1778. Part of the company followed him, the rest dispersed; in 1794 the city passed into the hands of the French and the bombardment of the following year laid low much of the town, including the opera house. Re-established under Venningen, the theatre had won itself a good reputation, though the conductor, Peter Ritter, was said to be an ineffective organizer, and according to Weber did not give the orchestra a strong enough lead.[1]

But if official music was still recovering from the effects of the war, there was no lack of amateur activity in the town. In 1803 Mannheim had passed into the hands of Carl, created Grand Duke of Baden by Napoleon, and married by him to Josephine's niece Stéphanie Beauharnais as part of the grand design for harnessing Germany to French interests; and in the same year there was founded a club named the Casino, with a library, card-room and smoking room. It was the wish of some of its members to admit ladies from time to time that led to the formation of a rival concern dedicated to 'Literature, Music, Female Graciousness, all the Arts and every means of Sociability'; this met in the Hillesheim Palace, and by virtue of the interest taken in it by the Duke and Duchess was named the Carl-Stéphanie Museum. Here were given concerts that rapidly reasserted the Mannheimers' interest in good instrumental music. Moreover, amateur performers were not lacking in a town that had been compelled by the fortunes of war to democratize itself at unusual speed. Taxation had borne heavily on the aristocracy—even

---

[1] Weber praised his opera *Der Zitherschläger* in a notice written that autumn, boldly (considering the political situation) admiring it for resisting weak French influences in a truly German work (Kaiser 9).

the Duke and Duchess were forced to live in comparative modesty—and the effect of so many soldiers billeted in the grandest houses and with the richest merchants, coupled with the influence of Freemasonry and of the secret societies, was to bring classes much more closely together than was possible in the feudal backwater of Württemberg. Though Napoleon's censorship was still in force and open political or philosophical discussion was inhibited, there was nothing to hinder the arts. Men of all classes were glad to meet and make music together; even if Carl Theodor was another creature of Napoleon, here at least was fresh air for Weber, a composer whose art could never have flourished in the stifling, archaic atmosphere of Stuttgart.

In charge of the Museum concerts was the energetic amateur musician Gottfried Weber, who had been born in 1779 at nearby Freinsheim and had studied law and philosophy at Heidelberg and Göttingen, becoming a barrister and judge at Mannheim, Mainz and Darmstadt. As a boy he had abandoned the piano for the flute, at which he became expert, later adding organ and cello to the list of instruments he mastered. His other activities included the foundation of the Mannheim Conservatory, the publication of several learned treatises including the highly successful *Versuch einer geordneten Theorie der Tonkunst* (1817–21) and a study of the authenticity of Mozart's Requiem, the foundation in 1824 of a music magazine, *Cäcilia*, which he edited to his death, the invention of a new kind of metronome and a wealth of conducting and composition. A few weeks before Franz Anton and Carl (to whom he was no relation) arrived in Mannheim, he had married his second wife, the singer Augusta von Dusch, sister of the amateur cellist Alexander. Gottfried Weber's own father was then seventy-six, and in their house lodging was readily found for Franz Anton. Having settled his father, and taken part in a musical evening as a pianist, Weber pressed on to Heidelberg with Gottfried to visit Alexander von Dusch and to present further letters of introduction from Danzi to the music director, Hoffman.

This was to plunge into one of the capital cities of Romanticism. As soon as Clemens Brentano had settled there with his wife Sophie in 1804, what Hölderlin called *jene gigantische, schicksalskundige Burg* became a rallying point for the poets of his circle. The beauty of the scenery, with its mediaeval atmosphere of castles rising through the deeply forested banks of the Neckar, the intellectual stimulus of the newly revived University, the literary traditions going back two hundred years to when Opitz had made it the centre of the German Renaissance, all combined to provide an ideal atmosphere in which the Romantics could gather. The Middle Ages were brought a stage closer when Görres edited his *Die teutschen Volksbücher*—a collection which, more than Herder's of 1778–9, strikes the nationalistic note typical of Romanticism. The impetus of Scott's *Minstrelsy of the Scottish Border* of 1802, which Achim von Arnim had discovered during his British travels, lay behind this and behind the famous collection of *Volkslieder* published by Arnim and

Brentano in 1805 as *Des Knaben Wunderhorn*—a mine of Romanticism that continued to give rich yields for many decades to come. In Heidelberg, too, Weber's old Eutin friend Voss was living, locked in deadly intellectual combat with his enemy Creutzer. In 1808 there appeared the second edition of *Des Knaben Wunderhorn*, together with the short-lived journal, *Zeitung für Einsiedler*—a collection of poems, tales, legends and oddities of old German lore to which a wider group of poets than the Heidelberg Romantics contributed; it foundered, however, on the Voss-Creutzer quarrel, and attempts to revive it were merely abortive. But the poetic glamour of the group attracted many contributors, among them the brothers Grimm (whose famous *Kinder- und Hausmärchen* followed in 1812–15), not to mention Rückert, Lenau, Gottfried Keller, Hebbel, and Eichendorff, many of whose best poems were written while he was studying at Heidelberg. The original movement was shortlived, for by 1808 the Heidelberg group had more or less disintegrated; but its influence on the younger writers, artists and composers was still potent by the time Weber arrived two years later and lasted far beyond his own lifetime.

Dusch gave Weber a most cordial welcome in Heidelberg, introducing him to a wide circle of friends that ranged from scholars, poets and musical theorists as well as Danzi's personal friends the Houts—a talented family who lived at Stift Neuburg, a twelfth-century monastery turned into a private house—and to the student fraternities of the University. Among the latter, Weber's talents were an immediate success: he arranged a serenade of students and joined in their activities so enthusiastically that he became involved in a riot between two rival *Korps* which the police had to quell. This resulted in the cancellation of the concert he had just secured from Hoffman and undid all his friends' good work on his behalf; he had made a good impression in the town, especially after playing his 'Vien quà, Dorina bella' variations at an amateur concert, but was now obliged to return to Mannheim.

Here Gottfried Weber had arranged a concert, which duly took place on 9th March: it included the First Symphony and several piano works which Weber played himself, and was evidently an artistic success though it added only thirteen gulden to his total capital of forty. The Stuttgart debts loomed; accordingly he set about arranging a further concert, writing on 19th March to Venningen to ask for permission and facilities. In Venningen's absence, an assistant answered curtly giving permission so long as it could take place that week so as not to interfere with Amateurs' Night; to which Weber replied that this was hardly possible as he could not raise an orchestra in time; moreover, he pointed out, the Amateurs would not suffer from his concert as they had only three more to give, at dates that did not in any way conflict with his own plans. He ended by putting in a good word for *Silvana*. Venningen regretted that he had no place for the opera, but allowed a concert on 2nd April in which Weber included a number of his own works, among them the Piano Quartet and First Symphony, plus the usual improvisations. The programme also included the première of *Der erste Ton*, with the famous actor Esslair to declaim Rochlitz's text—with such effect, writes Max Maria, that the audience burst into applause before the entry of the chorus. The Duke and Duchess were away, but the concert nevertheless netted Weber fifty-three gulden.

The concert's success was a highpoint of this brief but exceedingly happy period of expansion. Between arriving in Mannheim at the end of February and beginning *Abu Hassan* in October, Weber composed nothing larger than songs or canons except the First Piano Concerto and the Six Little Violin Sonatas (the cello variations, as we saw, were merely assembled from various sources). The canons were trivia: as Gottfried Weber wrote in *Cäcilia*, his circle had a private convention whereby letters between them should be in this form;[1] thus 'Die Sonata soll ich spielen' (J.89) is a reply to a request from Gottfried to play a new piano sonata dedicated to Weber, couched in a mock-mournful chromatic vein, satirizing the music's style;[2] 'Canons zu zwey sind nicht drey' (J.90) is an elaborate riddle canon which Jähns elucidates at great length in his catalogue; 'Leck' mich im Angesicht' (J.95) was probably a PS in a letter to Gänsbacher; and no doubt various others were exchanged. They are of no importance except as witness to the fact that Weber was now happy among musical friends. Of the three songs that were the only other music he wrote this spring, the guitar song 'Die Schäferstunde' (Op. 13, No. 1: J.91) also testifies to the pleasant tenor of his life.

Alexander von Dusch had returned to Mannheim at Easter on finishing his studies at Heidelberg; like Arnim and Brentano, who practically founded the German Romantic delight in the Rhine with their journey along it in 1802 to collect their folk-songs, guitars slung over their shoulders, so Dusch and the two Webers now spent much of their time in nocturnal wandering around Mannheim and Stift Neuburg and Heidelberg, singing and playing new songs and folk songs. Weber had become an excellent guitarist, and the closeness of his natural song style to the national folk-songs which had been made available to all in *Des Knaben Wunderhorn* and the other collections, is clear in the charming pieces of this and subsequent periods of his life. In the twentieth century we need no reminder of the direction in which such nationalistic ways of thought ultimately point; early nineteenth-century artists lived in the state of heady innocence characteristic of young movements, little considering the perils in elevating nationalism to an absolute principle, or that though Dionysus is an alluring god, he eventually drives his followers mad. As a reaction to the Napoleonic wars and the chaotic divisions of Germany, the young Romantics set about their task of personal rediscovery by way of the heroic past and the untainted elements of the present, fastening

[1] *Cäcilia* XV, Vol. 57, p. 37.
[2] Weber later wrote a cordial notice of the piece in the *AMZ* in 1812 (Kaiser 40).

upon the previous Romantic age of high chivalry and upon the songs and stories of the peasants in whom something essential of the nation was felt to be preserved. Folk-song and folk-tale were to prove a method of establishing national identity that was to last into our own century; in Weber's day they were an exciting novelty, and in an age that urged the arts towards greater unity there was every inducement to absorb folk-song and popular legend into the music the new composers were writing.

Hard work, lively mutual criticism and discussion of these topics went with the relaxed enjoyment of Weber's group of friends. He seems to have dominated them, despite what Max Maria concedes was his insignificant appearance;[1] now twenty-three, he was small, slight, lame, with a long, thin neck rising from narrow shoulders, though distinguished by the liveliness of his manner, his large voluble hands, expressive blue-grey eyes and faintly reddish tinge to his brown hair.[2] His normal dress was the tight trousers and 'cannon' boots, long black coat, white shirt and cravat familiar from his portraits. But though he clearly needed the relaxation and the encouragement of living among musicians of his own kind after the servitude of Württemberg, his career was not advancing. In the more regimented atmosphere of Darmstadt opportunities were greater, and established there was not only Gänsbacher but the Abbé Vogler.

Gottfried and Dusch accompanied Weber to Darmstadt and saw him set up in lodgings with a butcher, Klein, in the Ochsengasse, with arrangements to have his meals with a sergeant's widow, Frau Jenitzsch, for twelve groschen a day. His resources were low and he and Gänsbacher could not afford breakfasts, but there was hope that Darmstadt would provide him with more work than Mannheim had, for under the direct supervision of the Grand Duke Ludwig a long musical tradition was being strictly preserved. As early as 1670 a theatre had been set up in the former riding school, to be replaced in turn by an opera house, built by Lafosse, in 1710. Successive Landgraves had gathered singers and instrumentalists about them, and the present Grand Duke was himself a musician of considerable accomplishment; he could play the violin, piano, flute and horn, he had formed an amateur choir, and on succeeding to the throne in 1790 he assumed directorship of the opera, taking four rehearsals a week, carefully and strictly supervising his ensemble, though handing over to his *Kapellmeister*, Georg Mangold, for the weekly performance on Sunday. To add further musical lustre to his court, he had in 1807 invited Vogler to take up residence in Darmstadt. He awarded the old composer a Grand Cross, the position of Privy Counsellor, a house and a decent position of 2,200 gulden, making him also welcome at his own table, but shrewdly avoided seeking his musical advice and prevented him from having any say in the management of the opera.

[1] MMW, Vol. I, p. 191–2.
[2] Locks of his and Caroline's hair are preserved in *Weberiana*, Classe V, No. 1.

The situation suited Vogler well enough, for it flattered his vanity and allowed him to welcome his well-loved pupils Weber and Gänsbacher generously, providing them with music and supervising their work without charge. He had, moreover, acquired a profitable new pupil of eighteen, Jacob Beer, later to be known as Giacomo Meyerbeer—a precocious, hard-working, good-natured young man, free with his extensive library of scores and with the food hampers that arrived regularly from his wealthy banker father in Berlin. The three young composers rapidly became close friends, and in their excursions around the town Weber was able to recapture some of the gaiety of his Mannheim existence and to escape from the gloomy, garrison-like atmosphere of Darmstadt, trenchantly summed up by Gäns-bacher as 'von Gott vergessene und von Luther bessessene'. 'I take up my goose-quill', he wrote to Gottfried on 15th April, 'to tell you in boring words how bored I am with boring Darmstadt.'[1] They took their exercises to Vogler, first thing in the morning once they found that he was apt to fall asleep over them after lunch, analysed works by Bach and Handel with him and listened to him improvising elaborately in the churches of the town, often with Gottfried Weber accompanying them. Vogler took great pride in his pupils' individual talent: 'Gottfried knows the most, Meyer does the most, Carl Maria has the most ability and Johann [Gänsbacher, the former soldier] hits the mark most frequently', he declared, adding of Weber and Meyerbeer, 'Ah! had I been forced to leave the world before I had formed these two, I should have died a miserable man.'

As far as composition was concerned, this was still a fallow period for Weber; nevertheless, the time spent in renewed study and in absorbing new ideas was not wasted. Max Maria reports that the ideas for the main theme of the *Invitation to the Dance* and for the ballet music in Act 3 of *Oberon* sprang from popular tunes encountered on various wanderings; certainly, others which Weber came to know or to invent at this time were to emerge later in formal musical surroundings. On one of his visits to Stift Neuburg, he was leaning out of the window of the room he shared with Dusch one spring night humming tunes; Dusch remembered two of these next morning and took pleasure in allowing the startled Weber to overhear him singing them.[2] One was to become 'Light as fairy foot can fall' in Act 1 of *Oberon*, the other 'O Fatime! meine Traute' in No. 2 of the opera whose text he had already received from Hiemer but was neglecting, *Abu Hassan*. It was at Stift Neuburg, too, that Weber and Dusch came across a newly published volume of ghost stories, Apel's *Gespensterbuch*. The first tale instantly seized their imagination: it was *Der Freischütz*. They carried it off to Mannheim, where

---

[1] He was later to report that there was little genuine popular music life in the town, music being regarded as a service to be rendered the Grand Duke.

[2] MMW, Vol. I, p. 199.

Dusch sat up all night sketching out the libretto they had both immediately seen in it. They even outlined some scenes; but pressure of business kept Dusch from completing the work and so allowed the idea to wait for a time when Weber was able to master it fully.

Vogler's kindnesses to Weber included the arranging of a concert at Aschaffenburg, though this brought him in only a small profit. On a visit to Amorbach, where another opening apparently presented itself, he heard that his old patron Duke Eugen of Carlsruhe was due to pass through Frankfurt on 3rd May, and accordingly he hurried off to explain his dismissal from Stuttgart. Eugen seems to have received him with the greatest friendliness, keeping him up all night talking and on their parting presenting him with a ring. At Frankfurt, too, Weber found a publisher in the firm recently established by Nikolaus Simrock, to whom he sold for one hundred and fifty gulden his Polonaise, Piano Quartet, Cello *Potpourri*, *Der erste Ton* and six songs: out of the Polonaise alone Simrock soon made a profit in thousands of gulden. By the end of May, Weber was back in Mannheim, where he attended the première of a symphony by Gänsbacher and contributed to the same concert some music of his own, including the Adagio and Finale of his new Piano Concerto. A notice he wrote praises Gänsbacher's work and ignores his own contribution.[1] A Heidelberg concert on 30th May included the new Cello Variations for Dusch which he had finished in Mannheim two days previously, and was a triumphant success, not least among the students. Immediately after it, Weber hurried back to Darmstadt to prepare for the celebrations of Vogler's sixty-first birthday on 19th June. For these the three young composers had agreed to collaborate on a cantata. Lots were cast for the uncongenial task of writing the words, which fell to Weber; two solos were contributed by Gänsbacher, a trio and chorus by Meyerbeer, whose sister Therese was allowed to take part (Weber complained that she sang out of tune). Despite this and other demonstrations, the day was overcast for Vogler by the failure of the Duke to send any message (there had been a tense scene earlier when Vogler had offended him at a rehearsal), and he seems to have received his homage coldly. He did, however, take the three composers through his latest work, a Requiem, and asked Weber to write the introduction to his new edition of twelve Bach chorales, revised and lamentably re-harmonized. This was a task which Weber rightly foresaw (in a letter to Gottfried) would 'bring a whole pack of hounds upon my back'. Like the revisions, it seems more concerned to honour Vogler than Bach.[2] Vogler further invited Weber to accompany him on a concert tour to Frankfurt and Mainz—an invitation

[1] *AMZ*, dated by Weber 12th June (Kaiser 12).
[2] Kaiser 14, where two instances of Vogler's chorales are shown. Weber was later to make handsome amends with an article for Ersch and Gruber's *Enzyklopädie der Wissentschaften und Kunst* (Vol. 7, 1821), in which he praises Bach as 'a Gothic cathedral of art' and goes on to argue that he is a more Romantic artist than Handel (Kaiser 147).

eagerly accepted since there had been a hint from the director of the Frank-furt Theatre of a production of *Silvana*. The latter came to nothing; as did a chance re-encounter with Gretchen Lang, from whom he finally parted after a concert at which he heard an aria of Paer's sung by a new young soprano—Caroline Brandt. Vogler's concerts were successful, and the brief tour was concluded by way of Hanau and Offenbach, where Weber sold to the publisher André[1] several works including the First Symphony, the unfinished Piano Concerto and six as yet unwritten sonatas. On Vogler's advice, he next made a trip in the company of Gottfried and Augusta Weber to Baden-Baden, where Crown Prince Ludwig of Bavaria was staying (it was felt that an introduction might prove useful at Weber's next intended port of call, Munich). A cheerful letter to Gänsbacher reports a happy journey and pleasant days in Baden-Baden: despite the failure of concert plans, which made the trip an expensive one, he met once more his brother Fridolin and a circle of his Stuttgart friends, he came to know Tieck, he spent much time in the company of the Crown Prince, especially on more night wanderings with a guitar singing serenades, and he was invited by the publisher Cotta to write an article for his *Morgenblatt für gebildete Stände*.[2]

This was not the first time such an approach had been made, for Weber's fame as a composer was now being rivalled by his reputation as a critic. His earliest encounter with the printed word went back to the controversy with Fischer in Freiburg over *Das Waldmädchen*, though presumably his father was largely responsible in that instance; but various more important literary plans had occurred from time to time. As early as 1802 Susann proposed to him a scheme for a musical journal, and he in turn wrote to Susann on 30th June 1803 suggesting collaboration on a musical dictionary. Nothing came of this, though Gerber's *Lexicon der Tonkünstler* (1812–14) contains articles by Weber on Salzburg musicians: possibly these represented some of the work done on the original plan but later given to Gerber. Various other references in his letters suggest literary work in hand, though the only substantial outcome is the fragmentary semi-autobiographical novel *Tonkünstlersleben*.[3]

Weber began work on what he originally meant to call *Tonkünstlers Leben, eine Arabeske* in 1809, and published one episode, Chapter 4, as *Fragment einer musikalischen Reise* over the name Carl Marie in the Stuttgart *Morgen-blatt für gebildete Stände* (No. 309, 27th December 1809). Other parts were published in Kind's monthly *Die Muse* (1821) and W. G. Becker's *Taschen-buch* (1827, also edited by Kind), and smaller extracts appeared elsewhere. From time to time between 1809 and 1820, when he seems finally to have abandoned it, Weber worked on the book, often taking it up again under the

---

[1] Johann Anton André had recently taken over the firm and developed it by allying himself with Senefelder in order to apply the processes of lithography to printing music.

[2] A lively account of Baden-Baden, published 1st August 1810 (Kaiser 16).

[3] Kaiser 160.

influence of writer friends—Rochlitz in Leipzig, Duke August in Gotha, Brentano in Prague, Tieck in Prague and Dresden, while a reading of Hoffmann's *Tales* in Prague in 1816 caused him to write excitedly to Rochlitz that the idea was in his mind again. Two plans for it were outlined and several chapters completed; there remain fragments or summaries of the others, with a synopsis. The latter omits Chapters 4, 5 and 6, though it seems that twenty-three chapters in all were intended. There was to be an epilogue in the form of *The Artist's Last Will and Testament*; and beneath each chapter heading, a musical note was to appear, the complete cycle making up a chorale in the form of a *canon cancrizans* that was, Weber appears to have felt, 'to some extent a picture of human life' since it read the same backwards as forwards.

Hoffmann's particular influence is here less marked than that of the *Künstlerroman* which had by now become a highly popular Romantic form. Possibly the immediate inspiration was Brentano's famous *verwilderte Roman, Godwi*. But Hoffmann's manner—in particular the jumbling of verse and prose, seriousness and parody familiar from *Kater Murr*—certainly colours the later episodes, with their elaborate fantasies and coincidences; and in general the style has grown much brighter, more pungent and amusing than in the earlier writings, which (as Weber admitted in an 1817 sketch for *Tonkünstlersleben*) had been 'gaudy, somewhat precious and bombastic'. It is not exactly an autobiography in the accepted sense, though the composer-hero—known as Felix or sometimes simply A—shares with his author the early loss of a mother, a lax father who delighted in showing off his talented son, and some experience of minor German Court life. What the book most vividly gives us is a series of glimpses into Weber's states of mind, above all when composing. The opening describes little more than an adolescent daydream, with its 'vague longings for the dim distance where one hopes to find alleviation without quite knowing how; painful excitement of inner power on which the knowledge of a high ideal lays heavy fetters from which one sometimes abandons all hope of release; irresistibly violent impulses to work, with vast pictures and hopes of accomplishment that immediately dissolve into vacancy of mind . . .' But later he grows more precise. He contrasts the composer at the mercy of his piano-fingers with the one 'whose inner ear is the judge of things simultaneously imagined and criticized. This spiritual ear, strengthened and upheld by wonderful musical capacities, is a divine secret belonging only to music and incomprehensible to the layman: for—it hears whole passages, even whole pieces at a time, taking no notice of little breaks or unevennesses which are left to be filled in and smoothed out at a later thoughtful moment . . .' But Weber did not believe that a Romantic temperament meant composing in a fevered, impetuous rush: on the contrary, composition was for him a highly ordered process requiring the greatest intellectual application. Indeed, this was possible while attending to other more superficial matters. He describes the creative impulse as 'a basic element of that peaceful mood which is, so to speak, able to abandon the individual Ego entirely and pass over to the creative Ego'. This meant that he was quite capable of composing while carrying on a conversation: 'I find it perfectly simple to talk connectedly about quite different subjects, yet my whole soul, fully absorbed in its subject, forms musical ideas and composes.' He gives a very revealing account of how these ideas may come:

> The contemplation of a landscape is to me the performance of a piece of music. I feel the effect of the whole, without dwelling on the details which produce it; in a word, strange as it may seem, the landscape affects me in the dimension of Time. The pleasure to me is successive.
> But this has its major delights and pains. Delight because I never quite know where the mountain, the tree, the house—or whatever else it may be—could occur, so that at every contemplation a new performance is experienced. But great pain when I travel. Then begins a fine confusion in my soul, for everything becomes a whirl and a muddle. How the ideas chase each other and criss-cross and shatter themselves! If I see a view steadily in the distance, the picture always conjures up a parallel musical image in the sympathetic world of my imagination, one which I can perhaps then happily grasp and secure and develop. But good heavens! when Nature is gradually unrolled before my eyes, how the funeral marches and rondos and furiosos and pastorales somersault after each other!

This faculty for imposing imaginative order upon Nature (and conversely the sense of disorder when an arbitrary succession of images is imposed upon the mind) is quintessentially Romantic, as Wordsworth recognized in that Romantic key poem of 'the growth of a poet's mind', *The Prelude*:

> To every natural form, rock, fruit or flower,
> Even the loose stones that cover the highway,
> I gave a moral life, I saw them feel,
> Or link'd them to some feeling: the great mass
> Lay bedded in a quickening soul, and all
> That I beheld, respired with inward meaning.

The soliloquies and conversations from which these examples are taken are the essence of the book. There is little attempt to characterize Felix except as an artist of over-weening temperament, and the plot on which his musings are hung is really no more than a string on which may also be threaded odd verses, pieces of melodrama, outbursts of annoyance or sarcasm, and parodies. The most entertaining of the latter is the scene in Chapter 6 (written in 1818). Felix has fallen for a girl he knows only as Emilie, and the confusions of a masked ball at which they find themselves are interrupted by the appearance of Hanswurst to introduce operas of various countries. First comes the Italian, which Hanswurst sardonically praises for having developed a kind of melody that can be sung in any key, with any decoration and for any situation—the fatal indictment for Weber, to whom dramatic expression was all-important. The opera begins with 'a noise made in the orchestra to shut the audience up—that's called an overture in Italian'. Italian scoring he lampoons as: *Oboi coi Flauti, Clarinetti coi Oboi, Flauti coi Violini, Fagotti col Basso. Viol. 2e col primo. Viola col Basso. Voce ad libitum. Violini colla parte.* When she appears, the heroine wears an expression that remains identical whatever her role or emotion. The ensuing aria uses a minimum of words, completely banal, purely as vehicle for the music, and comes to an end on the word *Felicità* with a ten-bar trill on the last syllable that brings the house down. The French opera, based on a skit published in Paris in 1670, mocks the unities ('The action takes place between twelve o'clock and mid-day') and is formal beyond endurance, with choruses that automatically echo stereotyped situations of joy or grief ('Chantons, dansons, montrons notre allégresse/douleur') and an ending on the obligatory *deus ex machina*. But Weber is equally capable of attacking German opera, even though a good many of his missiles seem like boomerangs. Hanswurst berates German opera for trying on an absurd unsuitable selection of foreign costumes, all of which enfeeble real German art; and the so-called *romantisch-vaterländisch Tonspiel*, set 'im Herzen von Deutschland', tilts in lively manner against the current nationalist excesses. Agnes Bernauer, the eponymous heroine, begins, 'Ach! meine Seele ist müde, matt und abgetragen', and the *galère* of characters includes ghosts, minnesingers, hermits, Schilleresque robbers and even Brunhilde. Hanswurst irritatedly breaks off complaining that he will fare better in ten years' time . . .

The story running behind these incidentals occupies less of Weber's attention. Even when Felix manages to establish a relationship with Emilie (he naturally turns out to be the mysterious author of her favourite piano pieces), matters quickly go wrong: she leaves him for a dissolute Prince who has figured earlier and who has engaged Felix as court composer; whereat he turns his back on it all—for Art. Weber, in fact, despite his lively prose style and quick ear for parody, is no novelist. *Tonkünstlersleben* was as much diary and common-place book as novel; yet he impressed his contemporaries with his literary ability, and it was even claimed by Theodor Hell (who has left an interesting appreciation of Weber in his preface to the *Hinterlassene Schriften* which he collected) that if he had not been a composer, Weber might have been a significant writer. Hell pays tribute to how much he had himself learnt from Weber while working with him on *Die drei Pintos* and on the translation of *Oberon*.

In the burst of new found assurance 1810 brought him, Weber was ready to set pen to paper with the ideas that were humming in his head; and credit must go to Vogler for his encouragement in this direction as well as in so many others. The verses he wrote for Vogler's birthday ode are fluent (though there is a more personal edge to the cutting wit of some epigrams he wrote the following week). In the same month of June he published *Ein Wort über Vogler*,[1] a brief essay that was destined as the sketch for a full-scale biography: he wrote to Gottfried on 20th June, 'Between ourselves, I shall *perhaps* write a biography of Vogler, if the seat of my trousers holds out',[2] and to Gänsbacher on 9th October, 'Papa's biography is begun'. But this, too, was to be unfinished. Also in June, he sent André four translations from the Italian for Gänsbacher's songs, the first evidence of what was to prove a remarkable flair for languages. Despite repeated requests from editors, chiefly his old friend and ally Rochlitz, he never plunged regularly into criticism; but he was always ready to turn out a notice of an interesting work or to produce an occasional or polemical essay when cause arose. The two chief periods of this activity came between 1810 and 1812, when perhaps he felt urged to define his aims to himself and others; and between 1815 and 1820, when there was the need to explain his motives to audiences during his time as Director of the Opera at Prague and Dresden.

For a musician of his day, Weber's opinions were strikingly original and advanced; and his mature style contrasts very favourably in its clarity and grace of expression, especially in its ready sense of humour, with that of most of his contemporaries. His writings reveal much about his outlook and his preoccupations, above all his determination to repel Italian influences in favour of a national form of opera. This made him excessively intolerant of foreign influences, as even Wagner admitted, and is at once his strength and his weakness as a critic: generous to a fault with many new German works he was called upon to criticize, he was dominated in his views by this desire to see German opera established. Invariably he wrote from a firm critical standpoint; and it is in this light that we should judge the comments on Beethoven that have won him a great deal of discredit.[3]

These do not include the oft-quoted remark about Beethoven's Seventh Symphony, 'the extravagances of this genius have now reached the *non plus ultra*, and Beethoven must be quite ripe for the madhouse.' This was cited by Schindler in his Beethoven biography but immediately challenged in two reviews protesting against Schindler's obsessive attacks on Weber. Schindler replied in one of these journals admitting that 'perhaps Weber was not the author of those bitter criticisms of Beethoven's works which originally the

---

[1] Kaiser 13.

[2] The 'perhaps' is heavily underlined: BM Add MS 33, 610.

[3] Notably in Anton Schindler: *Biographie von Ludwig van Beethoven* (1840: 3rd edn., 1860, trans. Constance S. Jolly and ed. Donald W. MacArdle as *Beethoven as I knew him*, 1966). Georg Kaiser: *Beiträge zu einer Charackteristik Carl Maria von Webers als Musik-schriftsteller* (1910) goes to great pains to refute the attacks on Weber by Schindler, whose possessive adulation of Beethoven is well known.

well-known composer and writer living in Vienna, Baron von Lannoy, considered had come from C. M. Weber's pen (he having received the certain information from Beethoven's friends). In this matter I was only a reporter.'[1] Nevertheless, Schindler did not amend his remarks in his *Beethoven in Paris: ein Nachtrag zur Beethovens Biographie* (1842), and even in the third edition of the biography (1860) still repeated the allegation while dismissing objections with the comment that Weber's remark had appeared in print (no reference is given) and would sooner or later turn up. It never has; but meanwhile Schindler had caused the remark to pass into legend, and it still continues to be repeated. There is no shred of concrete evidence for it, and the evasions practised by Schindler in the matter are unfortunately characteristic of his behaviour when feeling obliged to defend Beethoven.

What can be taken as fact is part of Chapter 4 (1809) of *Tonkünstlersleben* and the letter written to the publisher Nägeli (21st May 1810). In the former (a chapter that foreshadows Berlioz's method and even style in *Les Soirées de l'Orchestre*), the author dreams he is overhearing the instruments chatting among themselves. Argument is silenced by the arrival of the orchestral porter, who threatens that they are soon going to be given the *Eroica Symphony*, 'after which we shall see who can move a limb or a key'. 'Not that!' beg the instruments: a viola counter-proposes, 'Rather an Italian opera, then we can at least drop off from time to time.' The porter proceeds to describe in derisive terms the opening of the newest symphony arrived from Vienna:

> First, we have a slow Tempo, full of brief, disjointed ideas, none of them having any connexion with each other, three or four notes every quarter of an hour!—that's exciting! then a hollow drum-roll and mysterious viola passages, all decked out with the right amount of silences and general pauses; eventually, when the listener has given up hope of surviving the tension as far as the Allegro, there comes a furious tempo in which the chief aim is to prevent any principal idea from appearing, and the listener has to try and find one on his own; there's no lack of modulations; that doesn't matter, all that matters, as in Paer's *Leonore*, is to make a chromatic run and stop on any note you like, and there's your modulation. Above all one must shun rules, for they only fetter genius.

This passage is always taken, even by Kaiser, to refer to Beethoven's Fourth Symphony, presumably on the grounds that it immediately follows the satirical reference to the taxing nature of the *Eroica* and that the Fourth Symphony had appeared in Vienna only the previous year. Nevertheless, the description does not fit. The complaints about lack of ideas and surfeit of modulations are too vague for identification, and it is hard to see how the passage attacking the 'three or four notes every quarter of an hour' could apply, even satirically, to Beethoven's opening Adagio. More specifically, there are no silences longer than a quaver until just before the Allegro, no

[1] *Blätter für literarische Unterhaltung*, 31st December 1840.

general pauses at all, nor are there any 'hollow drum-rolls' (*dumpfer Pauken-wirbel*) or 'mysterious viola passages' (*mysteriöse Bratschensätze*)—the violas invariably play with other instruments, in a doubling or purely harmonic role, and the timpani do not enter at all until the two *ff* chords immediately before the Allegro. It seems most likely that, since Weber deliberately avoided mention of any particular work here but did not hesitate to name the *Eroica* previously, he was attacking a generalized target.

The letter to Nägeli, written in answer to one of several contemporary comparisons of Weber and Beethoven, states his objections straightforwardly:

> You seem to see me from my Quartet and the Caprice[1] as an imitator of Beethoven, and flattered as many might be by this, I don't find it in the least pleasant. Firstly, I hate everything bearing the mark of imitation; secondly, my views differ too much from Beethoven's for me to feel I could ever agree with him. The passionate, almost incredible inventive powers inspiring him are accompanied by such a chaotic arrangement of his ideas that only his earlier compositions appeal to me; the later ones seem to me hopeless chaos, an incomparable struggle for novelty, out of which break a few heavenly flashes of genius proving how great he could be if he would tame his rich fantasy. Though of course I cannot take pleasure in Beethoven's great genius, I do at least believe I can defend my own music from a logical and technical point of view, and produce in every piece a definite effect.

At the time when he wrote these two comments, Weber was twenty-three —an age at which any critic would be grateful for indulgence. It is important, moreover, to remember that he was far from alone in holding such views: most of his colleagues had found the greatest difficulty in following Beethoven beyond the First Symphony, and the musical journals of the day are depressingly unanimous in their failure to understand what he was about. Without at all excusing these writers, we may perhaps understand how, nurtured on rationalism, they were left genuinely baffled and afraid by this sudden new explosion. But unlike the phalanx of lesser critics who were trying to cry halt to music by insisting that Mozart and Haydn were exemplars of style for all time, Weber believed that he had glimpsed a way forward with the new century; and like all critics who have incompletely penetrated an unfamiliar style, he concentrates on superficial aspects of Beethoven and fails to understand either the new expressive aim or the new extensions of form which this brings about. Later, as well as coming to admire Beethoven personally, he fully acknowledged his genius, and it is the greatest pity that the letters they exchanged—four from Weber, three from Beethoven—are lost. He regularly played and conducted Beethoven's music, and was enraged when the Prague public failed to appreciate *Fidelio*; though his old doubts about Beethoven are expressed privately in a letter to Gänsbacher of 26th December 1822,

[1] Presumably the *Momento Capriccioso*, with its superficial resemblance to the *Eroica Symphony*'s scherzo.

finding fault with 'the number of modulations, of complexities in the counter-point and many harmonic details'. As well as reflecting some of the points in which his style most markedly suffers by comparison with Beethoven's, these comments shed light on Weber's consuming faith in the path which he believed German opera must follow. Anything, however glorious, which was irrelevant to the complete theatrical work of art troubled him; and the very sublimity of much of *Fidelio*, in conflict with the residues of *Singspiel* form, led him to worry about its 'absence of scenic life'. We can see most clearly the point of view from which such doubts could arise in his famous comments on Hoffmann's *Undine*, when he rejects the notion of single pieces of music, be they never so magnificent, whose failure to connect properly disturbs the pattern of the complete opera, and goes on to plead for 'the type of opera Germans want: a self-contained work of art in which all the elements, contributed by the related arts in collaboration and merged into one another, disappear and, submerged in various ways, re-emerge to create a new world.' A composer with a vision of the *Gesamtkunstwerk* so vividly fixed before his eyes would naturally resist what he felt to be a movement in the wrong direction, the more violently when it was shot with such obvious genius.

Regrettably, the only criticisms Weber published of Beethoven's later music are confined to some of the weakest works. He was understandably cool about *Christus am Oelberg*, the Choral Fantasia and *Wellingtons Sieg*. Though the first performance he heard of *Wellingtons Sieg* was made nearly inaudible by the uproar of cannon, he acknowledged that it showed 'obvious traits of genius, such as are never absent from the work of this mighty com-poser'; unfortunately he could not be any more enthusiastic when another performance allowed him to hear the music more clearly. Obviously Weber, like almost every other composer criticizing a massive rival, allowed himself to be too greatly upset by the different course Beethoven was pursuing, and was thus led to underrate the scale of his achievement; but he is far from being alone among avant-garde critics (for such he was) in passionately dismissing a fine composer who has successfully continued to develop forms and techniques of a previous age into times that seem unable to support them. From the nature of his hopes for music, Weber could not bring himself to accept Beethoven as a greater genius than his own Romantic movement produced. It was left to Hoffmann to suggest to his fellow Romantics their closeness to Beethoven and to indicate the true scale of his genius in his fine essay, *Beethoven's Instrumental Music*.[1]

It was to formulate and propagate the principles of Romantic music as he saw them that Weber founded in the autumn of 1810 the *Harmonische Verein*, an association of like-thinking artists somewhat on the lines of

[1] Originally in the *Zeitung für die elegante Welt* (Dec. 1813), reprinted in *Fantasie-stücke in Callots Manier* (1814). English translation in Oliver Strunk: *Source Readings in Music History* (1950).

GOTTFRIED WEBER

Engraving by Devrient, after Müller

JOHANN GÄNSBACHER

*Lithograph by Matthias Tretensky, after the
drawing by Josef Bücher*

Reproduced by permission of the University of Basel

E. T. A. HOFFMANN

*Engraving by Johann Passini, after the
portrait by Wilhelm Heusel*

GIACOMO MEYERBEER

Portrait by Franz Krüger

Schumann's fictitious *Davidsbündler* dedicated to upholding certain beliefs and to overthrowing the ranks of *Philistertum*. The notion for this was sketched out early in 1810, and a highly formal set of twenty-one statues was drawn up dated 30th November. Weber was to be the leader, Gottfried the secretary, treasurer and archivist; certain contributions to cover expenses were to be exacted; new works were to be presented to the director and lodged in the archive; there was to be open criticism of each 'brother's' work as well as propagation of it; and in sections 14 and 15 the aim of the society is stated, to 'uphold and prosecute the good ... and especially to take account of promising new talent', while on the other hand, 'since the world is inundated with so many bad works, often upheld only by authorities and by wretched criticism, there is the duty to expose them and warn about them ...' Each brother was to adopt pseudonyms. Weber was to be 'Melos' or 'M – s', 'Simon Knaster', and 'B.f.z.Z'[1]; Gottfried Weber was 'G. Giusto' and 'Julius Billig'; the other original members were, of course, Meyerbeer ('Philodikaios' and also 'Julius Billig'), Dusch ('The Unknown') and Gänsbacher ('Triole'). Further members recruited were the tenor Berger, later Danzi and the Breslau organist Berner; it was also planned to invite the pedagogue Joseph Fröhlich, the Munich actor Max Neigel, Nägeli, and the poet Heinrich Zschokke. These and other plans never came to fulfilment; indeed, the society soon began falling apart and was no longer effectively operating by 1813. It was emphatically not a mutual admiration society, as one of the statutes went out of its way to make clear; indeed, only six reviews of members' works survive as compared with dozens about others'. Much correspondence and exchange of ideas ensued, though the plans for the obvious need, a journal, to be entitled *Der harmonische Bund* (later *Zeitung für die musikalische Welt*) and due to start on 1st May 1811, never came to anything. Weber later told Rochlitz that this was out of respect for the Leipzig *AMZ*.

On 26th August Weber made his third journey of the year to Frankfurt in order to supervise the delayed production of *Silvana*. There was much to be done, especially since Gretchen Lang was now capriciously hesitating over the part of Mechtilde specially written for her: this she eventually sang, while the title role, with its difficult dance-cum-mime nature, was taken by the young artist Weber had previously heard in a Frankfurt concert, Caroline Brandt. Like the rest of the company except for Gretchen Lang, she seems to have admired and believed in the young composer (though there is no evidence of any more personal feelings on either side as yet); and all was going well up to the dress rehearsal on 13th September when a totally unforeseen hitch occurred. By an unhappy coincidence, 16th September, the day of the première, was announced as the day on which the celebrated Mme.

---

[1] Knaster was a kind of cheap tobacco, also slang for an old grumbler; B.f.z.Z. stood for Weber's motto, *'Beharrlichkeit führt zum Ziel'* or 'Perseverance leads to the goal'.

4

Blanchard would make a balloon ascent—an event sensational enough to dampen interest in the new opera.[1] Consequently, the theatre was filled with chatter about the thrilling event of the day; even the singers were distracted, and though in the circumstances the opera went well, with several encores, Weber was distressed over the lost opportunity and only with difficulty could Caroline persuade him to acknowledge the applause for him led by a group of his champions.

Meanwhile, on a brief return to Darmstadt during rehearsals, Weber had been completing his Piano Concerto No. 1 in C (Op. 11: J.98), to which he was finally able to put the date 4th October. It was the largest-scale piece he had yet written for the instrument that was closest to him; and if it cannot be numbered among his finest works, it epitomizes much that was going into the formation of his mature style. At the back of his keyboard manner lay the example of composer-virtuosos such as C.P.E. Bach, Cramer and especially Hummel and Dussek. However much Weber may have resisted Beethoven, ignoring the example of the five piano concertos he must have known by this time,[2] however much he designed his own concertos not as symphonic experiences but purely in order to give pleasure, there is an element common to the two composers in the balance of the piano with the orchestra, in the avoidance of an improvised cadenza (a self-deprivation in Weber's case even more than in Beethoven's), in the effort to give greater weight to slow movements, all of which goes back to Dussek. How closely Weber must have studied the technique of his predecessors, taking exactly what he needed as the basis of his own novel manner, is immediately evident from their music.[3] If his feeling for keyboard colour and richness probably found most stimulus in Clementi, much else shows a fascination for the technical advances exploited by Cramer, Dussek and Prince Louis Ferdinand. In their works are found many ways of the habits associated with Weber, which he made the basis for his own entirely new approach to keyboard style—among them, the passagework in thirds, the arpeggiated leaps over a wide span (often imme-

[1] Marie-Madeleine-Sophie Blanchard (b. 1778), widow of the pioneering balloonist Jean-Pierre Blanchard, who had made the first aerial crossing of the Channel in 1785, was the first professional female balloonist. She was eventually killed in Paris in 1819 when her balloon caught fire as she was discharging a firework from it in mid-air. She had made an ascent in the presence of Napoleon in June 1810, and Frankfurt was a natural choice for another demonstration since Blanchard had made one of his first flights from there. There is unhappily no foundation in the legend that Weber called on her to ask her to alter the date, and, finding himself left alone with her child when the nurse went to fetch her, composed his *Wiegenlied* 'Schlaf, Herzenssöhnchen' (Op. 13, No. 2: J.96) in order to soothe it. According to W. de Fonvielle: *Aventures Aeriennes* (1876), she was childless. Mozart, too, had previously been inconvenienced by one of Blanchard's ascents (see letter to his wife, 6th July 1791).

[2] His diary records the acquisition of the score of the *Emperor* Concerto early in 1811.

[3] This question has been examined in detail by Walter Georgii in his *Karl Maria von Weber als Klavierkomponist* (1914).

diately repeated), the rapid staccato figures arising from the old toccata but completely different in expressive effect. These and a host of other devices he matched to his own fluency of manner and love of virtuosity, and to his own brilliant technique as a pianist.

Weber's piano music is always superbly written and usually extremely difficult to play. There is no contradiction in terms here: his difficulties are invariably pianistic, never written against the natural possibilities, though they often take their nature from the exceptional size of his hands, already mentioned. An etching and an engraving of the twenty-six-year old composer[1] shows clearly his long fingers and narrow nail-beds, with extraordinary thumbs that reach the middle joint of the index finger. It is this which makes possible the octave glissandos of the *Konzertstück* and the frequent four-part chords covering a tenth, even making allowance for the keyboard of the day, which was not only lighter in touch but substantially narrower.[2] As Benedict was to describe it, 'Having the advantage of a very large hand, and being able to play tenths with the same facility as octaves, Weber produced the most startling effects of sonority and possessed the power, like Rubinstein, to elicit an almost vocal quality of tone where delicacy or deep expression were required.'[3] Whereas Chopin's writing makes allowances for natural characteristics of the average human hand such as the weakness of the fourth finger, Weber was happy to make the most spectacular use possible of his own hands; and in this lie many of the difficulties in playing his music. He was, nevertheless, to exert a profound influence on Chopin and still more on Liszt, whom Weber foreshadows in this sphere as strongly as he does Wagner in his

Ex. 15

[1] *Weberiana*, Classe VIII, Vol. I, Nos. 7 and 8.
[2] Weber's piano, a Brodmann (Vienna), had an octave span of 15.9 cm. as against the modern 16.5 cm.
[3] Benedict: *Carl Maria von Weber*, p. 140 (1881).

dramatic works. His use of ornamentation, in particular, hints at Chopin's infinitely richer use of decorative figures to cause the music to lean away from the tonic key—a procedure that was, in the last music of both Chopin and Liszt, to prove as insidious a threat to tonality as was Wagner's attack by way of long suspensions, delayed resolutions and ever remoter added notes. In this early concerto we can only see suggestions—a sudden modulation or Weber's familiar tendency to give passing or alternating notes prominence in the melodies. And if there are clearly traceable ancestors and descendants, the personality that marks this uneven but attractive work is entirely Weber's own, whether in the reconciliation of folk-inspired tunes to salon elegance or in the technique that makes (for other pianists) almost impossible use of his giant stretch to suggest the clever, charming guitarist of the Heidelberg serenades (Ex. 15, p. 99).

No less typical is Weber's ability to fit into such a classic structure an authentic Romantic shudder:

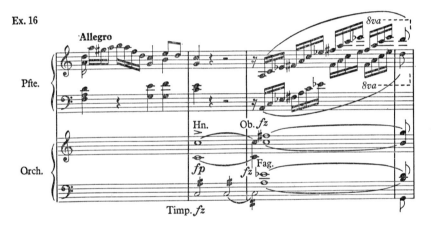

The movement is curiously military and challenging for the rest of the work until we remember the atmosphere in which Weber was living, with Napoleon a potent force and the war of liberation still lying ahead. Yet salon charm wins easily over Beethovenian defiance, as is made unmistakably clear when the piano takes over the opening theme from the aggressive orchestra. The Adagio looks back to the two symphonies, contrasting pianistic delicacy with the dark hues of horns, violas, two solo cellos and double basses—had Weber the Andante of Beethoven's Fourth Piano Concerto somewhere remotely in mind? The finale is really a fast waltz with charming episodes, a rondo based on the common arpeggio figure that turns up in the sonatas of Clementi, Steibelt, Dussek and other contemporary composers (Ex. 17, opposite page).

The touches of chromatic harmony are purely decorative, part of the

pervading charm and wit, in the Six Progressive Sonatas, described as 'for
piano with violin obbligato' (Op. 10:[1] J. 99–104) which Weber was now
required to grind out in fulfilment of André's commission. They were
composed in Darmstadt between 20th September and 17th October, and the
effort of writing fifteen numbers in twenty-eight days bore heavily: we find
him telling Gottfried on 23rd September, 'I've got a swine of a job in hand
[*eine Hundsföttische Arbeit*]. Six little sonatas with a violin for André; it's
costing more sweat than as many symphonies, but what's to be done?' A
further letter told of difficulty in getting them finished, especially the last
one—much the most ambitious of the set. Then on 1st November an exasperated letter to Gottfried reported André's reaction: 'The — has sent
my sonatas back on the splendid grounds that *they're too good*, they must be
much more ordinary.'

Presumably André had in mind a set of graded pedagogical works. What
Weber wrote was a simple, completely charming group of pieces in which the
piano generally has the major and technically more demanding part, with the
violin ingeniously given a role that shows off an average-to-good amateur
technique to excellent advantage. Indeed, they are, with the possible exception of the last, scarcely sonatas at all so much as sonatinas for domestic
music-making, where they still have a place. To lend as diverse a character
as possible to them, Weber imported into five of the movements the exotic
influence that the Romantics (and especially Vogler) found so stimulating. No. 5
ends with a pleasant Siciliano; No. 2 has a first movement marked *Carattere
Espagnuolo*, skilfully turning the graceful opening theme into a bolero. As
elsewhere, Weber's 'Spanish' manner is based on little more than conventionally jaunty rhythms, though it was to act as a model for many another

Ex. 17
Presto

---

[1] Originally numbered by Weber Op. 17.

German composer, even to the point of actual turns of phrase. Schumann, who deeply admired Weber, may well have had one of these pieces in mind when he wrote his song 'Der Hidalgo'.[1]

Ex. 18

The finale is one of two 'Polish' movements in the set, in this case making use of an alleged *Air Polonais*; the finale of No. 6 is another of Weber's many Polaccas, much in the manner of Aennchen's 'Kommt ein schlanker Bursch'. Between these two movements of No. 2 comes a strange Adagio in which, over bare, steady part-two piano lines, the violin creeps in low quavers. Both the *Air Polonais* and the unevenly phrased *Air Russe* of No. 3 suggest to Weber some engaging harmonic swerves; and given the small canvas, it is an agreeable surprise to discover how much harmonic scope he was able to allow himself. Mostly this is as incidental strokes of colour, principally designed to be 'effective', though there is a more serious formal purpose at work in the last of the set. No. 5, one of the three in only two movements, opens with a somewhat grandiose set of variations on the subsequently discarded No. 10 of *Silvana*, Mechtilde's 'Warum musst ich je erblikken'. Perhaps the aim was to popularize the opera after its inauspicious première; Weber also used the theme for his clarinet variations (Op. 33: J.128). The sonatas have been arranged for piano duet by Czerny and published in England in a revision by Moscheles.

Silvana had earned Weber 100 gulden, which with other earnings of the autumn he sent to Stuttgart to pay off his debts; ironically, he had in August made a start on Hiemer's libretto for *Abu Hassan* with the Creditors' Chorus 'Geld! Geld! Geld!', and the rest of the year was largely given to

---

[1] Schumann originally included in his *Album für die Jugend* an arrangement of Caspar's 'Hier im ird'schen Jammerthal' from *Der Freischütz*. Later he crossed the MS out; but the 'Kleinen Fuge' from the same collection suggests a knowledge of Weber's 3rd Piano Sonata and the fughetta in the finale.

finishing the new opera. Darmstadt had grown more oppressive since Gänsbacher's departure to a new post as factor to Count Firmian in Prague, and the opportunities for travel were poor. A concert planned in Frankfurt for 20th October promised well, but on arriving there after delivering the ill-fated sonatas to André on the way, Weber found the town in uproar. Napoleon's determination to intensify the blockade of England had led to a decree (12th September 1810) banning English imports and ordering the destruction of all English goods discovered in store, and this was in the process of being carried out: the streets were filled with French soldiers smashing, looting and burning the contents of Frankfurt's well-stocked shops and warehouses. A concert was clearly out of the question. Gottfried was able to arrange a replacement concert for him in Mannheim, and efforts were made to dispense with Ritter, now grown even lazier, and replace him with Weber. This proved impossible. Further difficulties were caused by Ritter, who had presumably learned of the attempts to unseat him and now singled Weber out as the victim of a regulation declaring that outsiders could not be accompanied by the orchestra during the winter concerts (other visitors were not thus treated). Weber did not help matters by attacking Ritter in print;[1] and although so hard up that he secretly had to sell a pair of trousers in order to pay for an excursion with his friends, there was no alternative but to leave. In Dusch's rooms, a few days before his departure, he composed the song *Des Künstlers Abschied* (Op. 71, No.6: J.105). Back in Darmstadt, he finished *Abu Hassan* on 11th January and took Vogler's canny advice to dedicate it to the Grand Duke. As he wrote to Gottfried on 15th January, 'Yesterday I dressed the rogue up in neat red morocco, dedicated him to the Grand Duke and sent him over. What he'll say about it, one can't tell, but I hope he'll say, "Musje, je tien bocop de ce!" '. He was in luck: perhaps taking the opera's hint about regal munificence towards a poor but worthy debtor, the Grand Duke accepted the dedication, offered him a concert and sent a payment of forty gold pieces as well as buying a hundred and twenty tickets for the court. For the concert Weber composed the Duett 'Se il mio ben' (Op. 31, No. 3: J.107), as he told Gottfried 'in such a wretchedly Italianate style that it might have been by Farinelli; it was hellish successful'. The singers were the *Kapellmeister* Mangold's daughter Charlotte and Mme. Schönberger, both contraltos, the latter 'one of the most beautiful, the fullest and most resonant contralto voices',[2] of such depth that she had actually sung tenor roles at the correct pitch; the orchestral accompaniment had an obbligato clarinet played by a new friend of Weber's, the virtuoso Heinrich Bärmann. Weber made 200 gulden out of the concert, and was delighted to find that Dusch, Gottfried and Meyerbeer had come over for it. But they had to return home; and the failure of prospects in Darmstadt

---

[1] *AMZ*, 1811 (Kaiser 20).
[2] From an article on Schönberger (Kaiser 54).

turned Weber's thoughts in new directions. It had been a busy year, also one filled with disappointments; but he had settled part of the Stuttgart debt of 2,500 gulden, he had produced one opera and written another, he had begun to find himself, through the company of like-minded artists, poets and musicians. They had made his life worthwhile, he wrote in his diary, and he had grown better. When Dusch and the others parted from him, he made another entry, 'Shall I ever again find such good men and loyal friends?' Sixteen years later, shortly before his death, he was to add a large 'NO'.

CHAPTER SEVEN

ABU HASSAN

Allah upon thee, O my sister, recite to us some new story, delightsome and delectable, wherewith to while away the waking hours of our latter night.

The Thousand and One Nights, trans. Burton

T HE ARRIVAL of *The Thousand and One Nights* in Europe in the early 1700s was to have an effect upon poets and writers comparable to that of Scott at the beginning of the following century. Essentially, the book is a collection of tales from different lands—India, Persia, Greece, Syria and Egypt, principally—and from different, times between the tenth and fifteenth centuries, arranged by unknown Arabian hands into the framework of Shahrazad, or Scheherazade, nightly entertaining a misogynist Caliph with a series of stories so as to save herself from death in the morning; and it was brought to Europe by Antoine Galland, an attaché-secretary of the French Ambassador at the Sublime Porte who had travelled extensively in the Levant. The twelve volumes of his *Mille et Une Nuits, Contes Arabes traduits en François* appeared at irregular intervals between 1704 and 1717, and in various pirated editions instantly swept Europe. The exoticism of the tales, their open treatment of sex, perversion, cruelty and corruption, their simple fantasies of wish-fulfilment were all novel flavours that the reading public found greatly to its taste; and before long the influence began to show in imitations such as Beckford's *Vathek*, as an example to works ranging from Voltaire's *Zadig* to the English pantomime, and in general as an encouragement to collections of fantastic short stories that was still highly potent by the time Hoffmann came on the scene. To the Romantics, the exotic thrill had of course a particular charm.

The collection was, naturally, much altered and added to in the course of its history. The MS used by Galland did not include what is usually entitled *The Tale of Abu-al-Hasan-al-Khalia*,[1] or the *Sleeper Awakened*; but when short of further material for his series of volumes in 1709, Galland happened to meet in Paris a man from Aleppo who told him eleven more stories, thus enabling him to open his Vol. IX (1712) with *Le Dormeur Eveillé*. A less fully embellished version appears in other MSS unknown to Galland; and according to E. W. Lane, in a note to his translation of 1839–41, the earlier part of the story (not used in Weber's opera) is even recounted as fact in Ishak's history of 1623. The full story is, in outline, as follows:

[1] Al-Khalia means, roughly, The Wag.

Having wasted half his inheritance on worthless friends, Abu Hassan resolves only to entertain strangers, for a single night each. He is seated by a bridge when the Caliph Harun al-Rashid and his chief sword-bearer Masrur appear disguised. Having accepted and enjoyed Abu Hassan's lavish hospitality, the Caliph asks if he wishes anything; Abu Hassan's only desire is to be Caliph for a day so as to punish his false friends. The Caliph drugs him, takes him to the palace, and arranges for him to be treated as Caliph. Awakening, the surprised Abu Hassan greatly enjoys himself and duly has his former friends beaten and banished. Drugged again, he is returned home, but refuses to believe he is no longer Caliph; he attacks his mother for disbelieving him, and is briefly imprisoned. Seated once more by the bridge, he is annoyed to re-encounter the Caliph and Masrur; but when the Caliph points out that his wish to be rid of his false friends was granted, however mysterious the 'sorcery', he agrees to be their host again. The Caliph repeats his trick, but next day interrupts Abu Hassan's Caliphate and reveals the truth, rewards him, makes him his chief cup-bearer, and marries him to Nuzhat al-Fuad ('Heart's Delight'), treasurer to his own wife Zubaydah.

Abu Hassan soon exhausts his money, and decides to recoup his losses and repay the Caliph's tricks at the same time. He and his wife in turn feign death while the other goes separately to the Caliph and Zobaydah for the funeral grant of a hundred dinars and a silk shroud. Argument develops in the palace as to who really is dead; Masrur and an old woman, sent in turn by the Caliph and Zobaydah to settle the wagers that are now being made, report differently. When the entire retinue arrives at Abu Hassan's dwelling, both occupants appear to be dead. Puzzled, the Caliph offers a thousand dinars to whomever can tell him who died first, and this is instantly claimed by Abu Hassan; Nuzhat follows him 'back to life'. The Caliph is delighted to find them alive and amused at the trick; he reproaches them for not telling him of their needs, and all ends happily.[1]

It was the second part of this tale which Hiemer saw as a likely subject for Weber, and which became his *Singspiel* in one act, *Abu Hassan* (J. 106). Not only were Turkish operas popular—there was the example of Vogler's *Kaufmann von Smyrna* as well as Mozart's *Entführung* and many others—but the notion of a witty debtor outmanoeuvring a monarch had a rueful appeal to both librettist and composer. Though he does not trouble to explain why it is that Abu Hassan has such a claim on the Caliph's affection, Hiemer greatly strengthens the part of the story he uses by emphasizing the serious-

---

[1] The spelling of the names is taken from the best English version of the story, to be found in Supplemental Vol. I of Sir Richard Burton's famous translation *The Thousand Nights and a Night* (16 vols., 1885–8). But Galland's version contains several elements, in none of the English translations, that were carried over into Hiemer's libretto, notably a strong emphasis on the love between Abu Hassan and Nuzhat and on the quantity and quality of their food and drink; while a mention of their fondness for accompanying their songs on the lute may have suggested to Weber the guitars used in Abu Hassan's first aria.

ness of the couple's debts and introducing a new character in the money-lender Omar who lusts after Abu Hassan's wife (renamed Fatime).

After an Overture using material from the opera, the curtain rises on Abu Hassan's (ten.) room in the palace. He and Fatime (sop.) are lamenting their sorry, hungry state (No. 1, Duett: 'Liebes Weibchen, reiche Wein'). Fatime reveals that Omar is wooing her—unsuccessfully, to Abu Hassan's relief (not that he is above making use of her charms). He now hits upon the notion of them each 'dying' in turn while the other claims from the Caliph (speaker) and Zobeide (speaker) the funeral money and shroud. Fatime leaves at once to carry out this plan, and left alone, Abu Hassan reflects on the delights that lie ahead (No. 2, Arie: 'Ich gebe Gastereien'). He is disturbed by the arrival of a horde of creditors, with Omar (bass) at their head, demanding instant pay-ment (No. 3, Chor der Gläubiger: 'Geld! Geld! Geld!'). This is interspersed with negotiations between Abu Hassan and Omar, who agrees to settle with the creditors upon hints of Fatime's interest in him being held out; he leads them off to his house. Fatime returns with ten thousand dinars and a shroud from Zobeide, and they sing a love duet (No. 4, Duett: 'Thränen, Thränen sollst du nicht vergiessen'). It is now Abu Hassan's turn to go to the Caliph; left alone, Fatime reflects on her love for Abu Hassan, whose enslavement of her heart is her true freedom (No. 5, Arie: 'Wird Philomele trauern'). Omar reappears and begins wooing Fatime; in the ensuing number (No. 6, Duett: 'Siehst du diese grosse Menge') he explains that he has settled their bills, and makes further advances, which she repels (though not so far as to discourage him utterly). Seeing Abu Hassan returning, she bundles Omar into a cup-board; she explains the real situation *sotto voce* to Abu Hassan, who has also been successful in getting funeral money, while aloud they pretend to quarrel about the cupboard being locked. In the ensuing trio (No. 7, Terzett: 'Ich such' und such' in allen Ecken') they build up the fiction of Abu Hassan the jealous husband demanding that the cupboard be opened, while the terrified Omar regrets his rash action. They are interrupted by catching a glimpse of Masrur (speaker) on his way to find out the truth: Fatime feigns death, and Abu Hassan sorrowfully confirms this to Masrur, who hurries away to inform the Caliph that he has won his bet with Zobeide. When Zobeide's confidante Zemrud (speaker) is seen approaching, Fatime sings a mock lament about the loss of Abu Hassan (No. 8, Arie: 'Hier liegt, welch' martervolles Loos!'). The former scene is now enacted in reverse, with Zemrud sent off to report that it is Zobeide who has won the wager. All three left behind are now somewhat alarmed—Abu Hassan and Fatime because they realise the truth is bound to come out, Omar because he is still apparently imprisoned and at the mercy of a jealous husband. Panic develops when they hear in the distance sounds of the Caliph's retinue approaching, and both Abu Hassan and Fatime take up the position of corpses (No. 9, Terzett und Chor: 'Aengstlich klopft es mir im Herzen'). Finding both of them evidently dead, the puzzled Caliph offers ten thousand golden dinars to anyone who can solve the riddle of who died first. Abu Hassan leaps up to claim it, declaring that he died second: they explain all to the highly amused Caliph, including the fact that their bills have now been settled by Omar (still in the cupboard) out of his hopes of winning Fatime. The Caliph orders cupboard and contents to be taken to the city prison, gives Abu Hassan the promised ten thousand dinars and appoints him cup-bearer at an increased salary. All ends happily in a chorus of praise to the Caliph (No. 10, Schlusschor: 'Heil ist dem Haus beschieden').

Weber received the text from Hiemer on 29th March 1810; but his diary indicates no work on it until the beginning of August, when he records that he composed the Creditors' Chorus. The date finally given it, however, is 3rd September: 'componirt' for Weber meant that the idea had been worked out in his mind, in more or less complete form, but was not necessarily then written down, or 'notirt'. Four more numbers were finished during September—No. 6 on the 4th, Nos. 9 and 10 on the 10th, and No. 7 on the 12th. The remaining items of the original score followed at a distance. No. 2 is undated, but No. 1 is marked 2nd November and No. 5, 13th November; while the Overture and with it the whole opera have a final date of 12th January 1811. This makes a total of an overture and eight items; Weber later added No. 4 (composed December 1812, scored 2nd January 1813) and No. 8 (2nd March 1823) to complete the opera as we know it.

This haphazard working plan could never be deduced from the finished opera. Though it is a small-scale piece, *Abu Hassan* has an inventive security that reflects the new confidence Weber had gained during his months away from Stuttgart. He could even view that period and its legacy of debt with good humour: he chose to begin work on this *Arabian Nights* daydream of a wish fulfilled with the chorus demanding an immediate settlement of accounts. 'Geld! Geld! Geld! ich will nicht länger harren' opens with two insistent rising scales, leading into a brusque male voice chorus not so remote in style from the student shouts Weber must often have joined in during his Heidelberg evenings, and which were to become the background of his later male-voice and patriotic choruses. When, by means of a hint of Fatime's complaisance, Omar is talked into settling up, the chorus accept with 'Ja! Ja! Ja!' now on a repeated unison F, continuing with their previous abrupt and ill-humoured counterpoint now smoothed out into placid block harmony over which Omar congratulates himself on the promise of delights to come while Abu Hassan takes off in exuberant ornamental flights of counterpoint. It is a neat musical analogue of the altered situation.

The best of *Abu Hassan* deserves the comparisons with Mozart which many of Weber's biographers are keen to underline. There is a Mozartian tenderness running through the work, in the goodnatured portrayal of Omar as well as in the treatment of Abu Hassan's and Fatime's love for each other, however brilliantly this is maintained on the level of light sentimental comedy. More than one casual phrase could have come from Mozart; and the opening of the delightful Terzett (No. 9: 'Aengstlich klopft es mir im Herzen')

Ex. 19

suggests that Weber had been impressed by an accompaniment figure in
Belmonte's 'O wie ängstlich' (Ex. 19, p. 109).

But there is no element of Mozart imitation in the treatment of this figure;
and the growing alarm of the three principals, as their fears of exposure are
sharpened by the sound off-stage of a Turkish March on oboes and horns

signalling the Caliph's approach, is superbly handled. There is, again, a
Mozartian nervy inventiveness in the Terzett (No. 7: 'Ich such'') that
originally preceded this number, with the violins showing Abu Hassan's and
Fatime's suppressed laughter as they go through their charade of jealousy
and outraged virtue for the benefit of the terrified Omar (Ex. 20, p. 110).

But again, the development is completely Weberian, even to the point of
using a thrusting triplet ostinato that first appeared in *Silvana* and turns up
again in *Euryanthe* and *Kampf und Sieg*:

Ex. 21

And there is a characteristic *Abu Hassan* stroke in the return of the off-beat
violin figure, on bassoons to lighten Fatime's mock-despairing appeal to the
'jealous' Abu Hassan.

Ex. 22

Weber was right to sense later that a solo aria was needed to separate these
two trios, even at the cost of continuity. For the Dresden production of 10th
March 1823 he composed Fatime's 'Hier liegt' (No. 8), soliloquizing over the
supposed death of Abu Hassan.[1] It is a beautiful little lament, heavy with

---

[1] In his English version (1959), David Harris moves this aria so that it occurs after
Zemrud's entrance instead of immediately before: thus it is sung not as a soliloquy but as
if to convince Zemrud of Abu Hassan's death and Fatime's grief.

chromatic woodwind, violas and throbbing double basses, over which Fatime utters her plaint in wide flung arpeggios; but it does not really suit the style of *Abu Hassan*. Weber was busy with *Euryanthe* at the time, and evidently found it impossible to recapture the lighter manner of over twelve years previously. Yet the piece has its place in the opera, if only on its own merits; so, more importantly still, does the magnificent duet 'Thränen, Thränen' (No. 4) which Weber added at the very beginning of 1813 for a private performance at Duke Friedrich of Gotha's private theatre. Once again, this does not recapture the authentic pace and lightness of the original *Abu Hassan* numbers, and comes forward with a full-scale love duet between a couple who otherwise tend to keep their affection on an almost bantering level, while reserving for solo arias, when alone, their real depth of feeling for each other. Yet it manages not to disturb this convention too much: the opening Andante is soon dispelled with one of Weber's gayest themes; and the lovers emphasize their dependence on each other, but their refusal to take matters too seriously, by coursing cheerfully along with lively figures linked in thirds.

The more essential note of the opera, however, is found in the two original solo arias. Fatime's 'Wird Philomele' (No. 5) begins with Minette's Romance from *Peter Schmoll* (No. 3: 'Im Rheinland eine Dirne'), rescored, principally with cello replacing the bassoon obbligato, and slightly reharmonized; it breaks off with a brief passage of recitative leading into one of Weber's polaccas that gives the singer plenty of chance to show off her coloratura. All the same, this has a precise expressive function to play, Fatime answering her serenade describing the nightingale's longing for freedom with delight in the freedom she herself can only find when bound by love to Abu Hassan. When she slyly attempts to distract his attention from his hunger with vocalization for its own sake in a serenade *all'Italiana* in the opening duet, Weber-Hassan sharply brings her to heel (Ex. 23, p. 114).

Abu Hassan's solo aria looking forward to the delights of a solvent life together with Fatime is still more successful, and shows how even in this brief work Weber could link sharply contrasted tempos to make an effective larger structure. His musings on his love for Fatime, and his plans for making her queen of the banquet they will arrange, break naturally into an effervescent little Vivace 6/8 outburst a mere nineteen bars long; this in turn gives way to a serenade in which the elegance of the tune is charmingly set off by the accompaniment on two guitars, and, ensuring we do not mistake this engaging character for a Great Lover, a gently grotesque bassoon. The final Allegro keeps the tenor's coloratura score even with the soprano's.

Abu Hassan is a *Singspiel* by description and intent. Yet like *Entführung*, if a good deal more modestly, it transforms the genre with invention of a lightness and tenderness, with a pace and a range of effect, that set it in another category altogether from the earthy, routine humours of most *Singspiele*. The

resources with which this is achieved are modest, showing again that Weber
had won a confidence which allowed him to forgo experiment or theory, and
simply relax with an entertaining story that could engage his invention at its
purest. The scoring is light—double wind, two horns and trumpets, a trombone, string quintet and the two guitars for No. 2. There is not even a very
large allowance of percussion—in addition to timpani, he uses the bass drum,
side drum and triangle of the *Türkische Musik*, but quite reticently—and there
is very little reliance on 'exotic' effect. Instrumental obbligatos are few and
kept brief (except for the dancing violin of No. 6); the melodies have a liveliness and at the same time a more positive character than anything in the
previous operas; and harmonically the piece is kept exceedingly simple in
the interests of speed and lightness of emotion—so much so that Omar's
ninth-chord and Fatime's seventh-chord at the mention of love and death
respectively have in context the unmistakable flavour of parody (Ex. 24,
opposite).

All these qualities are found at their best in the brilliant overture, composed in abbreviated sonata form on music from the opera. Only the difficulty of fitting one-act operas into repertory can stand in the way of *Abu*

Ex. 23

Hassan's revival, for occasional performances have shown how excellently it comes across in the theatre. It was an immediate success at its première at the Munich Hofbühne on 4th June 1811: among the other towns which took it up in the next two years were Berlin, Dresden, Frankfurt, Gotha, Königsberg, Prague, Stuttgart, Vienna and Würzburg. It did not reach England until 1825, in a version by T. S. Cooke; Castil-Blaze's French version is almost accurate, and Nuittier and Beaumont's merely alters the order of numbers. Weber had found his touch in the form closest to his heart, and Germany was quick to recognize the fact. If only circumstances had allowed him to follow up this success, if only he had discovered librettists to match his rapidly expanding imaginative powers, the whole course of his career and indeed the evolution of Romantic opera might have been completely altered. Yet he was compelled to put his energies into other aspects of opera, to waste much of the little time he had left in hackwork and in supporting other men's enterprises even when he was not trying to foster German opera by precept and performance rather than example. Ten years, a quarter of his life, were to pass before his next opera, and that was *Der Freischütz*.

Ex. 24

CHAPTER EIGHT

TRAVELS: 1811–1813

Ja, wohl bin ich nur ein Wanderer, ein Waller auf der Erde! Seid ihr denn mehr?
GOETHE: *Werther*

WEBER HAD been expelled from Stuttgart in disgrace, banished as *persona non grata*; he left Darmstadt on 14th February 1811, almost exactly a year later, with the optimism of a conqueror. Though disappointed in the hope of a permanent post—the Duke liked conducting too well to contemplate such formidable rivalry—he had gained the self-assurance and self-knowledge to be confident of success as a touring virtuoso. Arming himself with the conventional letters of introduction, he accordingly set off on a concert tour that was grandly intended to embrace Munich, Prague, Dresden, Berlin, Copenhagen and St. Petersburg. In the event, he described a broad curve across southern Germany that brought him to rest in his next port of call, Munich.

First he travelled north to the little university town of Giessen, where despite a contemptuous reception by the police, he gave a triumphant concert; in Aschaffenburg he met a famous virtuoso, the Abbé Sterkel, another former Vogler pupil whose playing had greatly impressed the young Beethoven; in Würzburg he talked with Joseph Fröhlich, a renowned teacher who was later to carry out Weber's plan for a biography of Vogler; and arriving in Bamberg on 3rd March, he met, over the first of many glasses of wine in *Die Rose*, the music director and scene painter of the theatre, E. T. A. Hoffmann. They did not become close friends, though Hoffmann seems to have enjoyed Weber's company and Weber was undoubtedly fascinated by the Romantic aura Hoffmann cultivated in his conversation and behaviour. Journeying on by way of Erlangen and Nuremberg, he paused in Augsburg to discuss business with his old publisher Gombart, though (as he wrote to Gottfried) the lack of success over a concert and hence the shortage of money, coupled with his natural restlessness when unoccupied, caused him to move on quickly. He reached Munich on 14th March.

As the capital of the new Bavarian state, Munich was in a somewhat comparable position to Württemberg *vis-à-vis* the French. Having been made into a kingdom by Napoleon, largely through the efforts of Maximilian I's minister Maximilian Josef von Montgelas, Bavaria was closely dependent on France: she had twice fought with the French against Austria, and a further bond was tied with the marriage of Maximilian's daughter Augusta to Napoleon's adopted son and heir Eugène Beauharnais, in 1806. But while no-one could have called Friedrich of Württemberg the Father of his People, Maximilian did much to earn this title from his Munichers. Supported by Montgelas, he had in 1808 put through a new constitution bringing about economic, administrative and legal reforms; and if not personally greatly devoted to the arts, he recognized their importance, encouraging art galleries and the theatre, and fostering the activities of architects, writers, composers, painters and philosophers. Chief among the latter was Schelling, whose works Weber had studied with enthusiasm in Stuttgart. He was soon writing proudly to Gottfried of his warm friendship with 'this truly great man'.

Among Weber's letters of introduction was one to Montgelas, who received him courteously and arranged an immediate interview with the Queen; this in turn led to the promise of a concert. Other opportunities abounded. The two leading musical societies were the Harmonie, where music formed part of the social scene, and the Museum, which under the direction of Ferdinand Fränzl was more seriously inclined. The opera was one of the most prominent in Germany, with an ensemble that had, until now, been under the enlightened control of Joseph Maria Babo: unfortunately Babo had come into conflict with the Court Superintendent, Count Törring-Seefeld (according to Max Maria, over the question of the prominence allowed to Italian opera), and coincidentally with Weber's arrival, he was replaced by the more docile Carl August Delamotte. Nevertheless, Weber was able to report hopes of production of two operas to Gottfried on 22nd March, despite the equivocal attitude of the music director, Peter Winter. A violinist in the Mannheim orchestra at the age of eleven, Winter had later become director of the theatre before following the court to Munich with many of the most famous players; the National Theatre was to include opera, and the opera repertory was to be given in German. Among his many stage works, *Das unterbrochene Opferfest* (1796) long retained popularity; but Winter's mild manner evidently concealed a powerful sense of jealousy, for he had damaged Mozart's chances in Vienna by spreading slanders, and though at first he received Weber cordially, on discovering that this was no amateur to be patronized but a highly professional colleague, his manner changed sharply.[1] Winter's orchestra had maintained its Mannheim traditions of excellence, and among its most distinguished artists was the clarinettist Heinrich Bärmann.

Weber met Bärmann again at the house of the head of the public works, Wiebeking (another letter of introduction had secured the entrée to Wiebeking's

---

[1] Spohr has left a lively thumbnail sketch of Winter's odd combination of meekness and violence, recounting how he would spend hours decorating his Christmas crib with dolls until bustled off by his bullying housekeeper to get on with an aria (*Selbstbiographie*, Vol. 1 (1860–1)).

house and the task of teaching the piano to his daughter Fanny). Born in
1784, Bärmann had trained at Potsdam, served in a military band, been cap-
tured at Jena and after his release had come to Munich: a tour that covered
England, France, Italy and Russia had won him wide fame. Bärmann's personal charm as well as his virtuosity on Weber's favourite wind instrument
drew the two musicians together; and immediately Weber set to work on a
Concertino for Bärmann to play at the projected concert. This was duly held
on 5th April. The Court took fifty tickets, and the hall was sold out. Weber's
own contributions to a long programme included the First Symphony and
Der erste Ton—the latter misfiring somewhat since the intended speaker,
Max Heigel, was taken ill and had to be replaced by an inferior performer
named Kürzinger. But the Concertino was delightedly received, so much so
that the King forthwith ordered two full-scale clarinet concertos.

The reasons for Weber's attraction to the clarinet are not hard to find. As
in the case of other instruments, its technical maturity coincided with the
appearance of a school of virtuosos; and despite various shortcomings,
chiefly of intonation, it was rapidly accepted in other orchestras besides that
of Mannheim during the last quarter of the eighteenth century. The great
Joseph Beer set the German style—soft, rich and full in tone, in contrast to
the shriller and more brilliant French manner—and his immediate pupils
and followers won the enthusiasm of a wide circle of composers who explored and extended the new range of sounds. What Beer had been to
Stamitz, so Stadler was to Mozart, Hermstedt to Spohr and Bärmann to
Weber. Two years before their Munich meeting, Bärmann had acquired
a ten-key clarinet that allowed greater flexibility and smoothness; and in
Bärmann's clarinet Weber found an instrument that with its French incisive-
ness and vivacity and its German fullness seemed to express a new world of
feeling, and to match both the dark romantic melancholy and the extrovert
brilliance of his own temperament.

From this close affinity the Concertino (Op. 26: J.109) takes its nature and
indeed its form. With the two concertos that followed—No. 1 in F minor
(Op. 73: J.114) and No. 2 in E♭ (Op. 74: J.118)—Weber felt obliged to make
use of the normal three-movement form, and thus come to grips again with a
sonata first movement. Working to a royal commission, he doubtless considered innovations to be out of place, effectiveness within understood forms
a more certain passport to success. But no matter how deftly he brought off
the two opening movements of these concertos, the fact remains that he
found sonata form basically incompatible with his own ways of thought.
There was, of course, the example of Beethoven; but quite apart from questions of stature, the distance Weber felt to exist between himself and
Beethoven is charted in their different approach to sonata form. However
lofty and far-reaching the extensions Beethoven made, however profoundly
he matched it, from the *Eroica Symphony* right on to the last quartets, to the

infinitely varied expression of a new movement of the human spirit, sonata was for him the natural inheritance, the source from which the vast river of his invention might swell. With Weber we immediately sense a lack of belief in the form. This shows itself in various ways. It was to him a convention that a skilled composer should be able to use; but in his sonatas and concertos the true colour and weight of his invention lies elsewhere, in the grave, strangely-hued slow movements or the dashing charm of the finales, while the first movements are measured more by the degree to which such qualities can be accommodated than by the mastery of form that grows from real instinct and faith in it. Internal evidence apart, this is revealed in the fact that he often left the opening movement until the last to compose. In more than one instance (for example the Adagio and Rondo for Harmonichord, and the Andante and Rondo for viola, both with orchestra) he in effect simply omitted it altogether. Further, the last of his piano sonatas is formally the most successful because geared to a hidden programme, while the last of his concertos, the famous *Konzertstück*, abandons traditional forms altogether and sets a pattern for later Romantic composers in its use of a programme to provide a shape that will also be satisfying in strictly musical terms. The internal drama of sonata has been left behind; if, instead, theatricality sometimes overtakes Weber's instrumental music, this is the less happy outcome of the heightened sense of effect, visual, poetic and dramatic, which he introduced into Romantic currency.

Ex. 25

In so far as a 'programme' exists in the Concertino, it is one reflecting the
human voice as well as Bärmann's own personality. With the Second
Concerto, a sense of the instrument's operatic affinities causes the lyrical song
of the Andante con moto to acquire an increasing degree of coloratura
ornamentation until the logical outcome is a passage candidly marked
'Recitativo ad lib.'. The brief Cadenza at the end is not a display of instrumental or creative virtuosity but the singer's scalic flourish on the dominant
before the final tonic. The Concertino already reflects this capacity to
'vocalize' melodies; though in his first essay for the instrument Weber is
concentrating on showing off the fascinating tone-colour and the new
flexibility of Bärmann's technique—by the seventh bar of its entry the
clarinet is required to slur up from a written low F to the A two octaves
and a third higher, a startling enough effect even if it was to be excelled by
the leap of three octaves and a third in the Quintet from low E to high
G (Mozart, though a good part of the invention in his Concerto and
Quintet springs from the effect of contrasted chalumeau and high register,
preferred to avoid slurring across the leaps). It is significant that Weber is at
his most natural with a form arising from display of an instrument's character, and that in discovering a new quality in the instrument's tone colour by
matching it to divided violas he should find his inventiveness with the theme
at its most original (Ex. 25, p. 119).

The Adagio of the First Concerto ends with a comparable tonal effect,
when, the darker side of the clarinet's tone having been emphasized with
chorale-like passages on bassoons, later joined by oboes and then flutes

Ex. 26

against murmuring strings, a brief animated section leads to a sombre hymn against three-part horn harmony.[1] (Ex. 26, opposite page).

This liking for the dark, mysterious quality produced by the careful combination of two tone colours in the right instrumental register goes back to the Adagio of the Second Symphony (see Music Example No. 6, p. 58); and though it had become something perilously near a cliché by the time he wrote the Bassoon Concerto that November, four months after the Second Clarinet Concerto, his sure ear for timbre carries him through with distinction:

Ex. 27

It is in these slow movements that we find the most intense and most characteristic side of Weber, indulging his instinct for colour and implicitly

[1] For a concert homage to Weber in 1831, Bärmann arranged the whole of this section for clarinet and three male voices, who sang words by Eduard von Schenk:

Er ist dahin, der Schöpfer dieser Klänge!
Der Hohe Meister, der von hinnen schied,
Er lehrt den Engelchören nun Gesänge;
Doch ewig lebt auf Erden auch sein Lied!

revealing his longing to be back at work on opera (the Bassoon Concerto's Adagio also ends with a vocally inclined cadenza). Of the finales to the clarinet works, that of No. 1 is lively enough but can hardly compare with the unaffected gaiety of the Concertino's Allegro, still less with the verve and wit Weber conjures out of his favourite Polonaise rhythm for No. 2. After a display of fireworks scintillating enough to dazzle any audience and burn the fingers of most clarinettists, this ends with a hurtling passage of sextuplets that he need scarcely have troubled to mark *brillante*.

The success of the Clarinet Concertino was not confined to the King. By the end of the month Weber was writing to Gottfried,[1] 'Since I composed the Concertino for Bärmann the whole orchestra has been the very devil about demanding concertos from me . . . two Clarinet Concertos (of which one in F minor is almost ready), two large arias, a Cello Concerto for Legrand, a Bassoon Concerto. You see I'm not doing at all badly, and very probably I'll be spending the summer here, where I'm earning so much that I've something left over after paying my keep . . . Besides, the orchestra and everybody would like to see me appointed *Kapellmeister*.' The Cello Concerto was never written, perhaps partly because Weber's thoughts were inclining more towards wind instruments. As well as composing for clarinet and bassoon, he published an article giving serious technical appraisal of Johann Nepomuk Capeller's improved flute;[2] and an entirely novel timbre came his way when on an excursion to Nymphenburg with some friends he met Friedrich Kaufmann and heard the new Harmonichord. Invented in 1808, this was one of many contemporary attempts to make a so-called Sostenente Pianoforte that would overcome the normal instrument's disadvantage of losing power from the moment of a note being struck. It was, more or less, a hurdy-gurdy with piano action: when the keys were depressed a rosined leather cylinder revolved by a footpedal came into contact with the strings. Degrees of tone and of loudness were controlled by finger pressure on the keys. Weber's enthusiasm for the novel sound seems to have evaporated as he came up against the technical problems of writing music for it, since he only finished the ensuing Adagio and Rondo for Harmonichord and orchestra (J.115) early on the morning of the day before Kaufmann's concert of 13th June, which included the première of the First Clarinet Concerto; and on the 27th he wrote to Gänsbacher that 'it was damned hard work composing for an instrument whose tone is so original and strange that one needs the liveliest fantasy in order to blend it properly with other instruments. It is a stepchild of the Harmonica,[3] and has the peculiarity that with every sustained note its octave is prominently heard.' Since the instrument is extinct, one can

---

[1] Letter of 30th April 1811.

[2] In the *AMZ*, 1811 (Kaiser 23).

[3] Presumably Weber is referring to the Glass Armonica, for which Mozart and others wrote pieces.

scarcely judge the effect of Weber's music, except as a characteristically elegant piece of melodic writing; it was used by Kaufmann as a demonstration piece for many years.

Meanwhile *Abu Hassan* was due for production in Württemberg, though, to Weber's irritation, with his name suppressed because of his exile; and in Munich on 4th June, after only four rehearsals, it was given its première at the Hofbühne. Josepha Flerx-Lang, a Munich artist since 1807 and according to Weber 'a fiery artist', sang Fatime; the title role was taken by Georg Mittermaier, who also made a considerable reputation as a bass; Omar was sung by an older and very experienced artist, Joseph Muck. Despite a false fire alarm, which emptied the theatre during the first number, the opera went excellently on its resumption, five numbers being encored. Weber's confidence in his calling as an opera composer reasserted itself: as he wrote to Gänsbacher, 'I am waiting in agony for a good libretto. I don't feel right when I haven't got an opera in hand.' But none came, and the remaining works of the first half of 1811 are small—four guitar songs for the character of Goswin in the production on 9th June of Kotzebue's play *Der arme Minnesinger* (Op. 25, Nos. 2, 3 and 5, one MS: J. 110-3); and the *Trauer-Musik* (J.116) for the actor Max Heigel, who had died on 9th June and for whose funeral on the 26th, Winter's Requiem was instead chosen owing (wrote Weber bitterly in his diary) to scheming by Heigel's son. It is a solemn obsequy for baritone, chorus and wind band; the close is a rescoring of the *Grablied* of 1803 (J.37), and parts were later used for the E♭ Mass (J.224).

Apart from the simple song *Maienblümlein* (Op. 23, No. 3: J.117), this is the sum of his compositions during these months. Other activities abounded; but the social round was intoxicating rather than nourishing—he wrote to Gottfried complaining how much he missed having real friends around him, despite the welcome visit of Danzi, and despite his various love affairs, often recorded in his diary with the accompanying entry 'A. W. T. N.' ('Alle Weiber taugen nichts'—'All women are worthless'). A new bout of restlessness coincided with an offer, by way of Gottfried, of the post of *Kapellmeister* at Wiesbaden. Weber replied with detailed questions on 8th July, proposing conditions and a salary of 1600 gulden to the Wiesbaden Intendant on 16th July. The answer on 3rd August that he could not expect more than 1000 gulden decided him against accepting the offer—not an ungenerous one considering that as a summer resort Wiesbaden would leave his winters free—and instead he revived the idea of a trip to Switzerland to see Nägeli and to study Pestalozzi's ideas on musical education—more generally to investigate the country's musical possibilities. On 9th August he set off.

The direct route to Switzerland lay across the territory of Ravensburg, since 1810 part of the Kingdom of Württemberg. Trusting to luck, Weber presented his passport and had already had it cleared when he was recognized by a former Stuttgart Chief Inspector, Romig, arrested and confined in a room of the town's single inn. Paur, the postmaster, treated him kindly, sending for a doctor when he contracted a fever and even hunting up two of his former Stuttgart officer friends as company while word was sent back to the capital for instructions from the King. After three full days (11th to 15th August; he counted this as five days when writing to Gottfried) the sentence was delivered: Paur was dismissed the royal service, Weber was to be escorted to Mörsburg and put on a boat for Constanz. These were his exact plans in any case, for he was on his way to visit his Munich friend Baron Hoggner at Schloss Wolfsberg, two hours away from Constanz. Leaving a thank-you letter to Hoggner in the form of an Italian *canzonetta*, *D'ogni amator* (now lost), he next travelled down the Rhine to the music festival at Schaffhausen (where another *canzonetta*, *Ch'io mai vi possa* (Op. 29, No. 3: J.120) was written). The town was full—two hundred and fifty performers and some fifteen hundred listeners—and among the visitors Weber met Nägeli (who disappointed him by refusing to publish the planned journal of the *Harmonische Verein*) as well as Meyerbeer's family. Impressed by the parents but annoyed with Meyerbeer himself on account of some offhand behaviour, he left in their company for Winterthur, after a highly enjoyable series of concerts.[1] Here the orchestra proved so incompetent that he was compelled to rearrange his First Piano Concerto for solo and string quartet; he was also unable to find a decent piano. After an unprofitable concert, he travelled to Zürich, where Nägeli reaffirmed his refusal to publish the proposed magazine. But moving on to Bern, Weber now took up another project, a so-called *Musikalische Topographie Deutschlands* that would provide a kind of Baedeker for travelling musicians. Germany, Denmark, Sweden, Russia, Italy and France were to be covered, with details in all the important towns and music centres of who ran the concerts, how best to arrange them, the standard of the orchestra, which was the best day in the week to choose, what kind of music was most popular, and so forth. Providing his own report on Basel,[2] he wrote enthusiastically to Gottfried on 2nd September, to Gänsbacher on the 22nd, enquiring for details of Prague and reporting success in obtaining a publisher (Orelli and Fuessl of Zürich). But the other members of the *Verein* were tepid, and the project lapsed.

After a concert in Zürich, where he was delighted to make his first acquaintance with the newly patented Erard grand piano and disappointed at the standard of singing in the Institute run by Nägeli on Pestalozzian lines, he set off on a walking tour with a musical friend named Liste. For someone chronically lame and delicate it was an unpromising trip, but the four days seem to have done him good; and on returning to Berne he was happy to find letters from Danzi, Bärmann and his father—the latter still meddling in Weber's affairs and muddling his own. A second walking tour took him

[1] Weber's account of the Festival is Kaiser 33.
[2] The plan is Kaiser 34; Weber's Basel contribution is Kaiser 36.

through the Oberland. He bought souvenir boxes for Bärmann and Wiebe-king, made himself ill with some rich goat's-milk bought in a peasant's hut, and filled his diary with impressions of the spectacular Alpine scenery. To Dusch he protested his inarticulacy: 'Shall I describe it to you? That would drive me quite mad, no, I *feel* in God's free Nature, but I can't *speak* to you about it.' But the impression made by this intimate contact with nature at its most sensational went deep. Rousseau, being Swiss, had admired the Alps; and his Romantic successors likewise took pleasure in the dramatic, exaggera-ted nature of the scenery, its sudden alteration of intense, pastoral sweetness with the violent storms that 'irrationally' descend upon the lakes. Although the greatest painter of the German Romantic movement, Caspar David Friedrich, preferred the level countryside of North and Central Germany, choosing dusk, mist and autumn or winter as settings for his melancholy inner version, the Romantic fashion more generally was Wordsworthian, for the sounding cataract, the mountain, the deep and gloomy wood. In such surroundings poets and musicians could find something of their own sharply dramatized moods; and undoubtedly the Swiss interlude in his professional life allowed Weber to enrich and intensify his feeling for the natural world—however light and halting the notes in his diary. At Grindelwald: 'Indescrib-able the beautiful blue, underfoot like a diamond . . . Picked flowers by the glacier. The beggars are very plentiful, but one astonished me by bringing cherries on to the glacier, where I had the sensual pleasure of sitting and eat-ing them . . .' On returning, he spent some time near Solothurn at the Jegenstorf estate of the Bavarian minister Count von Olry. Here he com-posed, on 2nd October, the *Scena ed Aria d'Atalia* (Op. 50: J.121), a dramatic Andante and Adagio that kept his hand in at opera, so to speak, though intended for no known opera. But he thought highly enough of it to revive it for Mary Anne Paton at the London concert two days before the première of *Oberon*. Having missed Zschokke on a visit to Aarau to recruit him for the *Harmonische Verein*, he returned to Basel for a concert in mid-October—a success financially, netting 130 gulden, despite the fact that the attention of the nobility of the town was distracted by the presence in salons and drawing rooms of the popular Grand Duchess Stéphanie. Pausing briefly once more at Schloss Wolfsberg, he returned (by way of Lindau, this time) to Munich. The three months had spread his reputation still further, while strengthening him both physically and in self-confidence.

Back in Munich, life rapidly became as complicated as before, and to escape from the tangle of his love affairs he was thankful to fall in with Bärmann's suggestion of a joint tour of North Germany. But first, there were professional matters to be put in order. As well as making a petition for the usual letters of introduction from the King, he had to finish some critical articles, prepare for a concert and complete for the Queen a group of three *canzonette, Mille volte* (Op. 31, No. 1: J.123), *Ninfe se liete* (Op. 29, No. 2:

J.124) and *Va, ti consola* (Op. 31, No. 2: J. 125). These, with the other Italian pieces written on the Swiss journey, were presented to the Queen by the slightly abashed composer—their composition had been very hasty—but his apologies for such trifles were waved aside with, 'Hush! hush! nothing is little, nothing big! Everything which you do can be nothing but beautiful.' Italian songs play a small part in Weber's output. His aversion to Italian music is such a *Leitmotiv* of his life that it may seem surprising to find him setting the language at all; but the closeness of his melodic style to Italian song is unmistakable, and though he firmly avoided the elaborate ornamentations demanded by Italian singers, he showed in these and his concert arias to Italian texts a very real understanding of Italian grace and fluency of line. Most are pleasant trifles, usually cast in simple ABA form: the duets tend to be more freely handled.

Previously, on 8th November, he had completed his Overture, *Der Beherrscher der Geister* (Op. 27: J.122). Weber describes this in his catalogue of his music as 'a completely new working' of the now lost *Rübezahl* overture. The last eleven bars of the first violin part (all that survive) include two figures used in the new overture, one of them the opening repeated chords, though with a key signature in the minor. Some of the themes may well be the residue of sketches for arias in the unfinished opera; what seems certain is that in 1804–5 Weber could never have produced a piece of such brilliance and ingenuity. Essentially, the overture is an orchestral tour-de-force on the alternation and development of a hurtling violin theme with three slower wind themes (two of them closely related); the experience of *Abu Hassan* has been absorbed, but to pace and charm has been added a new contrapuntal skill— not of the bookish kind which appears in some of the earlier music but in a simultaneous play of wit, as when the strings divide up their opening theme to make a lively accompaniment for first wind theme, similarly broken up (Ex. 28, opposite page).

If any dramatic reason lies behind the odd central passage when the other wind theme is solemnly hymned on brass chorus with timpani, none has survived. It is more likely to be the result of Weber's fondness for a darker alternative colouring (as in the *Euryanthe* overture): later he satirically likened this section to 'an artillery park'. But he was pleased with the overture's 'strength and clarity', he told Gottfried,[1] re-titling it in its new form since it no longer had any operatic connexions. He nevertheless felt it to be dramatic enough to be used with the music he wrote for Müller's *König Yngurd* (Berlin, 1817); a year before that it had awakened a Milan audience to the existence of a hitherto unknown genius in Germany. Gottfried's answers, however, were chilly. He felt Weber to be neglecting the affairs of the *Verein* in favour of his own; Meyerbeer was no better. Weber's plea that he had been working on Gottfried's behalf with Winter and others did not

[1] Letter of 15th November 1811.

Ex. 28

convince; and relations remained clouded until the two managed to meet once more. The overture triumphed on 11th November at the royal concert, which included the *Atalia* scena (sung by Regina Lang) and an improvisation by Weber himself on a theme selected by the Queen from Méhul's *Joseph*, the Romance 'A peine au sortir de l'enfance'. On the 25th Bärmann gave the first performance—playing 'in a heavenly manner', according to Weber's diary—of the Second Clarinet Concerto at an 'Academy' arranged by the tenor Weixelbaum, who also sang another semi-operatic scena Weber had finished on the 22nd, the *Scena ed Aria, Qual altro attendi* (J. 126).

The operatic note recurs in the Bassoon Concerto (Op. 75: J.127), which Weber completed two days after the Academy. Still more than in the clarinet concertos, whose pattern it admittedly follows, there is a sense here of the bassoon presented as a dramatic character—indeed, one seemingly on the brink of words at the start of the Adagio. The middle section of this movement, the first to be written, has already been quoted (Mus. Ex. 27, p. 121); as well as the cavernous mystery in the instrument's tone, Weber also discovers tenderness and dignity shot with a curious pathos. Until the final bars of applause music (a natural conclusion to the clarinet concertos but a less appropriate device here), the wit of the Rondo retains this note of wistfulness. Partly this arises from Weber's feeling for the bassoon's high register, which in less sympathetic hands can so easily sound merely querulous, partly from the fact that although he uses the potentially comic contrast between high and very low registers, he does so sparingly and always to make a musical point. There is, in fact, no mocking of the bassoon for a cheap laugh; the musical wit arises from the instrument and is never directed against it. The opening Allegro was as usual written last and as usual does not match the succeeding movements. But it ingeniously uses Weber's favourite dotted rhythm to display the bassoon at its cockiest; and the solo entry is a highly imaginative stroke. After a very brief orchestral ritornello, ending on the dominant C, the drum beats out the crotchet rhythm on the tonic F, over which the bassoon enters with the march-like first subject; this time the close on the dominant is answered by the same effect a tone higher, on G, by pizzicato cellos and basses; and so the movement finally gets under way. It was the Allegro which Weber altered most when he came to revise the work in Dresden in 1822; the Adagio and Rondo were scarcely touched. The date of the première is not known. Since it was written for the Munich bassoonist, Georg Friedrich Brandt, a local performance is likely, but the first one mentioned is in Prague on 19th February 1813.[1] The first printed copy describes the work as 'Primo Concerto'; but apart from the *Andante e Rondo Ungarese* of 1813, nothing followed. Taken away from Munich by the tour with Bärmann, Weber abandoned such plans as he may have had for continuing the cycle of con-

[1] *AMZ*

certos—a sad loss, for the Second Clarinet Concerto and still more this Bassoon Concerto have an originality and charm that only Mozart among woodwind concerto composers has excelled.

On 1st December they set off, not by stage but in a comfortable new carriage they had combined to buy. Pressing on day and night, they reached Prague on the 4th, Weber completely exhausted but Bärmann in high spirits. They were welcomed by Gänsbacher, who had used his position in the service of Count Firmian to organize a concert and arrange a list of sponsors among the nobility. With Bohemia's musical traditions, this had proved comparatively easy, for though the tense political situation had brought about a decline in public standards, music remained among the nobles neither a duty nor an occasional recreation, but a natural pastime. Chamber music was part of daily life: servants were frequently engaged as much for their ability to fill a place in an ensemble as for their domestic skills, and the master of the house would not think it inferior to take a secondary role in a quartet. It was not so long since Burney had described the Bohemians as the most musical people of Europe; and the memory of Mozart and *Don Giovanni* was green. Only the year previously, despite all he exhaustions of the war, a *Verein zur Beförderung der Tonkunst in Böhmen* had been founded by eight nobles, among them Count Joseph Wrtby and Prince Georg Lobkowitz; in the year of Weber's arrival this society opened its music school, and together with the Union of Musical Artists for the Support of Widows and Orphans, founded in 1803, provided the city with its first regular public concert life.

In these surroundings, Weber and Bärmann found a ready welcome. Wrtby and Lobkowitz provided them with introductions to other houses, where their recitals and especially Weber's improvisations met with the greatest success; and generally did everything they could to support the coming concert. In Count Firmian's house on 14th December the first performance was given of the Seven Variations for Clarinet and Piano on a Theme from *Silvana* (Op. 33; J.128)—the same theme (from Mechtilde's No. 10a, 'Warum musst' ich dich je erblikken') that had already done duty for No. 5 of the Six Progressive Sonatas. The fact that this was only finished on the morning of the concert and makes use of similar variation material to the earlier sonata (Var. 2 is unaltered), though not the gracefully handled invention, suggests a hastily assembled piece that would both display Bärmann's talents and act as a trailer for the opera. For Weber had also called on Liebich, the director of the theatre. Confined to his bed with bad attacks of kidney stone, Liebich was accustomed to hold conferences with his artists in a kind of levée. He greeted Weber goodnaturedly, 'So you're that splendid chap, the Weber who plays the piano like the very devil; you want me to buy your operas? Gänsbacher tells me they're good; one fills an evening, the other doesn't, I'll give you 1500 gulden for the pair of them—

5

shake on it!' He made Weber promise to come back to Prague the following spring to conduct rehearsals.

Despite a blizzard, the concert on 21st December was well attended, and not only by the nobles. It included the First Clarinet Concerto, the First Piano Concerto and a poor performance of *Der erste Ton* with the popular Prague actress, Mme. Löwe. The next day, having made 1240 gulden out of the evening, Weber and Bärmann left for Dresden. But here they found the court absent; and moving on, they came to Leipzig on the 27th. Weber immediately sought out his old champion Rochlitz, who greeted him cordially; but as a pupil of Vogler he was treated coldly by the Abbé's old rival Johann Schicht, the Cantor of St. Thomas's; while Franz and Joseph Seconda, the brothers who jointly managed the operas of Leipzig and Dresden, sided too firmly with Italian opera for any success to be expected in that quarter. The publishers Härtel and Kühnel were more friendly; but with Bärmann idle and enjoying himself, Weber found the contrast with Prague disagreeable—'*Gohlis*[1], Merseburg beer, tobacco and bowls' were all they thought of, he wrote, adding that he found the balls a bore, the girls plain and the students uncouth. With Rochlitz's encouragement, he turned his thoughts towards criticism and began another chapter of the novel *Tonkünstlersleben*. But this, and projected work on editions for Kühnel and articles for newspapers, was interrupted by an invitation from the Duke to spend some time at the court of Saxe-Gotha. After a successful concert on 14th January that included *Der erste Ton*, Weber and Bärmann left for Gotha on the 17th.

That the Duke should prove not to be there after all when they arrived was the least of his many eccentricities. Arguing that for so tiny a state to raise an army, even in time of war, was absurd, he had devoted his exchequer to the peaceful improvement of his land—thus winning Napoleon's comment that he was the most intelligent prince in Germany—and to the arts. But here his interest became charmingly personal. He bombarded his intellectual friends, Jean Paul Richter among them, with long letters, had published a romance entitled *Kyllenion, a Year in Arcadia* among many other writings, and even attempted settings of his own verses with the help of visiting musicians. Once finding a proffered theme too cheerful in the major and too mournful in the minor, he asked for it to be half-major. He delighted in shocking his formal little court by addressing them in gibberish, dyed his hair a different colour every day, and dressed in a toga or (more often) in woman's clothing, which even the innocent Max Maria thinks may have had a connexion with his effeminate manner. But his interest in the arts was genuine: he was at this time maintaining Spohr as court composer and he passed his love of music down to his grandson Prince Albert, Queen Victoria's consort. When they

---

[1] *Goli* is Swiss German for a fool, and *golen* means, roughly, to roister. There is also a Swabian word *Gole* meaning a mask with a big head, suggesting carnival pranks.

eventually met, Weber was caught up in a whirl of musical activity by the enthusiastic Duke (to the cynical amusement of the more reserved Spohr) until, thoroughly exhausted, he fled to Weimar on 27th January to resume his concert tour with Bärmann, an invitation to return that autumn in his pocket.

At Weimar the pace was more gentle. The Grand Duchess Maria Paulowna, sister of the Tsar, welcomed them and made arrangements for a series of musical evenings. It was during one of these, when Weber and Bärmann were playing the *Silvana* variations, that Goethe entered, and sitting down began to talk to the lady next to him; when the music finished, he rose to leave. Weber was presented to him, but was upset to find Goethe lofty and dismissive; he noted briefly in his diary, 'I did not like him' and though Goethe recorded his admiration for the 'fine talent' of the 'clever musicians', he never showed any subsequent interest. Relations were more cordial with the aged Wieland, whose last important poem, *Oberon*, had appeared over thirty years previously, and whom Weber sought out on the evening of his arrival; and with Pius Alexander Wolff, whose Spanish plays included the *Preciosa* for which Weber was to provide incidental music in 1822. Nothing came of the Grand Duchess's efforts to have *Silvana* staged (Max Maria scents intrigue on the part of the *Kapellmeister*, August Müller), and after a formal concert the two musicians returned to Dresden on 5th February. Matters went no better here: despite a flurry of calls on influential people, only a single concert could be arranged. Weber otherwise occupied himself with an article for the *Zeitung für die elegante Welt*,[1] noting the snobbishness and the preference for Italian opera that were subsequently to prove such obstacles. He also paid a visit on his Munich friend Friedrich Kaufmann, whose latest invention was a mechanical trumpeter in Spanish costume which played two simultaneous notes at set times.[2] The public concert was not a success, Weber's style being declared a pale imitation of Spohr's and after a private recital before the Royal Family on 18th February, Weber and Bärmann left for Berlin.

Arriving on the 20th, Weber was given a warm welcome in the Charlottenburg house of the Beer family, and set about trying to make his way in the musical life of the city—a far more competitive atmosphere than he had yet come across. Used to dealing with minor German princelings whose favour completely controlled the arts in their province, he had armed himself with a letter of introduction from the Crown Prince of Bavaria to Friedrich Wilhelm III: and though the king was well disposed towards him, attending the concert given with Bärmann on 15th March, the busy intellectual life of the

[1] No. 198, signed 'Melos' (Kaiser 49: an altered version is in MMW, Vol. I, pp. 331–3).
[2] Subsequently this Hoffmannesque creature went off unexpectedly, knocking Kaufmann senseless and blinding him in one eye. Thereafter Weber took pleasure in speaking of the trumpeter's sinister powers with his voice lowered.

city went very much its own way. Neither Righini nor Bernhard Anselm Weber, the directors of the opera, gave him any encouragement in his hopes of getting *Silvana* produced, declaring it crude and in need of revision.[1] Iffland, whose dramas had featured in the repertory of the old Weber Theatre Company and who had brought the Prussian National Theatre to the position of the most important in North Germany, was pointedly cordial to Bärmann while ignoring Weber. Zelter, the Director of the *Singakademie*, was hardly more friendly, though he did introduce Weber to his *Liedertafel*, a group that met once a month to dine and to sing choruses under his direction. Here it was that Weber first met Friedrich von Drieberg, the theorist and composer whose *Don Tacagno* was produced on 15th April. Weber praised this in the *AMZ* on 24th April,[2] adding the hope that his few reservations about some lack of character in the melodies and the weight of the scoring would be taken in good part. Drieberg seems to have done this, for although he had similar strictures to make about *Silvana*, Weber in his turn accepted these as coming from a friend, however much they depressed him.[3]

But pressure was now being brought to bear by the Court on B. A. Weber (Righini's health, in decline since the death of his son in 1810, had by now broken down and he had left for Italy). Accordingly *Silvana* went into rehearsal, though spasmodically (six weeks intervened between first and second rehearsals) and with quarrels raging as to which Weber had the right to conduct. It is not hard to see why Bernhard Anselm resisted the work so strongly. As a vigorous champion of German opera against the prevailing Court fashion for Italian opera, he might have welcomed this ally: but his colleague Righini was a pupil of the rival faction's leading light, Spontini; *Silvana* is admittedly immature, and its novel effects might leave an older man of rigid views somewhat unimpressed; worst, rumours were beginning to suggest the younger Weber as the new conductor of the Opera. In the end *Silvana* was produced on 10th July, with the composer conducting; it was a striking success. Weber wrote brief accounts to Danzi and Rochlitz, to the latter complaining that Bärmann had now given up the tour and returned to Munich, leaving him among strangers. To both he laments the absence of a libretto to work on.

Meanwhile, he had received a shock in a letter from Gottfried: on 16th April Franz Anton had died, seventy-eight years old, his mind by now almost totally confused. However burdensome a father he had been, Weber recognized, beneath all the interference and petty ambition, a depth of affection whose absence would be felt the more acutely in the present

---

[1] Hinrich Lichtenstein (see p. 134) rather oddly attributes this lack of success to Weber's frail physical appearance, which he alleges irritated them when combined with such vitality in other respects. Perhaps we should read into this a euphemism for arrogance.

[2] Kaiser 43.

[3] See p. 80.

wandering, hopelessly insecure life. 'He has fallen peacefully asleep,' the diary records. 'May God send him, there, the happiness he lacked here. It is an enduring grief to me that I have been unable to give him happier days. God bless him for all the great love he had for me, which I did not deserve, and for the education he gave me. *Requiescat in pace.*' To Rochlitz, who had been suggesting that so much wandering was bad, Weber wrote admitting the fact but asking sadly how else he could find an arena in which to practise his art. There was no alternative but to keep on in his search.

Work on *Silvana* provided some distraction, but his dependence on friends became even greater, as he told Rochlitz. For the *Liedertafel* he wrote a vigorous male-voice chorus, *Das Turnierbankett* (Op. 68, No. 1: J.132), the first of many pieces that caught the note of open patriotism being more freely expressed in Berlin, and especially at such gatherings, than in any town Weber had so far visited. The idiom is scarcely more subtle than that of the Heidelberg student songs, but Weber lends even this simple manner a certain distinction, hinting (not only in the trick of a rhythmic bass 'la-la-la') at the bracing freshness of the *Freischütz* choruses. To the soldiers and students, they were irresistible: when Weber produced his *Kriegs-Eid* on H. J. von Collin's words 'Wir stehn vor Gott' from *Liedern österreichischer Wehrmänner* (1809) (J.139) as the finale of an afternoon's singing by the soldiers in the Oranienburg Barracks on 20th August, so Weber noted in his diary, it brought tears to the eyes of the Captain and the Chaplain. Another of the period, the *Schwäbisches Tanzlied, Geiger und Pfeifer* (J.135) was later (so Weber wrote to Caroline) to move the Lord Chamberlain at Dresden to seize the Mistress of the Household and waltz round the room with her. Undoubtedly these choruses catch the mood of the moment with music whose earthy tunefulness comes directly from German folk-song, matching patriotic sentiments with recognizably national sounds. For the first time the whole of Germany was gripped by a common emotion, and it was above all in the more stimulating intellectual air of North Germany that artists and philosophers, soldiers and statesmen, shopkeepers and merchants combined to feel that the moment was upon them when the horrors of conscription and the blockade might be flung off and the French finally checked by a newly united nation.

Yet Weber himself was interested in politics only from a romantic point of view, and these choruses reflect a somewhat forced note of camaraderie in his own person. His need for real friends is a theme that runs through his whole life. Berlin high society provided cordial acquaintances such as Prince Radziwiłł, whose compositions Weber helped to revise; he came to count many writers and intellectuals among his companions; among his women friends there was Beethoven's admired singer, Amalie Sebald; but it was Zelter's *Liedertafel*, and especially the success of *Das Turnierbankett*, that won him the lasting friendship of the Professor of the Zoology and co-director of the Berlin *Singakademie*, Hinrich Lichtenstein, to whom he remained faithful all his life and to whom some of his best letters were written.[1]

Lichtenstein stands out from all the friends of Weber's Berlin circle. Though one of the lesser lights of the formidable intellectual group that Humboldt was gathering around him at the new University (founded when Prussia lost its University of Halle to Napoleon's new Kingdom of West-phalia), Lichtenstein seems to have recognized in Weber something essential of the new spirit that was suffusing his countrymen, a popular musical voice to accompany the University's intellectual bracing of the nation's mind for action; for the first cracks in the French Empire had begun to widen, and by mid-August Napoleon was well on his way to Moscow. Lichtenstein's memoir gives a charming picture of Weber at this period, surrounded by an admiring circle to whom he would play, yet curiously alone in their midst

> Weber was as great a master of the guitar as of the piano. His songs, which were not yet well known, and which he would sing with incomparable expression in his weak but uncommonly sweet voice and accompany with real virtuosity on the guitar, were perhaps the most perfect of their kind and won all hearts. When he had worked the group around the open-air tea-table up to a pitch of high excitement, he would go to a piano and taking any one of the masterpieces lying there, would use his powers to make everyone feel he had never heard the work until then. Next, to give the singers a rest, he would play some of his own piano pieces, of which the favourite was the as yet unpublished Sonata in C... Schneider's pupils would fall on their knees before him, others put their arms around his shoulders, everyone gathered round him until instead of a circlet of flowers he seemed crowned by a ring of happy, friendly faces; and the passionately melancholy style he assumed on these occasions would ring on far into the night in the most profound and serious manner . . . His improvisations in this vein differed greatly from that of greater (or rather, more accomplished) pianists like Hummel and Kalkbrenner, with whom, however little they may have meant it, there always seemed a desire to please. With Weber the impression at such times was that he had above all found a means of revealing his deepest feelings to his closest friends, and that his whole being was concentrated on making himself understood . . .[2]

This characteristic scene gives us the clue as to how best to approach the new Piano Sonata, No. 1 in C major (Op. 24: J.138). Though he may not principally have desired to please after the alleged manner of Hummel (whose style of playing he did not admire), his invention could never entirely separate itself from virtuosity and drama. In this early sonata there is a sense of expressive elements struggling against pure virtuosity and, frankly, losing.

[1] *Briefe von Carl Maria von Weber an Hinrich Lichtenstein*, ed. Ernst Rudorff (1900).
[2] Written as foreword to his collection of Weber's letters (1833), and reprinted by Rudorff, *op. cit.*

The dramatic diminished seventh introduction to a lyrical first subject is set against a more tinselly piece of finger-music for a second subject; and though there is much to admire in the way the final tonic is established from the surprise re-entry of the first subject in the re-capitulation in E♭, there is no real sense of a battle between warring elements in Weber's character being waged. The chromatic adventures are decorative rather than organic. Similarly in the Adagio, a serene opening promising a movement of considerable depth soon gives way to what is a barely concealed amiable guitar song:

Ex. 29

Nevertheless, the movement is well handled, with piano sonorities giving rise to a satisfying formal plan, particularly in the use of an obsessive throb in the bass; this is the movement in which Weber most nearly deepens melancholy into a more profound emotion. The minuet continues the contrast between dynamic and virtuoso elements, with an admirable trio whose chiming opening chords seem to hint at the world of *Oberon*. But the whole sonata is allowed to collapse into the brilliant effect music of the Rondo (which was written first). Weber himself called this piece *L'Infatigable*, and it is a tireless *perpetuum mobile* in his most charming *Abu Hassan* manner (it has frequently been published separately as *Moto Perpetuo* or under some such title, as well as in a version for left hand by Brahms (1852) and another for left hand with a new right-hand part by Tchaikovsky (1874)). Significantly, it is this most showy of the movements that contains, almost to the point of anthology, a wide range of piano figuration taken directly from Dussek and Prince Louis Ferdinand, as a pair of examples will show (Exs. 30 and 31, p. 136).

These are, of course, no more than technical tricks making virtuoso piano figuration out of simple harmonic patterns; they give little indication of the new expressive colour Weber brought to them, which belongs more to the world of Mendelssohn's scherzos than the piano pyrotechnics of Dussek and his contemporaries. But that Weber felt the menace of mere virtuosity in his style is indisputable. In *Tonkünstlersleben* he has a passage deploring that 'these damned piano fingers, which through endless practising take on a kind of independence and mind of their own, are unconscious tyrants and despots of the art of creation'; and he goes on to make a contrast with the composer whose invention springs from a deeper level. He was accustomed, when ill and finding his fingers rusting up, to loosen them by playing this finale, at full speed, in C♯. There is still a whiff of the salon about, in fact; and the interest of the sonata derives from the effort Weber was making to free himself of it. There is a more warmly personal note than in any of his previous piano music; and characteristically he achieves this by exploiting quasi-vocal sonorities in his piano writing. This is not the purely musical drama of Mozart or Beethoven's sonata movements, and by that much Weber is separated from them, but something closer to the rhetoric and pathos of the opera house. The melodies have a vocal cut to them; the alterations and contrasts of texture are deliberately picturesque; the harmony tends to be geared to a sensational effect; and what is the finale but a brilliant ringing

Ex. 30

DUSSEK: Piano Sonata Op. 35, No. 2: 3rd movt.

WEBER: Piano Sonata No. 1: 4th movt.

Ex. 31

PRINCE LOUIS FERDINAND: Piano Trio, Op. 2: 1st movt.

WEBER: Piano Sonata No. 1: 4th movt.

WEBER: Piano Concerto No. 1: 1st movt.

down of the curtain? The novelty of the work is that this is all enacted directly to a sympathetic group personally interested in the artist-performer. However unobtrusively, the salon has been dislodged for a concert-room in which composer and listener meet on equal human terms. It was this quality, as much as the individual mixture of elegance and *Volkstumlichkeit* which Weber brought to his major keyboard works, that gave so much nineteenth-century piano music its character. It is no surprise to find Liszt preparing editions of Weber's piano music for his own use, nor Chopin enthusiastically including Weber in his recitals—perhaps even remembering the downward rush of semiquavers that opens this sonata when he came to write his *Revolutionary* study.

If Lichtenstein was Weber's closest kindred spirit in Berlin intellectual and artistic circles, the aesthetic leader was Count Carl von Brühl. When Iffland died in 1814, Brühl was to succeed him as Intendant; already he had begun to take the interest in Weber that led to his championship of *Der Freischütz* as the epitome of German opera. He was the philosopher of the movement, as well as its aristocrat; and in him Weber recognized with relief an artistic seriousness of purpose quite different from the elegant dilettantism of Munich, Mannheim and Stuttgart. Berlin introduced him to ways of thought kindred to his own, but for which his background and his peripatetic life had not adequately prepared him. Despite his personal popularity among the admiring acquaintances who always seemed ready to gravitate towards him in any musical centre, and who here formed themselves into bands of *Webergesellen* and *Musikalischen Baschkiren* (Musical Cossacks) to go serenading and carousing with him, he was unable to make his way in Berlin's musical life with his usual facility. The experience served to deepen him, to assure him of the truth in Rochlitz's reproach about his wandering life as a mere virtuoso. His moodiness in the Berlin months is surely more to be attributed to doubt over the course of his career than to the death of his father or money worries: from now on the need to settle and put down roots became paramount. When his friends gave him a surprise party on the eve of his departure to finish his interrupted visit to Gotha, he embraced them, sat down at the piano and after a long improvisation sang a new song to his own words giving thanks for friendship.[1] Lichtenstein's memoir records him as unusually gloomy and moody, but emphasizes the good his Berlin stay had done him. Apart from anything else, he had established good relations with the publisher Schlesinger; and at the Berlin opera he had heard a number of works that were to be influential on his own style as the background of the emergent Romantic opera—among them, operas by Mozart, Gluck, Méhul, Cherubini, Paer, Spontini, Winter, Salieri, Benda, Paisiello, Weigl and Sarti.

At the end of August, Weber took leave of the kindly Beers—by whom, he

---

[1] Later (29th January 1813) fitted to Tieck's words 'Sind es schmerzen' and published as Op. 30, No. 6 (J. 156).

wrote, he had been treated like the son of the house—and travelled to Leipzig. 'My first business, 2nd September,' he wrote to the *Webergesellen*, 'was to attack my old enemy, Kühnel the publisher, where he was entrenched in his camp behind the usual excuses of bad times and poor receipts.' He did manage to sell several pieces, including the Second Clarinet Concerto and the overture *The Ruler of the Spirits*. Rochlitz gave him the words for a new Hymn, *In seiner Ordnung schafft der Herr*; and moving on he received the warmest welcome in Gotha on the 6th.

Here the pace was as hot as ever. The Duke kept Weber and Spohr by his side on his movements from one house to another, demanding songs, marches, arrangements of his own compositions or new improvisations at a moment's notice. When he fell ill, the entire court was obliged to carry on its business in his bedroom; and though he was extremely appreciative, showering Weber with presents, the contrast with Berlin was depressing. 'It is like a dream,' Weber wrote to Lichtenstein,[1] 'that I have left Berlin and all that which is so dear to me. I can't convince myself that I've left you for long; I fancy myself simply out for a walk, about which I shall have all the more to tell you when I come home . . .' The Duke's importunate requests for music and offers of collaboration were fortunately interrupted by a brief trip, and Weber found the much-needed time to work. Though the Duke's brother, Prince Friedrich, required him to go through a mass of Italian music, there was time to write, between the 16th and 19th, a set of Seven Variations on a Theme from Méhul's *Joseph* (the popular Romance 'A peine sortir' on which he had improvised for the Queen in Munich and which many composers used for variations—Op. 28: J.141). They form the most ambitious and elaborate set he had yet composed. Dedicated to Fanny von Wiebeking and naturally designed for show, they are nevertheless considerably more passionate and personal in tone than his previous sets; and they suggest great capability on the part of his former pupil. The Grand Duchess Marie Paulowna, on the other hand, whom Weber visited at Weimar during the autumn, confessed herself beaten by the C major sonata he had dedicated to her; and Weber privately reported to Lichtenstein that if she had not been Grand Duchess he would have agreed with her.[2] Here he again met Goethe, who was somewhat more polite, though Weber commented drily, 'It's a wonderful thing, familiarity with one of the great spirits. One ought only to view these heroes from afar.' As before, he was more successful with Wieland, whom he overwhelmed with his improvising: Weber's final crescendo brought the old man gradually to his feet until he stood trembling with excitement, and as the music ceased fell back exhausted and burst into tears.[3] But Weber's letters are full of complaints, so much so that Lichtenstein was moved to

[1] Letter of 12th September 1812.
[2] Letter of 1st September 1812.
[3] MMW, Vol. I, pp. 382–3.

reproach him with unnecessary melancholy. It was presumably a result of restlessness in absurd surroundings, for the substance of the complaints is lack of solid work (that is, on an opera) yet self-doubt as to his ability to tackle it, coupled with irritation at the petty demands being made upon him. His time was drunk up with improvising for the Duke, once on a Minuet from *Don Giovanni* to which the Duke maliciously added two entirely different themes. Max Maria records its stunning success. After the concert, Weber and Spohr were walking home in the small hours when they heard soldiers of the Spanish garrison singing their national songs—melodies which so impressed Weber that he leaned against the barracks wall listening and, it is said, humming tunes that found their eventual way into *Preciosa*.[1] Once more, the nearest Weber was able to come to opera was a large-scale concert aria, a Scena ed Aria from *Inez de Castro* (1st. Op. 53: J.142), written for Prince Friedrich to sing accompanied by two choirs and orchestra. It is based on a scene in the Third Canto of Camõens's *Lusiads*, and despite the existence of a later *Inez de Castro* Scena ed Aria *Non paventar* for soprano, comes from no known opera. He also composed a pleasant but inconsiderable set of Six Favourite Waltzes (J.143–8);[2] and for the Duke's birthday on 17th November wrote another waltz for wind, with his song *Maienblümlein* as trio (J.149) as well as scoring, also for wind band, four of his previous songs, *Ihr keine Vögelein*, *Lebe wohl*, *Die verliebte Schäferin* and *Beim kindlichen Strahl* (J.150–3). He further produced, in December, for the local production of *Abu Hassan* the Duet No. 4, 'Thränen sollst du', having in the previous month completed the Hymn *In seiner Ordnung schafft der Herr* (Op. 36: J.154) on Rochlitz's words. These praise, in turgid tones, God and his justice;

Ex. 32

[1] Spohr, who had had one of the Spaniards billeted with him, used a song he overheard in his house for the finale of a violin concerto.

[2] No. 1 was later used as No. 4 of *Preciosa*.

and Weber sets them, without much conviction, for the most part in square choral harmonies. There is a brief lyrical interlude for soloists after the opening exordium and an operatically inclined bass recitative; thereafter Weber settles for a dull harmonization of the famous chorale *Befiel du deine Wege* and a final fugue—of which, it must be said, he was rather proud. But as a whole the piece suggests one of the Berlin *Liedertafel* choruses with operatic inclinations rather than a genuinely religious utterance.

Weber had finished the Rondo for a new piano concerto in Munich the previous autumn, and even played it as the finale to his First Piano Concerto—though, as he admitted to Gottfried,[1] 'it has a completely different character and is much more brilliant and difficult than the first, a really bold piece of *Sturm und Drang*'. It is indeed a piece of altogether more forceful and serious nature, though the necessity of selling music by way of virtuosity is still felt even in the theme itself, which requires the right hand to hop in a manner almost foretelling Liszt's *La Campanella* (Ex. 32, p. 139).

But even here we have come some way from the finger music of the First Concerto and its passages in which the virtuoso is clearly meant to be seen at least as much as heard:

Ex. 33

Weber picked up the threads of his Second Piano Concerto (Op. 32: J.155) in October with a powerful opening sonata movement, scoring for normal orchestra less oboes (which to judge from the other works for Gotha, did not feature in the ducal orchestra). The keyboard writing is geared much more closely to novel tonal effects rather than merely to the player's fingers; and not surprisingly this gives Weber greater freedom to bend sonata form more convincingly to his own uses. Although he had trouble with pianos in Gotha, his relish of piano tone in this work suggests an excellent instrument as when in a cadenza-like passage tremolos introduce the massive gestures of the soloist's first entry (Ex. 34, opposite page).

The Adagio is one of the finest movements Weber ever composed. Comparisons with Beethoven are, once again, not so much odious as simply irrelevant. By 1812 Beethoven had finished with the piano concerto and was turning in ever greater isolation towards the last great sonatas. Beside his contemporaries, he seems like some vast rock around whose base the tide has

[1] Letter of 15th November 1811.

begun to swirl in another direction; and Weber was undoubtedly the composer who led the new movement, evolving a new technique in order to do so
(at the time Schubert had hardly written anything; and indeed his greatest
sonatas came after Weber's death). The piano writing in this Adagio shows
not merely a liking for subtle effects of colour but the ornamental, vocal
quality that was to characterize much of the nineteenth century's piano
music. Mendelssohn was to find much of his lightness of touch in Weber's
scherzos; Schumann, who narrowly missed becoming Weber's pupil, echoes
many of his effects of sonority; and if Chopin took from the Rondo his
liking for brilliant upward leaps and from the Adagio of the First Concerto
Weber's trick of matching held and staccato notes, it is in the Adagio of this
Second Concerto that he found the limpid, decorative brilliance which hints
so strongly at the human voice that it has been repeatedly attributed to the
influence of Bellini. Chopin's fondness for letting ornamentation play the
role of variation, for allowing the piano to sport like a fountain around a
theme, has its roots in Weber's quasi-vocal writing, with its arpeggios,

Ex. 34

written-out portamentos and—reflected especially in Chopin's own concertos—piano 'coloratura' and finger virtuosity transformed into intense
poetry. The difference between this and the example from the First Piano
Sonata is crucial (see p. 135, Ex. 29). The entire movement is a locus classicus
of Romantic technique.

Ex. 35

Col Vla., Vlc., Db. F♯

Weber played the new concerto in Gotha on 17th December, when according to his diary, it 'made a furore and went excellently; I didn't play it badly either'. Pressed by the Duke, he stayed on until the 19th; but apart from the obvious impossibility of remaining in Gotha, there were still debts to be settled and now his father's funeral expenses to be repaid to his Mannheim friends. The Duke (not a rich man) contributed towards these the sum of 40 Friedrichs d'or tactfully described as 'an honorarium for instruction in the spirit of music'; and after the usual hectic farewell parties, Weber left Gotha. Pausing briefly in Weimar, where he again played to the Grand Duchess, he reached Leipzig the day after Christmas and set about preparing for the New Year's Day première of the Hymn *In seiner Ordnung*. He played his new concerto at the concert, with great success, and his diary notes that the Hymn 'went well until the Choral, where Mlle. [Albertine] Campagnuoli sang so appallingly flat that I came out in a cold sweat; it was much applauded.' He sold the *Rübezahl* overture, the *Joseph* variations and the Clarinet Concertino to Kühnel, and with eighty-eight more thalers in his pocket, set out for Prague on what was intended to be a two years' tour of Europe.

CHAPTER NINE

FROM PRAGUE TO DRESDEN: 1813–1817

Wir suchen überall das Unbedingte, und finden immer nur Dinge.

NOVALIS

W EBER ARRIVED in Prague[1] on 12th January 1813, to be greeted by Gänsbacher with the news that Wenzel Müller had resigned the Directorship of the Opera and that Liebich was offering him the post. At first he was by no means enthusiastic; but under Gänsbacher's tactful pressure the notion of settling began to seem more attractive than the projected concert tour. Above all, as he noted in his diary, there was the chance of finally discharging the Stuttgart debts. Gänsbacher saw to it that he was suitably flattered by the Prague musical Establishment, and matters were clinched by the persuasiveness of Liebich himself, who had clearly had his eye on Weber since the previous visit with Bärmann. An agreement was concluded whereby Weber would receive a salary of 2,000 gulden (to begin immediately), a benefit of 1,000 gulden, three months' annual leave and full powers to reorganize the company. The old company was to be disbanded at Easter and reconstituted during the summer with the addition of new talent to be recruited by Weber; and the new season was to open in September. He wrote to his Berlin friends, 'The entire nobility and Board of Directors gathered eagerly around me and called me the saviour of the Opera. In fact, they gave me so little time to think things over that I allowed myself to be completely bowled over, with the result that I am under a three-year contract to stay, with unlimited powers.'

There was much to be done. Wenzel Müller's five years had failed to halt the decline in standards brought about by the tensions of wartime, with its impoverishment of operatic life and its tendency to divide the public into national and political factions, as well as into separate classes who neither exchanged ideas nor formed genuine societies of their own. In his article on Prague[2] Weber was to complain of the lack of vital intercourse between the social strata. But alarmed though he was when he began to appreciate the scale of the work demanded of him, he remained confident that with Liebich's vigorous backing he could rekindle the Prague audience's famous devotion to music. The theatre to which he was appointed had itself a distinguished,

---

[1] The fullest account of Weber in Prague has not yet been translated from the Czech; it is Zdeněk Němec: *Weberova Pražská letá* (*Weber's Prague Years*) (1944).

[2] *AMZ*, July 1815 (Kaiser 61).

if brief, history. Founded under Joseph II by Count Nostitz, it was built during 1781–3 to plans by Antonín Hofenecker and opened on 21st April 1783 with Lessing's drama *Emilia Galotti*. It was, and still is, a charming example of baroque theatre architecture, compact and well laid-out with a pretty wooden gallery running round the outside of the building. 1784 saw the start of a new Italian opera company under Pasquale Bondini, who, as well as giving works by Cimarosa, Gazzaniga, Traetta and others, had early recognized the genius of Mozart and on 29th October 1787 followed up his successful *Figaro* production with the première of the newly commissioned *Don Giovanni*; *La Clemenza di Tito* was to follow for the coronation of Leopold II in 1791. German *Singspiel* flourished alongside the Italian reper-tory, and indeed after 1807 the theatre was reserved for German works, even to the exclusion of the occasional Czech language performances that had begun.

Having settled into new rooms—with a great deal of domestic enthusiasm, according to Max Maria—Weber now set about making preparations for the concert on 6th March. He finished two of his finest songs, *Sind es schmerzen* (Op. 30, No. 6: J.156) and *Unbefangenheit* (Op. 30, No. 3: J.157), continued work on the Clarinet Quintet for Bärmann which had been begun two years previously in Jegisdorf, and for his old Munich friend Brandt revised the earlier viola *Andante e Rondo Ungarese* (J.79) for bassoon (Op. 35: J.158); this Brandt played with great success, Weber's diary notes, on 19th February. However, it is not a piece to set seriously beside the Concerto. Though pleasantly written, with some amusing and characteristic touches and a lively melodic spring, it lacks the confidence of idiom Weber was shortly to find in his Darmstadt and Munich months—for the revision is so slight, with scarcely any attempt to rethink the solo line in bassoon terms, that the piece must be considered as belonging to 1809 rather than 1813.

A few other songs and minor pieces are the sum total of his works for 1813. Helped by Gänsbacher, he strengthened his contacts with the city's musical notables, among them Prince Isidor Lobkowitz, Count Nostitz, the banker Kleinwächter, the doctor Jungh, and Count Pachta, a leading force in the recent foundation of the Conservatory; and he busied himself so thoroughly in plans for the new operatic regime that little time was left for composition—so little that Max Maria firmly describes 1813–17 as his father's 'years of bondage'. Nevertheless they gave him a new freedom from other worries as well as his first mature taste of opera management; and if he was unable to contribute any opera of his own to the busy repertory he founded, he was at least enabled to put into practical form some of his ambitions for German opera and clarify his own ideas as to how he might as a composer express them. The task was very far from being easy—or even welcome to his audience. Already at the concert on 6th March, a brilliant success netting him 609 gulden, he encountered some hostility; as he wrote to Rochlitz (reporting on the success of the Second Piano Concerto and First Symphony but concealing the poor reception for the *Hymn* to Rochlitz's words), 'I already find plenty of adversaries. That doesn't matter. The gentlemen don't bother me. I go my own quiet way. If I get any truth from them, I make a mental note and let the rest vanish. One finds my music "mystical" etc., another regards it as wrong of me to play almost exclusively my own works in the concert. Tomašek and Co. have been pulling wry faces ever since they knew I was to stay here.' Armed with a document of authority from Liebich, Weber was on the point of leaving for Vienna to search for new artists when a letter arrived from Caroline Brandt, enquiring if there was any chance of a place for her in the new company. Remembering her as Silvana with pleasure, he engaged as the first member of his new team the singer who was soon to become his wife.

Weber left Prague on 27th March and arrived to find Vienna filled with musical friends. Vogler was back there, Bärmann was giving successful concerts; and both complained, with justice Weber thought, of the vain and touchy manner that had now come over Meyerbeer, who was in Vienna to study with Hummel. He made friends with Moscheles, his future champion Mosel, the ballet-master Duport (who was to figure in the production of *Euryanthe*), and the violinist Franz Clement, dedicatee of Beethoven's Violin Concerto, whose feat in making a piano score of Haydn's *Seasons* prompted only by the libretto, after a few performances (including one they attended together), so impressed Weber that he promptly engaged Clement as leader of the Prague orchestra. But he refused to yield to Vogler's pressure on him to meet Salieri, around whom the rumours of his having poisoned Mozart had been circulating. He was welcomed by Viennese society, and in the house of the poet Ignaz Castelli found a congenial circle of artistic friends. The whirl was terrific, as a letter to Gänsbacher in the form of a diary makes clear; but there was also much to be done in the way of auditions and contracts, new works to be heard, scores to be acquired and copied. He even arranged a morning concert of his own at the Redoutensaal on 25th April; but his performance in his Second Piano Concerto was on all sides unfavourably compared with the playing of Hummel and Moscheles. In fact, he had risen from a sick-bed to play; depressed, he left Vienna precipitately and fled back to Prague. Here he lay in his rooms in delirium, unattended, until Count Pachta chanced to visit him. At once a litter was summoned, and the invalid taken to Pachta's own house and nursed through a slow convalescence. Though he had begun to complain of pains in his chest in the previous year and was troubled intermittently by rheumatism, especially in his lame hip, this was the most serious illness he had yet suffered.

Scarcely was he able to move about again than he plunged into an exhausting regimen of work. He rearranged the conditions of employment in the company, laid down a thorough system of duties for the staff, and in general so re-disciplined the entire organization that in the ensuing storm of protest he was compelled to dismiss more of the original company than he had at first intended. 'The orchestra is in rebellion!' he wrote to Gottfried on 21st May, describing his activities. 'Corresponding with new members of the company, both singers and instrumentalists; organizing all the contracts, new regulations for orchestra and chorus, bringing a muddled library into order and cataloguing it, and so forth, as well as being overrun by a horde of people —it's indescribable. Correcting scores, describing décor to scene painters and wardrobe staff, etc. etc., I ought really to go to Eger for four weeks to set myself up completely in health, and can't because the pressure of business is so great that the smallest delay is too much. I get up at six and often work through till midnight. I shall thank God when the machine begins to function; then half the battle will be won.' Finding a good many of his staff took refuge in Czech when they wished to grumble, he set himself to master the language and within a few months was able to understand and make himself understood in it.

Prague had by now begun to assume an almost Viennese gaiety. With Napoleon's Russian disaster, hopes were running high; and a general optimism that the time was at last at hand to be rid of the French set the mood of the moment. Reasonably isolated from the war and nominated for an abortive Peace Congress, the city was filled with the nobility and even royalty—Friedrich August and the Dresden court had taken refuge here when the Allies invaded Saxony, and the Emperor of Austria was living nearby—while artists and intellectuals also thronged in. Weber renewed friendships and formed new ones with Humboldt, Barthold Niebuhr, Tieck, Brentano, the actor Ludwig and his sister Rahel Varnhagen, the Prussian statesman Baron vom Stein and the Austrian commander-in-chief of the Allies' Grand Army of Bohemia, Prince Schwarzenberg. There is no record of his expressing any concern in the political situation uppermost in everyone's mind: his interest in getting rid of the French was a normal patriotic attitude intensified by his absorption in his own art, his response was chiefly to the excitement of his friends. Brentano and Tieck were a more potent influence than Stein or Schwarzenberg: a letter to Gänsbacher on 28th July reports the pleasure one of the latter's songs gave Tieck and dilates on the charms of the *corps de ballet*.

Weber himself now became embroiled in a tumultuous affair with one Therese Brunetti, who had graduated from the ballet to singing soubrette parts in the opera. Married to a dancer and the mother of five neglected children, she was thirty-one at the time Weber met her, with red-gold hair, blue eyes and a widely-appreciated figure. She was capricious and unscrupulous: she threw herself in Weber's way by hanging about the theatre at all rehearsals, and before long he was completely ensnared. He defied gossip by setting up house with her and her complaisant husband, where Therese, soon

tiring of her conquest, proceeded to amuse herself by tormenting the luckless
Weber with grotesque demands on his good nature. He was sent about Prague
in all weathers on trivial errands, dragged off to dances, compelled to listen
to marital squabbles and to put up with domestic squalor. His diary makes it
plain that he fully recognized her worthlessness but was unable to escape her
influence. Violent scenes were common, together with equally violent
reconciliations: it is a pathetic record of jealousy and misery, on which
Therese delighted in playing by her association with new lovers, especially
a rich banker named Calina. Weber had done her many services—as well as
finding her attractive little presents, such as a watch hung about with
romantic symbols, he secretly taught her eldest daughter the piano as a
birthday surprise—but he could not compete with this wealthy rival. Not
even his absorption in his work could extinguish the loneliness that put him
so much at Therese's mercy.

Rehearsals by the nearly completed new company had begun on 12th
August with Spontini's *Fernand Cortez*, the first of sixty-two operas by more
than half as many composers that Weber was to produce during his Prague
intendancy. He had assembled a troupe which, rather than containing the
best-known singers of the day, was designed as a versatile and well-knit
ensemble. With his usual methodical approach, he kept a notebook[1] of his
repertory and staff; and this document contains invaluable comments on his
singers as well as details of all his productions. The women included Wenzel
Müller's daughter Therese Grünbaum; Czeka (Mozart's Countess, Donna
Anna and Sextus); subsequently Caroline Brandt (whom Weber notes as
good in 'simple, gay and so-called *Spielrollen*; also acts a lot in plays'—she
was his Zerlina and Cherubino, as well as taking the lead in works such as
Isouard's *Cendrillon*); Allram (Donna Elvira); Ritzenfeld ('old and comic
roles'—Marzelline); and Böhler ('young roles'). A later, and famous,
recruit was Henriette Sontag. The men included Grünbaum as first tenor,
Kainz as first bass, the tenors Stöger, Seidl and Löwe and the basses Gned,
Zeltner, Allram and Dorsch.

Spontini's opera may seem a curious choice, not only in view of his later
rivalry with Weber but since it was a French opera in which Napoleon had
taken a personal interest at its original Paris production four years previously,
feeling it could help to influence public opinion towards his Spanish war.
Yet the operas with which Weber filled his repertory at first were almost
exclusively French. *Cortez* was succeeded by a full dozen works by Spontini
and Cherubini (both based on Paris, the latter since 1788), Isouard, Boïeldieu
and Dalayrac. There were only three exceptions to this succession, in the
first six months: Fränzl's *Carlo Fioras*, a piece Weber had found popular
in Munich in 1810, and introduced when his public began complaining
at the number of foreign works; Mozart's *Don Giovanni*, in which

[1] Now in the Library of the Rudolfinum, Prague.

Prague took justifiable pride; and Fioravanti's *Le Cantatrici Villane*, which as *Die Dorfsängerinnen* was immensely popular in Germany. No other Italians ever appeared in his repertory, with the exception of Salieri, a Viennese figure whose *Axur* (produced by Weber on 20th January 1815) was a version of his *Tarare* to Beaumarchais's libretto, and Paer, another composer who worked in Germany and indeed had some influence on Beethoven, as well as setting Bouilly's libretto for Gaveaux's *Léonore* as his own *Leonora, o L'Amore Conjugale* and thus preceding *Fidelio*. Not until a full year had elapsed did Weber really begin introducing a substantial number of German operas; and he never produced one of his own.

Weber was in fact almost literally setting the scene for the appearance of German Romantic opera; and to this end it was necessary to go to French opera. Signs of a new direction in taste had already been gathering in France before the cataclysmic upheaval in humanitarian feeling of the Revolution, which was to give Romanticism a clear field. Rousseau, held in such veneration by the Romantics of Germany, had himself written in *Le Devin du Village* (1752) a little pastoral opera for Fontainebleau, musically of small moment but indicating the new flow of feeling towards Nature that was demonstrated even at Versailles itself with Marie Antoinette's mock-shepherdesses of the Petit Trianon. Still more revealing is the choice of subjects made by Grétry. As well as developing in such works as *Zémire et Azor*[1] (1771), *La Caravane du Caire* (1783) and *Raoul Barbe-Bleue* (1789; Prague, 19th June 1814[2]) the growing cult of the exotic which Gluck's *Rencontre Imprévue*, Mozart's *Entführung* (and even *The Magic Flute*) and Weber's own *Abu Hassan* also adopted, Grétry turned for librettos to purely sentimental comedy, Gothic horror and mediaeval chivalry. *Richard Cœur de Lion* (1784; Prague, 5th February 1815) is Grétry's most Romantic opera, set in vaguely mediaeval dress in the heart of Germany: it skilfully exploits the use of folk-influenced choruses and ballads, such as Blondel's song to his lost master, which Weber was to integrate into a style whose influence had the profoundest effect on his successors right up to Wagner. Alongside Grétry stood Dalayrac, whose operas include *L'Enfance de Jean-Jacques Rousseau* (1794), and show increasing fascination with the exotic. Weber included two in his repertory—*Adolphe et Clara* (1799: Prague, 6th February 1814) and *Les Deux Petits Savoyards* (1788: Prague, 26th June 1814): the frequent appearance of Savoy in operas of the period is another tribute to Rousseau. Dalayrac also played his part in the cult of the Rescue Opera that reached its apotheosis in *Fidelio*. One of the earliest composers to

[1] Marmontel's libretto, with its story of magic intervening in the lives of an 'exotic' Persian family, held a particular fascination for the Romantics. As well as being re-worked as a 'Romantic-Comic Opera', for Baumgarten as early as 1776, it was used by Spohr in 1819.

[2] The Prague dates given in this section are those of Weber's first productions, not necessarily the first in the city.

adopt this topical form was Henri Berton with *Les Rigueurs du Cloître* (1790) (in which a young nun is saved in the nick of time from being walled up), and other practitioners included Gaveaux (*Léonore*, 1798) and Cherubini (*Les Deux Journées*, 1800; Prague, 17th Oct 1813)—all of them composers who featured in Weber's Prague repertory.

Not only Gluck's classicism but the Romantic pressures that also show in his music were to influence Cherubini. In their different ways, he and Spontini developed a new love of the startling and spectacular. Beside the stern classicism of Cherubini's early Metastasian operas and his *Médée* must be set two works that strongly affected Weber. *Lodoïska* (1791) includes several minor features that were to influence him (including the *Polonaise* colouring and some of the arias for secondary characters), as well as the crucial figure of Dourlinsky, who set an example of operatic villainy that Beethoven and Weber were both to learn from (see Mus. Ex. 50, p. 217–18). *Lodoïska* is also significant for showing, with its climax in a fire, how natural forces may play an organic role in the drama; this is also the case with *Elisa* (1794), which stresses at every turn the Rousseau-inspired Romantic admiration of Switzerland and culminates in an avalanche (Cherubini was later, in 1809, to set a version of Rousseau's *Pygmalion*, with its archetypically Romantic fable of warmth of heart overcoming classical remoteness). Not surprisingly, Weber had a special affection for *Elisa*, which introduced into operatic currency the so-called *musique d'effet*, and like several of Cherubini's best-known works was more successful in Germany than in France. But the works of Cherubini that he chose to produce were *Les Deux Journées* and *Faniska* (1806, in Vienna, where Beethoven and Haydn led the applause; Prague, 7th November 1814). Not only are both Rescue Operas, but both include simple ballad-like interpolations in their dark and dramatic plots, and both make an exceptionally rich use of the orchestra to carry the story and the emotions of the characters (with a suggestion of *Leitmotiv* in *Les Deux Journées*), as Weber recognized in an article of his Munich days.[1] His detailed praise of the orchestration of *Les Deux Journées* was to find practical expression in his own mature operas, which take their example from the new importance Cherubini gave the orchestra, even to incidents of scoring. Still more striking, in *Euryanthe*, is Weber's reflection of Cherubini's formal methods in the use of extended and linked numbers to carry forward the dramatic action. Not even in *Richard Cœur de Lion* could Grétry, with his simple, separate numbers approach the dramatic truth and accurate portrayal of character which Cherubini's far richer and subtler structures embody. *Les Deux Journées* is also a people's opera; for as in the case of *Der Freischütz* in Germany, it offered a distillation of an everyday life, idealized but sufficiently close to everyone's common experience to provide an immediate point of reference. The combination of simple Savoyard water-carriers

---

[1] *Gesellschaftsblatt für gebildete Stände*, 3rd July 1811 (Kaiser 28).

singing, like Anton, the pretty, consciously pathetic ballad 'Un pauvre petit Savoyard', and a Rescue Opera with peasants now no longer comic servants or *ingénus* but human figures proposing righteous moral sentiments, found a ready public—most impressively in Goethe and Beethoven, who both considered Bouilly's libretto one of the best of its day. Beethoven is said to have kept the score of *Les Deux Journées* on his desk.

The cult of the exotic was further taken up by Boïeldieu, whose *Le Calife de Bagdad* (1800: Prague, 7th August 1814) had won an easy success for which Cherubini publicly rebuked the composer; whereupon Boïeldieu immediately placed himself under the older man for a stiff course of counterpoint. Weber never lived to have the chance of producing his most famous and most Romantic work, *La Dame Blanche* (1825, based on Scott), though he was delighted with it in Paris in 1826 and urged it upon Dresden; but he did find a place for *Jean de Paris* (1812: Prague, 1st January 1814) and *Le Nouveau Seigneur de Village* (1813: Prague, 3rd August 1815), as well as for five light works by Boïeldieu's great rival Isouard, one by the less significant Catel and three by Méhul. Of the latter, *Uthal* (1806: Prague, 19th October 1813) and *Joseph* (1807: Prague, 20th September 1813) are the most important. Though in Méhul the search for local or exotic colour at all costs sometimes strains too far after effect, in his 'Ossian' opera *Uthal* there is a sense of Northern gloom and darkness in the scoring (assisted by the total omission of violins) that must have appealed to Weber—not least in the sinister tremolos and swirling scales of the overture, which raises the curtain on a mist-wrapped forest. He had, of course, already shown his appreciation of 'a real masterpiece' by his piano variations on 'A peine sortir' from *Joseph*, a work in which he praised 'the antique, simple Biblical spirit so admirably sustained throughout, with no superfluous tinkling to tickle the ear; everything works towards the highest truth and by judicious control over the scoring . . . a minimum of means produces the maximum effect'.[1]

Alongside Bouilly's libretto for *Les Deux Journées* Beethoven ranked Etienne Jouy's[2] for Spontini's *La Vestale* (1807), the work with which Weber on 3rd October 1813 followed up the success of *Fernand Cortez*. At first condemned in Paris by all concerned with it, from the selection committee (including Cherubini) to the singers, as merely noisy and odd, the backing of the Empress Joséphine forced for it a hearing that led to the most brilliant success imaginable. Spontini's novel 'spectacular' was to propagate a fashion that the Paris Opéra has never wholly shaken off—grand opera with a compulsory ballet, elaborate realistic scenery, a large chorus to provide vast pageant-like effects and a full team of personality soloists to lead the giant ensembles. Only Meyerbeer was to exceed the scale and din of Spontini's operas. Reflecting the pride and size of Napoleon's Empire, their brilliance of

---

[1] *Gesellschaftsblatt für gebildete Stände*, 10th July 1811 (Kaiser 29).
[2] It had been refused by Cherubini, Méhul, Boïeldieu and Paer.

effect and sheer dramatic thrill, which depended as much upon sensational orchestral effects as upon the vocal writing, impressed not only Weber but Friedrich Wilhelm III: having heard *Cortez* in Paris in 1814, he instantly ordered it for Berlin and set about arranging for Spontini's engagement there. Weber's act in opening the Prague season with his two most monumental works was part of a calculated policy first to seize the attention of his public and then to introduce them to works that were the foundation upon which German Romantic opera might be built.

That he failed in his enterprise was scarcely his fault. Apart from the apathy he was to encounter, there was simply not enough German opera worthy of taking the centre of the stage he had so carefully set, until the time was politically and socially ripe and until he himself had shown the way. It is true that *Singspiel* was a flourishing tradition, to which Goethe had himself contributed. With the Emperor Joseph II's establishment of a *National-Singspiel* at the Vienna Imperial Theatre in 1778 it had even acquired new prestige; Mozart had contributed his *Entführung* and it had shown itself capable, in its apotheosis with *The Magic Flute* and *Fidelio*, of becoming the vehicle of the greatest spiritual experiences the operatic stage has to show. These are the transcendental exceptions which only genius can provide. Not until Wagner was a means to be found of fully reconciling and unifying all the demands of the German operatic stage; and his indebtedness to Weber is acknowledged. Before Mozart, German opera has a thin history. The national movement opens with the publication in 1749 of *Thusnelde* by Johann Scheibe, which though never set to music initiated works such as Wieland's librettos for Schweitzer's *Alceste* (1773) and *Rosamund* (1780) and Klein's libretto for Holzbauer's *Günther von Schwarzburg* (1777). These and other operas of the period may perhaps be called hopefully patriotic rather than genuinely national, even though many of the Romantic traits are beginning to show themselves—as in Wranitzky's Wieland opera *Oberon, König der Elfen* (1789) which was not displaced until Weber's work on the same theme. Only Mozart and Beethoven possessed the power to give German opera a national identity before its time was really ripe: they naturally figured prominently in Weber's Prague repertory, but the gap in achievement between them and the works of the other German composers who feature there—such as Fränzl, Fischer, Himmel, Weigl, Winter, Poissl and other lesser lights—shows up all too vividly the effort Weber was demanding of himself.

One other minor feature of the repertory deserves mentioning—the melodramas of Jiři Benda. These had been much admired by Mozart and, despite the failure of more elaborate plans for a full-length *Semiramis*, the technique was actually used by him in *Thamos* (1779) and *Zaide* (unfinished), as well as by Beethoven in *Egmont* and especially in the grave-digging scene of *Fidelio*. Possibly Weber took it up as a sop to Czech taste, which has remained intermittently loyal to it, but certainly he responded to its especial powers of mysterious effect when he came to compose the Wolf's Glen scene in *Der Freischütz*.

Throughout the autumn Weber worked to develop and strengthen his company. On 11th December Caroline Brandt arrived, and on New Year's Day, 1814, she made an extremely successful début in the title role of Isouard's *Cendrillon* (a work Weber did not greatly admire). This comparatively slight part seems to have suited her soubrette talents ideally: she was evidently lively (to the point of quick-temperedness, Max Maria admits in his catalogue of his mother's qualities), charming and graceful, with a natural stage presence. Born in 1794 to an actress mother and a violinist-cum-tenor father who had a streak of Franz Anton's charlatanry in his make-up, she had like Weber grown up on the stage, making her début at the age of eight as 'little Salome' in Kauer's *Das Donauweibchen*, an early treatment of the popular Romantic *Rusalka* theme. By the time she played Silvana in Frankfurt at the age of sixteen she was already a seasoned performer, with a career of successes and mishaps almost as chequered as Weber's own early life. Her success as Cendrillon won her the unusual honour of a curtain-call, the entrée to the houses of Prague's music-loving nobles, and the fierce jealousy of Therese Brunetti, with whom Weber was still embroiled. But this affair was nearing an end. When Therese ignored his present of the watch but fell voraciously upon a barrel of oysters he had also brought her, he was shocked; but to separate him finally from her it took the news that she was proposing to set up a new *ménage* with Calina and had urged upon Caroline a similar profitable arrangement with his fellow banker Kleinwächter. Weber's letters reflect utter personal and professional despair; composition was virtually at a standstill, despite rumours that he might write a Bohemian historical opera, and the daily routine at the theatre was as demanding as ever. He produced nine operas in the first three months of 1814, coaching the singers himself and supervising details of production, dances, scenery and costumes, as well as taking every rehearsal from start to finish. For his Benefit on 15th January he chose *Don Giovanni* (with Caroline as Zerlina): but in an access of economy Liebich refused to authorize the expense of the small stage bands, and for the opening night Weber angrily paid the extra himself. He made 1,200 gulden towards the Stuttgart debts. Exhausted by the dragging routine of putting on an opera virtually every other night throughout the year, he was further depressed by the news of Vogler's death on 6th May. It was natural that he should find himself turning increasingly towards Caroline: she was attractive and talented, she lived quietly with her mother and resisted all the advances of Prague's smart young aristocrats, she seemed exceptionally goodnatured (he had as yet no inkling that she could very nearly match Therese in jealous tantrums). When she caught her foot one day in a scenery-groove and was thrown by a flat being abruptly shifted, Weber took her home and began a series of calls that her mother, and on a later visit her father and brother, cordially approved. Therese promptly redoubled her efforts, and Weber now found himself caught in the struggle between them. His health gave way under the accumulated strain, and leaving the conductorship in Clement's hands, he thankfully set off on three months' holiday at the beginning of July.

From the spa of Liebwerda, where he had gone with Frau Liebich and another elderly lady, Weber wrote a somewhat indecisive letter to Gänsbacher: he mentions girls known privately to them as 'F major' and 'D minor', dismisses the rumours of his marrying that had been buzzing round Prague, and openly declares that he is in love with Caroline but is resolved to put the situation to the test. In fact, the three months' absence was to be punctuated with an exchange of letters (only his are preserved) that chart an uneasily developing depth of involvement—passionate love on Weber's side, of an intensity that is perhaps partly responsible for Caroline apparently feeling somewhat overwhelmed and being driven to elementary coquetry to test her own reactions as much as her feminine powers.

On the last day of July, Weber set out for Berlin, arriving to find the city seething. Napoleon, having been crushed at the 'Battle of the Nations' at Leipzig the previous October after his failure to follow up his defeat of Schwarzenberg outside Dresden, had by now been forced back to Paris and, having signed his abdication, had departed for Elba that April. Berlin awaited the triumphant return from the Treaty of Paris of Friedrich Wilhelm and the Tsar, and flung itself into an orgy of celebration. At a gala performance at the *Singakademie*, Weber found Blücher and other war heroes among the six hundred people gathered there; but he was immediately spotted by Lichtenstein and given a welcome which was warmly echoed by the Beer family when he called on them the following day. On the 7th the King was due. A military ballet with a prologue by Kotzebue was to take place at the Opera; the city was illuminated; nearly crushed by the crowd under the wheels of a passing carriage, Weber looked up to see Tieck, who hauled him in to safety and shouted in his ear, 'Now I understand the reasons for the illuminations and why I'm in Berlin!' Brentano was also in Berlin, and to him Weber turned as he found the rest from Prague responsibilities encouraging new ideas for composition. Searching mediaeval legends for a suitable opera libretto, Brentano came upon the story of *Tannhäuser*. Weber was delighted with its possibilities and asked Brentano to begin work immediately; but other pressures intervened, though a substantial part of the book does seem to have been written. Among friends, Weber was busy and popular again, though he insisted to Caroline that he was lonely and depressed; he was caught up in aristocratic as well as artistic circles, meeting among many others Baron Friedrich de la Motte Fouqué, who had found time between his campaigns as a cavalry officer to produce his long series of romances, Hardenberg, recently back from Paris, Prince Radziwiłł and

Queen Victoria's uncle, the Duke of Cumberland, soon to be King of Hanover. His concert on the 26th was a success, especially for his own playing of the E♭ Piano Concerto, though he was by now exhausted. Preparations for *Silvana* went less smoothly; but against the old opposition he could set the warmth of the company and the orchestra, who dropped hints that a new deal following the death of the aged Iffland would favour Weber. The performance, on 5th September, went badly: the house was full, but found this gentle piece of woodland mediaevalism little to its taste in such heady times. The same night Weber left Berlin in a downpour for Gotha.

Once more he travelled by way of Leipzig and Weimar, where he found a letter from Liebich urging a speedy return to Prague to take over from the inadequate Clement. Deciding to stick to the terms of his leave, he pressed on to Gotha and to the nearby castle of Gräfen-Tonna where the Duke was taking the waters. To Caroline he wrote, 'The ancient castle where I am now staying and where I write these lines, in a grim room with rattling doors and windows, comforts me with its peace . . . On the 13th I wrote two new songs, set my papers in order and spent the whole day from eleven in the morning to eleven at night with the Duke, when of course both fingers and throat had to turn to . . .' The songs were the first of the set that make the three books of *Leyer und Schwerdt* (No. 1, Op. 41: J.174-7; No. 2, Op. 42: J.168-73; No. 3, Op. 43: J.205).

In responding to the mood of the moment that was expressing itself in dozens of ephemeral victory pieces—Hoffmann's *Die Schlacht bei Leipzig*, Gottfried Weber's *Morgenlied der Freien* and many another such—Weber naturally turned to the *Singakademie*. There were even, ready to hand, the verses of a young poet fallen in combat—Theodor Körner, killed at Gadesbusch the previous year at the age of twenty-two. His extremely simple, not to say banal, songs exactly hit off the current emotion, and provided Weber with texts upon which he could hang music very much in the manner of the *gesellige Lieder* at which he had already shown his aptitude. It was a piece of patriotism he later paid for when Friedrich Wilhelm took offence at the songs being adopted by the Landwehr, who were sharp rivals with the King's regulars; while subsequently at Dresden he was to find Friedrich August, as an ex-ally of Napoleon, taking a poor view of Prussian victory songs. Most of them were composed during the autumn at Prague, with the exception of Book 3, written at Berlin the following November. Loudly hailed in their day, and for many years to come capable of stirring German enthusiasms at moments of national crisis, they are of wider interest now only for the inventive skill with which Weber handles a limiting set of demands. In a letter to Rochlitz of 14th March 1815, he emphasizes that something more than mere imitation lay behind the stormy, writhing demi-semi-quaver accompaniment that runs through *Gebet während der Schlacht* (Op. 41, No. 1: J.174)—'I don't like scene painting', he declares, adding that he is attempting to reflect the stress not on the battlefield but in the soul. Few of the others are so striking. The rest of Book 1 consists of a broad Adagio setting *Abschied vom leben* (Op. 41, No. 2: J.175); a vigorous use of dotted rhythm to add not the gaiety with which it is often associated in his music but strength and resolve in *Trost* (Op. 41, No. 3: J.176); and a strophic piano song, answering recitative questions at once aggressive and sentimental, for *Mein Vaterland* (Op. 41, No. 4: J.177). The songs of this book are all for voice and piano. Book 2 is set for four-part male chorus (TTBB), in one instance (No. 4) with piano. They are for the most part considerably duller, though there is a lively spirit in the chorus of No. 4, *Männer und Buben* (Op. 42, No. 4: J.170) when Weber sets with less than complete conviction sentiments urging 'No kissing or singing or drinking—stand by me!' The best known of the Book is No. 2, *Lützows wilde Jagd*[1] (Op. 42, No. 2: J.168)—a vigorous 6/8 hunting chorus, part of which Weber later introduced into his patriotic cantata *Kampf und Sieg*. This it was, with the *Schwertlied* (Op. 42, No. 6: J.169), that Weber wrote during his stay in Gotha. The third book, *Bei der Musik des Prinzen Louis Ferdinand von Preussen* (Op. 43: J.205), is more ambitiously laid out as a kind of cantata for voice and piano, divided into clear sections but musically continuous. It was a natural gesture of homage on Weber's part to salute Prince Louis Ferdinand, who, having been killed in the action at Saalfield before the Battle of Jena in 1806, was a national hero as well as a personal one to Weber, whose piano style he influenced considerably.[2] Seven quotations from the Prince's works, chiefly from the F minor Piano Quartet, are marked by Weber with the initials P.L. in the first printed copy (the MS is lost); but there is plenty of Weber's own material as well, and the quotations are by and large allowed to stand as interpolations, sometimes with a Weber counter-melody, rather than act as the subject of development. The whole is prefaced by an introductory poem in Weber's name by Brentano.

When another and more pressing letter arrived from Liebich, Weber felt obliged to return—not without opposition from the Duke, who had discovered a new pleasure in sitting by Weber's side at the piano and describing fanciful scenes in his mind's eye to an improvised accompaniment. At least, Weber pointed out to Caroline, it allowed him to get on with working some ideas out. Reluctantly, despite the attraction of seeing Caroline again, he abandoned the final weeks of his leave and set off, arriving on 25th September. 'I cannot describe to you', he wrote to Rochlitz on 8th November, 'how gloomy I was at returning a fortnight earlier than expected . . . *Believe only half a director's lamentations and stick out your leave to the last minute.*' It was true, however, that discipline had sagged in his absence; and with Liebich's grateful support Weber swiftly brought matters under control once more.

---

[1] Ludwig von Lützow had in the previous year raised a famous corps of *Schwarze Jäger* who had taken an active part in the war and with whom Körner had served.

[2] See p. 135-6.

His spare time was spent in writing out the *Leyer und Schwerdt* music, most of which was already in his head, and in clarifying his relations with Caroline. To Lichtenstein, who had written with news of his own engagement, Weber replied 'God grant you a good wife who will make you happy—or at least, not unhappy, which is in itself much. Day by day I am more remote from this hope. I love like a drunkard who's skating on thin ice and persuades himself against his better judgement that he's on solid ground . . . I love her with all my heart, and if there's no sincerity in her feelings, then the final chord of my whole life has sounded. I shall live, perhaps even marry: trust, love—nevermore!' Part of the difficulty lay with the *Leyer und Schwerdt* songs themselves. Having been born in Bonn, Caroline was a Bonapartist and sharply objected to Weber's alignment, even if this was emotional rather than seriously political. To contribute to his unrest, a letter arrived from Berlin: Iffland had at last died, on 22nd September, and Count Brühl was offering him the appointment about which studied hints had already been dropped. Keen as he was to accept, Weber wrote a careful reply asking for further details and stressing that he could only take the job on if he felt the arrangements fitted in with his own ideas. He also approved Lichtenstein's action in telling Romberg, his rival for the post, what was afoot so as to avoid any feeling of jealousy or intrigue. Weber meanwhile declined, in favour of Romberg's brother, an offer from Kotzebue to take on the theatre at Königsberg; as he wrote to Lichtenstein, he was amused at the thought of the frantic anxiety over the appointment that would be shown by 'my fat namesake' B. A. Weber, who would certainly of two such terrible evils prefer the lesser—that is, the slightly built Weber to the obese Romberg, who did in fact secure the post.

In November, as Vienna set about disporting itself while the Congress worked out a new structure for Europe, Weber produced *Fidelio*. It was coolly received on the 27th—to Weber's fury, as he declared in a letter to Gänsbacher on 1st December. Fourteen rehearsals (an altogether exceptional number) had gone into a work he especially admired, yet although 'there are truly great things in the music—they understand nothing. It was enough to drive one mad! *Kasperle*,[1] that's where they find truth.' His once high opinion of the Prague audience was reaching rock-bottom, he told Gottfried: 'every day and every hour I find myself more and more separate from other men and feel that there are too many rotten souls in the world. Bohemia has really become a spiritual hospital for me.' Not even the success of *Lützows wilde Jagd* and the *Schwertlied* at his concert on 6th January 1815

---

[1] Kasperl was the Punch-figure invented, or at least made famous, by the Viennese actor Johann La Roche, who played him with great success, possibly as early as the 1760s. *Kasperle* became so popular that they even gave their name to the 34 Kreuzer piece charged for admission to the Kasperl Theatre. Kasperl is normally a comic servant, often timorous, cheeky, shrewd, endearing and far more positive than the upper-class characters.

cheered him. Contemptuous of public opinion, he committed the indiscretion of announcing that he would himself sit in the theatre box-office and sell tickets for Caroline's benefit performance of *Cendrillon* on 11th January; the ensuing storm of gossip roused the fury of Caroline's mother and Weber felt obliged to propose marriage. But Caroline hesitated: she was, after all, an established and popular artist, while he was still a struggling composer whose career would probably extinguish hers. She demanded time to think, so Weber decided to leave Prague—yet she was upset to think that he might go on her account. Once more he confided in Lichtenstein: 'My wife must belong to me, not to the world; I must be able to support her without a struggle. No devil of a mother shall come between us. You might think that shows want of love, but passion shall never lead me to accept a happy present that may bring with it the misery of a lifetime.'

He plunged himself back into his work. The *Leyer und Schwerdt* songs fetched only twelve Louis d'or from Schlesinger in Berlin, but his own Benefit performance of *Così fan tutte* on 4th March—the sixth new production of the year—brought in 1204 gulden. The clarinettist Hermstedt visited Prague and gave a concert for which, Max Maria records, Weber wrote a *Savoyard Song* and a Concert Movement, both now lost; Caspar and Anton Fürstenau, father and son flute virtuosos, also came, and for them he wrote a piece that is in all probability the original of the *Schäfers Klage* Andante of the Trio for piano, flute and cello which was subsequently dedicated, from Dresden in 1819, to Dr. Jungh, an excellent amateur cellist whose house Weber frequented.[1] From Gottfried came news of a new device he had evolved during work on the *Versuch einer geordneten Theorie der Tonkunst*, a so-called Chronometer for measuring tempo by means of a pendulum with calibrated knots on the string. This form of metronome was viewed by Weber with some misgiving: while commending Gottfried for its use in helping musical idiots, he felt that real musicians would always find the right tempo and in any case allow themselves some freedom (see also p. 304). He did, however, make use of it for the numbers of *Euryanthe*, possibly feeling the necessity of correct relationships between tempos more important here than in his other operas.

Apart from a *Scena ed Aria, Ah! se Edmondo fosse l'uccisor* (Op. 52: J.178), written for Therese Grünbaum's Benefit performance of Méhul's *Héléna* on 4th January, Weber completed no new works in the first half of 1815 except the variations for piano on a Russian theme, 'Schöne Minka', a popular Ruthenian song also known as 'The Cossack Ride' (Op. 40:[2] J.179). This is the largest and most elaborate of all his sets of variations: though the theme

---

[1] Weber's diary for 16th October 1814 notes the composition of an Adagio and Variations for Jungh (and presumably himself), which Jähns supposes to be the original of this version of the *Schäfers Klage* (J Anh 42).

[2] Later editions give Op. 37, as which the work has also been known.

CAROLINE VON WEBER
From the portrait by Alexander von Weber

itself is but a simple little two-strain melody, Weber treats it not as a peg on which to hang virtuosity but a musical cell to set his imagination working. An Adagio introduction makes the seriousness of the work plain, and ingeniously introduces many of the figures that are to distinguish the individual variations. These are all in the original key, C minor, except for a *dolce grazioso* treatment and an over-long, more virtuosic *Espagnole* finale in Weber's polacca vein; both are in C major. If the harmony remains somewhat unadventurous, except possibly in the chorale Var. 4, with its Voglerian chromatics, the piano writing has a richness and range that are new to the variation works, indicating that the 'damned piano fingers' have lost their ascendancy over the imagination. That they still contribute to it is indisputable; but the relationship is closer to that in Chopin's Etudes, whose greater sophistication and emotional range they adumbrate. It is difficult not to see the 'Schöne Minka' variations as an expression less of Weber's virtuosity than of his current unhappiness and indecision.

Further troubles came to accelerate his departure from Prague. His brother Fridolin, who seems to have inherited Franz Anton's more difficult characteristics, turned up having abandoned a job in Frankfurt apparently with no reason except the hope that his more successful brother might find him a better position; Weber managed to place him at Carlsbad (Karlovy Vary), some seventy miles away, if only to get rid of him. A thief broke into his rooms and stole money and clothes. Worst, Caroline had become jealous of a recently engaged actress named Christine Böhler and the ensuing rows led them to agree that they had better separate. Weber decided to anticipate his leave, and on 6th June departed for Munich.

Despite their angry parting, Weber and Caroline were soon exchanging letters. His despair was profound, for it was not only the loss of Caroline that he feared. The letters proved too painful for Max Maria, who suppresses them on the grounds that they present a distorted picture of his father; in fact, they give a moving insight into the mind of an artist who is brought so low as to doubt the very nature of his chief purpose in life. They are indeed painful letters, couched in the dramatic, half-incoherent exclamations that *Werther* had put into lovers' currency, mingling a touching superstition in the fact that their letters crossed (meaning that they wrote to each other on the same day) with anguished cries fearing the extinction of his gifts, alarm at his coldness towards his own works, and scorn for the petty social dance being performed by the puppets all around him, perhaps as meaninglessly as in his own efforts to achieve something with his life. Certainly Munich could offer plenty of social gaiety to contrast with his own condition. The day he arrived, 18th June 1815, was the day of Waterloo; and when the news came through the city flung itself into carnival. Through streets lit by special illuminations and echoing to fireworks and the salvoes of victory cannon, Weber made his way to the Michaeliskirche for a thanksgiving service; and on emerging with the idea of a victory cantata in his mind, he ran into the actor and poet Johann Gottfried Wohlbrück. They discussed the plan, and by 2nd August the text of *Kampf und Sieg* was ready. The composition went more slowly, for differences with Caroline continued—her letters are lost, but Max Maria reports that she made another and final break with him—and, as he told Rochlitz, his creative powers seemed to have deserted him. He occupied himself in discussions with old friends and new: Poissl solicited his advice over *Athalia* (which Weber produced in Prague the following 16th May), Rahel Varnhagen tried to cheer him up by taking him to a farce, there were further lessons for Fanny Wiebeking, and concert plans with Bärmann, in whose house he was staying. He played before the King and Queen at Nymphenburg and before Napoleon's stepson Prince Eugen, who had taken up residence in his wife Princess Auguste Emilie's city; and gave a very successful public concert, playing the First Piano Concerto and what Max Maria calls the Duo for Piano and Clarinet—presumably the newly written Andante and Allegro of the *Grand Duo Concertant*, to which a first movement was added in November 1816. Three of the *Leyer und Schwerdt* songs were given as encores and the concert proved a financial success—unlike one a few days later in Augsburg arranged by a bookseller uncle of Bärmann's.

For Bärmann, too, Weber at last completed on 25th August, the day before its première, the Clarinet Quintet (Op. 34: J.182) on which he had been sporadically engaged at various times and places since Jegisdorf in 1811. This lack of sustained concentration undoubtedly shows in the final result, a highly enjoyable but imaginatively lightweight virtuoso work to show off Bärmann's skill—his well-known agility, in the difficult final applause-music; his song-like tone and phrasing, in various episodes but above all in the fine Fantasia (an Adagio clarinet aria); particularly his evident fluency with chromatic scales. The Fantasia twice breaks off to introduce a dramatic contrast between chromatic scales, *ff possibile* and *ppp*, rising from low D to the B♭ almost three octaves above; scales play a strong part in the invention as well as the passagework, and indeed provide the elegant little theme for the final Rondo. The Capriccio Presto minuet is an engaging little rhythmic tour de force with one of the several nice examples of almost Schubertian modulatory sideslips that occur in this otherwise harmonically straightforward work. It is less as a piece of genuine chamber music that the Quintet is rewarding—for the strings scarcely escape from a purely accompanying role—than as a pocket concerto, written purely for delight in virtuoso effect.[1]

The Horn Concertino (Op. 45: J.188) which he finished on the last day of the month is likewise written to show off the talents of a virtuoso, originally the Carlsruhe player Dautrevaux. This 1806 version is now lost, presumably

---

[1] An 'Introduction, Theme and Variations' for clarinet and string quartet, published in various editions in modern times, as composed for Bärmann in 1815, is spurious.

destroyed by Weber when he now revised it for the Munich player Rauch, but internal evidence suggests that the changes cannot have been very radical. Though the loose form—Adagio-Andante introduction, Andante theme with variations, Recitative, Polacca—already shows a wish to move away from the three-movement concerto, the result is considerably more stilted than in the Clarinet Concertino. Weber had not then mastered the art of linking contrasted sections: the introduction is simply a lilting 6/8 tune leading into variations that do little but increase the number of notes per variation to demonstrate the horn's agility. The final Polacca chiefly tests its ability to make quick accurate leaps. The most interesting section is the Recitative, possibly an 1815 addition in the light of the similar passages in the Second Clarinet Concerto and Bassoon Concerto written for Rauch's fellow virtuosos in Munich. It ends with the horn being required to play a passage in chords, a trick already well known to horn players but held in some scorn as a freak.[1]

By 7th September the reluctant Weber was back in Prague. But at least Gänsbacher was there, recruiting musicians for his Tyrolean battalion of *Jäger*; and his anxieties about meeting Caroline again seem to have been partly damped by the excitement of the new cantata. He had already told Gottfried, 'I shall send you a copy of Wolhbrück's *excellent* text, which you must know, in my next letter, then I'll send the score to all the Sovereigns. The local English Ambassador is sending it to the Prince Regent, and seeing to an English translation. You can imagine how much this kind of work, which justifies my career in the world, occupies me day and night, and— THANK GOD!! during the past few days that I have been thinking about it I've been feeling the return of my powers and the hope that I may still do something useful in the world.' Only a few minor pieces interrupted his work on the cantata. Two songs were written for Anton Fischer's farce to a text by Giesecke, *Der travestirte Aeneas,* which had been produced in Weber's absence on 24th August—*Mein Weib ist capores* (J.183) which calls for a falsetto yodel and *Frau Lieserl, juhe!* (J.184) which he also arranged as an orchestral waltz (J.185). He produced two more patriotic songs for a play by Gubitz, *Lieb' und Versohnen oder die Schlacht bei Leipzig,* produced in Prague on the anniversary of the battle, 18th October—these are *Wer stets hinter'n Ofen kroch* (J. 186) and *Wie wir voll Glut* (J.187). Finally there is the Ballad *Was stürmet die Haide herauf?* (Op. 47, No. 3: J.189) for Reinbeck's *Gordon und Montrose,* produced on 18th November. The only other diversion to his energies was the writing of articles for the Prague papers. Perhaps finding opposition more serious than he had anticipated, he hit upon the idea (on

---

[1] This is achieved by humming another note at a fixed interval above or below the one played, which has the acoustical property of strengthening some normally inaudible partials so that one or two other notes are also heard. For technical accounts, see Robin Gregory: *The Horn* (1961) and R. Morley-Pegge: *The French Horn* (1960).

6

13th October, he later told Gänsbacher) of publishing an introduction to each of the new works he was producing: he announced this in the *K.K. Privilegierte Prager Zeitung*[1] on 20th October, following it up with an article in the same paper on the following day on Meyerbeer's *Wirt und Gast*, staged as *Alimelek*. It is not one of his most successful essays, being more concerned with recommending Meyerbeer and everyone else involved by any means, including snobbish ones, than with preparing the audience for a new work.[2] It failed to win a success for the work, though Weber persevered and eventually began drawing audiences.

Apparently for private circulation only, Weber also wrote an introduction[3] to his cantata *Kampf und Sieg* (Op. 44: J.190), which he had virtually finished on 11th December—almost exactly four months since an entry in his diary for 17th August notes the completion of the first chorus. The essay is a full description, pointing out the absence of arias as part of an attempt to keep the drama of battle moving rapidly before the listeners' ears. There is nevertheless opportunity for two extended numbers, both instrumental and both the finest sections of the work. These are the overture and the *Schlacht-musik* (No. 7). In contrast to the lively scenes literally evoked in the choral numbers, these have a depth and seriousness, achieved by purely musical means and through close thematic development, that are strikingly Beethovenian. Until the end of No. 7, when the *Ça ira* is heard under a chanting of anxious soldiers, Weber is concerned with dramatizing the emotions rather than the events of battle, as he had already declared to be his aim in connexion with the *Gebet während der Schlacht* in *Leyer und Schwerdt*. But at such a time, some kind of musical report from the front was also strongly in demand; and Weber's powers of illustration and of organizing brief scenes into a large work are well evidenced. The *Chor des Volkes* (No. 2) presents national anxieties at the renewal of conflict, met with reassurance in a Recitative (No. 3) by Faith (bar.) who is joined by Hope (ten.) and Charity (sop.) in a Terzet (No. 4) urging 'noble anger' against the enemy, and, to a gentle characteristic cello melody, promising God's favour. No. 5 is a chorus of North German soldiers, into which irrupts the sound of an Austrian grenadier march denoting the arrival of allies. But in No. 6 the South German soldiers hear the march of the enemy (in 6/8) and cheer themselves with Körner's prayer *Wie auch die Hölle braust*. As the battle (No. 7) ends, the third soldiers' chorus, of South Germans again (No. 8), brings in five authentic Prussian horn calls—Enemy Sighted, Advance Guard Forward, Advance, Form Ranks, and Charge. During the Charge, the soldiers break

---

[1] Kaiser 64.

[2] Kaiser 65: Weber's subsequent criticism of the work in the *AMZ* (1815; Kaiser 66) is much more valuable.

[3] 'Meine Ansichten bei Komposition der Wohlbrückschen Kantate *Kampf und Sieg*, für meine Freunde niedergeschrieben' (Kaiser 75).

into the melody of Weber's *Lützows wilde Jagd*. This leads straight into No. 9, a united soldiers' chorus subtitled 'Battle renewed' in which an elaborate chromatic struggle with the *Ça ira* theme ends in the routing of the enemy and, in tribute to the presence at Waterloo of the English, the full-scale orchestration of *God save the King* (or *Heil dir im Siegerkranz*) that Weber was later to use in his *Jubel-Ouvertüre*: he claimed it was particularly appropriate here as denoting thankfulness to Heaven 'as opposed to the devilish joy of the enemy.' In No. 10, Faith urges the wounded to forget their pain at the thought of what they have won, and with Hope and Charity promises the soldiers honour and recompense. No. 11 is a brief number praising unity; No. 12 rams the message home by pointing out that only in unity was victory won; and the cantata ends with a large Chorus of all Nations (No. 13) begging for peace, culminating in an extended fugue (in preparation for writing which he had renewed his fugal studies).

There is much that is obviously now difficult to accept in this cantata. The sentiments are belligerent, for all the final courtesy gesture towards peace, in a manner that is explicable in the excitement of a great victory won in aggressive times, but, with its exaltation of a God of Battles and a Holy Fatherland, is distasteful outside the immediate time and place which gave rise to it. Yet this is a skilfully composed piece, foreshadowing Berlioz's technique in *La Damnation de Faust* of mixing illustration, symphonic meditation, narrative by soloists and active choral participation into a kind of concert opera. Faith, Hope and Charity play a small role, appearing only to draw moral conclusions from the events expounded narratively; and their observations are, significantly, less convincing than those of the choruses in the large dramatic design Weber builds up from his short numbers. His declared aim was to 'unify the contrasting and emotionally opposing parts without the theatrical help of the eye'; and whatever its inaccessibility now, *Kampf und Sieg* shows that the years in which he was unable to write an opera are years of loss.

With Weber's familiar ill-luck, the first performance fell on a day, 22nd December, when a storm kept at home many of those who were not already occupied with Christmas parties. But the thin audience warmed to the work, and in the loud applause at the end General Nostitz, a veteran of Leipzig, walked over to Weber and observed, 'In your music I hear the voice of the Nations, in Beethoven's big boys playing with rattles'. (Some of Weber's biographers have followed Nostitz in attempting to draw conclusions from the superiority of *Kampf und Sieg* to *Wellingtons Sieg*.) Neither this success nor the reconciliation with Caroline during the autumn did anything to alter his decision to leave Prague, which had been strengthened by a statement 'On the Decline of the Theatre' which the directors had addressed to Liebich. Weber defended himself with dignity in his reply,[1] pointing out the

[1] Kaiser 67.

personal sacrifices he had made, the difficulty of the times, and despite all troubles the high position to which he had restored the Prague Opera. He goes on to re-emphasize his view on national opera: 'I found a musical taste formed by older Italian opera and then that of Mozart's time. There was a restless mood that could not seem to decide what it really wanted. The nature of Italian opera demands few but outstanding artists. A few brilliant gems, regardless of their setting. Everything else is secondary and unimportant. The German digs deeper; he wants a work of art in which all parts form themselves into a beautiful whole . . . I consider the presentation of a good ensemble to be of the first necessity; I consider nothing secondary, for art knows of no trifles.' His letters to his friends were already full of complaints about his exhausting duties. The success of the cantata and Caroline's increasing warmth did nothing to change his mind; though he plunged with his usual enjoyment into the winter round of parties, composing for masked balls little waltzes now lost but, according to Max Maria, long remembered by fellow-guests, and even arranging an elaborate masque of death on the theme 'Carnival's *Love's Labour's Lost*', at which Caroline, as Columbine, was borne on a bier by sorrowing Harlequins and Pierrots, with Weber himself as Death. This was one of many at the house of Liebich, who continued to press him to stay. Finding him suffering from his lame hip and sore throats in the damp, cold Prague winter, Caroline persuaded her mother to take him in as a lodger; yet a letter of 20th January to Gänsbacher, who had left Prague in the autumn reports continuing doubts about marriage. At Easter he sent in his resignation, with effect from the autumn. The early months of 1816 were spent almost entirely in attending to his theatre duties; a visit from Hummel set him practising two hours a day, but the only music written was a *Tedesco* (J.191) and a few songs. *Kampf und Sieg* was due for performance in Berlin; and despite Brühl's failure to secure him the appointment to the opera there (Max Maria implausibly suggests by reason of the King's jealousy of anyone else receiving attention over the recent victory) he set out on 5th June.

Travelling with a young pupil, Weber passed through Dresden, where the King's equerry Count Heinrich Vitzthum presented him with a snuff-box in acknowledgement of his gift of a score of *Kampf und Sieg*; and reached Berlin and the Beer family's house on the 9th. Brühl had done everything possible to help, B. A. Weber the reverse—even to the extent of performing Beethoven's *Wellingtons Sieg* shortly before Weber's cantata. As before, bad weather affected attendance, but as before the work was a success, above all with Friedrich Wilhelm at the introduction of *God Save the King*; but Weber's lobbying for a title as Court Composer proved fruitless. All Brühl managed to arrange was some guest appearances for Caroline. At a second performance attendance was equally thin owing to the arrival in Berlin of Catalani for a concert. Weber met Hoffmann again, suitably enough in a thunderstorm, and was given a copy of the newly finished *Die Elixiere des Teufels*; to Rochlitz and Caroline he reported his fascination with Hoffmann and his *Phantasiestücke*, while criticizing the casualness of their forms. With the youngest of the Beer sons, Hans, he left for Carlsbad on 9th July, passing through Leipzig, where he declined an offer of the opera there from the manager, Küstner, on the grounds that he did not wish to contract himself again to private enterprises. Possibly he hoped to treat his rheumatism at Carlsbad; there was also the opportunity of a further meeting with Count Vitzthum. Ostensibly this was to negotiate about the engagement of a tenor; but Vitzthum had recently been appointed Intendant of the Royal Theatre at Dresden, with the chance of establishing a German Opera there. Disgraced by the role it had played as an ally of Napoleon during the war, despite the desertion to the allies of its contingent during the Battle of Leipzig, Saxony had been treated as a conquered country and occupied by the Russians; and indeed only the pressure of Austria, France and Britain at the Congress of Vienna had prevented it from being annexed by Prussia. On 8th June 1815, King Friedrich had allied his reduced kingdom to the German Confederation; but the only hope Saxony had of regaining some of its former position lay outside the political or economic field. No-one understood this better than Vitzthum. Writing to his brother from Carlsbad, he emphasizes the general opinion that, 'Saxony ought now more than ever to make use of every means to distinguish itself in the arts and sciences since every other hope of winning honour and respect is lost to us.' This is the close of a letter in which he reports negotiations with Weber, whom he was in no doubt would prove the right man for the post. Weber in turn was attracted to the offer: disillusionment with private enterprise had led him to turn down the Leipzig offer, and conditions at Dresden seemed promising. But apart from some preliminary negotiation, nothing was firmly concluded.

On 18th July, Weber returned to Prague to find Liebich now permanently bedridden, the affairs of management in the hands of his unpopular wife. Weber did his best to rally his companion and maintain standards. On 1st September he produced Spohr's *Faust*, prefacing it with an article[1] in which he drew approving attention to the manner in which the overture is made a symphonic exposition of the events of the opera. Much of his time was spent in clearing up the affairs of the theatre and documenting matters thoroughly for his successor, Triebensee. He set the library and archives in order, and left in his notebook full notes on the singers, orchestra, scenic resources and costumes, with suggestions and details of his plans and comments on the public. Max Maria reports that it was while engaged on these chores that he worked out the Adagio of his new Piano Sonata in A♭. Having fully prepared the way for his successor, Weber finally placed his resignation in the hands of Liebich, who was by now too ill to respond. On 7th October the company

---

[1] *K.K. priviligierte Zeitung*, 1st September 1816 (Kaiser 98).

gathered to see him off to Berlin. Caroline, and her mother, travelled with him to take up the engagements he had arranged for her.

By now a widely respected figure in Berlin, Weber was given the warmest of welcomes on his return there. Max Maria records that this new evidence of his standing greatly impressed Caroline and her mother; and that when, returning home from a party one evening, Weber asked Caroline's permission to announce their engagement, 'mother and daughter regarded as a gift from Heaven what a few months previously they had hesitated to accept'.[1] Caroline had already appeared with success on the stage and made a good impression on his friends; they were delighted when he told them the news at a party given by the newly-married Lichtenstein—on a day of total eclipse of the sun which, by a piece of a dramatic timing not lost on Weber, shone out again at the moment of his announcement. On 20th November, Caroline left to fulfil engagements arranged with Vitzthum in Dresden. With both his private life and his career entering upon happy phases, Weber was able to give most of the autumn to composition.

As often before, when moved by some event connected with his personal life, he turned to song. Ever since *Die Kerze* ('Ungern flieht') (J.27) of 1802, he had produced *Lieder* in varying quantities and under the pressure of various events. The Darmstadt and Heidelberg days encouraged guitar songs; the Swiss trip and contact with singers in Munich sent him to Italian *canzonette*; but like a thread through his whole output—and one to which insufficient attention has been given—runs his interest in the German *Lied*. Up to Stuttgart times, when the affair with Gretchen Lang resulted in some of his most charming pieces, they had generally been simple in manner and light in matter. The songs of *Leyer und Schwerdt* are exceptions in his output, though not on that account uncharacteristic; his songs are mostly intended neither to rouse popular emotion, nor to explore an inner world of feeling in the manner that was to characterize the greatest in German *Lied,* but were written for companionship or to answer the mood of a moment.

With Weber's flowering as a song writer coinciding with the discoveries of Arnim and Brentano in *Des Knaben Wunderhorn*, it was naturally the folk element that drew him. Song had been discerned as part of the simple life that was suddenly found admirable and even important; now it came to make this life its subject and hence to draw close to folk music so as to lend the setting an authentic flavour. But Weber had no interest in scene painting, as he made a clear *à propos* the Körner songs, not even the richly detailed, atmospheric scene reflecting the singer's mood that is the especial glory of German *Lied* from Schubert onwards. Discipline counted for more than passion, he declared, even in an outburst like *Klage* ('Ein steter Kampf') (Op. 15, No. 2: J.63), the evocation of sentiment and the creation of dramatic life for more than exploration of the inner poetry. To Schumann's future

[1] MMW, Vol. I, p. 535.

father-in-law Friedrich Wieck, who sent him a cycle of eight songs (Op. 8) with a dedication, he replied with a thorough and candid criticism, observing, 'the creation of a new form must arise from the poem one is composing. In my songs I have always made the greatest efforts to render my poet truly and correctly declaimed so as to produce new melodic forms.'[1] It is accuracy of declamation rather than depth of meaning upon which he fastens; and indeed he never went to great poetry for his texts. His friends provided verses as well as the occasion for their setting—Lehr and Hiemer in Stuttgart, Dusch in Mannheim, Rochlitz in Leipzig, the *Liedertafel* and Gubitz in Berlin, later Kind and the *Liederkreis* in Dresden, together with a host of minor figures, Bürger, Voss, Matthisson, and so forth. His literary awareness caused him to regard great poetry as self-sufficient, less of a stimulus to music than would be the verses of an occasion. Naturally this led him into setting some poetry which is either downright feeble or of the sentimentality that was a by-product of Romantic ways of thought. But the occasions that often prompt his songs give them exceptional vividness—irritation at being locked up, as with 'Ein steter Kampf'; departure from a city full of friends, as with *Des Künstlers Abschied* ('Auf die stürm'sche See') (Op. 71, No. 6: J.105) and the two-part *Abschied* ('O Berlin ich muss dich lassen') (Op. 54, No. 4: J.208); a cradle song, a dance song, or a serenade. Humour continually breaks in, whether in *Ich sah sie hingesunken* (J.41) which begins solemnly and ends with a peal of laughter or (which, like Beethoven, he could have protested was *mehr Empfindung als Malerei*) the fairground band of *Reigen* ('Sagt mir an') (Op. 30, No. 5: J.159), filled with droning bagpipe fifths, wrong notes, a lurching bass and clumping clogs.

Ex. 36

---

[1] Kaiser 62. Weber reaffirms the point at the start of his answer to Müllner's criticisms of his songs for the playwright's *Yngurd*—a fascinating discussion of the whole question of prosody (Kaiser 122 and 124).

Many, like *Reigen,* are in varied strophic form. Weber was not afraid of allowing his melody to stand over simple accompaniments repeated exactly for several verses, as in the famous *Wiegenlied* ('Schlaf, Herzenssöhnchen') (Op. 13. No. 2: J.96) or the *Minnelied* ('Der Holdseligen sonder Wank') (Op. 30, No. 4: J.160), or in the dialect songs such as *Mein Schätzerl is hübsch* (Op. 64, No. 1: J.234) or the *Bettlerlied* ('I und mein junges Weib') (Op. 25, No. 4: J.137), which he wrote in vigorous dance rhythms and with Swabian or Bavarian melodic inflections. But the more serious songs, and the more dramatically vivid of the comic ones, soon take him beyond exact repetition into the new forms mentioned in the reply to Wieck—especially the device of varying the strophes so that a dramatic tension develops between the expected repetition and the variation. In this he was one of the pioneers in German *Lied.* And above all it was, as he indicated, his dramatic sense which guided his sense of form. *Reigen* is a brilliant little developing strophic drama; the hesitations to the questions in Meine *Farben* (Op. 23, No. 1: J.62) are composed into the music as naturally as the abrupt utterances of *Unbefangenheit* ('Frage mich immer') (Op. 30, No. 3: J.157); in *Er an Sie* ('Ein Echo kenn ich') (Op. 15, No.6; J.57) there is no mimicry of the echo, such as almost any other composer might have allowed himself, but a skilfully varied strophic structure again reflecting the development of the emotional rather than the literal scene. Whether in formal melody or in near-recitative, whether in *Der kleine Fritz* ('Ach wenn ich nur') (Op. 15, No. 3: J.74) or *Das Röschen* ('Ich sah ein Röschen') (Op. 15, No. 5: J.67) hitting off the note of German folksong as no other composer had previously done, or whether suggesting the fluency of an Italian tradition in the more operatic of his songs, the melodies and the forms have an elegance and distinction that is entirely personal.[1]

There remains a number of songs which suggest an altogether larger artist. Obviously Weber cannot be compared as a *Lieder* writer to his great contemporary Schubert as far as the general level of his output goes—for one thing, the erratic nature of his life diversified his aims too much and other ambitions prevented him from developing his best vein. But there are songs which can stand comparison with much of Schubert, from as early as Stuttgart in 1809 and *Meine Lieder* (Op. 15. No. 1: J.73) and still more the heartfelt *Was zieht zu deinem Zauberkreise* (Op. 15, No. 4: J.68) of the same period, with its throbbing Schubertian chords and wistful falling piano phrases between vocal entries (Ex. 37, opposite page).

The same quality shows in a song from the unhappy early months of 1813, the agitated *Sind es Schmerzen?* (Op. 30, No. 6: J.156), and in *Frage mich*

---

[1] Wilhelm Müller's poems of *Die schöne Müllerin* and *Winterreise* were published in 1821 and 1824 as part of *Gedichte aus den hinterlassenen Papieren eines reisenden Waldhornisten,* dedicated to 'Carl Maria von Weber, master of German song, as token of friendship and admiration'.

Ex. 37

immer with its hopeless appeal to a Schubertian *Bächlein*. Later, with his private life contented and with the prompt of the texts offered by the Dresden *Liederkreis,* Weber was to revert to a more folk-like vein: the present period is a culmination of his more intense manner, and it produced two masterly sets of songs completed within a fortnight of each other in the autumn of 1816. The simplicity of the pair of Op. 47 (J.197–8), *Die Gefangenen Sänger* and *Die freien Sänger* is of a kind that must have appealed to Weber's great admirer Mahler; but they are overshadowed by the only group Weber wrote that comes near being a song-cycle, *Die Temperamente beim Verluste der Geliebten* (Op. 46: J.200–3). These *Four Temperaments* consist of sketches of abandoned lovers, done with a depth of feeling that is

Ex. 38

chastened with an engaging humour. *Der Leichtmüthige (The Sanguine)* waves the old love off with a jaunty little melody ending in what the piano suggests as a carefree whistle. *Der Schwermüthige (The Melancholic)* is intense and heartbroken, pouring forth sorrow in soaring D♭ phrases that look beyond Schubert almost to Schumann; it includes one effective drop from D♭ into A major (Ex. 38, opposite page).

Der Liebewüthige (The Choleric) sets off with a positively Beethovenian burst of fury, 'Verrathen!', and ends with an ironically amused farewell; and in contrast to these subtly *durchkomponiert* songs the final *Der Gleichmüthige (The Phlegmatic)* is a calm strophic air expressing the relief of not having to bother with all these emotional scenes any more. Perhaps they are curious songs from a man newly engaged to be married (though he had planned them and even written some as much as a year previously); but it may be that his new emotional security gave him the confidence to look back with such perception for the last time on what had, after all, been a good many partings from lovers.

Certainly there is a wholly new confidence in his handling of the sonata form opening movement of the *Grand Duo Concertant* (Op. 48: J.204). It was with this movement, as usual left until last, that he finished the piece whose other two movements had been completed in the July of the previous year. It is accurately titled: this is not a sonata for clarinet with piano accompaniment but a full-scale concert work for two virtuosos, and the music is deployed accordingly. This is evident in the cut of the themes for the opening movement, which are cunningly contrived to suit each instrument equally and indeed only assume their full character in this double handling: as throughout the work, there is much writing of brilliant scales in unison or thirds or sixths, and the piano frequently takes the lead in shaping the course of this furiously inventive movement. Even the Andante, where the *cantabile* qualities of the clarinet can hardly be overlooked, ingeniously brings the instruments into equal status. After the serene opening clarinet song over throbbing chords, the piano embarks on an ornate episode of its own built upon rich semiquaver figuration which remains to colour the music on the clarinet's return. This draws gradually towards the beginning of a restatement of the piano episode, to which the clarinet adds no more than a thickening of colour. But the song theme reassumes prominence, and it is on this that the movement ends. With the Rondo the clarinet seems to be dominating, but the partnership is in fact ingeniously maintained on equal terms by way of a quick-witted distribution of the material: it includes a mock-sinister D♭ episode with the clarinet declaiming in *Freischütz* vein over thunderous piano tremolos, whose menace is dispelled by the appearance of the skittish rondo figure in the bass; this gradually leads back to a restatement of the main theme. The writing throughout is in Weber's most entertaining 'brilliant' vein; but this should not conceal the extraordinary skill and originality of a work which bases its entire material and form on the demands of shared piano and clarinet virtuosity. Characteristically, it was in dramatizing their relationship rather than in matching them to an abstract concept that Weber found his invention most powerfully stimulated.

The two Piano Sonatas which he also completed this autumn—No. 2 in A♭ (Op. 39: J.199) and No. 3 in D minor (Op. 49: J.206)—mark a striking advance over the first. With the opening bars of the A♭ sonata a new breadth of imagination is revealed, perhaps more suggestive of orchestral effect than the keyboard, but setting out an ambitiously designed sonata form movement that was the most successful he had yet produced. The element of theatre is by no means absent, but the development of the broadly arpeggiated first theme and the slighter, more winsome second theme over a lengthy movement shows a new ability to think in extended musical paragraphs and to sustain a dramatic argument markedly lacking in the equivalent movement of the D minor sonata. Here, a violent march-like opening theme (marked Allegro feroce) and a more feminine and song-like second theme hardly make enough constructive musical contact throughout the movement. The respective Andantes have more in common, the suggestion of variation form in that of No. 2 coming frankly into the open with No. 3; but thereafter all similarity between the works vanishes. The A♭ sonata continues with a rather too regular scherzo, or so-called Menuetto Capriccioso,[1] in which the four-bar phrases remain unbroken all the way; and ends with a graceful Rondo in which the element of showmanship gives way to a relaxed charm that is also new in his music. The D minor sonata has only one further movement, a showpiece (sometimes published and played separately as *Allegro di Bravura*) which brilliantly combines three themes in a *tour de force* that is as much compositional as pianistic.

Once again, to compare these sonatas with those being written by Beethoven, who was finishing his Op. 101 in A major in the same November, is absurd. But if we except Beethoven as an isolated phenomenon, Weber's achievement as a keyboard composer beside that of his contemporaries is extraordinary. He towers over them, and in his anticipation of the new worlds of feeling to be explored by Schumann, Chopin and Mendelssohn in their piano works, he need fear no comparisons at all. The finale of No. 3 has the gentle Romanticism and indeed much of the technique of a Schumann Novelette; that of No. 4 is really a brilliant succession of moods suggesting each of these composers in turn. The devices taken from his forerunners, still evident in the C major Sonata, have been entirely absorbed into a new richness and authority of language; and it is Weber's turn to provide examples for his successors, whether in simple technical devices such as the use of staccato and legato in the same hand in the Andante of No. 3, a trick to be taken up with enthusiasm by Chopin (e.g. in his Etude, Op. 25, No. 4), or in

[1] Orchestrated by Tchaikovsky in 1863–4.

his ability to turn the traditional forms of a three or four movement sonata into a dramatic statement of feeling. There is no evidence to support those who have sought to wish programmes on these sonatas; but the impulse is understandable. Had Weber felt able to move away from conventional outer forms, the music would undoubtedly have gained in freedom and originality; as it is, he conferred a degree of unity on his sonata movements less by any conscious thematic relationship than by intensity of mood providing a similarity of idea within all the diversity. Thus many of the themes of the A♭ sonata, and much of the subsidiary material, spring from the idea of a falling scale—less a thematic relationship than an inventive tendency which continually comes over the music. Even when Weber feels obliged to end so massive a movement as the Allegro of this sonata with a couple of pages of display, the effect is quite different from the frank applause music of earlier works: this lightness is a genuine thematic outcome of the second subject, a satisfying conclusion to the argument. The salon has receded out of view, and if the stage still seems vaguely to frame the events, it is as an essential part of Weber's musical thinking, providing dramatic and colouristic contrasts which can be shaped into pure form.

Weber had been working spasmodically on the A♭ sonata ever since February, when he completed the Rondo; the first movement, as usual written last, came at the end of October and some extra work on the Adagio brought the work to completion on the 31st. He gave the first performance himself in a private house on the 10th, having the previous day begun work on the D minor Sonata, which he finished on the 29th (in this case the order of composition was Allegro-Rondo-Andante). It was the last important work of his stay in Prague: apart from five folksongs, the only other piece to be written was the *Divertimento assai facile* for piano and guitar (Op. 38 J.207)—an odd combination that is possibly explained by a reference in his Prague diary for 8th March 1814 mentioning an Andante for piano and guitar he had written for Therese Brunetti's daughter Resi. This would explain the simplicity of the piano part, which is within the capacity of any schoolchild, and the comparative difficulty of the guitar part. It is a straightforward little piece in several movements—an Andante; a Waltz with two trios; and Andante with five variations; and a Polacca.

Throughout the autumn negotiations had been proceeding with Vitzthum and the King of Saxony. On Christmas morning Weber received a letter from Vitzthum. He tells that he stared at it for a long time before summoning up the courage to open it; but shortly afterwards he in turn wrote to Caroline, remarking at the end that she should address any answer to,

The Royal Saxon Kapellmeister
Herr Carl Maria von Weber
Dresden—Post Restante.

CHAPTER TEN

DRESDEN-I: 1817-1820

O eine neu zu schaffende Deutsche Oper! Auf Menschlicher Grund und Boden;
mit Menschlicher Musik und Declamation und Verzierung, aber mit Empfindung; o grosser Zweck! grosses Werk!

J. G. HERDER: *Journal meiner Reise im Jahre 1769*

IN TRAVELLING from Berlin to Dresden, Weber was transferring himself from the intellectual capital of the new Germany to a backwater
that had deliberately, and disastrously, cut itself off from the stream of
national feeling. More than with most of the German states, Saxony's
history was one of turbulent relations with its neighbours; and the alliance
with Napoleon that had now brought it low was only the most recent of many
unwise political moves. Its Catholic traditions had lost it much of its importance among the German states after the Thirty Years' War; and by himself
becoming a Catholic in order to accept the throne of Poland in 1697,
Friedrich August I (Augustus the Strong) forfeited much of the authority
this royal title gave him.

His new religion served to strengthen his attraction towards Italian music.
The traditions were rich, going back beyond Schütz's reorganization of the
Kapelle on Italian models in 1617. Schütz's *Dafne*, the earliest German opera,
was produced for a royal wedding at nearby Torgau in 1627 (Rinuccini's text
was translated by Opitz; the music is lost); but after the Thirty Years' War
he was replaced by Bontempi and Albrici, and the flourishing line of opera
that began with the opening of a Kurfürstliche Opernhaus in 1667 with
Moneglia's *Il Teseo* was wholly Italian. In 1707 this theatre was converted
by Friedrich August into the Hofkirche; performances were given in the
Ritsensaal of the Castle; in 1719 Friedrich opened an enlarged Grosse
Opernhaus. Here, under Friedrich August II, Hasse and his wife Faustina
Bordoni found themselves the victims of much jealousy from the Italians
who were established as court favourites, despite his own Italian operas and
his popularity in Italy itself as *il caro Sassone* (he was not in fact a Saxon). In
1750, Galli-Bibiena altered the opera house; in 1755 Pietro Moretti completed the Komödienhaus (Kleine Hoftheater) that lasted until 1841 and was
the scene of Weber's work; while previously in 1746 Angelo Mingotti, one
of two impresario brothers in whose troupe Gluck had visited Dresden, had,
inside the courtyard of the Zwinger (originally planned as the vestibule to a
palace), opened a small wooden theatre designed for a more popular type of

opera. This was burned down in 1748; and for *Singspiele* and other popular pieces between Hasse and Weber, the Dresden public was largely dependent on the many little touring companies that visited the town. The transition from Hasse to new times is marked by the work of Naumann, Schuster and Seidelmann, three Dresdeners who visited Italy on a royal grant in 1765; on his return Naumann made some attempt to influence the opera in a German direction, doing much to reorganize the orchestra.

But with the courts providing the richest opportunities, the best singers were always attracted to the established Italian opera, so that Frederick the Great was voicing the average German court's feelings about *Singspiel* when he declared that his horse could sing an aria better than a German prima donna. Opportunities were no better for librettists. Poissl, the most energetic worker for German opera besides Weber, was driven to writing his own; while Weber's difficulties have already been described. But if the visiting German troupes did poorly, the Italians always fared well: companies under Locatelli, Moretti and Bustelli, among others, appealed to the fashionable taste of the Saxon court; and in a traditionally conservative city, used to an atmosphere of paternal absolutism, the citizens were content to follow the royal example. Friedrich August's act in throwing his opera open to the public as an economy measure set a wider fashion for Italian opera; though some slight erosion of this was caused by the presentation of *Singspiele* on non-opera days, from 1770, by Johann Christian Wäser, who fostered a taste for Hiller, Benda and Schweitzer. Joseph Seconda's theatre, opened on the Linckesche Bad in 1790, encouraged this, and in 1813–14 E. T. A. Hoffmann was director of the company the Seconda brothers ran in Leipzig and Dresden. But the Italians held their ground under Naumann's successor, Paer, supported by a court that continued to find in *opera seria's* formal trappings and elaborate tiered hierarchy of gods and heroes a reflection of its own order. *Opera seria* was, indeed, a true expression of the Saxon court's inability to understand the movement of the times, and of its tendency to make political moves merely as provision for the easiest possible continuance of the old order. Having shared in the Prussian defeat at Jena in 1806, Friedrich August III ('The Just') accepted Napoleon's offer of neutrality and the status of King of Saxony, committing himself to the Federation of the Rhine and the promise of troops to the French. In 1807 Napoleon took away Paer, who was succeeded by Franz Anton Schubert (who has had the ill luck to be remembered only by his contemptuous remarks when a copy of his namesake's *Erlkönig* was sent to him by mistake) and in 1810 by Francesco Morlacchi. After the Russian disaster of 1812, in which 21,000 Saxons took part, Friedrich fled to Prague when the Allies invaded Saxony, refusing even then to declare against Napoleon. His army having deserted to the Allies at Leipzig, his country was occupied by the Russians; he himself was taken prisoner, and only the desire of Austria to see Prussia kept at a reasonable distance prevented Saxony's total annexation when the Russians withdrew. Hopes for the establishment of a German national opera in the King's absence, and Morlacchi's diplomatic retirement—the Russo-Prussian government had brought all theatres into one organization under Carl Winkler (Theodor Hell)—were dashed by his return in 1814. In the following year he became a full member of the German Confederation that extinguished the hopes for a united Germany.

Dresden had suffered acutely during the war. Napoleon had made it a centre of operations in 1813, occupying it with as many troops as there were inhabitants; and the conditions following failure to bury the bodies of the dead led to an epidemic of dysentry. To cap all, the harvest failed in 1816 and 1817. But throughout everything, loyalty to Friedrich held. With a backward economy and lack of external trade, the life of the country was inward-turning by comparison with the rest of Germany; and in the conservative atmosphere people were accustomed to look to the king as an example and a leader. The court clung to antique formal dress and *ancien régime* manners, and a strict division of classes was perpetuated: the nobles tended to meet in the Casino or the Ressource, the merchants and middle classes in societies such as the Harmonie, the Albina or the Kaufmannsverein, while the labourers simply used the beer-cellars. There was no mingling of these strata, scarcely even by way of the large numbers of artists and writers who thronged Dresden. The *Dichtertee* that met, under the protection of the Minister Nostitz (who wrote under the name of Arthur von Nordstern), included Eduard Gehe, Friedrich Kind, the poetess Therese aus dem Winkel (a supporter of Italian opera and hence to be an enemy of Weber's), the archaeologist and drama critic C. A. Böttiger, and Theodor Hell—but not Tieck, who held aloof in some scorn and used to refer to it as 'The Incense Institute'. The society took its title from the regular meetings to consume bread and butter and read the members' works aloud; later renamed the *Liederkreis*, it in turn reflected the complacent, insular tone of Dresden life in the 'cliquish exclusiveness, mutual admiration and humdrum attitude of these commonplace tea-drinkers who like good family men were always home punctually by nine o'clock'.[1] It was for one of these meetings that Weber wrote a story, a 'Humoreske' entitled *Der Schlammbeisser* (The Mudfish).[2]

Vitzthum's negotiations for the setting up of a German opera in these unpromising surroundings were to test all his diplomatic skill. His conviction of its importance was by no means shared at court, where ranged against him he had not only the weight of royal prejudice but the Cabinet Minister Count Detlev Einsiedel—a powerful figure dismissed by Max Maria as an evil genius but in fact hardly more than an ultra-conservative politician who did try to develop his country's industry within the strict framework of the

[1] H. A. Kruger: *Pseudoromantik* (1904).
[2] Kaiser 130.

accepted order. Nevertheless, his mistrust of change set him in opposition to the 'German' party; and it was not until the King made a false economic move that Vitzthum saw his chance. In taking over the control of the Leipzig opera administration from the Seconda brothers on 1st April 1816, Friedrich found himself landed with a substantial deficit. To wipe it out, Vitzthum immediately proposed his German opera, and on 18th April the decree was granted (just at the time when the re-instatement of Italian opera was decreed in Munich). Vitzthum managed to fend off suggestions of cheaper rivals for the directorship in favour of Weber (Klengel, Schneider and Sutor were named), and on 14th December the decree went through Einsiedel to appoint Weber as *Musikdirektor*. The term had a significance of which Vitzthum kept Weber in ignorance; for Morlacchi's post with the Italian opera was the higher-ranking one of *Königlich Kapellmeister*.

Unaware of these crucial niceties, Weber arrived in Dresden on 13th January and settled happily into his new accommodation near the theatre. The so-called *Italienisches Dörfchen*, built in the early 18th century to house the Italian workers on the Zwinger, was one of the quietest and most picturesque quarters of one of Germany's most beautiful old cities, and soon Weber was able to write to Caroline with a contented description of his new domestic surroundings. The theatre was less promising; the 1755 Komödien-haus originally held 350, and though it had been enlarged to a capacity of 814 in 1783, with a bell-shaped auditorium providing excellent acoustics, the back-stage accommodation was miserable, with cramped, shabby dressing-rooms and a poor range of facilities. Vitzthum had been petitioning the King to enlarge it still further or to build a new house altogether but was compelled to settle for the third alternative he put forward, permission to stage opera seasons in the theatre on the Linckesche Bad, in the public gardens across the Elbe. However, Weber's optimism was still high. He was cordially welcomed, with invitations to embassy parties and calls from colleagues—including Morlacchi, with whom he decided he would be able to work. Their subsequent rivalry was genuine, but it has been exaggerated by German writers who, following Max Maria's loyal lead, have tended to underline every pettiness of Morlacchi's and pass over the irritability that was beginning to mark the increasingly ill and exhausted Weber. In other circumstances he could probably have co-operated with Morlacchi, a somewhat vain and idle but by no means wholly unsympathetic character. Another caller was the great bass Luigi Bassi, Mozart's original Don Giovanni, now fifty and almost voiceless; and from him Weber learned, on 16th January, the truth about his appointment. Vitzthum confirmed the situation, whereupon Weber presented his resignation on the point of principle that a German appointment should not rank as inferior. Vitzthum took the matter to the King, and, to Morlacchi's chagrin, was after the success of *Joseph* able to achieve equal status as *Königlich Kapellmeister* for his protégé.

There were six performance days in the Dresden theatre week. By
tradition Friday was free, with Wednesday and Saturday reserved for the
Italians and the remainder shared between German plays and opera. The
'Monday public' was drawn from high society, pro-Italian and reserved in
its applause; the 'Sunday public' consisted largely of merchants and work-
men who applauded heartily and indiscriminately. These audiences Weber
was required to satisfy with resources that were plainly inadequate even for a
less exacting task. The orchestra included some very weak members, and
could not be fitted complete into the cramped pit; while the lean times and
lack of sympathy for German opera meant that casting presented insuperable
problems. Most of his singers were ex-actors from the Seconda troupe, and
according to a later arrival, Eduard Genast, nearly all defective in some way;
while his nominal right to borrow singers from Morlacchi was easily refused
with various excuses. For his first production he chose Méhul's *Joseph*
partly since it makes minimal use of the chorus and needs only one leading
female part; nevertheless, he was obliged to cast as one of the hero's sons a
singer engaged for 'noble father' roles. The severity of his opening speech to
the company caused some antagonism; but he quickly won respect for the
discipline he imposed not only on his team but on himself, studying costume
designs for the production from old books, supervising the scene-painting
personally, and publishing, as in Prague, articles drawing attention first to the
need for a German style in opera and then specifically to *Joseph*.[1] The
performance on 30th January was well received, both by the King and the
critics; the opposition was represented by Therese aus dem Winkel, whose
hostile article in the *Abendzeitung* drew from Weber the retort 'This lady has
a regrettable disease: she can't hold her ink.' Privately he was far from
satisfied. The lack of a proper chorus was particularly worrying (by September it had not risen above thirty-two, and even in 1820 the strength was only
7.7.9.12), since it was upon this element that he was to lay much stress in his
formation of a German style. He was also the prey to personal worries, as a
letter to Gänsbacher on 10th March shows: he was at once unhappy about his
contract for a year only (though this was renewable) and upset over the lost
opportunities for travel, which marriage would hamper still more—he
recommends independence and the careful avoidance of the wiles of the girl
known to them as 'F major'.

If the *Dichtertee* with which he was associating had disclosed an enemy in
Therese aus dem Winkel, it also brought new association with Friedrich
Kind. After one evening's dramatic reading, they left together discussing
librettos. Happening again upon Apel's *Gespensterbuch*, Weber revived the
idea of an opera on the *Freischütz* legend. On 19th February Weber was able
to write to Caroline with news of the project. Kind set to work on what was
provisionally entitled *Der Probeschuss*, producing the first act within a week

[1] *Abendzeitung*, 29th January 1817 (Kaiser 107 and 108).

and the whole opera by 1st March. A copy was despatched to Caroline, who had some sensible comments to make: it was she, initially to the annoyance of Weber and enduringly to that of Kind, who suggested that the planned opening on a scene with the Hermit would be much less effective than raising the curtain on the village merrymaking. On 28th May he wrote to her pointing out what a serious rival she had in Agathe. After a little negotiating, he bought the rights of the book from Kind for thirty ducats.

There was, however, little time for composition. Much work on revising the opera house's organization had to be done, including the foundation of a library; and such time as he could spare for writing was absorbed in answering a request from Count Brühl for incidental music for a Berlin production of Müllner's *König Yngurd* (J.214), eleven very short inserts of which only the final number, a song *Lasst den Knaben,* is of any substance. There was also his own private house to be set in order for his bride.

Two unsuccessful productions followed—Fischer's *Das Hausgesinde* and Himmel's *Fanchon*—before Weber left for Prague to engage some singers from the now insolvent company there. He conducted a performance of *Silvana* with Caroline in the title role, and left having arranged engagements for the Weixelbaums, Eduard Genast and Therese Grünbaum; the bass, Gned, fared less well owing to his unfortunate resemblance to one of the King's political enemies, and he had to be disposed of to Berlin. Thither Grünbaum followed, despite a success in *Jean de Paris.* Weber's detailed recommendations to Vitzthum for the establishment of a proper company were only partly accepted; he did manage to secure the appointment of the bass-buffo Metzner as chorus-master, with the task of instructing the group in mime and dance as well as singing. Not until September did Weber have his first full rehearsal with them. More troubles began piling up on his return. The Prague bank in which he had invested his and Caroline's savings collapsed; he covered her losses without telling her. A demand that the Germans should remove to the Linckesche Bad was overruled only with great difficulty and due to Einsiedel's illness. More seriously, a quarrel with the Italians arose over a concert Vitzthum had asked Weber to conduct in the Frauenkirche. Morlacchi, with Einsiedel in support, claimed it as his right, and in an interview with the Minister, Weber once more threatened resignation. But this time the King upheld Weber's right. Nevertheless, the endless bickering with the Italian faction over petty supremacies so wore him down that he was easily tempted by an offer of the Berlin opera from Count Brühl in June. Though negotiations fell through when the Berlin Theatre was burnt down on 31st July, he made the time-honoured use of an outside offer to strengthen his hand in his current appointment, and Vitzthum was able to confirm his engagement for life. Work on *Freischütz* (now provisionally known as *Die Jägersbraut*) continued from 2nd July to 25th August; while on the 26th he completed his last set of piano variations, on a genuine gipsy song (Op. 55: J.219)—a brief and comparatively uninteresting work. In September Morlacchi took the first of the many long leaves that were to lay such a burden of extra work upon Weber, not returning until the following June. In the Italian's absence, Weber was engaged by Vitzthum to celebrate the wedding of Princess Maria Carolina of Saxony to the Grand Duke of Tuscany (also a German) with music for a festival play by Kind, *Der Weinberg an der Elbe*; but Einsiedel intervened and demanded in its place an Italian cantata.

The result was *L'Accoglienza* (J.221), assembled in a fortnight to highly formal words by the Abbé Celani. Allegorical figures of Agriculture, Science, Art and Commerce greet the festive day; the Spirit of Florence follows with a lengthy address to the bride, while in the background the Boboli Gardens and a view of Florence were to be revealed; and finally the citizens are led in prayer by an Old Man. Weber drew more heavily than usually on previously composed music, especially from *Peter Schmoll* and its overture, *Rübezahl* (the quintet) and some songs; but enough worthwhile music also went into it for re-use in *Oberon*—No. 6, the chorus of Tuscans, reappears slightly altered as the Chorus and Ballet (No. 21) and No. 3 in part as Reiza's cabaletta to the Slaves' Chorus in the Act 1 finale. But *L'Accoglienza* is inevitably patchwork, and Weber never regarded it as anything than a piece of musical journalism.

The cantata was finally performed on 29th October, after various post-ponements of the royal marriage that in turn meant the postponement of Weber's own marriage in Prague. The King approved the work and sent a diamond ring; but just as all was ready for Weber's departure, this was followed by a message that Kind's festival play was wanted after all, and with it some music. Weary and ill, he left for Prague, composing as he neared Prague the song *Hold ist der Cyanenkranz* (J.122). Caroline and her mother met him at the last posting station. On 4th November the couple were married, surrounded by friends and with the surprise present of a four-part chorus sung for them by members of Weber's former company.

Since Vitzthum had asked Weber to engage more singers, part of the honeymoon expenses could be charged to the German Opera. The couple tried to cover the rest by giving concerts. Travelling first through Eger, Bayreuth, Bamberg, Würzburg and Heidelberg, they came to Mannheim on 14th November. Here they left Caroline's mother with her son Louis and the husband from whom she had long been separated; Weber also made her a generous allowance of 100 thalers. In Mainz they found Gottfried Weber, established there in a legal post, but the meeting was not a success: new interests and the feeling that his own compositions had been neglected made Gottfried somewhat distant. A concert in Darmstadt on 1st December went poorly, but in Giessen on the 5th the couple had a joint success. In Gotha and Weimar, Weber was able to present his bride to his former patrons; in

WEBER CONDUCTING IN THE DRESDEN KOMÖDIENHAUS
Aquarelle by F. A. Kannegiesser

Leipzig they met Rochlitz once more; and by the 20th they were back in Dresden to a well-appointed flat in the Altmarkt, which Weber had teasingly allowed Caroline to expect would be in chaos. He had ended the year married and in a distinguished appointment; late at night on 31st December he entered in his diary a promise to honour both achievements.

The new year began with an incident that severely tested his resolve. Early in his appointment, Weber had realised that the disposition of the orchestra in the pit made it difficult to maintain proper control over players and (equally important to him) the stage action as well. On the extreme left, the pit extended under a box used by the Princes; on the right it extended under the King's box, and in the space were fitted the trumpets and the percussion, almost out of the view of the conductor, who sat at the piano in the middle of the orchestra with a cello and a bass reading his score over his shoulders. With the other instruments scattered equally haphazardly around him—another cello and bass in front of him; trombones seated among the violins and violas; woodwind and others far left—the conductor's difficulties seemed complete. For *L'Accoglienza* Weber set the upper strings to his right, the wind and brass to his left, keeping the lower strings behind him and moving his desk up to the prompter's box. In this way he hoped to improve his view of more of the most important players and his immediate control of the productions. In the excitement of the wedding festivities, the innovation passed off unnoticed, but at a performance of *La Vestale* soon after Weber's return the King was disconcerted by the noise of the brass, now no longer muffled beneath his feet. After a bout of furious lobbying by Vitzthum and by the Italians, the latter up in arms over an offensive reference by Weber in the *Abendzeitung* in reply to an attack by Therese aus dem Winkel, instructions were received that the old order must be restored. Not until 1820 was Weber to get his way.

During the first two months of the year he was also working on a royal commission for a Mass for soloists, chorus and orchestra, a routine task for Saxon *Kapellmeisters* which he approached willingly and conscientiously, so he told Lichtenstein on 14th May. From internal evidence, however, the Mass in E♭ (J.224) only really came to absorb him as it progressed. The opening movements have a certain stiffness that reflects the demands made upon him, which he in turn relayed to Gänsbacher on 24th and 26th December 1818 when the latter was approached for a Dresden Mass: it must be short, so as not to weary the King; the court liked *galant* style (but did not get it from Weber); sudden contrasts of loud and soft or rapidly shifting harmonies were useless in the highly reverberant acoustics of the church. Not least important, there must be a fine soprano solo for the favoured castrato Giovanni Sassaroli, and Weber continues drily: 'The singers are Italians, so not too strong, everything as singable as possible. The alto is a dog. Soprano [Sassaroli] excellent in elaborate music; breathes like a horse.

Don't forget to give him a top F or G *ad lib*. He's best between G and top A or B.' Sassaroli's characteristics are faithfully reflected in the Offertorium *Gloria et honore* (J.226) for soprano, chorus and orchestra which Weber wrote at the King's wish, to be inserted in his Mass.[1] The use of earlier

Ex. 39

music in the first part of the Mass also suggests an initial lack of absorption in the work. Between the two related choral movements of the Kyrie he used the arioso from the opening entry of the *Jugendmesse*; the movement also makes use of six bars of the *Trauermusik* written for Heigel (J.116); and no fewer than three of the Six Fughettas that were his very first published work turn up in various guises. The first (altered from 3/4 to 4/4) makes the traditional fugue for the Cum sancto spiritu in the Gloria, which is bound together by a *Leitmotiv* opening and finds room for a soprano solo Qui tollis. The Credo is a rondo in which the constant use of staggered fughetta entries suggests the endless circling of voices raised in faith: the sixth of the Fughettas is the subject of the Et incarnatus est passage.

Hitherto, however skilfully Weber reconciles the imposed demands with his use (as in the *Jugendmesse*) of forms to reflect a structure of faith, there is comparatively little real personal involvement. The Mass's composition dates are 4th January to 23rd February (1st March for the Offertorium): Weber did not resume the actual composition of *Der Freischütz* until 17th April, though, as we have seen, ideas were constantly turning in his mind, and this gives a certain common background to the thematic invention (the Mass is sometimes known as the *Freischützmesse*). When a more personal note begins to show in the Mass, it is distinctly dramatic in nature. Though a practising Catholic, Weber saw the rituals in a dramatic light more readily than as an inner act of faith; for like Verdi, as a born opera composer it was in this way that his imagination naturally took shape. The opening of the Sanctus is a superb dramatic stroke fashioned out of the simplest means. The

plain chords and hushed beat of the drums and pizzicato basses demand a
rich echo, such as the Dresden church provided, for its effect of awe before
the Godhead; one might see this as the 'good' obverse of which Samiel's
diminished sevenths and throbbing drums are the reverse (its example
was not lost on Berlioz when he came to write the Agnus Dei in his
Grande Messe Des Morts and the opening of his Te Deum) (Ex. 39, pp.
182–3).

The Sanctus is cast as a three-part progress towards jubilation, with the
opening two bars providing a strong bass figure for the Pleni sunt coeli and
finally revealing themselves as the theme of the first of his Op. 1 Fughettas,
now worked out in an *allegro* Hosanna. The ensuing Benedictus concludes
with the identical Hosanna, but the first part is a gentle aria with chorus,
written for Sassaroli but suggesting the womanly blessings of Agathe and
her 'Und ob die Wolke'. The first six notes here, essentially a turn around
the dominant before a leap to the tonic, are a Weber fingerprint that
marks the Mass, and is, for that matter, identical with Agathe's 'Himmel,
nimm'.

Cello,
Db. & Org.

The Agnus Dei, which opens on a progression similar to this same Agathe
theme, contains the richest choral and solo writing; but though the C minor
Largo gives way to an Andante in the relative major, there is curiously little
sense of consolation. It is as if the prayer ended on a note of depression, a
feeling reinforced by the return in the final three bars of the heavy throbbing
rhythm on which the movement began.

If the professional difficulties continued unabated, Weber's personal life was now set on a contented course. There were, however, some early awkwardnesses with Caroline, who, despite her very real devotion to Weber and his interests, only learnt to cook by trial and error and showed continuing symptoms of jealousy: Weber dealt with the latter by allowing her to build up a jealous fantasy upon a mysterious series of absences and then producing his bust by Matthäi together with a list of the times of his sittings signed by the sculptor. He enjoyed, as ever, evenings in the tavern run by an Italian, Chiappone, as well as the *Liederkreis* meetings; but his health suffered in the hard winter, and with spring the couple found a house with a five-roomed flat to let at Klein-Hosterwitz, near Pillnitz, the site of the royal castle where a good deal of Weber's summer work was called for. Being too poor to furnish both houses, they had to move their furniture to and from Dresden in spring and autumn; but from the moment they moved into Hosterwitz on 18th June, they fell completely under its spell. Picturesquely set, with fine views and dramatic walks in the nearby 'Saxon Switzerland', it became highly popular among his friends—the *Liederkreis*, visiting writers such as Fouqué and Jean Paul Richter, Prince Anton and Princess Amalie (who had written an opera which was performed at Dresden), members of his company and even of the Italian group, especially the fat castrato, Sassaroli, who touched the Webers' hearts by his gentleness in playing with children, whom he pathetically adored, while tears poured down his cheeks. Sassaroli was widely popular, and is said to have hated only one man, the father who was responsible for his mutilation. Weber's circle at Hosterwitz was eventually completed by various well-loved domestic animals—a large dog, an Angola cat called Maune, a starling rescued from some boys by Caroline, a monkey and a raven which charmed Weber by its trick of croaking 'Good evening' at him. The surroundings were enchanting—indeed, enervatingly so, for as he later told Rochlitz, a less attractive situation would have stimulated harder work. Nevertheless, he found time for a steady stream of songs and other pieces, mostly in connexion with his work in the theatre or as a royal employee. For a production of Eduard Gehe's *Heinrich IV, König von Frankreich* he wrote nine brief pieces of incidental music (J.237) of which all but Nos. 1, 3 and 4 have found their way into subsequent works, chiefly *Oberon* and *Preciosa*; for these he also used a dance and song 'In Provence' on a genuine Spanish tune originally written for Hell's *Das Haus Anglade* that April (J.227). July and August at Hosterwitz also saw, among other pieces, a chorus for Grillparzer's *Sappho* (J. 240), some work on the piano duets that were to comprise Op. 60; and two cantatas written to the royal commission.

The first of these, *Natur und Liebe* (Op. 61: J.241) was written for the King's name-day, *Augustus-Tag* (3rd August), and consists of nine songs for S S T T B B and piano to words by Kind. For the most part they recall the manner of his *gesellige Lieder* of the Berlin period, some with introductory

WEBER'S HOUSE AT HOSTERWITZ

Anonymous drawing

recitatives: they include a pretty duet (No. 3) for two sopranos and a charming Nightingale Song (No. 7) addressed to the Queen and sung by solo soprano over the other voices. No. 5 is a lively 3/8 sextet in which the tune passes from voice to voice over a rhythmic accompaniment by the others: of a simple and pleasing but inconsiderable cycle, it is this number which most looks forward to the manner of Brahms's *Liebeslieder* waltzes. An attempt by Herklots to perpetuate the songs beyond their immediate purpose with a new text as *Freundschaft und Liebe* has not succeeded.

The *Jubel-Cantate* (Op. 58: J.244) of the same August, written to celebrate the fiftieth anniversary of the King's accession of 20th September, is a more ambitious affair, the largest of the total of thirteen pieces which Weber wrote to the royal command. Scored for SATB soloists, SATB choir and orchestra to another of Kind's texts, it shows some signs of the intense hurry in which Weber wrote it. The music is by and large little more than an efficient setting that does its best to lend distinction to Kind's platitudes. There is some attractive woodwind writing in No. 2 (a tenor recitative leading to an Allegro), but the most interesting movement is No. 5, a bass solo lamenting the horrors which nature, no less than war, can inflict on mankind. It was the dominantly pastoral note in the cantata that led to an attempt to rescue this occasional piece also, with a text refashioned as *Ernte-Cantate* (*Harvest Cantata*) by Amadeus Wendt and printed below the original in the Schlesinger first edition of 1831. The unhappy legacy of the war and the double harvest failure is clearly reflected in Kind's text, which makes the most delicate possible reference to the King's behaviour in deserting his country by observing how his children missed their father: Wendt's text alters this to 'seek' their father, and in general God is substituted for the King in a purely pastoral rather than political context. An English version was prepared by Hampdon Napier as *The Festival of Peace* for Weber's last concert in London on 26th May 1826; and a revision of this to bring it closer to Wendt's text has also been published by the Rev. John Troutbeck. There is no link between the *Jubel-Cantate* and the *Jubel-Ouvertüre* (Op. 59: J.245) which Weber composed on his return to Dresden at the end of August for the concert on the 20th: apart from anything else, the cantata is basically in E♭, the overture in E major. A celebratory Adagio leads into a Presto whose jubilations are recognisably the work of the composer of the *Freischütz* and *Oberon* overtures. Weber is, characteristically, more personally involved when given a free hand with the orchestra than when required to make the best of a formal text; and he completes his homage to the King with a *pièce de resistance* as his climax, the wholesale importation from *Kampf und Sieg* of his orchestration of *Heil dir im Siegerkranz* (*God save the King*).

Weber returned to Dresden exhausted by the concentrated effort of work on the cantata and with symptoms of tuberculosis asserting themselves, to find that other arrangements had been made for the concert on the 20th. Immediately he withdrew the overture also; but at Vitzthum's urgent request he gave his permission, mounting the cantata himself in the Neustadt church as a benefit for the destitute peasantry of the Harz Mountains. Among the audience was the Duke of Gotha, whom Weber persuaded to grant a title to Kind. The rest of the year was, apart from work at the theatre and a few small pieces, given to a second Mass, in G, this time to celebrate the royal pair's Golden Wedding on 17th February.

Less dramatic in vein, the Mass in G (Op. 76: J.251) has a simpler charm to it and is a more even work. As a so-called *Jubel-Messe* it was required to utter its sentiments in an atmosphere of worldly celebration, which the almost Haydnesque directness and tunefulness of the opening Kyrie and still more the ensuing Gloria immediately make clear. The latter shows the increased skill with which Weber was able to bind his solo and choral forces into one movement: by the time the Cum sancto spiritu fugue has arrived, each has had a brief entry—in the case of the tenor, a beautiful extended solo to the accompaniment of one of Weber's grief motives—and the final fugue itself is conducted under brilliant passage work from the soprano, doubtless a delight to the King in Sassaroli's handling. The Credo is constructed as a series of bold choral entries against the working out of a *Leitmotiv* on which the violins open; its central section, the Et incarnatus est, reintroduces the soprano in a passage over chromatic harmony which has been praised as anticipating Wagner but has now been coloured by its associations with Mendelssohn's English oratorio manner at its most sentimental. After the brief Sanctus, the Benedictus and Agnus Dei once more suggest the voice of Weber's operatic heroines. The Benedictus, a beautiful four-part solo, again hints, as in the previous Mass, that the personality of Agathe was beginning to take shape in the composer's mind; while the Agnus Dei is a short and charming cavatina for contralto leading directly into the brief, graceful Dona nobis pacem. For this Mass, too, Weber wrote an Offertorium, *In die solemnitatis* (J.250) another insertion (of no great distinction) to demonstrate Sassaroli's talents.

Despite its almost sunny nature, the Mass was written in the face of a series of personal troubles. Caroline was pregnant and far from well, while in his own lowered state of health Weber allowed the petty irritations of co-existence with Morlacchi and the Italians to upset him unduly. His cantata had been cancelled, and now he found his attempt to stage the first of his own operas in Dresden, *Silvana*, frustrated by Morlacchi putting singers he needed on to the sick list or arranging coincidental rehearsals and claiming priority. Weber reacted with a series of angry notes to Einsiedel that can have done his case no good. On 22nd December, after a difficult confinement, Caroline bore him a girl. The child was baptised Maria Caroline Friederike Auguste on 26th December; but instead of sending the conventional high-ranking deputy to show respect, the royal godparents sent a valet and a woman of the bedchamber—a disappointment if only on the grounds of lowered prestige for his office. On 28th December the Webers received the news of the death of Caroline's father. Then, a few days before the performance, Vitzthum was obliged to tell him that his Mass was to be given with sections of it replaced with music by Morlacchi and Polledro. It needed all the persuasion of Prince Anton, with whom he was in close contact, to persuade him to accept the situation. More than enough compensation seemed to be made when he received a commission for an opera to celebrate the marriage of Prince Friedrich August to the Archduchess Caroline of Austria; Kind insisted to Vitzthum on being chosen as librettist, and of his three subjects, historical, mythological and fairy, the last was selected. In ten days he had delivered the bulk of a libretto on *Alcindor*, based on a tale from the *Thousand and One Nights*. But Weber was too feverish to work: he took to his bed on 18th March, the news of his daughter's illness kept from him by Caroline. At the end of the month the child died, and Caroline too collapsed. Not until the beginning of May were they well enough to move out to Hosterwitz. Caroline recovered more quickly than her husband, who was cast into a depression in which he was unable to compose at all, rousing himself only to irritation at the hunger brought about by the near-starvation diet prescribed by his doctor, Hedenus. Max Maria records that it took sympathy for another bereaved father to cure him; for on a visit from Munich, his old friend Wiebeking told him of the death of his former pupil Fanny. He occupied himself with making piano reductions of *Abu Hassan* and the *Jubel-Cantate* and with some preparatory ideas for *Alcindor*. Then, at the end of June, Vitzthum appeared with the news that the order for the opera was cancelled. The reason given was that the King had been assured by the Italians that it was filled with superstition; the intriguers' agent was none other than Seconda, whose merchant brother-in-law had a quantity of blue cloth for disposal and acted on the hint that *Alcindor* called for a chorus of spirits in pink. At this, the outcome of a showdown between himself and Einsiedel, Vitzthum had resigned. Weber walked down to the Pillnitz ferry with him, and there they parted, their joint hopes for the success of a German opera in Dresden apparently in ruins.

The effect of this blow upon Weber was unexpected. Instead of relapsing into depression or turning immediately back to the interrupted *Freischütz*, he poured the invention that had been lying stagnant for the first half of the year into a stream of dazzling instrumental pieces which were completed in the space of a month—the *Rondo Brillante* (Op. 62: J.252) was finished the day after Vitzthum's departure, work was continued on the piano duet pieces, the Piano Trio (Op. 63: J.259) followed on 25th July and the *Aufforderung zum Tanze* (Op. 65: J.260) on the 28th. Apart from one day, 13th March, on which he had sketched Caspar's 'Schweig, Schweig!' and planned Act 1 of *Freischütz*, the only references in his diary to preparatory work on these pieces concern the Trio, on which he spent a single day each in April and May. Together with them one may bracket the Eight Pieces for piano duet (Op. 60: J.248, 264, 253, 242, 236, 265, 266 and 254) completed on 10th August; and rounding off the group of his most scintillating piano works, the *Polacca Brillante* (Op. 72: J.268), completed at Hosterwitz on 25th August before the Webers' return to Dresden. In the last days of the month, 28th and 31st, he had also finished the Scherzo and Allegro of what was, three years later, to be his Fourth Piano Sonata.

Whether or not ideas from the abortive *Alcindor* found their way into these pieces, as Max Maria hints, it is impossible to say. Conceivably some of the song-like episodes in the solo piano pieces are tentative operatic ideas put to new use; but essentially the *Rondo* and the *Polacca* are such brilliant pieces of pure piano virtuosity that no other impulse is evident apart from a sense of release and of new exuberance of spirit guiding Weber towards his own instrument. The Rondo, subtitled by Weber '*La Gaité*', is hardly more than a dazzling tour de force in the salon style of his predecessors; the Polacca, which he subtitled '*L'Hilarité*', is no less entertaining as a concert squib but has considerably more substance to it, and anticipates to a striking degree the virtuoso polonaises of Chopin. But Liszt's intended homage in orchestrating it with the addition of the introduction from the earlier Grand Polonaise, as already mentioned in connexion with that work, is misplaced since a thematic relationship is broken—a curious failure of perception of the part of a composer with Liszt's concepts of thematic metamorphosis. His edition of the *Rondo Brillante* confines itself to suggestions in phrasing and dynamics; but to the *Polacca* he added alternative readings that add further to already dizzy difficulties of execution.

If the *Polacca* anticipates the Romantic concert Polonaise, the famous *Aufforderung zum Tanze* is the first and still perhaps the most brilliant and poetic example of the Romantic concert waltz, creating within its little programmatic framework a tone poem that is also an apotheosis of the waltz in a manner that was to remain fruitful at least until Ravel's *poème choréographique*, *La Valse*. According to Mosco Carner,[1] it was Hummel who first produced a suite of purely concert dances for piano with his *Tänze für die Apollo Säle* of 1808. Even Schubert's delightful sets retain a direct connexion with actual dancing, and rustic *Ländler* at that, compared with the concert sophistication of Weber's piece. His own previous waltzes had given no hint of how inventively he was to develop Hummel's scheme, and his idea of making the conventional few bars' introduction into a miniature drama is one of genius. He himself provided the key when he first played it to Caroline (to whom it is dedicated), and hence this has come down to us:

[1] Carner: *The History of the Waltz* (1948).

First approach of the dancer [bars 1–5] to whom the lady gives an evasive answer [5–9]. His more pressing invitation [9–13: note the insistence of the added grace-notes]; her acceptance of his request [13–16]. Now they converse in greater detail; he begins [17–19]; she answers [19–21]; he with heightened expression [21–23]; she responds more warmly [23–25]; now for the dance! His remarks concerning it [25–27]; her answer [27–29]; their coming together [29–31]; their going forward; expectation of the beginning of the dance [31–35]. The Dance. End: his thanks, her reply and their parting. Silence.

This provides a framework for the suite of waltzes by the eventual return of the opening music; and the waltzes themselves are cast in the novel form of a rondo with a clear and satisfying balance of speed, character and key. Despite the wonderfully sympathetic orchestration which Berlioz made for use at his Paris performance of *Der Freischütz* in 1841, and which has given the piece its widest currency, it is essentially a bravura keyboard work in Weber's most dashing and elegant vein, and at one stroke it placed the waltz in the Romantic repertory alongside Polonaise, Nocturne and Scherzo setting a direct example to Chopin and Liszt and fathering a vigorous line of characteristic genre pieces.

The Trio for piano, flute and cello (Op. 63: J.259) which Weber completed on 25th July is almost certainly based on the reworking of an earlier piece, the *Schäfers Klage* Andante which he had probably rewritten in March 1815 from an 1814 original composed for Dr. Jungh (see p. 158). The 1819 diary records composition dates for all the movements but this one, and the dedication of the whole work to Jungh further suggests a Prague origin. The movement casts its note of melancholy over the rest of the work. Jähns claims that it is not a real song, merely a Shepherd's Lament in general character; but it has been variously identified as *In einem kühlen Grunde* and *Dort droben auf jenem Berge*.

Ex. 41

In the space of 59 bars this little melody is made to bear the weight of a far more intense melancholy than its wistful lilt might suggest. Its first statement is answered by a more richly harmonized piano solo; a sharp wrench into D major produces a passionate flute decoration to the theme in the left hand of the piano, which then subsides to heartfelt throbbing under another version of the theme before issuing a call to order and leading the movement to a quiet but still somewhat restless close.

The unexpected contrasts against a basic note of anxiety characterize the rest of the work still more strongly. It is one of Weber's strangest and most affecting works, and the one which exercises him most in keeping a classically based formal control over very diverse material. The Allegro moderato is perhaps the most successful of his sonata movements in setting a Romantic character in classical form; but with the G minor-major Scherzo its grave melancholy is sharply dispersed with a gesture of Beethovenian gruffness. Yet the continuation is nothing less than a waltz that might equally well have found its way into the *Invitation to the Dance*.

Ex. 42

Weber senses accurately that the contrast here is more than enough to allow him to dispense with a Trio; but there is undeniably a danger that the charm of the 'waltz' may come to seem merely trivial after such a powerful opening gesture, instead of suggesting the consolations that gaiety can provide against the attacks of fate—despite the fact that gaiety is totally vanquished in a final burst of the opening violence.

The concluding Allegro, after the *Schäfers Klage*, compresses into the opening piano 12-bar statement five distinct themes (including at [d] some of the trills that were to be put to sinister use when he came to write Caspar's 'Hier im ird'schen Jammerthal', at the end of November). Each of these might have furnished Beethoven with material for a complete movement. (Ex. 43, opposite page).

But again Weber has a consolatory flute alternative (Ex. 44, p. 194).

The burden of this movement is really an engagement between the two elements, carried on in a more elaborate contrapuntal manner than anything Weber had yet written and with the separate parts of the piano statement providing a bewildering variety of material. The Trio is an odd work, whose weakness lies chiefly in the fact that distraction and consolation seem too readily available given the context of harshness and melancholy; and that the working out of the two, though as ingenious in each of the movements as anything Weber wrote, provides exciting, charming and intellectually stimulating incident, but hardly charts any real emotional progress. Yet with familiarity, the work's virtues come to dominate—the originality of its chamber music writing, superior to that in the Piano Quartet, and the completeness with which even in its awkwardness it expresses the character of a composer surviving intense unhappiness and on the brink of his greatest achievements.

No such tensions mark the Eight Pieces for piano duet which Weber completed on 10th August. He had written them at odd times since 29th May 1818, the first (No. 5) as an alternative version of the Dance (No. 2) in his music for Gehe's tragedy *Heinrich IV*, the remainder for no particular purpose—though No. 6, a Theme and Variations on the song *Ich hab' mir eins erwählet* (Op. 54, No. 3: J.212) which he had written in Berlin on 8th January 1817 and dedicated to Caroline, had for this reason a special place in his affections. The duets are much the finest of his three sets, their simplicity and direct charm concealing a high degree of technical control. Though aimed at domestic consumption, there is no whiff of either salon or schoolroom; in their limited but graphic character, they look forward to the genre pieces of Schumann or even, in the beautiful song-like Adagio (No. 3), hint at the grace of a Chopin Nocturne. No. 2, Allegro, is a pungent little march sometimes known as *Alla Militare*. Another march, No. 7, is a

Ex. 43

7

Marcia Funebre, but one with a sinister jollity that attracted Hindemith when he came to write the last of his Weber Metamorphoses for orchestra: the wild, exuberant *Allegro all'Ongarese* (No. 4) went to make the first of them.

Despite this flurry of summer activity, Weber was also anxious to fit in the work of writing music to celebrate the wedding of King Ferdinand of Spain to the Princess Maria Josepha, a girl of sixteen who was well-liked among the inhabitants of Pillnitz and Hosterwitz, including Weber. But the request, transmitted through Vitzthum's brother to Einsiedel, was denied in favour of a cantata by Morlacchi to words by an Italian courtier. Weber's stock sank lower after an incident on 1st August when the King of Prussia came to pay a reconciliatory visit to the King of Saxony. All Dresden drove out to Pillnitz to witness the meeting of the two old enemies. Friedrich Wilhelm drove up in an open carriage, accompanied by an adjutant; he wore a military cap, with a plain grey uniform under his military cloak, which he left in the carriage as he walked up the steps to greet Friedrich August, who was in full court attire with buckles, powdered wig and pigtails. Weber's remark to Caroline, 'My God, it looks as if the Past and the Future are greeting one another', was unfortunately overheard and rapidly brought to the ears of the King. The summer visitors to Hosterwitz included the young Heinrich Marschner, whose *Heinrich IV und Aubigné* he had sent to Dresden the previous year. Weber had admired the opera and determined to stage it; his first contact with Marschner's somewhat bluff manners was less happy, though he came to value the younger man's qualities and became firm friends with him. Back in Dresden for the autumn, he was also visited by Spohr, there for a court concert before leaving for England. The major part of the autumn that he could spare from the theatre was given to work on *Der*

Ex. 44

Freischütz (still provisionally known as *Die Jägersbraut*). Act I was finished on 30th November, and by 6th December Weber was able to write to Brühl with the promise that the whole work would be ready by March. But on the 21st came a disappointing answer from Berlin: the new Berlin Schauspiel-haus was to be opened not by Weber's opera but a work of Goethe's; the new opera would, however, be the first musical piece. He continued up to the 20th, then breaking off until the following February. He spent a happy Christmas with Caroline and his friends, writing them verses to go with their presents and appearing in a masque. His diary for the year closes, 'So the year that has brought so many sorrows has ended gaily. May God continue his blessings; thanks and praise to Him for the strength to bear His trials.'

The New Year of 1820 began hopefully with, amid all the official exchanges of greeting, a pacific letter from Morlacchi. Weber responded cordially; but the truce was brief, and broken by Weber. When he produced Meyerbeer's *Emma di Resburgo* in Italian on 26th January, ahead of a production of *Alimelek* on 22nd February, he preceded them with articles in the *Abendzei-tung* on 21st and 22nd January regretting Meyerbeer's Italianization with some force: 'There must be something seriously wrong with the digestive powers of Italian stomachs for a genius of such original powers as Meyerbeer to have felt it necessary, not merely to have set nothing but sweet, luxuriantly swollen fruit on the table, but also to have sugared it over in this fashion-manner.'[1] The Italians were up in arms about the alleged attack on their artistic honour, and violent sides were taken. Einsiedel tried to play the affair down, and succeeded in placating Weber somewhat without losing the loyalty of the Italian faction. In the middle of this upsetting affair, Caroline miscarried; Weber was to some extent consoled by the attentions of his friends, and by visits from Anton Fürstenau, Hummel, and Mozart's younger son Franz Xaver, a fellow-pupil of Vogler. It was Hummel's visit which led to an evening at the palace of Prince Friedrich in which Weber gave the first public hearing of the *Freischütz* music, the Agathe-Aennchen duet. He was also visited by his villainous ex-groom from Stuttgart days, Huber, now down on his luck; without mentioning the matter to Caroline, Weber gave the man clothes and money. In gratitude for producing their son's operas, the Beer family sent a handsome pair of silver candlesticks which they had heard Weber coveted; but his scruples about receiving a reward for producing an opera from its composer's relatives compelled him to insist, twice, on the gift being returned. A further difficulty arose over Caroline's singing lessons with Johann Miksch, who Weber thought was forcing her voice too high; but the quarrel did not prevent him appointing Miksch, with great success, as chorus master of the opera that summer. A happier incident was the granting of permission through Vitzthum's succes-sor, Hans Heinrich von Könneritz, for Weber's plan for reseating the

[1] Kaiser 140.

orchestra over which there had originally been so much trouble. But from 22nd February his energies were concentrated on finishing *Der Freischütz*. On 13th May he was able to record, 'Overture to *Die Jägersbraut* finished and with it the whole opera. God be praised and to Him all the honour.'

No convenient repertory catalogue to match that of the Prague years exists to cover Weber's Dresden period. But evidence from his diary and letters and from old theatre bills in the Dresden archives build up the picture of a repertory that was very similar—heroically so, given the nature of the Dresden audience. Even in the three and one third years he had so far spent in the town, he had managed against all setbacks to exercise some influence on taste, compelled though he was to accept many compromises. The lack of good singers, still more the undeveloped Dresden taste that leaned on vaudevilles, farces and melodramas for entertainment in the vernacular made for greater difficulties. There were, in any case, only about twenty serious German operas on stages anywhere. But apart from his own *Freischütz* and *Euryanthe* in subsequent years, Weber was able to produce *Lodoïska*, *Faniska*, *Les Deux Journées*, *Héléna*, *Fidelio*, *Jessonda*, Weigl's *Die Schweitzerfamilie*, Winter's *Das unterbrochene Opferfest*, as well as Mozart's *Clemenza di Tito*, *Figaro*, *Seraglio*, *The Magic Flute* and *Don Giovanni*. Statistics for 1817–21 are unavailable; but those for 1822–26 show that 68% of the prèmieres were of German works, there being very little demand for repeats: Italian works averaged fifteen performances, German ones seven—soon discovered to be the maximum number of times a German work could be repeated without a sharp drop in receipts.

In the poor conditions in which he was obliged to work, Weber's responsibility as Director was naturally the greater. He took upon himself even more attention to detail than at Prague, looking after planning, casting, production, costumes, scenery, even lighting. His rehearsal schedule was exhaustive. It would begin with a *Leseprobe*, at which he would read the text to the assembled cast, explaining details and points of meaning, and acting out the drama so vividly that at the Vienna rehearsals of *Euryanthe* he was jokingly offered a permanent job by the impressed stage manager. Next would come *Zimmerproben*, private rehearsals with the singers, such as are now delegated to répétiteurs. He would normally follow these with two *Setzproben*—not the same as the modern *Sitzprobe* at which the singers sit on the stage singing from scores, but a placing rehearsal in which the *mis-en-scène* was translated into action and tableau. Lastly would come two to four *Generalproben* or Dress Rehearsals. The fewest number of rehearsals he ever managed with was three for Dalayrac's *Adolphe et Clara*; Spontini's *Olimpie* took twenty-three, and the average was ten to fifteen for a major work, five to seven for a smaller one.

This elaborate rehearsal pattern was the practical realization of the very firm theories about the nature of German opera which Weber had now consolidated. The importance he attached to the *Leseprobe* arose from his belief that it set in the participants' minds the essential meaning and spirit of the work that was to be realized with all the available theatrical means, and that the existence of this was the basic characteristic of German opera. He was fond of comparing his work with that of a painter, who might paint the same landscape at different seasons and different times of day, marking the essential difference with a character that was immediately appreciable. This was more than a convenient metaphor: he took up the Dresden fondness for including set tableaux and made them a structural feature of his productions, conceiving them as part of the design to heighten the text at certain points instead of purely as decorative visual groupings for their own sake. His décor he saw as mobile painting, playing a similarly precise expressive function, not merely as naturalistic furnishing. Much importance was attached to the visual side altogether as a conveyor of meaning; and his descriptions turn naturally towards comments about singers 'portraying' their roles with 'fine brush-strokes' or 'like a fresco'. Having a poor opinion of singers' intelligence, however easily he made friends with them, he attempted to improve their understanding of their roles by appointing in 1825 a *Literator* (what we should now call a *Dramaturg*) in the person of Ludwig Tieck, charged with the task of attending rehearsals, instructing singers in meanings and the pronunciation of foreign words, supervising the accurate portrayal of character and costume and reading new pieces submitted to the theatre. The novel idea failed not through any want of enthusiasm on Tieck's part, especially for reading the texts to his cast, but because he was no man of the theatre. Weber also appointed Miksch as chorus master, setting a new importance upon the role of the chorus. His friend Ignaz Mosel, vice-director of the Vienna Hoftheater, had observed that most choruses seemed to think their work done if they got *piano* and *forte* right; and the producer seldom troubled them with much more than standing them in either a line or a semi-circle. Weber believed that if they understood their parts properly they could be one of the crucial elements in the drama. The solo singers he attempted to deflect from their position as personalities answerable only to their God and their larynx into portrayals of the good or evil principle in the plot—a strongly moralistic concept that played an important part in his designs for opera and influenced the shaping of his own characters. But he asked that these distinctions should be made by subtler means than merely dressing villains in black or spotlighting virtuous heroines, and also made expressive use of contrast between a noble exterior and inner corruption, as in the case of Lysiart. He fastened with delight on the arrival in his company of Wilhemine Schröder (later Schröder-Devrient), whose Fidelio was to rouse the young Wagner to a sense of vocation as a composer. Her whole-hearted projection into her roles, which she always conceived from the start as dramatic rather purely vocal, won as much enthusiasm from Weber as hostility from the Dresden critics, who regarded it as a breach of good manners when she was seen to be actually weeping on the stage (she later became known in London as 'The Queen of Tears'). This preference for dramatic expression over vocal or even musical perfection was intensely sympathetic to Weber, who objected to the refined bass Franz Siebert, insisting that Caspar should be acted rather than sung, and went so far as to declare over *Euryanthe*, 'She who cannot sing the last passages of Eglantine's aria with blazing fire had better simplify the music so that the passion of the whole number is not chilled.'[1] His violent distaste for meaningless ornamentation was sharply brought home to his bass Genast, who once dared to put a small Italianate flourish into a phrase during *Joseph*. Catching sight of Weber's face, he rushed to his dressing-room on leaving the stage so as to change and get away from the theatre, but was caught still in beard and wig by Weber, who shouted, 'What was that stupid thing for? Don't you think that if Méhul had wanted that kind of *Schnickschnack* he'd have done it better than you? I won't stand for it! Do you understand? Good night, and sleep off your Italian frenzy.'[2]

Weber's care for detail extended to the lighting. Up to the rebuilding of the Hoftheater in 1821 and the replacing of the old stage machinery, this was by oil and candle. The new Argand lamps, named after a London maker who had invented them in 1783, used a cylindrical wick and glass that gave a clear flame without smoke, thus at once showing up the poor state of the torn and sooty old scenery and giving Weber a new range of visual effect. In all that he introduced into theatrical currency in these ways, he demanded above all clarity and simplicity in delineating the essential meaning of the work in hand. Though Weber never lived to have a free hand in an opera house with proper resources, there is no doubt that even in their limited application his theories were an astonishingly advanced sign of much that was to happen in the European theatre of the next hundred years and even beyond. While he did not make use of the term *Gesamtkunstwerk*, his rallying of all the arts into a new unity brought into the theatre what was already good Romantic theory. As early as 1797, Wackenroder's *Herzensergiessungen eines kunstliebenden Klosterbruders*, one of the sacred writings of the Romantic movement, had proposed a new aesthetic. Art, in reaction to the tidiness and materialism of the Enlightenment, was seen as divine revelation—a language of the soul requiring a devout approach from artist and audience alike, variously expressed but essentially an indivisible entity nationally orientated. Closely associated with Wackenroder in this and other enterprises was Tieck, who had settled in Dresden in 1819 and whose direct influence upon Weber is more obviously observed in his folk tales in which human beings fall victim to mysterious supernatural forces, often against the background

[1] Kaiser 151.
[2] Eduard Genast: *op. cit.*, Vol. 2, pp. 23–4 (1862).

of a curiously ambiguous relationship with nature; and in tales such as *Genoveva* which take their colour from the Romantic fascination with mediaeval chivalry.[1] Weber had already in his Munich days come powerfully under the spell of the philosopher of the Romantic movement, Schelling, with his view of Nature and Spirit as two aspects of a *Weltseele*—Nature as visible Spirit, and Spirit invisible Nature. In art Schelling had found the ideal fusion of the two, 'the infinite, finitely described'—a radical difference from the eighteenth century's careful distinction between man and nature.

It was Schelling who impressed Goethe with his description of architecture as 'frozen music', and in the new century's atmosphere of the arts drawing closer together in a mystical relationship, such contacts were keenly cultivated. Weber, as we have seen, was at pains to indicate the visual and narrative elements in his music as it contributed to a theatrical whole. It is quite possible that his comparison of his orchestral methods with the different atmosphere given by a painter to the same landscape at different seasons and times of the day derived from the work of the two leading painters of German Romanticism, both of whom had been established at Dresden. Philipp Otto Runge (1777–1810) had learned much from Tieck's promptings as to the place of poetry and music in painting, and the unity of God, Man and Nature in art, in turn influencing Tieck and Brentano with his illustrations; he saw his *Vier Tageszeiten*, with their images of Nature's growth and decay, as symbols of Christian redemption, paraphrasing them with verses and even intending to exhibit them in a Gothic temple to the accompaniment of suitable music. Caspar David Friedrich (1774–1840), the greatest of his generation, had also painted a cycle on the hours of the day and the seasons and at the same time the ages of man. Settled in Dresden from 1798, he was appointed to the Academy in 1816 and made Professor in 1825; his landscapes, predominantly autumnal or wintry and set in moonlight, mist or twilight, project his own melancholy vision on to a scene—often, as in the strange *Moon Rising over the Sea* of 1823, by the device of watchers in the foreground with backs turned to us. His *Felsenschlucht* might be a stage design for the Wolf's Glen. It was he who developed a method of painting which ideally expressed the Romantic attitude to nature; and this places him above the innumerable lesser figures of the movement. Their work in all its variety has in common a receptivity to literary influences. As Sir Kenneth Clark has observed, 'even when Romantic pictures do not actually illustrate a story, visual experience is coloured with thoughts and memories of a kind more usually expressed in words.'[2] Wackenroder, Tieck and Schlegel were the most direct local literary influences in Dresden; yet their own writings, as with those of so many of their contemporaries, in turn

---

[1] His version was one of the sources of Schumann's only opera, which is profoundly influenced by *Euryanthe*.

[2] *The Romantic Movement*: catalogue to the 1959 Arts Council Exhibition, p. 18.

looked to music as the condition to which all art aspired. Tieck's own poem
Liebe defined their attitude in famous lines:

> Liebe denkt in süssen Tönen,
> Denn Gedanken stehn zu fern,
> Nur in Tönen mag sie gern
> Alles, was sie will, verschönen.

Schlegel, Jean Paul, Novalis and Wackenroder were among those leaders
of the Romantic movement who shared his view that music was the truest
and most expressive language of Romantic feeling. It has often been pointed
out that Classicism was by tendency plastic, perceiving through the eye,
whereas Romanticism was musical, needing above all the power of music in
the ambitious synthesis of intellect and feeling it attempted.[1]

Considering Romanticism's instinctive association with the political
movement towards national unity, the inert atmosphere of Dresden might
seem an unlikely background for its leading musician. But Romanticism
took much of its fire from being in revolt, and it seems probable that the
irksome tensions of Dresden, to which Weber remained bound in the face
of other offers for a full nine years, were also fruitful in forcing upon him the
sense of artistic solitariness in the face of *Philistertum* which the Romantic
ego needed to feel. In its political structure and its everyday life, Dresden
presented almost a caricature of the formal, routine-governed pre-Revolu-
tionary society against which the revolt of individual instincts that is the
essence of the Romantic movement could be more sharply felt. It was this,
at least as much as the pastoral beauty of the countryside with its Romantically
'unspoiled' Rousseauesque peasantry and the charm of the ancient town, that
made it a centre for the Romantic school of painting, and attracted Romantic
writers and provided the stimulus to a composer of Weber's complex make-
up. To reach universal significance, *Der Freischütz* needed performance in
the intellectually alert atmosphere of Berlin; but for its actual creation, the
provincial country surroundings of Dresden were more congenial.

---

[1] For a full and authoritative discussion of these questions, which can here only be
touched on, see L. A. Willoughby: *The Romantic Movement in Germany* (1930), especially
Chapters 1 and 12.

CHAPTER ELEVEN

DER FREISCHÜTZ

Barely touched by the wand of the magician Weber, the realistic and natural scene for the most German of melodramas assumes a grace and freshness, a mystery even worthy of Shakespearian fantasy.

CLAUDE DEBUSSY, to ROBERT GODET
(*The Chesterian*—June 1926)

THE ORIGIN of the legend of the marksman who makes a pact with the powers of evil to obtain bullets that will go wherever he chooses is long lost—if indeed any origin exists outside the wishful thinking of the poor shot and rivals' jealousy for the good shot. Though it occurs in Scandinavia and Africa, it is naturally most prevalent in Central Europe, whose vast, game-filled forests have been the source of an endlessly rich folklore—the friend-enemy, provider-destroyer, mother-betrayer for Germans that the sea has immemorially been for shore-dwelling Celts.

The first historical mention of the kind of incident that was well-known in story occurs in the famous treatise against witchcraft published in 1484 by Jakob Sprenger and Heinrich Krämer, the *Malleus Malleficarum*.[1] Here is recorded the tale of an archer who was found near the castle of Hohenzorn, in the diocese of Constance, standing paralysed before a bleeding wayside crucifix at which he had shot in the belief that he would thereby obtain three or four arrows he could guide at will. Other references soon begin to mount up: an early one (1529) is the story of the Landsknecht Melchior Hauser who found a monk in Hungary using three or four such arrows a day. The term *Freischütz*, litterally a Freeshooter, seems to occur in writing first over the trial at Rostock in 1586 of Hans Cröpelin and Cersten Sasse for attempting to forge *Freikugeln*, or free-bullets. Other attempts are documented, and certain common elements in the story begin to emerge. Various dates are possible—Midsummer's Day or *Abdonstag* (30th July, the Day of Oaths) are usual—and various conditions, but two methods of obtaining the bullets are most frequently mentioned. One, as in the *Malleus*, involves the blasphemy of shooting at a crucifix, a picture of Our Lord, or the Host. More complicated rites attend the process of nocturnal casting, sometimes by use of the skull of a woman who has died in childbirth, so as to cast through the eyeholes bullets made of lead stolen from a church; elaborate and unpleasant *Macbeth*-like recipes for powder are also mentioned. Most accounts require

[1] *Malleus Maleficarum*, II, I, xvi (1484).

the casting to take place by night at a crossroads, when it will be accompanied by the sound of tears or a sinister rumbling, possibly a red devil, the clatter of evil birds and other apparitions. The resultant bullets can not merely be guided, even when shooting blind out of a window; they can turn a cat up the chimney into a hare, and will shoot a named person many miles away. Even the Devil himself flying through the air is not safe. But the Freeshooter cannot go to church, and will be shunned by his fellow men. The Devil may turn a bullet on him, and his end, always horrible, is the preface to his reappearance from his mysteriously opened coffin as a ghost, forever hunting.[1]

One of the references to attempts to get *Freikugeln* names an eighteen-year-old clerk, Georg Schmid, who is said to have been tried in 1710 for blasphemously casting bullets. The place of his trial is usually given as Taus, now Domažlice in Czechoslovakia; but the local records for that period have perished. At all events, his case became sufficiently well known for it to be included in the fifth discussion in a series that originally appeared monthly in 1729–30, and subsequently in three volumes in 1730, the *Unterredungen von der Reiche der Geister* by Otto von Graben zum Stein. The fifth of these discussions between Andrenio and Pneumatophilo, 'Von den Luft- und Feuergeisten', turns on the possibility of spirits taking earthly form and controlling the elements or making pacts with humans. Pneumatophilo is convinced of it, and to prove his point tells the story of Georg Schmid.

> Keen to profit by good marksmanship, Schmid agrees to go with an old mountain huntsman to a crossroads on 30th July to cast sixty-three magic bullets: sixty will succeed, three (it is not known which) will miss. The huntsman draws a circle and various indecipherable characters with his hunting knife, and tells Schmid to strip naked and deny his God and the Trinity, above all to make haste since Satan will claim him if the work is not done by midnight. He must also keep silent, whatever happens. At eleven o'clock the coals begin to glow mysteriously; an old woman appears, hung about with ladles which she tries to sell him. Then carriages drive like the storm-wind over his head. After the Wild Hunt, a rider on a black horse asks what he wants: the huntsman answers, 'We have cast sixty-three bullets in your name; three of them belong to you, the others you must give us.' When the rider is then refused the ladle and the bullets, he grinds his teeth and throws over the bullets something that causes such a terrible stench that the two men fall half-dead, remaining thus until dawn. The huntsman recovers first, takes the bullets and hurries to the nearest village to tell the inhabitants that a poor man is lying in the woods on the road; he then makes off for the Salzburg mountains. The half-dead clerk is taken to the town and under examination admits all. He is sentenced to be beheaded and burned; on grounds of youth this is commuted to six years' imprisonment.

Friedrich Kind gives his version of how he and Johann August Apel came

---

[1] For full details and references, see *Handwörterbuch des deutschen Aberglaubens* (1930–1).

upon this tale in his *Freischützbuch* (1843), a pathetically vainglorious piece of work that includes, with his original full libretto and various other items, a semi-fictitious account of its origins. Kind was born of a Leipzig legal family on 4th March 1768, and as a boy shared the general fascination with the *Thousand and One Nights* and with *Robinson Crusoe*, the translation of which had fired eighteenth-century German writers to a host of imitative *Robinsonaden*. But his bent was more towards the gruesome and fantastic, like that of Apel, born in the same town on 17th September 1771 and a student of music (he played the piano and glass armonica) as well as of science, theology and law. According to Kind, when they were fellow-students at the Thomasschule in the 1780s they delighted in poring over old books, and in the Ratsbibliothek came upon 'a browning, dusty quarto'— Kind tactfully could not remember which—where they found the story of Georg Schmid. Kind's motive in telling the story is clearly to suggest that this, and not the *Gespensterbuch* of 1810 which Apel went on to write with Friedrich Laun (Friedrich August Schulze), was the original of his libretto— in fact, to cut Apel out of the honour which he desperately sought for himself over the one success of his literary career. (When Count Brühl urged that the title of the opera should revert to that of the original tale, *Der Freischütz*, it was Kind who made objections). But the facts do not support him. The *Unterredungen* are actually not Quarto but Octavo: this might well be a slip of the memory, were it not that enquiries have shown that the book was never in the catalogue of the Ratsbibliothek. Apel did, however, at some time acquire a private copy, still in the possession of his family, as did Laun. When—as the outcome of a series of *Gespenster-Thees*, so Laun tells in his memoirs[1]—they collaborated on their *Gespensterbuch*, they worked up the tale of Georg Schmid as the first in their opening volume, and called it *Der Freischütz*.

Käthchen, daughter of the ranger Bertram and his wife Anne in Lindenhayn, against her father's wishes plans to marry the clerk Wilhelm instead of the huntsman Robert; but when Wilhelm agrees to become a huntsman, thus continuing the two-hundred-year-old line, Bertram promises to make another Kuno of him. His great-grandfather Kuno, he explains, was hunting one day with his master, the Junker von Wippach, when they saw a stag with a man bound to his back, a punishment for poachers. At the Count's order, Kuno managed to shoot the stag leaving the man unharmed, and was awarded the ranger's cottage in perpetuity. But envious voices said he had used a *Freischuss*, so it was decided that each new inheritant must make a *Probeschuss*, or shooting trial: Bertram had to shoot the ring from the beak of a wooden bird swinging from a pole. Bertram grows fond of Wilhelm, and gives his secret consent to the marriage; but meanwhile Wilhelm has been shooting badly, hitting trees and the wrong birds, even a dead cat and a herdsman with his cow. The ranger's boy Rudolf declares that it is not natural, and suggests going one

---

[1] Friedrich Laun: *Memoiren* (1837).

Friday night to a crossroads, drawing a circle with a ramrod or a bloody dagger and making a cross three times in the name of Sammiel.[1] Bertram angrily points out that Sammiel is one of Satan's host, and Wilhelm wants to hear no more. But in the morning he misses a stag at ten paces, twice his gun misfires, and once the game he hits disappears unharmed. He meets an old soldier with a wooden leg who declares his gun is bewitched, needing magic bullets to counteract the sorcery. He gives one to Wilhelm, who brings down with it a vulture that was but a speck in the sky. As seven strikes, he goes, leaving Wilhelm a handful of the magic bullets.

Wilhelm pretends that his better luck is due to a fault he had cured in his gun, but is alarmed to learn that the picture of Kuno in the house has fallen down on the stroke of seven. He tries in vain to save the bullets for his *Probeschuss*, but soon only two are left. These he has to use to fulfil an order from the castle for venison; he catches a glimpse of the soldier when shooting the deer, but cannot then find him after the last bullet has gone. He listens miserably that evening to Bertram's tale to Rudolf of Georg Schmid (briefly told at this point). Wilhelm asks what Schmid did wrong, and is told that he was frightened by the apparitions into jumping out of the circle, at which he was half torn to pieces by the Devil's claws. Bertram warns Wilhelm against the use of such bullets.

After a disturbed night, Wilhelm wrestles with his conscience in the woods, arguing that if man can rule the animals, why should he not control dead metal? Failing to find the soldier, he decides to make his own bullets. But that night the ranger is upset and insists that Wilhelm stay with him; and the next evening Wilhelm has an unexpected visit from his uncle. The third night is the last before the trial. Despite the omen of Kuno's picture again falling, wounding Käthchen on the forehead, Wilhelm sets out with the excuse that he has forgotten some game in the forest. Though he has drunk enough to give him courage, he is alarmed by the sinister aspect of the forest and hesitates. But going on, he comes to the crossroads, draws the circle and lays out skull and bones, putting into the pot three bullets that had found their mark. Bats, owls and other night creatures begin to flutter round the light, soon joined by more mysterious forms, wavering like mist with sorrowful gestures. He sees the sad face of his dead mother. Amid the rattle of bones and the croaking and hooting of birds, on the stroke of eleven he casts the first bullet. Up the road comes an old bent hag who tries to trade a spoon for the bones. A carriage with lightning flickering round the horses' hooves and phosphorus at the wheels drives at him, passing overhead; a boar follows. He thinks the time up, but it is a false alarm. Then he sees Käthchen fleeing the hag, with the soldier barring her way; he shoots and is about to jump out of the circle when midnight strikes and the scene fades. A form on a black horse rides up, but Wilhelm refuses his request for three of the sixty-three bullets—'Jene treffen,

[1] Samael (Sammael) is a demon prince in Jewish legend, the destroyer in Talmudic and post-Talmudic literature whose name means 'venom of God'; he is perhaps connected to the Syrian god Shemal or, thinks Kind, derives from the Turkish Semum or Samum, a destructive south wind. Prominent in Jewish mythology, he commands an army of demons and seeks to shame men. See *Jewish Encyclopaedia*, Vol. 10 (1895).

diese äffen' ('those hit, these deceive') observes the figure, parting with a promise that they will meet again.

Next morning Käthchen is alarmed by Wilhelm's corpse-like appearance. The ranger feels he must have seen something in the woods, but agrees not to press for an answer for nine days. When the Count's party arrives, they insist on going first with Wilhelm into the woods. Bertram is worried, Käthchen goes about the house as if in a dream. The Parson comes and reminds Käthchen about her wreath; Anne has locked it up and in her haste jammed the lock, so a child is sent for another, the best the wreath-maker can provide. Misunderstanding, the wreath-maker sends a funeral wreath, which frightens both the women. The lock to the real wreath is now found to work.

When the hunting party returns, all are full of praise for Wilhelm and regard his trial as a mere formality. He is invited to shoot a dove on a post, but Käthchen stops him, crying that she dreamt last night that she was a dove. Urged to shoot by the others, Wilhelm fires and Käthchen falls to the ground with a shriek, her forehead shattered by a bullet still in the wound. Wilhelm turns to see her lying in her own blood, with the lame soldier standing behind her laughing, 'Sechzig treffen, drei äffen'. Drawing his dagger he hurls himself forward, but falls senseless over his bride. The Parson and Huntmaster try to console the parents, but hardly has Anne laid the prophetic funeral wreath on her daughter than she too expires. Bertram follows her soon to the grave. Wilhelm ends his days in the madhouse.

There are several important new elements in this improved version of the story in the *Unterredungen*, chiefly the alteration of motive from simple gain on Schmid's part to love for Käthchen on Wilhelm's, and the introduction of a *Probeschuss*. Whether the latter was Apel and Laun's invention cannot be said: as Apel loved old hunting books and was himself a huntsman, he may well have taken up some hint. The *Gespensterbuch* was instantly popular in an age that could not have too many tales of folklore and the supernatural, not least with Weber himself, as we have seen; and the opening *Volkssage* of the book, *Der Freischütz*, was promptly turned into a 'romantic tragedy in four acts', *Der Freyschütze*, by Franz Xaver von Caspar, with music by Carl Neuner. The first version (Munich 1812; a second, five-act version of 1813 had a tragic dénouement) had a happy ending brought about by the redeeming love of Pauline (=Käthchen) for Wilhelm and by the intervention of a Hermit, thus routing the power of Abadonna (=Sammiel) Further similarities between Caspar's play and Kind's libretto lie in the development of Pauline as a character and Abadonna as a force for evil, with Robert as his tool and go-between, to balance the Hermit's force for good; and in quite a few details of the setting. There is, indeed, enough correspondence with Kind's libretto to arouse suspicions.[1] Certainly Caspar sent his play to Kind after the appearance of Weber's opera, and received a courteous

[1] These have been fully discussed, with Caspar's complete text printed, by Gottfried Mayerhofer: *Abermals vom Freischützen* (1959).

if somewhat lofty reply remarking on the manner in which they had reached similar conclusions by a different route—Kind points out that he felt the old hag to be too comic for the situation, for instance, but acknowledges the kinship of Robert and his own Caspar. Weber knew that the subject had already been dramatized, and there is at the very least a strong likelihood that he mentioned this to Kind, who then used both Caspar and Apel as his source. If he ever heard it, Weber may even have been unconsciously influenced himself by Neuner's music, which makes copious use of dances for the village folk (Neuner was best known as a ballet composer), is lively if unsubtle and has an overture whose opening bars could easily stand behind the invention of his own far superior work:

Ex. 45

NEUNER: Overture, *Der Freyschütze* (1812)

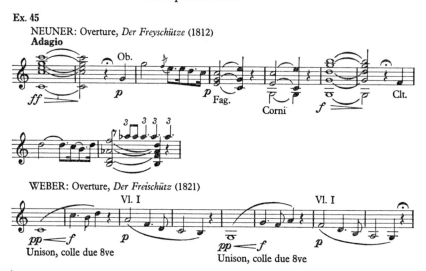

WEBER: Overture, *Der Freischütz* (1821)

Other versions followed. On 20th November 1816 at the Leopoldstheater in Vienna the tale was given (without much success) as *Der Freyschütze, romantische-komische Volkssage mit Gesang nach Laun bearbeitet* by Ferdinand Rosenau; and on 28th December this was followed in the Theater in der Josephstadt by *Der Freyschütze, Schauspiel mit Gesang in drey Aufzügen* by Aloys Gleich, with music by Franz Roser—its humorous parts kept this alive until 1828. A five-act tragedy by Count von Riesch was also produced on 17th August 1821.

Whatever Kind's debts to his predecessors, he responded to the story with a certain acumen. By transferring the time to the period of the Thirty Years' War, he avoided the possible accusation of placing superstitious practices before a rational modern audience; the setting 'in the Bohemian forest' further strengthens the connexion with the remote event of Georg Schmid. Even if he took the conflation of the lame soldier and Rudolf as his Caspar, and the introduction of the Hermit and other details, from Franz von Caspar, other changes are original. Apel's Mutter Anne becomes the soubrette Aennchen, a part eagerly welcomed by a composer who saw his bride as just such a figure; the number of bullets naturally has to be reduced from sixty-three to seven; the bridesmaids, the huntsmen[1] and the figure of Kilian are introduced; and the comparatively ordinary crossroads becomes one of the most famous inventions of Romantic opera, the Wolf's Glen, the legendary abyss in the depths of the *Urwald* where lurks everything vile and horrifying and evil.[2] From his first literary work, *Leonardo's Schwärmereien* (1793), Kind took the words for his chorus of spirits in the Glen; and in pursuit of his avowed attempt to strengthen the moral content of the work, he put uplifting sentiments into the mouth of the Hermit—'Guard the purity of your hearts'—and introduced him in two brief opening scenes.

Weber readily agreed with Caroline when she urged that these should be abandoned in favour of an opening on the crowded village merry-making. Citing Goethe's opening of *Egmont* on a crowd scene in Brussels and Schiller's of *Wilhelm Tell* in the Swiss countryside, he declared it a good maxim to set the scene of the action immediately before the audience—the matters in the exchanges between Agathe and the Hermit could emerge in subsequent conversation with Aennchen.[3] Kind was never convinced, and printed the missing scenes in his *Freischützbuch*. They show the Hermit interrupted in prayer by a fearful vision of a fiend clutching at a lamb; Agathe, whom the lamb represents, then appears with provisions for him, reporting Max's anxiety about the coming *Probeschuss*, and is given, for her protection from evil, roses from a tree the Hermit's predecessor had brought from Palestine; they join their voices in a pious duet. Though Weber never composed these scenes, an attempt was made to repair his omission in 1871 by Oskar Mörike, who set them to music based on themes from the opera: this was included in a production at Lübeck on 3rd November 1893. More recently, Gustav Rudolf Sellner's Berlin production (May 1966) restores the essence of the scenes as a brief spoken introduction; and W. H. Auden and Chester Kallman have contemplated a new version of the text to include the opening scenes. But as it stands, Weber's opera makes a satisfying structure without them.

> Act 1: After the Overture, the curtain rises on a clearing in the Bohemian forest before an inn; with his last shot, the peasant Kilian (bar.) wins a competition and is congratulated by the villagers (No. 1, Introduction: 'Victoria,

[1] A chorus of Huntsmen occurs in Paul Umlauff's *Die Bergknappen* (1778): and the Wild Hunt, together with scenery and other incidents and the somewhat unstable hero's redemption by her love, may have been taken from C. F. Bretzner's *Singspiel* to Johann André's music, *Das wütende Heer*.

[2] Vividly described by Wagner in the first of his articles for the *Gazette Musicale*, 23rd and 30th May 1841, translated for his *Gesammelte Schriftungen und Dichtungen*, Vol. 1 (1871).

[3] J. C. Lobe: *Gespräche mit Weber*, in *Fliegende Blätter für Musik*, Vol. 1 (1853).

Victoria'). Max, a forester (ten.), can barely conceal his fury and anxiety as the villagers form a procession (*Bauern-Marsch*) and mock Max as they pass, Kilian, with the backing of sneering laughter from the chorus, being especially contemptuous ('Schau der Herr mich an als König'). Max leaps angrily at Kilian, but the fracas is interrupted by the arrival of Cuno, Prince Ottokar's Head Ranger (bass), with some of his men, including Caspar (bass). Kilian protests that they were only giving Max the customary teasing for having missed every shot—at which Caspar mutters thanks to Samiel. Aloud, he opines that Max's gun must be bewitched and that he had better go next Friday to a crossroads, draw a circle round him with a ramrod or a bloody dagger and call upon the Great Huntsman. He is silenced with a sharp reproof by Cuno, who nevertheless feels obliged to warn Max that if he fails at the trial tomorrow, he will be refused the hand of Agathe, Cuno's daughter. To the enquiring huntsmen Cuno now tells the story (as in Apel) of his ancestor and the man bound to the stag, including the addition of the test by a shooting trial, before dismissing Max until sunrise. But Max is still depressed and (No. 2, Terzett mit Chor: 'O! diese Sonne') despairs of his good fortune; while Cuno warns him, Caspar urges a bold move, and the chorus try to encourage him before joining in praise to the open-air life of the huntsman. When they have gone, Kilian observes how dark and sinister the evening has grown, and wishing Max good luck for tomorrow urges him to find a girl and join the dance. When they have danced off, Max muses on his former happiness and success, now mysteriously removed, perhaps by dark powers—in the distance the watching figure of Samiel is seen (No. 3, Walzer [and Aria]: 'Nein! länger trag' ich nicht die Qualen'—'Durch die Wälder'). Caspar returns and orders wine for Max, secretly slipping something into his glass; Max's refusal is overridden by Caspar's insistence that they should drink toasts to the Head Ranger, Agathe and the Prince, between which he sings three verses whose earthiness upsets the highminded Max (No. 4, Lied: 'Hier im ird'schen Jammerthal'). It being now just seven, Max tries to make for home and Agathe, but stops when Caspar suggests that he might be able to help his shooting. He hands Max his rifle, and bids him shoot at a barely visible bird; as Max does so, a wild laugh rings out, he hears a noise on high like the wings of Hell, and a great eagle falls at their feet. The astonished Max is told that he was using a *Freikugel*, and learning it was the last, reluctantly agrees to meet Caspar in the Wolf's Glen at midnight to cast more, meanwhile to keep silence. Alone, Caspar sings of Max's impending doom and his own triumph (No. 5, Aria: 'Schweig! Schweig!').

Act 2: In the Chief Ranger's forest house, Aennchen (sop.) is cheerfully abusing the picture of Cuno which has fallen from its nail and hurt Agathe (sop.) who is prey to dismal fancies (No. 6, Duett: 'Schelm! Halt fest!'). Agathe is more frightened than hurt, and worried about Max's absence; Aennchen agrees that it is lonely with only themselves and the picture of an old gentleman—she prefers lithe young men and knows how to attract them (No. 7, Ariette: 'Kommt ein schlanker Bursch gegangen'). This cheers up Agathe, who has been gloomy since visiting the Hermit that morning, despite his gift of roses. Meanwhile, with Max's unexplained absence, she is sleepless, and prays to the tranquil light, which is troubled only by distant thunder, for his quick return; to her joy she sees him coming (No. 8, Szene und Arie: 'Wie nahte mir der Schlummer'—'Leise, leise'). But Max is wearing the eagle's plumes instead of the victory trophy, and though upset to find Agathe wounded by the picture falling at exactly seven o'clock, declares he must go out again to fetch a stag he has shot by the Wolf's Glen. Anxiety ensues (No. 9, Terzett: 'Wie? Was? Entsetzen!'), Agathe trying to restrain Max, Aennchen trying to comfort Agathe, Max trying to get away.

In the fearsome Wolf's Glen, Caspar is making a circle of boulders round a skull, a crucible, a bullet mould and an eagle's wing; while invisible spirit voices sing of the coming victims (No. 10, Finale: 'Milch des Mondes'), he lifts the skull on his dagger and as midnight sounds calls on Samiel (speaker), who agrees to accept Max as exchange for Caspar: he suggests that Samiel direct the seventh bullet, Samiel's own, on Agathe. Max arrives, filled with foreboding; he sees visions of his mother and then Agathe, but agrees to help Caspar, who now puts into the crucible lead, broken glass from a church window, quicksilver, three bullets that have found their mark, and the eyes of a hoopoe and a lynx. As he calls on Samiel, the crucible glows; each casting is accompanied by an echo as he calls out the number, and by apparitions— first flapping nightbirds, secondly a black boar, thirdly a hurricane, fourthly the cracking of whips and trampling of horses and fiery wheels, fifthly the Wild Hunt, sixthly thunder, lightning, hail, meteors and fire from the earth, and seventhly Samiel himself—as Caspar falls senseless to the ground, Samiel reaches a hand towards Max, and the clock strikes one.

Act 3: An Entre-Act (No. 11) introduces the sounds of hunting horns in chorus before the curtain rises on a forest scene. Two huntsmen comment on the glorious weather after the terrible storm of the night before over the Wolf's Glen; they greet Max, whose shooting that morning has been faultless. Alone with Caspar, Max, having had to fire three shots, asks for more bullets than the four Caspar gave him, but is refused; knowing that the seventh bullet belongs to Samiel, by covertly shooting a fox Caspar makes Max's remaining bullet the seventh.

In her room, Agathe is praying in her wedding dress, trusting to God (No. 12, Cavatine: 'Und ob die Wolke'). She has dreamed that she was a white dove; Max shot at her and she fell, but then the dove vanished, she was Agathe again and a great black bird lay bleeding instead. Aennchen tries to interpret this as coming from her white wedding dress and Max's eagle feathers; then, to dispel Agathe's fears that dreams may come true, she tells the tale of her cousin who dreamed of a terrible ghost with fiery eyes and rattling chain that turned out to be the dog (No. 13, Romanze und Arie: 'Einste träumte'). The Bridesmaids arrive and sing their song (No. 14, Volkslied: 'Wir winden dir den Jungfernkranz'); but Aennchen returns with news that Cuno's picture has again fallen, and the box she brings turns out to contain a funeral wreath. Even she is shaken, but agrees to Agathe's suggestion that they make a new one from the Hermit's roses.

In a romantic landscape, Prince Ottokar (bar.) and his retinue are seated at a table listening to the huntsmen singing of the joys of their life (No. 15, Jägerchor: 'Was gleicht wohl auf Erden'). He interrupts to hold the shooting trial, at Cuno's request before the bride arrives, and tells Max to shoot at a white dove on a bough; but as he takes aim, Agathe appears with a cry that she is the dove; the Hermit steps forward and touches the branch so that it flies off, to alight on the tree behind which Caspar is hiding. As Max fires, it flies off again, but Agathe and Caspar both fall to the ground. The Hermit raises Agathe, and withdraws. The people think Max has shot his bride (No. 16, Finale: 'Schaut, O schaut'); but it is Caspar who has been fatally wounded, and recognizing his failure as he sees Samiel appear, he dies cursing Heaven and Samiel. All agree that he always was a villain. Ottokar orders his body to be thrown in the Wolf's Glen and turns to Max for an explanation. Max confesses that he has been using free-shooting bullets cast with Caspar, and is immediately banished despite the pleas of Cuno, Agathe and the chorus. The Hermit (bass) now intervenes on his behalf (pointing out, incidentally, what no-one has hitherto seemed to notice, that it is the *Probeschuss* which, so far from preventing the use of free-bullets, has driven Max to such lengths out of his love for Agathe). He requests a year's probation for Max, and Ottokar agrees at the end of this period to officiate at Max and Agathe's wedding himself. All ends in a chorus in praise of God's mercy to the pure in heart.

When Weber sent the book to Count Brühl in Berlin on 12th August 1819, it was approved with a few minor reservations. The title was to be changed; and later Brühl asked for a second aria to satisfy Johanna Eunicke, the Aennchen. Agreeing, so long as it could be a small piece, Kind and Weber produced the aria about the cousin's dream, No. 13, which Weber finished on 21st May 1821. Weber had previously made a number of alterations to the libretto himself. He deleted a verse of 'Und ob die Wolke', added a second to the Huntsmen's Chorus ('Diana ist kundig'), made the Bridesmaids' Song into a solo and chorus rather than a quartet, greatly tightened up the Caspar-Samiel bargaining and other places in the dialogue, insisted on Kind's changing the three ravens in the Wolf's Glen into the Spirit Chorus, and deleted Kind's original aria with chorus for Cuno's narration of the founding of the *Probeschuss* in favour of dialogue, which he felt to be essential if the crucial background of the story was to be got across clearly.

Kind rose to the height of his modest powers with the material. He was, however, no dramatist. The age was not one in which major writers felt willing to give themselves to so journeyman a craft as libretto-writing—not even Goethe, who never made a major practical demonstration of his avowed longing for a great German opera. Regrettably Weber never approached Hoffmann, whose *Undine* to his own libretto greatly impressed Weber and had some influence on *Der Freischütz*, and who would seem to have been the ideal artist to play Boito to Weber's Verdi. Composers were obliged to fall back for the most part on theatrical hacks or on hopeful semi-amateurs such as Kind whose affiliations were less with the Romantic drama—itself the weak limb of Romantic literature—than with effective theatricality in a convention deriving, as we shall see, largely from French *opéra-comique*. The language of Kind's text is stilted and lame, even in an age that forgave much for the sake of an effective scene or moment; and there is only a minimal attempt at characterization. The point left Weber untroubled: he did not even feel obliged to demonstrate Max and Agathe's love at the obvious place, during his visit to her house in Act 2 before setting out for the Wolf's Glen. An opera about love without a love duet might seem an anomaly; but Weber was concerned with something besides the emotions of his characters, and as always the libretto stands or falls by what it means to its composer.

Weber himself pointed out that the essential course of the opera mirrors a struggle between the forces of good and evil, and in so doing describes a curve downwards into darkness and up into light again, in fact that 'half the opera plays in darkness. In the first act it is evening and its second half plays in the dark; in the second, it is night during Agathe's big scena, with moon-light through the window, and finally at midnight come the apparitions in the Wolf's Glen. These dark forms of the outer world are underlined and strengthened in the musical forms.'[1] He goes on to point out how impossible it would be to stage the work in a bright, elegant, modern setting in broad daylight. To reinforce a visual structure in the lighting, over which he took such great trouble, he devised a tonal pattern more elaborate than anything in his previous works. Broadly, C major stands for the powers of good, and for simple human goodness: it is the key of Aennchen's sunny Ariette 'Kommt ein schlanker Bursch' (No. 7) and of the Bridesmaids. C minor is the key of the demonic powers. D major is made to represent the joyful life of the village and the huntsmen, not in itself a force for good but the natural world in which the events take place, with a drop to E♭ (the relative major of C minor) usually signifying its darker side. The Huntsmen's Chorus is obviously in D major; and Caspar shows his huntsman's side with his drinking song that moves from B minor to a D major cadence (No. 4), though when Max is gone he drops into D minor for his next aria, 'Schweig! schweig!' (No. 5). The D major of the forest village life permeates the struc-ture of the entire opera, despite the overture and finale in the 'good' key of C major. The Introduction (No. 1), the first scene in the village, is firmly in D, with the March moving to the subdominant (G), also the key of Kilian's 'Schau der Herr'. Max opens his 'O! diese Sonne' in A minor, moving via its relative major, the C major chorus of pious exhortation, to a cheerful F major close. The Waltz reverts to D major, with Max's 'Durch die Wälder' in E♭ a transitory reflection on lost happiness before a modulation to C minor as Caspar moves in with his temptation. The second act opens in the dominant of D major, A ('Schelm! halt fest', No. 6), moving after Aennchen's C major No. 7 to its dominant, E major, for 'Leise, leise' and thence dropping to E♭ for the anxious Terzett, No. 9. This E♭ proves to be none other than

[1] J. C. Lobe: *op. cit.*

the seventh which completes the diminished seventh that is not only Samiel's *Leitmotiv* but the key-pattern of the ensuing Wolf's Glen scene, whose sequence of keys is F♯–C–E♭–C–A–C–A–C–F♯. The third act opens with the D major Entre-Act on the Huntsmen's theme, continuing with Agathe's prayer in the 'unearthly' key of A♭, the remotest from D major, 'Und ob die Wolke', and Aennchen's attempt to laugh at the spirit world in G minor, 'Einst träumte', resolving in E♭. There are few more effective strokes in a score filled with effect than the drop of the ensuing C major Bridesmaids' Chorus, after the funeral wreath has been discovered, into A minor, impelled by a Berliozian flattened sixth (A♭ in C major); despite the flutes' and violins' efforts to restore this A to being the dominant of a healthy D, it can only force (by way of the enharmonic G♯) A minor to D minor, remaining as a troubled mutter in the bass. The whole finale is essentially a dramatic resolution from C minor to C major; C minor – C major – A minor – G major – E♭ – B minor – B major – C major.

Weber planned the layout of his instrumentation with no less care, and his comments on the subject are worth quoting virtually in full.

> There are in *Der Freischütz* two principal elements that can be recognized at first sight—hunting life and the rule of demonic powers as personified by Samiel. So when composing the opera I had to look for suitable tone colours to characterize these two elements; these colours I tried to retain and use not only where the poet had indicated one or the other element but also where they could be made effective use of. The tone colour of the scoring for forest and hunting life was easy to find: the horns provided it. The difficulty lay only in finding for the horns new melodies that would be both simple and popular. For this purpose I searched among folk melodies, and I have careful study to thank if this part of my task is successful. I did not even shrink from using parts of these tunes—shall I say, as far as the actual notes are concerned? It will not have escaped you, for instance, that the last huntsmen's chorus conceals the second part of the tune of Marlborough . . . The most important part, to my mind, is in Max's words, 'mich umgarnen finstre Mächte', for they showed me what chief characteristic to give the opera. I had to remind the hearer of these 'dark powers' by means of tone-colour and melody as often as possible . . . I gave a great deal of thought to the question of what was the right principal colouring for this sinister element. Naturally it had to be a dark, gloomy colour—the lowest register of the violins, violas and basses, particularly the lowest register of the clarinet, which seemed especially suitable for depicting the sinister, then the mournful sound of the bassoon, the lowest notes of the horns, the hollow roll of drums or single hollow strokes on them. When you go through the score of the opera, you will find hardly any number in which this sombre principal colour is not noticeable, you will be able to satisfy yourself that the picture of the sinister element predominates by far and it will be plain to you that *this* gives the opera its principal character.[1]

[1] J. C. Lobe: *op. cit.* The dots represent a few unimportant omissions and Lobe's questions.

Weber's innate understanding of the quality of each individual instrument is here brought to its highest pitch of mastery. He was never an orchestrator after the manner of Wagner or Strauss, with their infinitely rich and subtly flecked textures; his primary colours arise from a delight in the nature of every instrument which never staled, and which enabled him to discover in each one unsuspected new timbres. The instruments have broken free from their appointed roles in the classical orchestra and now acquire independent, dramatic personalities which Weber studies as if they were live operatic characters, each with a complex psychology all its own, coloured by contact with its fellows but always retaining its individuality. In this he is the founder of methods which Mahler extended to new dimensions, and which Debussy warmly admired: 'He scrutinizes the soul of each instrument and exposes it with a gentle hand. Deferential to his resources they yield him more than he appears to demand. Also, the most daring combinations of his orchestra, when he makes himself most deliberately symphonic, have in particular the tone quality preserved in its original quality; such as colours superimposed without mingling and the mutual reactions of which enhance rather than abolish their individuality.'[1]

It seems doubtful whether the resemblance to *Malbrouk s'en va t'en guerre* would have been observed, unless as the coincidence of a simple melodic pattern, without Weber's confession:

Ex. 46

But Weber's tunes in *Der Freischütz*, especially of course as regards the world of the villagers and huntsmen, are by intention so close to folk melody as to generate a two-way traffic. The refrain of the Bridesmaids' Chorus derives from a *Volkstanz, Der Windmüller* (Ex. 47, p. 214).

The village march, too, is based on an actual original still extant in country inns and fairs in Weber's day[2] (Ex. 48, p. 215).

On the other hand 'Victoria, Victoria', and 'Lasst lustig die Hornen entschallen', as well as the Huntsmen's Chorus itself, idealize the manner of his earlier *gesellige Lieder* of *Leyer und Schwerdt* and other collections, and they promptly became part of German folklore; while Weber's Bridesmaids'

[1] To Robert Godet, reported in *Weber and Debussy, The Chesterian*, June 1926.

[2] Quoted in MMW, Vol. 2, p. 307 and in August Ambros: *Culturhistorischen Bildern aus dem Musikleben der Gegenwart*, p. 47 (1865). Ambros suggests this folk march may in turn have been based on Mozart's in *La Clemenza di Tito*.

Chorus joined the others in collections of folk and student songs, reappeared attached to different words, infuriated Heine by its ubiquity, and was parodied by Kurt Weill when Jim, Jack and Bill, on their way to Mahagonny, invoke the 'schöner, grüner Mond von Alabama'. Weber himself felt that the tune was so obvious that anyone could have lit upon it. But herein lay part of his genius, in discovering a natural melody which brought folksong in to the realm of art. *Der Freischütz* was not the first opera to reflect German feeling by actual use of folksong—many *Singspiele* drew upon it—but never before had folksong been so perfectly epitomized.

A demonstrable part of the ancestry of *Der Freischütz* certainly lies with *Singspiel*—the background of nature, the pure, naïve heroine and well-meaning, misled hero, the villain hoist with his own petard, the fatherly prince, not least the portrayal of characters so black or so white as to produce a monochrome result. But these are figures in the landscape on to which Weber was in turn projecting emotional sensations and a moral argument—an exact parallel with the pictures of Caspar David Friedrich mentioned in the previous chapter. The nature influence has no real origins in *Singspiel*, which for by far the most part dealt only with formal situations, but comes more from the Rousseau-inspired sentiments of *opéra-comique* and reaches Weber most directly by way of the two major operas of the year 1816. Spohr's *Faust*, often cited as the first real Romantic opera, is a comparatively undigested mixture of French influences; but Hoffmann's *Undine*, which

Ex. 47

Weber admired even more, draws many threads of Romanticism together into a pattern for opera—particularly, as far as *Der Freischütz* was concerned, the impingeing of the spirit world on that of humans. *Undine* was the first opera of its era to set a text of real literary merit; and Hoffmann's famous attack on *Der Freischütz* was largely motivated by his desire for a closer unity of literary and musical quality. Weber, for all his ideas about unity and for all his own literary gifts, was primarily a musician and thought about librettos from the point of view of the composer as the magnet around which the other elements should form. And after ten years without a libretto, he fastened the more eagerly on the subject that seemed ideal.

However German *Der Freischütz* appears, and however closely it matched the national moment, the lineage with French opera is much stronger. Weber's selection of a repertory for his Prague intendancy, discussed in

Ex. 48

Village March

WEBER: Bauern-Marsch (*Freischütz*)

(Weber)

Chapter 9, showed that he was well aware of where the true origins of Romantic opera lay. Aennchen owes less to the traditional comic servant of *opera
buffa* and of its *Singspiel* manifestations than to the *soubrette* of *opéra-
comique* (she is emancipated from being servant to actual relation of Agathe's);
hence comes her fondness for polonaise rhythm, in any case one of Weber's
favourites, and in parody the form of her Romanze und Arie (No. 13). Max,
too, especially by comparison with the very German Kilian, shows that a
good deal of French blood runs in his veins with the graceful sentimentality
of his melodies, above all in 'Durch die Wälder'—a tune which is of the
colour Weber knew well from Méhul's *Joseph* ('Champs paternels') and *Uthal*
('Tel qu'on voit sur nos montagnes'), though in fact it derives directly from
his 1817 setting of Kind's song *Das Veilchen im Thale* (Op. 66, No. 1: J.217).

Ex. 49

As for Caspar, if his artistic parents are Pizarro and Weber's own Adelhart,
his grandfather is Cherubini's Dourlinsky in *Lodoïska* (Ex. 50, p. 217–8).
   The device of melodrama for the Wolf's Glen, despite the Czech melodramas Weber had himself staged in Prague, is French, as was the insertion
of an Entre-Act [*sic*], a feature unfamiliar in German opera; and there is
generally the inclination, under the encouragement of the Dresden taste for
tableaux, towards picturesque situation rather than development. Moreover,
despite Weber's notorious antipathies, he was by no means untouched by
what he called the 'sweet poison from beyond the Alps', most openly shown
of course in the major solo numbers and above all in Agathe's Szene und
Arie (itself an Italianate designation), 'Wie nahte mir der Schlummer', in
parts of which the element of sheer display is less effectively kept under
control than in Max's big aria.
   From French opera Weber also developed the Reminiscence Motive which,
though by no means unfamiliar in German opera, had not yet reached the

full dignity of *Leitmotiv*. The C minor tonality of the powers of evil regularly expresses itself as a scale of C minor, so consistently and with such skilful modifications as to be virtually a *Leitmotiv*; and there is of course the opera's only true *Leitmotiv*, the famous Samiel diminished seventh, keystone chord of Romantic horror (and of practical use for its ability to modulate in almost any direction), variously applied with great subtlety throughout the opera from parody in the viola arpeggio opening Aennchen's No. 13, down to its basic form as first stated in the Overture (Ex. 51, p. 219).

Given Weber's interest not so much in development and conflict of character as in setting his persons as actors-out of a moral principle, there is little call for the full deployment of *Leitmotiv*, essentially a method of portraying the interaction and developing relationship of persons and ideas with each other. Weber was convinced that careful definition of the basic elements in his story by key, and exposition by instrumental colour, was a sound framework; and with his assured grasp of melody and of theatrical situation, he was for his own purposes undoubtedly right. By opting for primary colours with which to depict his characters, he may have deprived them of the rounded subtlety and unexpectedness and contrariness of real human nature, but he

Ex. 50

CHERUBINI: *Lodoïska*, Dourlinsky's Act 3 aria (1791)

BEETHOVEN: *Fidelio*, Pizarro's Act 1 aria (orig. 1805)

WEBER: *Silvana*, Adelhart in the Act 2 duet, No. 9 (1810)

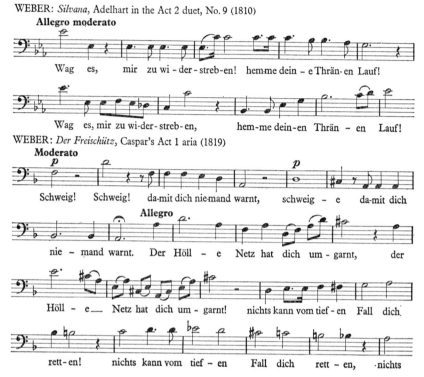

WEBER: *Der Freischütz*, Caspar's Act 1 aria (1819)

was enabled to define them for all time as types in which a delighted German nation found a reflection of its own qualities—Max a simple, brave hunter, for all his weakness and his proneness to melancholy and fantasies, an open-air figure of direct, unquestioned loyalties; Agathe a mixture of *ewigweibliche* and *Hausfrau*, patient, reflective, domestic, pious, faithful and (truth be told) a little dull; Aennchen the lively innocent, silly but charming and generous, all that is meant by the word *keck*; Samiel and his agent Caspar the embodiment of all that is dark and destructive in the elemental German wood spirits; Kilian and Cuno, villagers, Huntsmen and Brides-maids the familiar natural life upon which the aristocrat Ottokar imposes a human order and discipline that must in turn defer to spiritual order in the person of the Hermit, the Man of God. With *Der Freischütz* Weber succeeded where attempts by Tieck, Brentano, Schlegel, Arnim and Werner had failed—in bringing Romanticism into the theatre.

He was uniquely equipped among the musicians of his generation to do so. Hoffmann, who understood the problems as no-one else did, failed simply through inadequate musical gifts. But Weber had of all his generation the most acute ear for the sounds of the natural world, for the songs that were still very much alive both in town and country, for the instruments in whose tone-colours he was to find so much more than had been suspected. The opening number is itself a microcosm of the world Weber wished to set directly before the audience, with the first chorus yielding to a village band in which the shrill squeak of the C clarinet over horn colour and the solemn tonic-dominant sawing of the cello neatly catch the limitations of village players, in turn succeeded by Kilian's folk-type song 'Schau der Herr' with its jolly bassoon and its answering cackle of derisive laughter on major seconds Weber had heard from women misintoning the service at Pillnitz. Though there may seem a cruel note in the taunting of Max, Kilian is sincere when he protests to Cuno that it is all in good part—the natural roughness of the simple rustic life whose sunny nature is so vividly portrayed. It is with No. 2, the Terzett, that the first shadow crosses the scene, as the opening descending A minor phrase to Caspar's later 'Mag Fortunas Kugel rollen' and the ensuing dramatic *fp* on a diminished seventh make plain. Here is the first suggestion of the advance of demonic powers; and the inclusion of the hunting chorus 'Lasst lustig' serves to emphasize the happy norm from which Max has become separated. The *Walzer* (No. 3), foreshadowed in No. 1, is a typical South German Ländler; Hoffmann was the first to remark upon the superb stroke whereby it drifts away to a close in faintly sinister fragments, so that it comes as no surprise when we hear the anxious beat of violas and the turn to C minor for the solitary Max's scene. Weber told Lobe[1] that he wished to show Max torn between fear of his evil fate and love of his good angel Agathe; and in the context of lost happiness which the melody of 'Durch die Wälder' embodies, the tension of the scene is indeed pitched between the almost hymn-like G major section and the stormy C minor Allegro with his anxious 'Doch mich umgarnen finstre Mächte' and despairing 'O dringt kein Strahl' in the gathering Wolf's Glen motives: the first phrase accompanies his anxiety with the simplest Wolf's Glen C minor scale, while the second is destined to become the phrase with which Max first looks down into the abyss (Ex. 52, p. 220).

The double portrait of Caspar in Nos. 4 and 5 sets before Max the full nature of his adversary. Caspar's attempt to establish himself as a D major character from the opening B minor in which he sets off is immediately

Ex. 51

[1] Lobe: *op. cit.*

exposed by the devilish glitter of piccolos that answer his cadence—a classic
stroke of scoring (Ex. 53, opposite page).

Hoffmann thought this the crown of all Weber's songs, the most brilliant
number of the opera; and it was singled out by Beethoven when he expressed
his surprised admiration of *Der Freischütz*: 'That usually feeble little man[1]—
I'd never have thought it of him. Now Weber must write more operas, one
after the other, without any preliminary nibbling. Caspar, that fiend, is as
solid as a house . . .' As already indicated, it is Beethoven's own Pizarro
who is suggested in the ensuing 'Schewig! Schewig!' with which, soliloquizing in the manner of 'Ha! welch' ein Augenblick', Caspar reveals the
full scale of his commitment to evil, his piccolo glinting with a Wolf's Glen
figure that appears in various forms as he invites, 'Umgebt ihn, ihr Geister,
mit Dunkel beschwingt!' (Ex. 54, opposite page).

Ex. 52

¹ '*Der sonst weiche Männerl*'.

Caspar

trüg' der Stock nicht Trau - ben

Ex. 54

Caspar

um - gebt ihn, ihr Geist - er mit

Dun kel be -schwingt!

Wolf's Glen scene

With the area of battle defined and the forces of darkness fully advanced into position, Weber ends the first act. Shrewdly, he saves the appearance of the redemptive force of Agathe until the threat has been conclusively established; and so it is upon a new world of feeling that the curtain to Act 2 goes up in Agathe's house—though the influence of evil is shown in the action upon which Aennchen is engaged, nailing up the picture of old Cuno which has fallen and wounded Agathe on the forehead. The contrast between the two relations is immediately established in Agathe's initial restraint while Aennchen prattles happily away in a flowing 6/8 melody; they might almost be a rustic Fiordiligi and Dorabella. Aennchen is further defined with

Ex. 55

her *Ariette* 'Kommt ein schlanker Bursch gegangen', a *polacca* which may have had its origins in *opéra-comique* but is typical of the *Preziosa* music Weber was contemplating and indeed of many another polonaise in his output. She has acquired the skittish oboe from Silvana's liveliest side, together with the cello that in a neat exchange here mirrors the flirtatious wooing she describes.

When Agathe steps forward for her aria, it is of course a much more

substantial affair—indeed, this is the mid-point of the opera, the number in which we gain the most profound knowledge of her nature. Despite the Italian influences, the mastery with which linked episodes are held together is entirely Weber's own; as is the skilful economy of his means. The opening recitative tells us far more about Agathe than would a conventional *recitativo stromentato,* from the gentle melancholy of the opening sighs on clarinet, her special instrument, to the magical stroke as she opens the door onto the balcony, and with a modulation from (in E major) a seventh on G to a 6/4 on F♯, Weber spreads the whole beauty of the starlit night before us (Ex. 55, p. 222–3).

The low flute thirds that lead straight into 'Leise, leise' were a haunting sound that Berlioz was to remember when he came to write *Roméo et Juliette*; and as he pointed out in the *Grand Traité d'Instrumentation et d'Orchestration* (1844), a quite particular effect of gentleness is produced by confining the accompaniment of 'Leise, leise' to violins and violas. The course of the scene is poised between the exquisite lulling of 'Leise, leise' with the peculiar note of anxiety that underlies the stillness, and the joy with which her worries are resolved, by Max's appearance, into the prayer that is the antithesis of Caspar's in Ex. 54 and the most famous melody of the opera pre-Wagnerian in its rapturous turn round a single note before leaping to a higher one:

Ex. 57

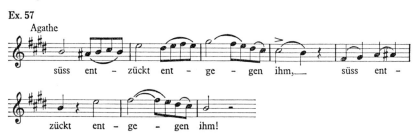

But Max's revelation of his intention to go to the Wolf's Glen dispels this with a violent C minor scale to introduce the first musical confrontation of Agathe, himself and Aennchen—whose simplicity is so far from the reach of evil that she can reply to Agathe's horror-struck exclamation with a disarmingly chatty remark about the Wild Huntsman in a light-hearted dotted rhythm, and even at the end, when the others have fully expounded their anxieties about his departure, can shrug her shoulders and prattle that a hunter's life is like that. A subtler character would not have missed the full import of the C minor scale figure that besets most of their exchanges, nor the fact that even Agathe is prone to the menace of Samiel's diminished sevenths.

The Wolf's Glen scene is the centre-piece of the opera, the gulf in which the work reaches its profoundest depth before the resolution into light. All its materials have by now been expounded; and indeed it is their close association with the human personages involved that elevates the scene above the conventionally picturesque, since it becomes a projection of their own disturbed emotions, their most appalling night fears. It is, moroever, Weber's genius for instrumental sound that enables him to avoid the cruder kind of imitation. For it is less upon the literalism of, say, galloping rhythms for the fiery carriage that the effectiveness of the scene depends than upon the subtle appreciation of instrumental tone—the shivering tremolo at the start over low trombones and clarinets in the chalumeau register, the shrill unison of woodwind over horns and the cries of 'Uhui!', the cunningly developed growth of tone as the bullets are cast. Nothing is more masterly than, at the Wild Hunt, the choice of register which produces from horns in B♭, F and E a vicious blare far removed from the warmth of the village scenes.

The Entre-Act immediately dispels these night horrors with the theme of the opera's most open celebration of the joys of forest life, the Huntsmen's Chorus. But we return to the village, as we left it, by way of the redeeming force as manifest by Agathe, who is discovered, over a Wagnerian throb of bassoons and horns, in prayer. Her obbligato instrument in this *Cavatine* (No. 12, 'Und ob die Wolke') is the cello, with the clarinet taking over from it. Aennchen is perhaps mocking her, as well as the Wolf's Glen, with the viola obbligato in the ensuing *Romanze und Arie*; its sinister huskiness is more effective with the opening Romantic irony of this innocent girl paro-dying the horror of the Wolf's Glen than when she tries more directly to cheer Agathe up at 'Trube Augen' (the tune of which originally appeared in Lucinde's Ariette, written for Huber's drama, *Das Sternenmädchen im Maidlinger Walde*). Given that Weber appreciated the need for another aria for Johanna Eunicke, perhaps even approved the chance of balancing the intense beauty of the melody of 'Und ob die Wolke' with a livelier piece for Aennchen, as in Act 1, he was being too indulgent when he accepted Kind's silly tale of the dog being mistaken for a ghost.

After the Bridesmaids and the Huntsmen—despite the superbly sinister ending to the Bridesmaids' Chorus, both are demonstrations of a return to the world of normality—the finale opens after the failure of Max's shot and the collapse of Agathe with the apparent triumph of Samiel on a rushing scale of C minor; and on her revival Agathe does not immediately shake off C minor before the hymn of thanksgiving. The finale is really concerned with the establishment of a conclusive C major; but it is the intervention of the Hermit that brings about the unexpected forgiveness in a key, B minor, which is completely unanticipated, an act of 'grace', so to speak, with the flute hovering about the Hermit's words as if, in Eliot's words, 'the dove descend-ing breaks the air'.

The overture describes the nature of the drama lying ahead in the opera with a characteristic reconciliation of the demands of programme music to sonata form. Gone are all Weber's difficulties with this form once he has

8

the substance of a drama in his mind and can visualize a dramatic rather than an abstract working out. Previous overtures had, of course, drawn on material from the opera they prefaced; but Weber took the art of symphonic synthesis of a drama to a new pitch of mastery. The overture's Introduction is not thematically connected to the opera—its bare octave figures suggest the emptiness of the primal forest, into which presently sounds the horn quartet not as a literal illustration of hunting life, as in the Huntsmen's Chorus, but as its distillation into a purer poetry. After the appearance of the spirit of evil with Samiel's diminished sevenths, the *molto vivace* begins a sonata form movement that is a dramatized struggle between two themes— Max's 'Doch mich umgarnen finstre Mächte' over heaving C minor scales, and Agathe's 'Suss entzückt entgegen ihm'. The recapitulation is abbreviated, and matters seem to have ended in Samiel's hands—until the sudden apotheosis and triumph of Agathe's theme whirls the piece home.

For all its originality and freshness of invention, *Der Freischütz* remains a problem. Weber and Kind may have avoided the accusation of superstition by removing the time of the action to the period just after the Thirty Years' War, when such beliefs were current; but they traded for a success on the susceptibility of their audiences to the exuberance of a newly free nation and still more to the Romantic shudder. Neither well stands the test of time, and indeed there were those of the authors' contemporaries who took exception to the naïvety with which the authors set about putting the horrors of the Wolf's Glen on the stage. Hoffmann was one; Beethoven, too, had his doubts: 'I see clearly what Weber means, but he's put some damned non-sense into it too. When I read it, for instance at the Wild Hunt—I have to laugh, but it must be right. One must *hear* that kind of thing, only hear . . .' (pointing to his useless ears).[1] However much Weber wished the incidents of the Wolf's Glen to reflect the assault of evil forces, he took elaborate pains over their literal detail (as with the wooden owl with lit-up eyes). Yet the effect of the Wolf's Glen remains amazingly sharp, since it represents some-thing very different from the picturesque storms and pastorals of the eighteenth century. Not only has nature—including a sadistically, romantic-ally perverted nature—become part of the action instead of a decoration to it, but the horrifying is made part of human consciousness, touching off psychological reverberations that obsessed the entire Romantic movement and did not begin to be properly understood until the age of Freud and Schoenberg's *Erwartung*. As Mario Praz has written, 'The discovery of Horror as a source of delight and beauty ended by reacting on men's actual conception of beauty itself; the Horrid, from being a category of the Beautiful, ended by becoming one of its essential elements.'[2] Hence pro-ducers who accept all the detail of the Wolf's Glen with the air of a resigned

[1] MMW, Vol. 2, p. 509.
[2] Mario Praz: *The Romantic Agony* (trans. Davidson, 1933).

shrug perhaps pay too much attention to the means whereby Weber knew he could obtain his effect with his own contemporaries and neglect the purpose to which he harnessed them. *Der Freischütz* should be no more inaccessible to a thoughtful and musical producer, one who understands Weber's carefully controlled curve down into a physical darkness that stands for a psychological darkness and up again into light, than its progeny, the scene in which Siegfried discovers that in the midst of the peaceful, sunlit wood there lurks the horror of Fafner. The very skill with which Weber matches something essential of the German spirit in this work has won it a permanent sentimental attachment from his countrymen that can in turn generate impatience from others. But the regular productions in opera houses all over the world show that this is by no means the most important or interesting aspect of the work, that we should heed Beethoven's suggestion and disregard the period trappings which were the product of an artist with a highly developed sense of effect, listening instead to dramatic music of timeless invention, freshness and point.

Of many subsequent attempts to improve upon Weber's opera, the most notorious is the concoction known as *Robin des Bois*. Castil-Blaze—in reality François Henri Joseph Blaze (1784–1857)—was a species of theatrical tomb-robber who, despite his attacks on poor translations and adaptations and the abuses of theatre managers, was himself guilty of pillaging numerous foreign works for the stage and modifying others to suit prevailing Parisian taste. This he took to include a preference for his own music, which he was not above introducing into the works of established masters. In the case of *Der Freischütz* his attack was upon a living organism, with a living composer to whose dignified protests[1] Castil-Blaze replied in the time-dishonoured tones of the *entrepreneur* that he was using his special understanding of the general public to ensure the acceptance of a work of art.[2] It emerged in 1866 that Thomas Sauvage, an old *vaudeville* writer, was the originator of the idea, claiming that he hoped to improve on Kind and avoid the censor;[3] but the musical alterations are Castil-Blaze's, and include the displacement of 'Schweig! Schweig!' and the interpolation of the duet 'Hin nimm die Seele mein' from *Euryanthe*, with an amended accompaniment. The new plot, set in Yorkshire at the time of Charles I, follows the outline of Kind's story very roughly, with Ottokar and the Hermit suppressed, Tony, Annette and Richard replacing Max, Agathe and Caspar, Dick (Kilian) in love with Nancy (Aennchen), the ruins of St. Dunstan's replacing the Wolf's Glen. There is also a new ending in which Richard actually wins Annette at the shooting trial, whereat the distraught Tony seizes a pistol and tries to shoot

---

[1] Kaiser 155.

[2] 'The wretch! . . . and to think that a miserable sailor is punished with fifty lashes for the least act of insubordination!' Hector Berlioz: *Mémoires* (1870).

[3] A confession made in the *Gazette Musicale*, 9th and 16th December 1866.

himself. In this he is frustrated by Robin (=Samiel) who guides the bullet onto Richard; thus all ends happily. It is difficult to exaggerate the degree of clumsiness in the versification of this libretto, with its cavalier distortion of the music to accommodate its banalities. But not content with this, Castil-Blaze also took it upon himself to alter Weber's scoring. He rewrote the wind parts of Kilian's aria and doubled clarinets with flutes an octave higher in Agathe's Act 2 aria, where he also substitutes a meaningless coloratura flourish at 'Welch' schöne Nacht' and adds a violin tremolo before the reprise of the verse. *Robin des Bois, ou Les Trois Balles* was produced at the Théâtre de l'Odéon on 7th December 1824, serving to introduce the music of *Der Freischütz* to an eager French public, and large sums of money into Castil-Blaze's pocket.[1] He further put about a number of arrangements of the music, including one of the Huntsmen's Chorus as 'L'armée française.' Doubtless the feeling that the Devil should not have all the best tunes led to adaptation of this piece also to fit church carillons, as was reported by a shocked traveller through Namur,[2] and even church choirs, who solemnly sang to its jaunty strains,

> Chrétien diligent
> devant l'aurore
> A ton saveur encore
> Addresses tes chants
> Ave Maria, gratia plena
> La, lala, la, lala, etc.

'Even in its mutilated form', wrote Berlioz of the Paris *Freischütz*, 'I was positively intoxicated by its delicious freshness and its wild, subtle fragrance.'[3] He promptly abandoned the Opéra for the Odéon and became one of its most passionate advocates. Those who raised voices against it were given no quarter. He invents a superbly macabre punishment to fit a young grocer's crime in hissing Agathe's aria—the skeleton of this malefactor, who has shortly afterwards died from overeating, is acquired fifteen years later by the Opéra and pressed into service:

> ... after that, at each performance of *Freischütz*, just as Samiel cries: 'I am here!', there is a flash of lightning, a tree crashes down, and our grocer, the enemy of Weber's music, appears in the red glow of the Bengal lights, enthusiastically brandishing his lighted torch.[4]

[1] 'The Odéon throve on the proceeds; and M. Castil-Blaze received over 100,000 francs for mutilating a masterpiece' Hector Berlioz: *op. cit.* For further details of *Robin* and other French versions, see Georges Servières: *Freischütz* (1913).

[2] Friedrich Kind: *Freischützbuch*, p. 270 (1843).

[3] Hector Berlioz: *op. cit.*

[4] Hector Berlioz: *Gazette Musicale*, 3rd December 1843, reprinted as the Fourth Evening of *Les Soirées de l'Orchestre* (1852). Berlioz's sense of humour preserved some features from his early days as a medical student: of course the tale is, as Servières solemnly shows in his *Freischütz* (1913), untrue.

However, Berlioz had by this time himself come under fire from Germany for his own version of *Der Freischütz*. In this case, the plea of defending the work's best interests is justified. When the Opéra decided to put on the work in 1841, in Emilien Pacini's translation, the question arose of recitatives to replace the spoken dialogue that was strictly forbidden in that theatre. Léon Pillet, the Director, approached Berlioz who, fearing that if he refused the task it might go to someone less familiar with Weber's style, accepted on condition that the work was to remain unaltered. He was never satisfied with the result, feeling that the simple, conversational exchanges were made far too weighty in the new form, however much he urged a rapid flowing manner upon the singers. There was also the question of the ballet so dear to the hearts of Parisian opera-goers. Berlioz managed to scotch the proposal that pieces from his own *Symphonie Fantastique* and *Roméo et Juliette* should be used; but he had to give in on the point of principle, and to his famous orchestration of the *Invitation to the Dance* he added dance numbers from *Preciosa* and *Oberon*. Nevertheless, he had to allow Mme. Stolz to transpose her two main arias down; and when his back was turned so many other cuts and interpolations were introduced that in 1853 a Polish Count Tyckiewicz, having paid good money for his ticket to *Der Freischütz*, sued the management before the Civil Tribunal of the Seine for misrepresentation on the grounds that he was not hearing the original work. His counsel, Maître Lachand, produced detailed evidence of the cuts; Maître Celliez, for the Opéra, protested that it was played according to the version prepared by Pacini and Berlioz. The tribunal dismissed Tyckiewicz's suit, but declared the mutilations of *Freischütz* regrettable; and this played into the hands of Berlioz's enemies in France and abroad.

His version is, in fact, very discreet—indeed, through fear of distorting Weber he has settled for a somewhat anonymous style that lacks the swiftness and character of Weber's own in the arias. When anything more than simple chords and running conversational lines in the recitative is called for, he refers to the original music, using the Samiel diminished seventh and once rather an effective allusion to the Bridesmaids' music before their entry, as if Aennchen can indeed notice their approach, as she says. He also reintroduces Aennchen after Agathe's 'Und ob die Wolke' with four bars of 'Kommt ein schlanker Bursch'; but his most substantial contributions are after 'Leise, leise', before 'Wie? Was?' and especially, where the drama obviously demands it, immediately before the finale at the shooting trial. Pacini was tactful, cutting as much dialogue as possible so as to reduce Berlioz's contributions, which were scrupulously marked with a B so that there should be no confusion. The most serious damage is done, of course, to the melodrama in the Wolf's Glen, though Berlioz insists on keeping in speech the counting of the bullets and Samiel's 'I am here!' For the rest, an undesirable necessity is handled with as much discretion as possible. The same cannot be said for other versions importing recitative—for instance, Franco Faccio's for Boito's 1872 La Scala version, which overplays the diminished sevenths and generally contrives to be pervasively Italianate, for instance bringing Max on in Act 2 at a lively Latin gallop quite alien to his nature.

Many other versions were made in the course of the work's triumphant progress across the stages of Europe, and it naturally laid itself open to the parodies that were at one time the dubious accolade of any opera's success. Munich's Isartor Theatre gave *Der Freischütz oder Stuberl in der Löwengrube* by 'Carl Carl' in 1822, and an anonymous German parody called *Samiel, oder Die Wunderpille* was published in 1824; better known, perhaps, is the English one of the same year by a certain 'Septimus Globus'. The nature of its fun is made clear from the full title: *Der Freischütz, a new muse-sick-all and see-nick performance from the new German uproar. By the celebrated Funnybear.* The hilarity reaches its depths in the Wolf's Glen, which is invaded by firemen, fire engines, a man from a Fire Office with a fire-policy etc., the conflagration being eventually attended to by the nightwatchman with his bucket. The printed version has twelve drawings by George Cruikshank, and rather surprisingly prints at the end a translation of Apel's original tale.[1]

---

[1] Studies of the *Freischütz* parodies and imitations were published by P. A. Merbach in the *Zeitschrift für Musikwissenschaft* (August 1920) and the *Zeitschrift für Musik* (1919–20).

CHAPTER TWELVE

DRESDEN – 2: 1820–1821

A wise man will make more opportunities than he finds.
FRANCIS BACON

ALREADY DURING the completion of *Der Freischütz* two other major projects were in Weber's mind, a set of incidental music for Wolff's *Preciosa* and a comic opera, *Die drei Pintos*, to a libretto by Theodor Hell. The latter he saw as congenial work for the summer, and accordingly set about finding a country house rather nearer to his work than Hosterwitz was. Choice fell upon a cottage, Kosels Garten, in the suburb of Dresden known as Antonstadt, close to the Linckesche Bad on the wooded banks of the Elbe; and on 13th April he moved in with Caroline, his animals and his belongings. But the spring was late in coming, and as well as fearing for her husband's health on his daily walk into the town, Caroline was alarmed because the lonely path passed a spot where an artist had been murdered. To pacify her, Weber armed himself with an enormous brace of pistols and a swordstick.

Here, twelve days after finishing *Der Freischütz*, he began work on the incidental music for a Berlin production of *Preciosa*. Though he had sworn not to write any more music for plays, the combined persuasiveness of Count Brühl and Wolff was too much for him—so he told Brühl in a letter on 20th February. He had evidently begun to give serious thought to it before the end of *Freischütz* since he protested to Brühl on 8th May that he found himself faced with something like half an opera. The music, an overture and eleven numbers (J.279), was begun on 25th May and finished on 15th July.

Pius Alexander Wolff was born in Augsburg on 3rd May 1782, and as well as pursuing a successful career as an actor—at Berlin, between 1803 and 1816, his roles included Hamlet—had won a small name for himself as a dramatist, in part owing to the recommendation of his teacher Goethe. Weber, who first met him at Weimar in 1812, later knew him in Berlin and admired him as an actor even above Devrient. In this role he is said to have followed the strict classical style approved at Weimar; but as a dramatist he had shared the fascination for Cervantes that overcame the Romantic writers with particular intensity at the turn of the century, in 1811 basing his prose drama *Preciosa* on *La Gitanilla*, the first of the *Novelas Exemplares* which Cervantes published in 1613. *Preciosa* was successfully produced in Leipzig with music by Traugott Eberwein, a choice of composer probably influenced by Goethe (settings of whose work the poet preferred to those by Schubert) but which Wolff thought mistaken; it was also set by Johann Schulz (Leipzig, 1812) and Ignaz Seyfried (Vienna, 1812). Encouraged by the success of this 1811 production, Wolff sent the play to Iffland in Berlin, without luck. But a reworking of it in verse was accepted by Brühl, who with Wolff's approval approached Weber for new music.

Doubtless the wish to please the impresario of his forthcoming opera loomed principally in Weber's mind; but the subject was one well calculated to appeal to him. Though *Don Quixote* had long been known in Germany, it was Tieck's translation of 1798 which became the classic; Cervantes also influenced and was translated by Schlegel, had been admired by Romantics from Wieland onwards with especial fervour and was a hero to the Romantics' prized philosopher Schelling. Even Helmina von Chézy took him as model for several of her tales. Part of their enthusiasm lay in the enjoyable trappings of chivalry throughout *Don Quixote*; but a deeper attraction was provided by its Romantic irony of the quest theme comically presented. As a major work on the influence of Cervantes on the Romantics puts it, his figures 'pursue, in an unending quest, the Blue Flower or the elect of their dreams, the absolute good which vanishes before them'.[1] Cervantes was also, of course, admired for his exact observation of the natural world and the simple people of his countrysides; not only his study of the customs of the gipsies, an exotic people in a Spain that was itself exotic to the Germans, but the construction of the tale itself caused *La Gitanilla* to be hailed as a model of story-telling. It is in fact simply a colourfully told anecdote, filled with vivid observation, of a fifteen-year-old gipsy girl whose fair looks and skilful singing and dancing make her the prize of her tribe and win her the love of a young aristocrat who abandons his home in order to follow her; eventually she is recognized as the daughter of a noble house who had been stolen as a child by the gipsies, and is restored to her birthright and the opportunity of a 'respectable' marriage to her lover. It shows a detailed knowledge of gipsy ways and is written in a style less sharply satirical, more warmly romantic than that familiar to readers of *Don Quixote* alone.

Weber responded to the detail of the story with an equally enthusiastic exactness. According to the Dresden librarian, he studied a collection of Spanish national tunes, which form the basis of the dances in Act 3 (No. 9), and even turned up some examples of genuine gipsy music. He claimed in the autograph of the score that the march was 'after an original gipsy melody'— perhaps the same one upon which Bizet based the march opening the Terzetto at the start of Act 3 of *Carmen* (Ex. 58, opposite page).

From his earlier music Weber borrowed two further pieces—the Allegro (No. 9) which he had based on a Spanish tune for his music to Hell's *Das Haus Anglade* (J.227) in 1818, and the Ballo (No. 4) which began life as the

[1] J. -J. A. Bertrand: *Cervantes et le Romantisme Allemand* (1914).

first (J.143) of his Six Favourite Waltzes of 1812 and was re-used as a *Tedesco* (J.191) for Liebich in Prague in 1816. Describing his music in a long letter to Wolff,[1] Weber emphasized the Spanish nationality he had portrayed at the start of the overture as well as with his genuine gipsy march (both recur immediately in Act 1, the first subject of the overture as the chorus 'Heil, Preciosa' (No. 2)). But his own knowledge of Spain was negligible, being based chiefly on his overhearing of a few Spanish songs in the company of Spohr from Spanish soldiers garrisoned near Gotha (see p. 139). Fascination with the exotic tang of national bolero rhythms largely did duty for any very serious identification with Spain, as becomes clear when the gipsies sing their beautiful Act 2 echo chorus 'Im Wald' (No. 5) in the exact tones of German foresters hymning the joys of the *Urwald*, and subsequently hail the sunrise (No. 8) and the pleasures of wine, women and song (No. 10) like so many forgathered members of the Berlin *Liedertafel*. Despite the transformation of its trio section to a crisper more 'Spanish' snap in the overture, the Ballo (No. 4) cannot disguise its *Tedesco* origins; and when Preciosa (who is asked to sing on this occasion as well as to speak and dance) stands with off-stage horns calling across her to the flute and proclaims her love in the charming Lied 'Einsam bin ich nicht alleine', we might be hearing the lost voice of Silvana. Nevertheless, *Carmen* is not a worse opera for its lack of a more thoroughgoing authentic Spanish atmosphere; and the value of the *Preciosa* music lies in the melodic charm the convention struck from Weber. There is still greater originality in the three melodramas (No. 3, 4a, and 11), where he makes skilful expressive use of the technique he had explored in *Der erste Ton* and brought to mastery in the Wolf's Glen scene. Preciosa is called upon to follow the music with notated speech rhythms, or at least with syllables marked with a strong beat to coincide with an orchestral chord.

Ex. 58

Preciosa (1821)

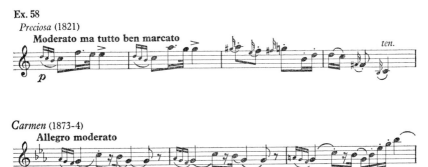

Carmen (1873-4)

¹ Kaiser 145.

Undoubtedly this is Weber's most important incidental music; and the success it won in the Königliche Hofbühne when the play was performed on 14th March 1821 substantially helped to pave the way for *Der Freischütz*.[1]

Simultaneously with work on *Preciosa*, he began sketching *Die drei Pintos*. But regrettably, news came from Berlin that delay in completing the new opera house, coupled with the sensational arrival in the city of Spontini, meant postponing *Der Freischütz* and his thoughts turned not towards composition but the notion of a concert tour. Funds were admittedly low, but the choice of North Germany and Denmark suggests that money was not his first object. He was quite unknown in Copenhagen (on his arrival the papers got the name of *Der Freischütz* wrong and confused him with B. A. Weber), and it was a substantial distance for a couple in poor health to travel—Weber's illness was gaining ground, and Caroline, having miscarried in the early part of the year, was now pregnant again. The need for a change from Dresden, the chance to visit his home town and simply the old *Wanderlust* were probably his main motives; at any rate, with the proceeds of the sale of a bundle of music to Schlesinger for 1,000 thalers and an advance of 40 Friedrichs d'or from Brühl for *Der Freischütz* he reckoned he could afford to take Caroline, and armed with the usual letters of introduction they set off on 25th July.

From Leipzig they travelled to Halle, where no doubt they were encouraged in the idea of visiting Copenhagen by the Danish poet Adam Oehlenschläger, an old acquaintance of Weber's and the future translator of *Freischütz* into Danish, who was currently installed in the town. A concert was arranged for Weber by Carl Loewe, and while the professors of the University showered their works upon him in such profusion that he privately remarked he could soon set up as a book dealer, the students gathered, four hundred strong, beneath his window to sing his choruses. Similar scenes attended him in Göttingen, and exhausted rather than refreshed they forged on by way of Hanover, after a carriage accident en route, to Bremen. Caroline, upset, managed to sing with success but was clearly far from well, and after concerts in Oldenburg and Bremen once more, he was compelled to leave her in Hamburg in the charge of a doctor. Also in Hamburg were his brother Edmund's son Carl Moritz and another brother, Fridolin, now violist[2] with the orchestra and with whom Weber pushed on to their birthplace, Eutin. Here they stayed from 11th to 14th September, pleased by the honour they found awaiting them; a concert was arranged by the Stadtmusikus, the

---

[1] A version by Castil-Blaze and George de Charlemagne cut the melodramas and shortened the numbers, altering their order. Other French versions followed, including one by Nuittier and Beaumont (1858) also altering the order and importing music from *Silvana* and the Second Symphony. The first English version (1825) had the music arranged by W. Hawes.

[2] Not music director, as in MMW, Vol. II, p. 252.

uncle of his Dresden flautist Anton Fürstenau. After being somewhat off-handedly received on his courtesy call on his godfather, Prince Carl of Hesse, Weber left with a letter to the marshal of the Danish court, Holstein.[1] He reached Kiel in an open carriage soaked to the skin, and gave an unsuccessful concert on the 20th. After two days hanging about waiting for the steamer, he left on the evening of the 22nd. Romantic indulgence in his emotion at his first sight of the sea, and at finding himself standing upon the heaving deck under the moon, with the Kiel lighthouse slipping astern, was abruptly dispelled by seasickness; but he seems to have enjoyed the trip, and arrived in Copenhagen in good spirits on the 24th. Oehlenschläger, back in Copenhagen ahead of him, had him well entertained during the delay before his concert caused by another pianist's arrival; he played to the King and Queen at Frederiksborg on 4th October, but despite the success of his *Rondo Brillante* and 'Vien quà, Dorina bella' variations, he was enervated at the loss of days which he was beginning to feel shortening menacingly. However, the success of the concert on the 8th was comforting, especially since the triumph of the evening was the première of the overture to *Der Freischütz*.[2] Picking Caroline up in Hamburg on the way home, together with a pet monkey named Schnuff, he set off for Dresden; but Caroline miscarried again, and there was opportunity for a concert only in Brunswick before they thankfully reached Dresden on 4th November. By the 19th Caroline was sufficiently recovered to celebrate her birthday with a grotesque fancy dress masquerade that included all their animals.

The rest of the year was spent quietly. No further work on *Die drei Pintos* was done until January, but Weber's interest in Spanish subjects was further stimulated by the dramatic readings which Tieck used to hold in his own rooms: that autumn he gave his listeners five-act tragedies by Calderón, Moreto and Lope de Vega. Pizarro, Don John of Austria and even Columbus were ideas for a major opera which came under Weber's consideration, and matters had reached the stage of a dramatic plan for *Le Cid* being drawn up by Kind when news reached them of a *Cid* opera *Rodrigo und Zimene* by the Munich conductor Johann Aiblinger (Munich, 1st May 1821). For the rest, his attention was given mostly to further work on *Tonkünstlersleben* and his duties in the theatre. Here he at last managed to impress the royal family when, discovering that the score of *The Magic Flute* had been forgotten just as the performance was due to begin, he calmly conducted the first act from memory.

But this success was followed by no practical royal help in his efforts to

[1] Not Schall, as in MMW, Vol. II, p. 259.

[2] Max Maria evidently knew nothing of this, for he describes a subsequent Dresden performance as the première (MMW, Vol. II, p. 268). See Erik Abrahamsen: *Carl Maria von Weber in Copenhagen* in *The Chesterian*, June 1926, for documentation of the whole visit.

establish the German opera more firmly, and it was only Hummel's persuasiveness that overcame his reluctance to distract his attention by taking
on a pupil. This was the sixteen-year-old Julius Benedict, who had been
brought to Dresden in February by his father, a wealthy Stuttgart banker,
expressly in order to study with Weber. Twelve lessons a month were
agreed upon; but soon Benedict found himself virtually a son of the family
as well as Weber's most talented pupil, and subsequently his first English
biographer. 'I shall never forget the impression of my first meeting with
him,' Benedict was to write:

> Ascending the by no means easy staircase which led to his modest house in the
> old Market place, I found him sitting at his desk, and occupied with the
> pianoforte arrangement of his *Freischütz*. The dire disease which but too soon
> was to carry him off had made its mark on his noble features; the projecting
> cheek-bones, the general emaciation, told their sad tale; but in his clear blue
> eyes, too often concealed by a few straggling locks, in the sweet expression of
> his mouth, in the very tone of his weak but melodious voice, there was a magic
> power which attracted irresistibly all who approached him.[1]

On 14th March, *Preciosa* had its Berlin première. Max Maria asserts that
the music was hardly noticed by the newspaper critics but well liked by the
public, thus paving the way for a favourable reception of *Freischütz*. Weber
did not take up Brühl's offer to let him cast the opera himself, feeling that he
knew too little about the Berlin singers; he agreed, however, to write the
extra aria Brühl requested for Johanna Eunicke (Aennchen's 'Einst träumte
meiner selgen Base'). The opening of the opera house was due at the end of
the month, with *Freischütz* scheduled for the end of May. At 8.30 on the
morning of 2nd May, beginning two months' leave made possible by the
redecoration of the Dresden theatre, Weber, Caroline and their dog set off,
sped by the good wishes of their friends and even, in a special interview, of
young Prince Friedrich. On 4th May they were welcomed once again at the
Beers' house in Berlin.

With him Weber brought the sketches of an F minor Piano Concerto he
had begun at the end of February—or rather, resumed work on, for its
origins go back to 1815, as he told Rochlitz in a letter from Prague on 14th
March of that year: 'I have an F minor piano concerto planned. But as
concertos in the minor without definite, evocative ideas seldom work with the
public, I have instinctively inserted into the whole thing a kind of story whose
thread will connect and define its character—moreover, one so detailed and
at the same dramatic that I found myself obliged to give it the following
headings: Allegro, Parting. Adagio, Lament. Finale, Profoundest misery,
consolation, reunion, jubilation.' At the end of May and in the early part of
June he continued work on what his diary now describes as his *Konzertstück*

---

[1] Benedict: *op. cit.*, p. 61.

(Op. 79: J.282), finishing it on the very morning of the première of *Der Freischütz*. Benedict, who had lately arrived in Berlin and happened to be sitting with Caroline, describes how Weber came into the room and played them the new piece with a running commentary expanded from the original outline:

> The lady sits in her tower: she gazes sadly into the distance. Her knight has been for years in the Holy Land: shall she ever see him again? Battles have been fought; but no news of him who is so dear to her. In vain have been all her prayers. A fearful vision rises to her mind;—her knight is lying on the battle-field, deserted and alone; his heart's blood is ebbing fast away. Could she but be by his side!—could she but die with him! She falls exhausted and senseless. But hark! what is that distant sound? What glimmers in the sun-light from the wood? What are those forms approaching? Knights and squires with the cross of the Crusades, banners waving, acclamations of the people: and there!—it is he! She sinks into his arms. Love is triumphant. Happiness without end. The very woods and waves sing the song of love; a thousand voices proclaim its victory.[1]

Despite the apparent intricacy of the detail, there is very little real expansion here of the rough outline Weber gave Rochlitz in 1815, or indeed much to differentiate it from the *Adieux-Absence-Retour* pattern which a number of composers, most celebratedly Beethoven in his Op. 81a Piano Sonata, found a convenient framework for the three movements of a sonata. In the same letter, Weber told Rochlitz that he hated pieces of music with labels attached and was a little nervous of being misunderstood over this one; and though he was prepared to admit, at any rate to his wife and pupil, the dramatic basis of his invention, he never printed the story or indeed gave any encouragement for the work to be treated as programme music. As in the past, most recently with the *Freischütz* overture, it was by way of his dramatic imagination that he was most readily stimulated to a satisfying formal design—not at all the same thing as following a preconceived story with illustrative music. With the exception of the March, much the weakest of the four sections, there is nothing in the work to betray anything more specific than generalized emotions: the very lack of any attempt to portray the quasi-mediaeval shows that he was not concerned with illustration. The *Konzertstück* is really his third piano concerto, and in its binding of four sections together to make a single-movement work, it joins contemporaries such as Spohr's *Gesangsszene* violin concerto in providing a model for the one-movement concerto of the later Romantics and above all of Liszt.

Such weaknesses as the *Konzertstück* possesses, then, cannot be attributed to the pressures of narrative; they arise rather from the risk that charm may become merely winsome, flashing brilliance merely flashy. The octave glissandos, the spectacular, ever-widening right hand leaps, the famous

[1] Benedict: *op. cit.*, p. 66.

crescendo leading into the Allegro passionato, the racing fingerwork over strumming chords are easily enough indicted as instances of the desire for effect overcoming invention. Yet this is to miss the very real originality and judgement behind them. As Tovey, who confessed himself thrilled by the finale, has pointed out, 'the four movements are astonishingly successful in covering the exact ground of their own ideas at such length as leaves each ready to lead to the next'.[1] This is a description of a composer perfectly in control of not only his material but his form, in this case an empirical one guided only by sure dramatic instinct. Consciously the centre of the stage himself, as virtuoso performer, Weber makes his gestures somewhat larger than life as he addresses his audience across imaginary footlights, but his technique never falters—indeed, it is the spur to some of his finest effects— and there is no doubting his sincerity. 'He may move awkwardly from one situation to the next; the stage carpenter may even appear in shirt-sleeves during the transformation scenes; but the emotions are unmistakable and commanding of respect.'[2]

But Tovey also praised the haunting bassoon plaint over shivering strings that connects with the March, and especially the skill with which Weber anticipates the theme of the Allegro as he nears the end of the opening Larghetto. There are plenty of parallels for linking movements in this way, but the method here is as sophisticated as anything in Liszt, who, like Chopin, also developed much in his actual piano-writing from Weber. The whole of the Larghetto is a *locus classicus* of Romantic piano style, from the use of staccato and legato in the same hand at the first entry (as in the Third Piano Sonata) to the elaborate fantasia which rapidly develops, discoursing in a manner somewhere between Chopinesque enrichment of a line with exploratory delight and the virtuoso thematic coruscations of Liszt. Yet this new technique is securely grounded in the manner Weber had developed from his predecessors in the first three piano sonatas, as already discussed. The *Konzertstück* is a keystone work of Romantic piano writing, crowning the bridge that leads from Dussek, Hummel, Kalkbrenner, Prince Louis Ferdinand and their contemporaries into the mid nineteenth-century and Mendelssohn, Schumann, Chopin and Liszt; while its influence was consciously acknowledged as late as 1929 by one of Weber's greatest modern admirers, Stravinsky, in his Capriccio.

The audience that began converging on the new theatre erected by Schinkel in the Gendarmenmarkt that evening was already divided into two factions. Behind Weber were ranged, for the most part, the intellectuals and middle classes, the groups from which had been drawn the most vehement patriots during the war and after. Despite the success of *Preciosa* on 14th

[1] D. F. Tovey: *Essays in Musical Analysis*, Vol, 4: reprinted from the programme of a 1931 Reid Concert at which Tovey had himself played the solo piano part.
[2] D. F. Tovey: *op. cit.*

March, not all were automatically Weber's supporters: outside his own circle of admirers there were many who feared that, having written his last opera ten years previously and having never had any very spectacular operatic success, he might not be powerful enough to represent them against the enemy—Spontini. He too was the unwitting champion of a cause, in this case upheld by the court and aristocracy. Ever since Friedrich III had opened the first opera house in Berlin in 1688, and the first public performances had followed there in 1702, there had been a tradition of royal patronage. Frederick the Great had resolved that one of his first works would be to erect an opera worthy of his capital; this he did in 1742. But latterly a decline had set in, Friedrich Wilhelm III showing a taste for spectacle that served to widen the gap between the elaborate court operas, reflecting the surviving panoply of royalty in a fashion reassuring to a post-Revolutionary aristocracy, and the increasingly popular German operas. The King's importation of a Franco-Italian composer in 1819 added to the impatience of the general public, and this was not in any way calmed by Spontini's overbearing manner, the open quarrels between him and Brühl, and the vast sums of money that were known to be being spent on his operas. For the Berlin production of *Olympie* Spontini had insisted on forty-two rehearsals covering a period of three months; yet he had failed to keep in proper touch with his ballet and chorus masters or even to allow adequate time to the translator (none other than Hoffmann). Even the King grew disturbed at the expenditure; but the first performance, postponed through Spontini's negligence from 5th March to 14th May 1821, was a triumph, by contemporary accounts one of overwhelming brilliance and sumptuousness. The division of opinion over Spontini sharpened, especially when the third performance already showed a falling off in attendance. The greater the satisfaction of the court, the more urgent the need became among the opposing party for Weber's opera to conquer. Each composer thus found himself cast in a role not of his seeking; personally they were perfectly prepared to be on good terms, and indeed Spontini had made a point of calling on Weber to welcome him on his arrival in the city.

Although Weber had been able to secure no more than sixteen rehearsals for his opera, matters had been going well. He was pleased with his charming and talented Agathe, Caroline Seidler, and with Johanna Eunicke (Aennchen) Carl Stümer (Max) and Heinrich Blume (Caspar). The staging caused more argument. Carl Gropius's sets portray, for instance, a substantial and lavishly appointed room for the simple forester's daughter and a forest redolent of a well-tended park, formalizing what needed to be informal, direct and natural. There was also some minor bother over the trappings of the Wolf's Glen, such as a mechanical owl that refused to lift one wing. Here Weber had overruled Gropius's intelligent suggestions that the spectral apparitions should be only vaguely discerned, hinted at as if produced by a convulsion of the elements; but in the end they reached complete agreement. He failed, unfortunately, to win his point over the dresses, whose ballet conventions were said to be to the taste of the Berlin public: he had wanted rough, simple costumes of the period, soon after the Thirty Years' War. But he seems to have approached the performance with equanimity of the artist who is satisfied that the preparations are complete, and spent the afternoon resting.

Benedict was not so easily calmed:

> As early as four o'clock I joined the crowd besieging the theatre; and when, two hours later, the doors were opened, I was literally carried into the pit by that surging human wave. The sterner sex prevailed on that evening. Many Iron Crosses were to be seen, and the students of the University mustered in large numbers. Frau von Weber was in a pit box with William Beer (brother of Meyerbeer) and his wife. E. T. Hoffmann (author of the Fantasie-Stücke), Professor Lichtenstein, Wollank, Gubitz, Heinrich Heine, and a host of literary and musical aspirants, amongst them little Felix Mendelssohn, with his parents and friend Dr. Caspar, occupied boxes and stalls.[1]

Heine, who had been busy with puns on Kind's name and the *kindische Verse* that would do for *Childe Harold*, has left a description of the figure that limped into the orchestra on the stroke of seven.

> Weber's appearance is not very prepossessing. Small stature, a shocking gait and a long face with no especially striking feature. But in this face is harboured the thoughtfulness, the confidence and the serene resolve that has so magnetic effect in pictures of the old German masters.[2]

The overture was greeted with loud applause, and encored; but despite occasional outbursts of enthusiasm, the rest of the first act was received with a certain puzzlement. Even 'Durch die Wälder' and Caspar's drinking song failed to make their expected mark, Max Maria records. The first interval found the Spontini party much reassured. But with the second act, it seems that the novel taste of the music had begun to be accepted. 'Kommt ein schlanker Bursch' went over well; but the turning point came with Seidler's singing of 'Leise, leise'; the applause and cheering stopped the show. The following Trio was also delightedly received; and the act ended on a sensation with the Wolf's Glen. The noise was deafening: a student beneath Caroline's box was overheard complaining, as he blew on his smarting hands, 'He's a devil of a fellow, that little Weber! It's hard work showing him how well he's done!' The last act went equally well: surprisingly the Huntsmen's Chorus failed to come over successfully, but the Bridesmaids' Chorus was encored, although nervously delivered by the First Bridesmaid, Henriette

---

[1] Benedict: *op. cit.* p. 66.

[2] Heinrich Heine: *Brief aus Berlin* No. 2, in *Sämtliche Werke* ed. Gerich, Vol. 2, p. 212 (1925). Heine contrasts Spontini's proud, dominating presence.

CARL MARIA VON WEBER
Portrait by John Cawse, painted between 14th March and 5th June, 1826

Reinwald; and by now the audience was so enraptured that, despite a certain coolness over the length of the finale, the evening ended in an overwhelming triumph. Wreaths, flowers and verses flew—including a verse whose satirical reference to Spontini's rival production was to cause unnecessary bad blood. Later that night Weber was able to note in his diary:

> In the evening, as the first opera in the new *Schauspielhaus*, *Der Freischütz* was received with the most incredible enthusiasm. Overture and *Volkslied* encored, of seventeen numbers fourteen uproariously applauded; but everything went excellently and was sung with love; I was called out and took Mme. Seidler and Mlle. Eunicke as I couldn't get hold of the others. Poems and wreaths flew.
> *Soli Deo Gloria.*

Earlier he had gone with his friends to celebrate at Jagor's Restaurant in Unter den Linden. The group included the Beer family, Lichtenstein, P. A. Wolf, Benedict, Rellstab, Gubitz and Hoffmann. The latter's behaviour over the whole première is somewhat enigmatic. Two days previously he had given a party for Weber at which he had raised his glass 'To my favourite composer—after Spontini' and invented a weird tale as he sketched a portrait of Weber about the latter's elopement with an innkeeper's daughter. When Weber, amused, came over to shake his hand, he cried out over the unfinished sketch, 'The face doesn't matter; the spirit is the most important thing!' At the second party, while Gubitz was reciting a set of ponderous verses in Weber's honour, Hoffmann sank slowly beneath the table between Caroline and Wilhelm Beer's wife, reappearing behind the composer, making a hideous face, to crown him with a laurel wreath as he exclaimed, 'Isn't he as grand as Tasso?' He further reduced Caroline to tears by his satirical comments on the supernatural effects—the 'fiery cab' and the 'Hermit who falls from the clouds', and so forth. Hoffmann has also always been accepted as the author of several articles on the work that appeared in the *Vossiche Zeitung*, notably two written on 26th and 28th June appraising the work levelly but with a distinct coolness. Having allowed Weber mastery of instrumental effect and profound understanding of the theatre, so that he knows how to win over his listeners with the slenderest means, this critical analysis then proceeds to praise certain numbers highly but to question others in a manner that must have been made more painful to Weber by its suggestions of influence by Spontini.[1] As the translator of *Olympie*, Hoffmann was of course in an awkward position. His baiting of Weber seems to suggest jealousy, and frustration at finding himself committed to the wrong camp, getting the better of genuine friendship and admiration.

Hoffmann's was not the only critical voice to be raised against *Der*

---

[1] Hoffmann's authorship of these famous criticisms is challenged in a long thesis by Wolfgang Kron: *Die angeblichen Freischütz-Kritiken E.T.A. Hoffmanns* (1957).

Freischütz. Zelter sent a characteristically grudging report back to Goethe, admitting that the music was good enough to make the public swallow everything but concluding that Weber had 'made a colossal nothing out a void'.[1] Tieck, surprisingly, called it 'the most unmusical hubbub that ever roared upon the stage'. Spohr expressed the view of several other critics when he wrote, a year later, that he could only explain its success by Weber's gift for writing for the general masses (he had himself abandoned work on a *Freischütz* with a tragic ending, to a libretto by Georg Döring, on learning of Weber's plans). The masses certainly remained entranced: within six months the work was heard the exceptional number of seventeen times, always to full houses. Max Maria enthusiastically declares that Weber was to friends of German opera in 1821 what Blücher had been to the whole German people in 1815—a reference to Waterloo and the *Freischütz* première both occurring on 18th June. No German opera has ever been taken up so widely and so rapidly. At least thirty different productions are recorded by the end of 1822, and there have been translations into at least twenty European languages. Berlin went on to have its five hundredth performance by 1884, its eight hundred and fiftieth by 1937; the tally must now be into four figures in that city alone. At one time during 1824 there were three productions running simultaneously in London, and there are endless tales of the work's incredible popularity, from the report in Kind's *Freischützbuch* of a newly discovered disease being named *Freischützenfieber* and of a traveller finding negro slaves singing the Bridesmaids' Song as they worked in the sugar plantations, to the advertisement inserted in a London paper by a nobleman with the rider that no-one who could whistle tunes from *Der Freischütz* need apply.[2]

Delighted by the success, Weber was nevertheless hurt by the repeated suggestion that he owed it all to the sensationalism of the Wolf's Glen. He was also troubled by the thought that Spontini believed him responsible for the poem, fluttering down on the first night, which observed that his shooting was likely to hit nobler game than an elephant—a reference to the most-publicized feature of *Olympie*. He even inserted a notice in the papers courteously suggesting that what might be a scratch to a more celebrated man had wounded him like a dagger, and that the famous elephant was in any case a considerably nobler beast than his poor owls. But Spontini was not to be pacified; and he had indeed been struck a mortal blow. As Philipp Spitta wrote, 'The immediate success of Weber's work may not have more than equalled that of *Olympie*, but it soon became evident that the chief effect of the latter was astonishment, while the former set the pulse of the

---

[1] Zelter was later to tell Goethe that Berlioz's *Huit Scènes de Faust* (1828) were a 'series of grunts, snorts and expectorations.'

[2] For statistics of the work's success, see Alfred Loewenberg: *Annals of Opera* (1943: rev. 1954), and for a fuller account, Hans Schnoor: *Weber auf dem Welttheater* (1942).

German people beating.'[1] Spontini was guilty of intrigues against Weber, but to no avail; and he had need of the censor to control the expression of public feeling against him. His reputation was on the point of decline, and the success of Weber's work served to underline how late it had grown for him. It is thus the more to his credit that he conducted the ninety-ninth performance of *Der Freischütz* for the benefit of Weber's widow and children, on 6th November 1826.

Weber did not have much time in Berlin to enjoy his greatest hour. Nine days after the première, on 30th June, he was to set out for Dresden once more; meanwhile, there was time for one concert, on the 25th. It was not a success, in spite of a warm reception for the new *Konzertstück*. The occasion was enlivened by the presence of the French violinist Alexandre Boucher, who liked to insist that he had been turned out of France because of his resemblance to Napoleon, whose triumphs on the field of battle he claimed to equal in the concert hall. Accompanied by Weber, he began the Variations on a Norwegian Air; but, recounts Max Maria:

> At a wave from Boucher, Weber stopped; and he and the astounded public suddenly heard tremolandos, pizzicatos and other coarser instrumental tricks, an imitation of the heavy drum-beats announcing Samiel's appearance, and then a whole firework display, an *olla podrida* of themes from *Der Freischütz*. Finally, after highly extravagant modulations, arpeggios and other pieces of tightrope walking, the good fellow lost his balance completely and could find no way of getting back to the original piece—so, as if inspired from above, he dropped his violin and leapt upon the stupefied, half irritated, half amused Weber, embraced him in front of everyone and shouted with a loud voice, as if choked with tears. 'Ah grand maître! que j'aime, que j'admire!'[2]

The return to Dresden was scarcely that of a conquering hero. The first need was to attend to Caroline, who was still unwell. On Dr. Hedenus's advice Weber installed her on 21st July with a friend, Charlotte von Hanmann, at the little spa of Schandau five miles away; but crossing the Elbe at Pirna, in a storm on his return, his horses took fright at the thunder and nearly plunged into the river dragging the carriage with them. Shaken, Weber drafted his will immediately on reaching home; in it he leaves everything to Caroline, specifically excluding his brothers and other relations. The following day he called to see Kind, but the poet had gone to Teplitz. A fortnight later he wrote a pleasant letter recounting their joint success. Kind replied after nearly another fortnight in a fit of the sulks; he was never persuaded that *Der Freischütz* was not really his own creation, decked with trivial and distracting music, and neither Weber's most eloquent assurances of his respect for the lofty role of the librettist nor even the offer to double the

[1] Article on Spontini in *Grove's Dictionary*.
[2] MMW, Vol. 2, p. 327.

original payment in proof of this would mollify him.[1] Meanwhile, Weber was approached with an offer to transfer to Cassel with full powers, a pension and a salary which at 2,500 thalers was a thousand more than he was getting at Dresden. Delicate negotiations with his new chief, the minister H. H. von Könneritz, resulted in a rise of 300 thalers, but not the decoration which Weber (in such matters very much Franz Anton's son) also craved. The pleasure of getting more money was also mitigated by the same rise being awarded to Morlacchi. The post at Cassel went instead to Spohr, at Weber's recommendation. He continued work on *Die drei Pintos* from July to November, breaking off in September for a festal cantata, *Du bekranzend uns're Laren* (J.283) to celebrate the birthday of the King's sister Maria Amalie of Zweibrücken. Composed for SSTB soloists, choir, flute and piano (presumably Fürstenau and himself) to a lame text by Kind, its eight numbers are pleasant enough but remarkable chiefly for No. 8, 'Sänge und Tänze', which was to reappear as No. 9, 'Fröliche Klänge', in the Finale to Act 1 of *Euryanthe*. The anxieties and annoyances began to mount again. Caroline was once more in the throes of a difficult pregnancy. Pleasure at the success of *Der Freischütz* was marred by reports of its emasculation by the censor, as at a Vienna performance on 3rd October, with the seventeen-year-old Wilhemine Schröder as Agathe, in which all firearms and the appearances of Samiel and the Hermit were banned. The renovated Dresden theatre was opened with Rossini's *La Donna del Lago* instead of his hoped-for *Don Giovanni* in German, with Bassi, Mozart's first Giovanni, helping in the production. *Der Freischütz* fell victim to intrigues to keep it off the stage. Finally, when he was refused permission to produce *Die drei Pintos*, which he had intended to dedicate to the King and stage at Dresden, Weber had his first haemorrhage.

---

[1] Kind received some support from Goethe, who told Eckermann that some honour ought to go to the author of such a good subject for music which might otherwise not have made its effect.

CHAPTER THIRTEEN

DIE DREI PINTOS

A prudent man will think more important what fate has conceded to him than what it has denied.

BALTASAR GRACIÁN

DEPRESSED BY the renewed volume of worries in the aftermath of his Berlin triumph, Weber was further upset to receive press reports disparaging the form of *Der Freischütz* and querying its composer's ability to tackle anything larger than this kind of *Singspiel*. As he told Helmina von Chezy, who had observed how pleased he must be by the Berlin reception, 'Praise lifts me up to a dizzy height; it delights me, but I am shattered by the smallest, even the most unjustified and ridiculous reproach.'[1] When on 11th November he received a letter from Domenico Barbaia, the Italian impresario who had that year taken over the lease of the Kärntnertor Theatre in Vienna, asking him for an opera for the 1822–3 season, he leapt at the chance of answering these criticisms. It was obviously the wrong moment for a comedy, and accordingly he put *Die drei Pintos* aside in favour of a grand opera, *Euryanthe*. But he never intended to abandon *Pintos* completely. On 17th May 1824 he told Lichtenstein that he was as fed up with it as with all music, and wrote again on 6th September saying that he still felt unable to rekindle his interest in it; however, his diary for 20th September observes laconically, 'GePintot'; and on 23rd December he wrote again to Lichtenstein saying that he was resolved to finish it that winter. In the eighteen months that then remained to him, there was no time to spare for it.

The idea for *Die drei Pintos* came from a *Novelle*, *Der Brautkampf*, by Carl Seidel, published in four consecutive numbers of the Dresden *Abendzeitung*, Nos. 299–302 for Wednesday to Saturday 15th–18th December 1819. The *Abendzeitung*, at that stage a small printed sheet folded once to make four pages, usually led with a story or a poem of some kind, the general level of which was more self-conscious and artificial than Seidel's quite simply, even drily, narrated comedy.

I. Don Pantaleon Roiz de Pacheco lives in an ancient palace in Seville, spending his time poring over the history of his family and their triumphs over the

---

[1] Helmina von Chezy: *Carl Maria von Webers Euryanthe*, in *NZfM*, Vol. 13, No. 1 (July 1840).

Moors. When he finds that a certain Don Carlos Fonseca had saved the last of his line in battle, he determines to marry his only daughter, Clarissa, to a Fonseca. Discovering one Capt. Don Nunno Mansos de Fonseca in Badajoz, he writes recommending his daughter's charms. But the Captain, a sexagenarian, suggests instead of himself his son Don Pinto—all this to the distress of Clarissa, who is secretly in love with Don Gomez Freires. Meanwhile, the adventurer Don Gaston Viratos is enjoying himself, together with his servant Ambrosio, in a tavern in Salvaleon. A curious figure now turns up dressed in a *mélange* of clothes from various centuries, military and knightly, and introduces himself as Don Pinto, on his way to marry the prettiest girl in Seville. Having eaten and drunk as heavily as he can be made to, he falls into a stupor. Gaston, removing his letters of introduction and identity, sets off in his place and is met on the outskirts of Seville by a servant who offers to conduct him to Pantaleon.

II. The house in which he finds himself turns out to belong to Gomez, who begs 'Pinto' not to pursue this marriage to a girl he cannot love, asks his friendship (with a fight to the death as an alternative) and offers his sister Laura as substitute. Gaston agrees to help and suggests that Gomez, whom Pantaleon has never met, take on the identity of Pinto while he himself be called, say, Don Gaston Viratos. Pantaleon prepares a feast, and introduces Gomez as Don Pinto to the astonished Clarissa.

III. The double pretence continues for a few days. But one day a tall, thin man limps through the door, and demands where Pinto is: it is Don Nunno. Gomez has to reveal his true identity, and assures the furious Nunno, who thinks they have murdered his son, that Pinto will be along shortly.

IV. The real Pinto is now announced, roundly abused by his father for abandoning his bride, and urged to fight for her. The bewildered Pinto obediently draws his sword to begin the bridal battle, and is lightly pricked by the amused Gomez. Pinto screams and gives up all claims to Clarissa. Gaston, fetched by her, disarms Nunno, disentangles Pantaleon from the armour into which he has been struggling, and confesses responsibility for the whole affair. Nunno threatens him and is again disarmed: when the furious old man attacks Gaston barehanded, he is put in a cupboard. In Pantaleon's eyes, the Fonsecas have disgraced themselves and the Pachecos come out well; he is thus reconciled to Gomez marrying Clarissa. All ends happily, with Gaston paired off with Laura, Ambrosio with Clarissa's maid, and even Pinto, on the journey home, finding consolation with the innkeeper's daughter.

Upon this story, Theodor Hell based a libretto in three acts,[1] slightly altering the order of events so as to open in Pantaleon's house before introducing Gaston at the inn and dropping one or two other features.

Don Pantaleon de Pacheco of Seville (bass) has promised his niece Clarissa (sop.) to Don Pinto de Fonseca (bass), son of his friend Don Nunno de Fonseca; neither Pantaleon, Clarissa nor her maid Laura (sop.) has ever seen

[1] Theodor Hell: *Die drei Pintos*. MS in *Weberiana*, Classe VII, No. 26.

him. En route to claim his bride, Pinto comes to an inn between Salamanca and Madrid where he meets the student Don Gaston (ten.) and tells him the purpose of his journey. Deciding to take his place, Gaston makes Pinto drunk with the help of his servant Ambrosio (bass) and the innkeeper's daughter Inez (sop.), and hurries off to Seville in his place. Before seeing Pantaleon, he meets Clarissa's lover Don Gomez (ten.) who takes him for the real Pinto. Gaston promises to withdraw his suit and support Gomez, giving him Pinto's papers and himself pretending to be the friend of this third 'Pinto'. Both are cordially received by Pantaleon; and Gomez becomes officially engaged to Clarissa. Suddenly the real Pinto appears outside the house, but is declared by Gaston to be a scheming interloper and is accordingly turned away by the servants. At the betrothal party organised by Pantaleon, Nunno de Fonseca unexpectedly arrives. Having gained admittance with him, Pinto has now to be recognised as authentic. Eventually all is resolved, and Gomez and Clarissa are betrothed.

In Weber's original plan this allowed for seventeen musical numbers, including an overture; but when work on the opera was dropped on 8th November 1821, he had only sketched seven:

Act 1

No. 1   Introduction: Chorus with Clarissa, Laura and Pantaleon, 'Wisst ihr nicht'.

No. 2   Recit. and Aria: Clarissa, 'Ach wenn dies du doch: Wonnigsüsses Hoffnungsträumen'.

No. 3a   Duett: Clarissa and Gomez, 'Ja sie wird'.
    3b   Terzett: Clarissa, Gomez and Laura, 'Geschwind nur von hinnen'.

No. 4   Duett: Seguidillos à dos: Inez and Gaston, 'Wir den Musen'.

No. 5   Terzett: Gaston, Pinto, Ambrosio, 'Also frisch!'

No. 6   Finale: Inez, Gaston, Pinto and Chorus, 'Auf das Wohlsinn'.

Act 2

No. 7   Duett: Gaston, Ambrosio, 'Nun da sind wir'.

As has been already mentioned, Weber's diary throughout his life recorded two separate processes in the preparation of a work. 'Componirt' applies to the stage when the music was actually invented, in many cases away from music paper or piano but composed down to such final detail that he could play the piece, completed in his mind, to his friends and even (as with his last song, *Gesang der Nurmahal*) in public without notes. The actual writing down was in many cases a purely mechanical process of copying which the diary describes as 'notirt'. Benedict has left us a vivid account of these working methods.

> Many a time he might be seen early in the morning, some closely written pages in his hand, which he stood still to read, and then wandered on through forest and glen muttering to himself. He was learning by heart the words of *Euryanthe*, which he studied until he made them a portion of himself, his own

creation, as it were. His genius would sometimes lie dormant during his frequent repetition of the words, and then the idea of a whole musical piece would flash upon his mind, like the bursting of light into darkness. It would then remain there uneffaced, gradually assuming a perfect shape, and not till this process was attained would he put it down on paper. His first transcriptions were generally penned on the return from his solitary walks. He then noted the voices fully and only marked here and there the harmonies or the places where particular instruments were to be introduced. Sometimes he indicated by signs, known only to himself, his most characteristic orchestral effects; then he would play to his wife or to me, from these incomplete sketches, the most striking pieces of the opera, invariably in the form they afterwards maintained. The whole was already so thoroughly developed in his brain that his instrumentation was little more than the labour of a copyist; and the notes flowed to his pen with the marks of all the shading of expression, as if copper-plated on the paper.[1]

Benedict has further testified to the completeness in Weber's mind of the whole of the music for Act 1 of *Pintos*.

It was the privilege of the writer of these lines not only to hear every piece of the first act as it came fresh from the brain of the author, but to become so familiar with them that he could remember every note, though they were penned in the usual hieroglyphic style of the master, who, having the whole, with all its instrumental and choral effects, perfect in his head, was satisfied with writing only the vocal parts, in many instances without even a bass, and with very scanty indications of the accompaniment. Had the task of completing the fragments been confided immediately after the death of the beloved master, or even one or two years later, to his pupil, he could have supplemented the deficiencies and omissions, and at any rate have presented a piano-forte score containing the harmonies and chief features of every number; but this was not to be.[2]

Benedict's obvious disappointment may have led him to exaggerate the contribution he could have made; but his evidence is supported by the surviving sketches, which match his descriptions. Some of them turn up in unlikely places, jotted on the staves left over from other works: for instance, part of No. 2 is found on a couple of staves under the original sketch for Agathe's 'Leise, leise'.[3] Others are isolated, but there is nothing approaching any full notation, and no orchestration apart from stray indications and, curiously, an eighteen-bar opening of the Introduction (a good number of the bars silent) scored in full. In most cases there is a fairly or completely

---

[1] Benedict: *op. cit.*, p. 83–4.

[2] Benedict: *op. cit.*, p. 173–4.

[3] This was Weber's common practice. The MS first draft of the *Invitation to the Dance* (in the State Library, Berlin) includes, on the back, parts of the Eight Pieces for Piano Duet.

full notation of the voice parts, but the accompaniment is sketched in as if needed only as a reminder to a composer for whom instrumental effects were in any case the most vivid. Thus, the chorus part of No. 1 is apparently complete, but the bass line is very tenuously marked in and often missing altogether. Similarly the solo voice parts may be accompanied by only a single line to mark the orchestral accompaniment, even when the latter comes between vocal entries. This process is repeated throughout the sketches, which were carefully collected and copied by Jähns.[1] They total, by his reckoning, 1,769 bars (as compared to 1,298 of the whole of *Abu Hassan*).

After Weber's death there developed a story that he had in fact finished the opera, or at any rate scored what has survived in sketch. In 1848 Caroline asked Benedict if he remembered seeing a full score, which she maintained had been completed, in the same neat handwriting as that of the *Freischütz* and *Euryanthe* scores, and taken with the composer on all his travels including the last one to London. Benedict had seen only sketches, but he shared her view; so did Lichtenstein, to whom Weber had played parts of *Oberon* and *Pintos* when in Berlin between 7th and 29th December 1823. On this occasion he told Lichtenstein that both operas were almost finished. Benedict thought it possible that one of those who had come to pay their last respects to the dead composer in Sir George Smart's house on the morning of 5th June 1826 had quietly removed the score, as Moscheles did with a small laundry list he found by the bed; and this impression was reinforced by the discovery of the eighteen bars of full score on the first side of a sheet of music paper used as folder for the sketches, leaving open the possibility that there had been more in full score. Further, there is the evidence of a table setting out Weber's outline for the opera, copied from his MS (now lost) by Theodor Hell and giving the following details.

Overture: 2/4 D major.

Act 1

No. 1   Introduction, 9 minutes. B♭. 4/4, 3/4, 6/8.
No. 2   Aria (Clarissa). 7½ mins. (± 1½ mins.). D major. C. 3/4.
No. 3   Duett and Terzett. 9 mins. (± 2 mins.). E♭. 4/4, 3/4.
No. 4   Canzonetta (Gaston and Inez). 5 mins. C major. 3/4.
No. 5   Terzetto. 9 mins. (± 3 mins.). B major.
No. 6   Finale. 9 mins. D major. 4/4, 6/8.
        Total: 70 minutes, of which 14 minutes dialogue.

Act 2

No. 7   Duetto. G major. 2/4.
No. 8   Aria (Gomez). C major.
No. 9   Duett. A major.
No. 10   Aria (Pinto). E major. 2/4.
No. 11   with Chorus. E♭.

[1] The fair copy is in *Weberiana*, Classe III, Bd. 5, No. 80.

No. 12 Finale. F major. 3/4, 5/6 [NB: the latter is inexplicable. There are no other durations given in this act, though it might still mean 5–6 minutes. Possibly Hell misread Weber's rapid scrawl.]

Act 3

No. 13 Quintetto. E major.

No. 14 Aria (Pantaleon). C major.

No. 15 Romanze A♭.

No. 16 Finale. D major.

Unfortunately the possibility that a score of the complete work may yet turn up does not survive the other evidence, some of which was expounded by Jähns.[1] In the first place, when Weber told Lichtenstein that the two operas were almost finished, more than half the work on *Oberon* remained to be done; the same could thus equally well apply to *Pintos*. Between the end of 1824 (when, as pointed out above, Weber wrote to Lichtenstein saying he meant to finish the work that winter) and his death eighteen months later, there was little time in which he could have done so much; and his diary, which throughout his life recorded the composition done during a day and had listed dates on which he had worked on various of the seven extant *Pinto* numbers, has nothing to say about any work done on the opera after 1824. The existence of a single sheet of full score really implies nothing about what else may have existed; and as for the table setting out his plans—as was seen in the case of *Der Freischütz*, Weber took the greatest care to plan his works systematically, so that sensible proportions and if possible an expressive key pattern were laid down as the foundations of his invention. It will be noted that the timings cease with the end of the first act, and that the time-signatures become less frequent. There is also the point that No. 13 is marked in the original libretto as an extensive musical number, but was later struck out by Hell; naturally it would have been replaced by something substantial, but this was never written, and Hell is unlikely to have crossed out a number that had, as 'Quintetto. E major' already been set by Weber. All in all, it has to be assumed that nothing beyond the sketches and the solitary page of full score was written down.

Naturally there arose the problem of what to do with the sketches that had survived. Various musicians took an interest in them, including Weber's Dresden successor, Carl Reissiger; but Caroline was persuaded (against her will, she later told Benedict, whom she first wanted to approach) that the best chance of working them up into some performable version lay with Meyerbeer. For twenty years he kept them, eventually confessing that he could do nothing with them. In 1847 they were accordingly returned to Max Maria von Weber, on whose death in 1881 they passed to his son Capt. Carl von Weber, then stationed in Leipzig. Through the Director of the Opera,

[1] In an article written for the *Vossiche Zeitung* in 1867, variously reprinted including in his catalogue of Weber's works (J.).

Staegemann, Capt. Weber met the new young *Kapellmeister*, who arrived in 1886 to assist Nikisch, Gustav Mahler. Whether Capt. Weber was also aware that Mahler soon became embroiled in an affair with his wife is unknown; but matters eventually reached the pitch when Frau Weber considered eloping with Mahler. At all events, in 1887 Capt. Weber handed over to Mahler the *Pintos* sketches, together with a version of the libretto he had himself devised. Mahler was already a great admirer of Weber: his *Das klagende Lied* of 1880 reflects this, and he had recently composed the first of his *Des Knaben Wunderhorn* songs from the copy of Arnim and Brentano owned by the Weber family. One of his first tasks on arriving in Leipzig was to prepare a centenary cycle of Weber's operas; and highly interested in the *Pintos* fragments, he took them away to study during his summer holiday. He was immediately captivated by the charm of the melodies, and decided that enough music existed to make two acts; the third could be spoken. The impracticability of this became evident to Mahler, Capt. Weber and Staegemann at the first *Zimmerprobe*; accordingly it was decided to supplement the original with some of Weber's little known pieces, which Mahler would select and score, together with his completion and scoring of the sketches, so as to make a thoroughly revised three-act opera.

In its new form, the libretto ran as follows:

Act 1: On the terrace of an inn at Penaranda, students from Salamanca are gathered to say goodbye to Don Gaston Viratos (ten.) who has graduated and is leaving with his servant Ambrosio (bar.) to become a lawyer in Madrid (No. 1, Chorus: 'Leeret die Becher'). He wonders how to brighten his future, and calling for the bill, thinks of the chances and attendant difficulties of finding a girl (No. 2, Rondo à la Polacca: 'Was ich dann tu' '). The Landlord (bass) produces a bill which makes Gaston and Ambrosio wonder how so much can have gone in one day (No. 3, Terzettino: 'Ei! ei! ei!'). He demands more wine to cheer himself up; Ambrosio discovers the landlord's daughter, Inez (sop.), who sings them a parody song about a lovesick tom-cat (No. 4: *Romanze vom verliebten Kater Mansor*: 'Leise weht' es'). Gaston recounts to her the pleasures of the carefree student life, to her cynical comments on the woman's angle of this (No. 5, Seguidilla a dos: 'Wir die den Musen dienen'). There now appears the grotesque, loutish figure of Don Pinto de Fonseca (bass), a young nobleman from Castille, who stumbles in saddlesore and demanding refreshment. He tells Gaston of his coming marriage to Don Pantaleone Roiz de Pacheco's daughter, whom he hasn't seen, and shows his letters of introduction. He is worried about his wooing technique, in which Gaston promptly gives him a lesson, using Ambrosio as stand-in for the lady (No. 6, Terzett: 'Also frisch). They then settle down to eat and drink. In the closing ensemble (No. 7, Finale: 'Auf das Wohlergeh'n der Gäste') Gaston determines that he cannot let a gross fool like Pinto claim the girl; he presses more and more wine on Pinto, who is eventually carried off to bed in a stupor while Gaston and Ambrosio depart with his papers for Madrid.

Act 2: The Introduction (No. 8, Introduction and Ensemble: 'Wisst ihr nicht')
is set in Don Pantaleone's house in Madrid, where the servants are gathered
for an announcement. Clarissa (sop.) with her maid Laura (mezzo) trying to
comfort her, is apprehensive about her father's threatened plans for her
'future happiness', which for her depends upon the absent Don Gomez: and
indeed Don Pantaleone (bass) announces that she is to be married to Don
Pinto in settlement of an old debt of honour to his father; all congratulate the
unhappy Clarissa. Laura tries to cheer her up by making her think of Gomez's
constancy (No. 9, Ariette: 'Höchste Lust ist treues Lieben'.) When Laura
goes off to find Gomez, who cannot present himself formally as he is in
disgrace following a duel, Clarissa muses on her hopes and fears (No. 10, Arie:
'Wonnesüsses Hoffnungsträumen'). Laura returns with Gomez (ten.) who
swears to stand by Clarissa (No. 11, Duett: 'Ja, das Wort'); in the ensuing
ensemble (No. 12, Terzett. Finale: 'Geschwind nur von hinnen'), Laura
urges them to flee since Pantaleone is approaching, and despite his protestations, Gomez vanishes.

Act 3: Laura and the servants are busy decorating the hall of the house with
flowers (No. 13, Lied mit Chor: 'Schmücket die Halle'). Pantaleone sends
them off saying that Pinto has arrived: enter Gaston and Ambrosio in high
spirits, ready to enjoy themselves whatever turns out (No. 14, Duett: 'Nun
da sind wir'). Ambrosio is not quite so optimistic as Gaston, but is cheered by
meeting Laura; both of them make up to her, but she is as cynical about men
as Inez was (No. 15, Terzettino: 'Mädchen, ich leide'). Gaston laughs at her
rejection of Ambrosio, who is not a whit put out (No. 16, Ariette: 'Ein
Mädchen verloren'). Gomez now arrives and demands that Gaston/Pinto
shall give up Clarissa, which after some resistance he agrees to do (No. 17,
Rondo-Terzett: 'Ihr, der so edel'). Gaston suggests that Gomez now become
Don Pinto, since Pantaleone does not know him; he himself will become Don
Gaston, the best man. The servants enter for the feast, and Pantaleone leads
in Clarissa (No. 18, Chor: 'Habt ihr es den schon vernommen?'). Gomez/
Pinto is welcomed and given Clarissa, as the girls come forward with wreaths
(No. 19, Mädchen-Chor: 'Mit lieblichen Blumen'). Suddenly the real Pinto
is announced. In the first finale (No. 20, Finale A: 'Was wollt ihr?'), he claims
his bride, to the general confusion. Gomez is enraged, Gaston amused; soon
Pantaleone becomes affronted by Pinto's manners and orders him out of the
house. When Pinto hesitates, Gaston threatens him with a dagger, and, much
alarmed, Pinto is ejected. Pantaleone cannot believe that such a figure is
really a Fonseca; but the truth now emerges, and Pantaleone is glad to settle
for Gomez as a son-in-law (No. 21, Finale B: 'Heil sei Euch, Don Pantaleone!').

To supplement the seven original Pintos numbers, Mahler searched
diligently through Weber's songs and choruses and, devised a very ingenious
three-act pattern:

Act 1
No. 1   Chor. *Das Turnierbankett* (J. 132: 1812).

No. 2   Rondo à la Polacca. Rondo alla Polacca for tenor, for insertion in *Der Freybrief* by 'Haiden' [*sic*] (J.77: 1809).[1]

No. 3   Terzettino. Three-part folksong 'Ei, ei, ei' for TTB (J.249: 1818).

No. 4   Romanze: *Alkansor und Zaide*, for voice and guitar, for Kind's drama *Das Nachtlager von Granada* (J.223: 1818).

No. 5   Seguidilla a dos. Orig. *Pintos* No. 4.

No. 6   Terzett. Orig. *Pintos* No. 5.

No. 7   Finale. Orig. *Pintos* No. 6.

Entr'Act Composed by Mahler on themes from the *Pintos* sketches.

Act 2

No. 8   Introduction and Ensemble. Orig. *Pintos* No. 1.

No. 9   Ariette. Triolett for voice and piano (J.256: 1819); and Waltz from *Ariette der Lucinde*, for Kauer's *Das Sternenmädchen* (J.194: 1816).

No. 10   Arie. Orig. *Pintos* No. 2.

No. 11   Duett. Orig. *Pintos* No. 3a.

No. 12   Terzett. Finale. Orig. *Pintos* No. 3b.

Act 3

No. 13   Lied mit chor. No. 7 of *Jubel-Cantate* (J.244: 1818).

No. 14   Duett. Orig. *Pintos* No. 7.

No. 15   Terzettino. Canon for three voices, *Mädchen, ach* (J.35: 1802).

No. 16   Ariette. Comic song, *Mein Weib ist capores* for Anton Fischer's Singspiel, *Der travestirte Aeneas*, for baritone (J.183: 1815).

No. 17   Rondo-Terzett. *Romance, Elle était simple*, for voice and piano (J.292: 1824); and, middle section of *Gesang der Nurmahal* from Moore's *Lalla Rookh*, 'From Chindara's warbling founts I come', for soprano and piano (J.308: 1826).

No. 18   Chor. Orig. *Pintos* No. 1 (as above, No. 8).

No. 19   Mädchen-Chor. No. 4 of Cantata *Den Sachsen-Sohn* (J.289: 1822).

No. 20   Finale A. Composed by Mahler on themes from Act 1.

No. 21   Finale B. Orig. *Pintos* No. 7 (as above No. 14).

Bald tabulation may leave the impression that Mahler's task consisted of little more than choosing suitable pieces, transposing and scoring them where necessary, and revising the rhythms to fit new words, then setting them beside the *Pintos* sketches he had completed from Weber's notes. His contribution is a great deal more substantial. Though he wrote no number developed exclusively on themes of his own invention, he had to supply a large amount of linking or filling-in music and was obliged to adapt the non-*Pintos* pieces to their new role. Not only did he revise the libretto without reference to Capt. Weber; he found that from his initial anxiety to sink

---

[1] Jähns assumes that *Der Freybrief* was a lost opera by Joseph Haydn. It was in fact a pasticcio put together by Fridolin Weber, based on Haydn's *La Fedeltà Premiata* but using a new text, and given by the family company at Meiningen in 1789 as *Der Freybrief von Joseph Haydn*. In November 1809 Fridolin wrote to his brother at Stuttgart asking for two pieces to insert in it. The above rondo was newly composed; a duet 'Dich an diess Herz' (J.78) was revised from No. 9 of *Peter Schmoll*.

Ex. 59

himself completely in Weber's spirit, he developed the boldness to use more of his own judgement and imagination.[1] The opening Chorus illustrates some of his methods. After twenty-one bars of his own he raises the curtain on the chorus singing the *Turnierbankett* music to his own accompaniment; Gaston's entry is Mahler, and the music proceeds (with a brief interpolation from No. 16 of the opera, Weber's original song *Mein Weib ist capores*) based on Weber music and incorporating stretches of the *Turnierbankett* chorus. The identification between the two composers is here so close that it is not always easy to define what is Weber, what Mahler basing his invention on phrases of Weber, and what Mahler's own. But not all the numbers are so complex in their make-up. No. 2 (Rondo alla Polacca) is virtually untouched Weber. For No. 3 (Terzettino) Mahler has added an accompaniment that simply doubles the voices discreetly. No. 4 (Romanze) was originally a guitar song based on a genuine Spanish tune that had been entered by a friend in Kind's commonplace book. The choice of this for the satirical song about the lovesick cat is brilliant—with only the slightest inflections on the singer's part, and a delicate underlining of them in Mahler's newly figured accompaniment, the trills and little leaning phrases of the original love-song unmistakably begin to mew. No. 9 (Ariette) is given a three-bar introduction, and, from about half-way, a more decorative accompaniment leading to an almost entirely new ending; the waltz refrain was originally one section of the *Ariette der Lucinde*, a song which provided a few phrases for Weber himself to re-use, in *Der Freischütz*. No. 13 is a comparatively formal item from the *Jubel-Cantate* entirely rewritten and rescored by Mahler to give an impression of much more relaxed gaiety. This is one of Mahler's most ingenious reworkings; by means of abbreviations, additions and some new counterpoint it is given a subtly new colour without altering its essential nature. In the case of No. 15 the brilliance lies in the choice itself—in spotting that a very plain little twelve-bar canon, written when Weber was sixteen, held the substance of a first-rate comic number for the stage. Weber told Gottfried Weber, in a letter of 16th May 1811, that he would never have been such an ass as to give it an accompaniment; all Mahler does is to add an ostinato of fourths on timpani and violas, later doubling up the parts, but the effect is as drily witty as in some of Sullivan's mock-academic ensembles (Ex. 59, opposite page).

No. 16 (Ariette) keeps close to the original. No. 17 brings two quite different songs together, altering them hardly at all until the last strophe, when Mahler produces an ingenious counterpoint in three voices on the music of the preceding song. No. 19, the last number directly imported, is virtually unaltered—Mahler skilfully sees that a pleasant number from a forgotten occasional cantata, *Den Sachsen-Sohn*, can be made to play a comparable role to that of the *Freischütz* Bridesmaids' Chorus.

[1] See Natalie Bauer-Lechner: *Aus einem Tagebuch über Mahler*, in *Der Merkur* Vol. III No. 5, March 1912.

Ex. 60

S.A.T.B. Chorus

mf Was wir lieb-en, was wir lieb-en, was uns hold und treu ge-blieb-en

Mässig traumhaft - leise

Woodwind

Brass

Triangle

Strings

W.W.

Brass

Str.

Two more numbers were composed by Mahler himself using the original *Pintos* music. No. 20 (Finale A) skilfully draws on material from Act 1, woven together with music of Mahler's own in a style that carefully preserves the manner of Weber's ensembles. With the Entr'Act, however, Mahler let himself go. Obviously he preferred not to attempt the overture that was in the original plan: not even his subtle and sympathetic identification with the material could produce a Weber overture. But the less spotlit Entr'Act gave him the chance for an original fantasy on ideas taken from all over the Pintos sketches; it is a kind of *hommage à Weber* by a composer who recognised with affection a musical ancestor. Although he naturally selects the themes that most suit his own invention, it is astonishing how close the two composers' natures are shown to be—how Mahler's already highly characteristic scoring reveals itself as a logical extension of methods developed by Weber, how immediately Mahlerian even a simple Weberian phrase becomes when recomposed in its new setting, as the very opening shows (Ex. 60, opposite page).

Mahler's work on the original *Pintos* is inevitably more controversial. Comparing the few faint scribbles left by Weber with the final Mahler version, one's first reaction is simply of admiration for the sheer feat of imagination in hearing the possibilities they might imply. Mahler's own personality was already, in 1887, well defined: aged twenty-seven, he had written *Das klagende Lied* and numbers of songs, including the *Lieder eines fahrenden Gesellen*; and the First Symphony and *Knaben Wunderhorn* settings were already in his mind. Yet except in the Entr'Act, he subdues his individuality without at the same time sacrificing his inventiveness. Nor is there any *pastiche*—simply a very intelligent musical deduction, based on close acquaintance with Weber's style, of what could have been expected. When one wants to take issue, it is always over points of detail rather than over the manner in which the work has been approached; and these are usually at moments when Mahler has seemingly feared to interpose too much of himself between us and Weber. The most striking instance occurs, perhaps naturally, in the largest solo aria, Clarissa's 'Wonnesüsses Hoffnungsträumen.' Originally a *solfeggio* written in Hosterwitz on 31st July 1818, this is set out in Weber's sketch as the opening theme after twenty-one bars of recitative (Ex. 61, p. 258).

All that Weber left here was the tune, the second strain very faintly sketched, with no indication whatever of how the accompaniment should go; and, especially since Mahler suggests by his transfer of the aria to its position in Act 2 and even by touches in the recitative that he takes this to be the equivalent of 'Leise, leise', it would seem more in character to accompany it with something richer than plain held chords with occasional passing notes— perhaps a steady crotchet motion on strings. Again, in the middle section Weber clearly seems to suggest that the *'bange Klopfen'* rhythm should

9

continue under the voice. Mahler resists this (his additions are in small notes) (Ex. 62, opposite page).

Obviously there is no end to the argument possible over individual examples, as over the scoring. Sensibly, Mahler has rescored even those imports into the opera which were already written by Weber with orchestral accompaniment, thus conveying a total character on the sound of the work rather than deferentially letting Weber's original stand where possible. Among those who were deeply impressed with this aspect of his work was the twenty-three-year-old Richard Strauss, who had just met Mahler and had the first act of *Pintos* played to him. He wrote enthusiastically to Bülow on 29th October 1887 of this 'masterpiece'—'most genuine, most likeable, and most gifted Weber! I believe you will be pleased with it too! Amongst other things, with Weber's technical mastery; completely free from dilettantism, such as crops up here and there in the other operas.'[1] Bülow, far from pleased, retorted on 27th March 1888 with a scathing attack on Strauss's lack of judgement about 'a monstrosity of syntactical and orthographical impurity . . . *wo Weberei, wo Mahlerei, einerlei*[2]—the whole thing, *per Bacco*, is infamous antiquated rubbish. I felt positively ill . . .' Strauss's answer on 17th April reads like that of a victim of brainwashing: 'How salutary for me was your justifiable reproach . . . It was terribly precipitate of me to recommend a work of which I only knew the first act . . . Mahler has committed some frightful stupidities . . . I only knew the first act, which Mahler played to me himself on the piano, with lively enthusiasm; this latter rather carried me away beyond myself, and so I now regret very much that you, most revered Master, should have been the innocent victim of my youthful impetuosity . . .' In his cringing anxiety to recant and return to a state of grace, Strauss adds some

Ex. 61

Clarissa

Langsam

Won - ne - süss - es Hoff - nungs-träum-en, wie ____ durch strö - mest

du   mein Herz!   willst die Wolk-en ros - ig__ säum - en,

Rüh - e__ ge - ben mein - em Schmerz.

[1] The quotations are from Hans von Bülow and Richard Strauss: *Correspondence* (ed. Willi Schuh and Franz Trenner, trans. Anthony Gishford 1955).

[2] The pun on their names, 'Weaver' and 'Painter', is untranslatable: literally, 'Where Webery, where Mahlery, it's all the same'.

detailed complaints about Mahler's scoring which do not stand up to investi-
gation—for instance, that Mahler 'constantly' writes for oboes up to high
F and G: there are only three high F's in the whole oboe part, and the G is
scrupulously avoided throughout. It is true, however, that the scoring lacks
the intense individuality of either composer; and given the amount that

Ex. 62

Mahler learned from Weber over the matter of writing for woodwind, especially, so that each voice in the choir gains rather than loses individuality by association with its neighbours, he was perhaps unnecessarily discreet. But *Die drei Pintos* in its Mahler form has a distinct character in sound as well as in material, and with such operations discretion is very forgivably the better part of valour.

One is perhaps the more anxious for Mahler to have taken a bolder hand at times since his complete rearrangement of the order of the music and events is so successful. By making Clarissa, like Agathe, delay her appearance until Act 2, he not only saves the big aria for this traditional place

Ex. 63

(No. 9 of Act 2 in Weber's original plan, the Duett in A major, was presumably to have been a love duet), but allows local colour and a comic atmosphere to be established from the outset—in accordance with Weber's own precepts when he dropped the opening scene of *Der Freischütz*. For Mahler also takes the opportunity of strengthening the Spanish flavour by importing another genuine Spanish tune (No. 4, Romanze) to match the Seguidilla a dos (No. 5)—itself a Spanish tune, and one that had been used by Beethoven as No. 20 of his *Lieder Verschiedener Völker* (WoO 158), where it is entitled 'Bolero a due'). This song, like the others, fits quite comfortably into the opera; for there is no substantial distinction in style between Weber's lighter individual songs and those he wrote for the secondary characters in his operas. The early insertion of a lighthearted song for Gaston not only establishes his carefree (and Spanish) nature: the piece obviously has a similar function and even manner to Kilian's 'Schau der Herr'.

Similarly, the opening chorus taken from *Das Turnierbankett* is perfectly effective, since it was upon the manner of these male voice choruses for the Berlin *Liedertafel* and other gatherings that Weber based the style of his operatic choruses, even in *Der Freischütz*. Clearly Mahler kept the example of that work in his mind; for though he naturally attempts no kind of imitation,

Die drei Pintos.
Gaston

Was ich dann thu', _ das _ frag' _ ich mich, frag' ich denn nicht recht _

wun - der - lich? Was ich dann thu', _ das _ frag' _ ich _ mich,

frag' _____ ich denn nicht _ recht _ wun - der -lich

he respects its precedents, and understands well the kind of proportions and relationships that can be made to work for Weber. It is as much his opera as Weber's in the end; and while we mourn the loss of the original, the major comic opera Weber himself had long wanted to write, there is enough operatic skill in the assembly and recreation of its fragments for us also to mourn the fact that Mahler's own youthful operatic plans proved abortive. The outcome is a unique collaboration between two related artists, a piece whose charm and humour fully earn it re-establishment in the repertory.

The first performance was given under Mahler in the Neues Stadt-Theater, Leipzig, on 20th January 1888, when it was declared almost impossible to discern which was Mahler's and which Weber's contribution. Subsequent performances followed in Germany and Czechoslovakia (including in translation), and in the early years of the century the piece occurred quite regularly in repertories. The English première was given by the John Lewis Partnership Music Society on 10th April 1962 under David Lloyd-Jones.

CHAPTER FOURTEEN

DRESDEN-3: 1821–1823

We succeed in enterprises which demand the positive qualities we possess, but we excel in those which can also make use of our defects.

ALEXIS DE TOCQUEVILLE

AT THE moment when Weber received Barbaia's letter on 11th November, requesting an opera for the 1822–3 Kärntnertor season, the Spohr family were with him. Champagne was sent for, and the new enterprise toasted. Weber's mercurial spirits immediately recovered and he set about searching for a subject. It is true that Barbaia had cautiously specified 'an opera in the style of *Der Freischütz*'; but Weber was determined to answer his critics with a grand opera. He wrote back enquiring about conditions and received an invitation to visit Vienna at the management's expense so as to study the available resources. Various subjects were already being considered for a libretto. The quarrel with Kind put a collaboration over *Der Cid* out of court; *Dido*, based on Rellstab, was discarded as having been used too often. Eventually he approached Helmina von Chezy, a figure in Dresden literary circles whom he already knew from the *Liederkreis* gatherings in Nostitz's house; and of her suggestions, he accepted *Euryanthe*.

Having set his new librettist to work, Weber resumed negotiations with Barbaia and took up the question of priorities with his employer. He was still hoping to finish *Die drei Pintos* and dedicate it to the King, and his letter to Einsiedel suggests that he would be willing to postpone the Vienna commission until the Dresden work was finished. If he hoped to bring pressure upon the King in this way, he was disappointed; the coming production of *Freischütz* was thought to be quite enough of his music for Dresden. Nevertheless, he was obliged to tell Barbaia that he could not finish a major new opera by July; as he wrote to his friend Treitschke, secretary of the Court Theatre, he was determined to produce the very best he could, and in addition to his normal duties there was the strain of trying to nurse Caroline successfully through her latest pregnancy. He devoted the rest of the year to an abortive scheme for subscription concerts and his duties at the opera; Morlacchi was once again on leave, which meant the usual amount of extra work. *Euryanthe* had already run into difficulties over an impossible first draft from Chezy, and not until 15th December, after prolonged discussions and alterations, did Weber accept the first act more or less as it now stands. The New Year found Weber in the throes of preparations for the Dresden première of *Freischütz* on 26th January. Lichtenstein sent him the eagle and the obstinate owl from the Berlin production; the costumes were carefully copied from some stone figures he found in a royal hunting lodge; and after ten rehearsals, disturbed by disagreements with Tieck over the necessity for his scrupulous attention to detail, he was able to pay a generous tribute to his cast and players: 'It will indeed not be the fault of you up there, nor you down here, if the opera does not please.' In the event, it was the greatest success; a vast laurel bush was passed up after the first act, and a team of couriers relayed the good news to the prostrate Caroline at home. There was only a small pinprick in the tasteless cartoon being sold in the town which showed the famous Raphael Sistine Madonna (in the Dresden museum) with Weber's and Kind's faces inserted and captioned with the notorious witticism, 'Was wäre Maria ohne das Kind?' Yet though warmed by his success, Weber was cast down by an attack in the *Wiener Zeitschrift*—a reprisal, suggests Max Maria, for his decision to withdraw from the polemics of criticism and, apart from *Tonkünstlersleben*, to concentrate his energies on composing rather than writing. It was a dangerous omen for *Euryanthe* in a city devoted as always to forming artistic factions, where the opposition was led by Grillparzer and currently given over to a passion for Rossini. Weber left for Vienna on 10th February, already troubled enough about his health to leave a moving farewell note in a sealed envelope for Caroline in case he did not return. On the 13th he reached Prague, where he was pressed into conducting a *Freischütz* that included as Agathe his future Euryanthe, Henriette Sontag— 'a pretty girl', he noted, 'but—still very much a beginner, and rather gooselike'. Vienna was reached on the 17th, and though exhausted by the journey he hurried straight to the theatre to see the performance and begin discussions with Barbaia's deputy, Duport. The following night came a *Freischütz* emasculated of hermit, demons and firearms: his diary merely records, '*Der Freischütz*! ACH GOTT!' But he was impressed by Wilhemine Schröder— 'pretty; superb voice, apt acting, pure intonation, though in many ways a deficient singer.'

Of his personal popularity in Vienna there was no doubt. His letters to Caroline record the enthusiasm of his welcome and the buzz of activity in which he found himself. Max Maria reports that he first met Schubert at this time; he even attempted to settle his old enmity with Salieri, though the meeting was not a success; he was taken up by the aristocracy as well as by literary and musical circles. In the middle of all this he pursued his negotiations with the Kärntnertor and gave some study to the new parts of the libretto that were arriving from Chezy in Dresden; but the pace proved too much for him, and he fell ill. He was still very weak when, at Wilhelmine Schröder's pleading, he conducted *Der Freischütz* on 7th March to such acclaim that he began to worry about it spoiling the chances of *Euryanthe*: he wrote to Lichtenstein fearing that 'that damned *Freischütz* will make it heavy going for his sister *Euryanthe*'. His concert on the 19th, generously postponed to avoid a clash with a colleague's Benefit, was not so well received. Meanwhile a letter of recall had arrived from Dresden, and on the 21st he duly set off for home, arriving on the 26th.

Immediately he was plunged into the usual round of work, Morlacchi's as well as his own. His spare time was occupied in moving house from the Altmarkt into rooms in the Galleriestrasse. Caroline, in the last month of her pregnancy, was in no state to help; but on 25th April he returned home after conducting a Mass to find that she had given birth to a son. Two days later the child was christened Max Maria Christian Philipp—'Max', so he always assumed, in honour of *Der Freischütz*. By 15th May the family was re-installed for the summer at Hosterwitz. Here, on the solitary walks described by Benedict in the previous chapter, Weber set about the composition of *Euryanthe*. There were, however, the usual interruptions from visitors. The most regular were Tieck and Jean Paul Richter (the latter Weber found unsympathetic); Wilhelm Müller and Wilhelmine Schröder, with her mother the actress Sophie Schröder, were more welcome; Spontini also came, evidently with friendly intent towards his rival, but his notorious loftiness of manner upset the touchy Weber and they parted coolly. Weber was in any case in a lowered state following an accident with his carriage, while returning from a *Preciosa* rehearsal, which had obliged him to walk most of the way home. *Preciosa* was given on 27th June, with a lack of success that further depressed the increasingly melancholy composer.

In this state he turned to the completion of what was to be his last piano sonata (No. 4 in E minor, Op. 70: J.287). Once again we are indebted to Benedict for elucidation of the work's background:

> The first movement, according to Weber's own ideas, portrays in mournful strains the state of a sufferer from fixed melancholy and despondency, with occasional glimpses of hope, which are, however, always darkened and crushed. The second movement describes an outburst of rage and insanity; the Andante in C is of a consolatory nature, and fitly expresses the partly successful entreaties of friendship and affection endeavouring to calm the patient, though there is an undercurrent of agitation of evil augury. The last movement, a wild fantastic Tarantella, with only a few snatches of melody, finishes in exhaustion and death.[1]

Certain puzzles remain. Weber's diary dates the completion of the 'Scherzo' on 28th August 1819 and the 'Allegro' (whether the opening Moderato or the Prestissimo finale is not clear) the period in which, recovering from the depression caused by the cancellation of *Alcindor* and following a fallow period of composition, he poured out some of his most exuberant piano music—the *Rondo Brillante* and *Polacca Brillante*, the *Invitation to the*

---

[1] Benedict: *op. cit.*, p. 155.

Dance and the Eight Piano Pieces, Op. 60. The Andante was written on 5th and 6th February 1822, between the Dresden première of *Freischütz* and Weber's departure for Vienna. For a work with such a precise programme to have been spread over such a long period and for its parts to be so dissimilar to the other music he was writing at the time is unusual; the supposition is that a good deal of revision was incorporated into the finishing of the sonata. It seems most likely that the Tarantella was the piece completed in 1819: not only did Weber prefer to leave his first movements until last, but the style of this finale is closer to the virtuoso pieces of that month, and it would not require too much revision to confer upon the gaiety the flushed, hectic quality it now possesses. If only in the context of the tragic running-down of the momentum and thinning of the textures at the end, there is a note of forced energy in the insistent galloping rhythms underlying a main theme that for all its apparent dotted-note brightness is nothing but the sorrowful descent of the sonata's opening:

Ex. 64

This Moderato is the most openly melancholy music Weber wrote for the piano, and as usual he produced one of his better sonata movements when motivated by a dramatic, or at any rate emotional, programme, however vaguely defined. Its sadness is only emphasized by the wistful lyricism of the second subject after a stormy linking passage; and taken a stage further in the second movement, which despite his original title Weber now describes as a Menuetto. It is no more a minuet than is a Beethoven scherzo, which it strongly resembles; though it is Weber's peculiar talent to bring into relationship with this a Trio whose sinister murmurings look in the other direction, towards Chopin, both in the figuration and the chromatic decorations of the harmony (Ex. 65, p. 266).

Although Chopin widens his harmonic spectrum and, characteristically, makes the rhythm flow over the bar-lines, the nature of his admiration for Weber is more evident in passages such as this than in their mutual devotion to the Polonaise.

The Andante quasi Allegretto is openly marked *Consolante*. Weber's instinct in avoiding placing the emotional centre of the work on a tragic Adagio is sound: he was not Beethoven, and in any case such a movement would have interrupted his dramatic scheme. Its curiously elliptical nature fits well enough into the scheme of the sonata, though this is by no means one of his most distinguished inventions. Yet whatever its unevenness, the E minor Sonata more than its predecessors suggests that an altogether larger artist was about to develop. At the age of thirty-five and a half, Weber was only four years from his death and in a state of increasing weakness. There is a sense in which all his works, up to and including *Der Freischütz*, are early works; from this achievement he sought to turn in a new direction, to enlarge his scope and enrich his potentialities. *Euryanthe* should have been the initiator of this middle period; and in the sonata we find similar evidence of a new, more direct feeling than is shown in most of the earlier keyboard music. The reliance on effect is sharply diminished; the old fingerprints—vocal aria melodies over guitar accompaniments, diminished sevenths, dotted rhythms, orchestral textures hinted at in the keyboard writing—are all transmuted into a language of new flexibility. In its own right the E minor Sonata is a touching and fascinating work; it also has all the marks of a transitional work into a period that was never to be.

The same day that he finished the sonata, 29th July, also saw the completion of a little *Marcia Vivace* for ten trumpets, written for the Prussian Black Hussars. Parts of this were subsequently incorporated into *Euryanthe*, on which he had begun serious work in May and which occupied much of his time until the end of August. Back in Dresden late that September, the Webers were able to give more attention to the new house: the music had

Ex. 65

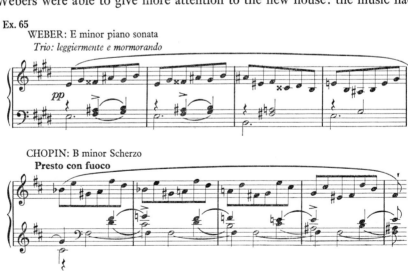

WEBER: E minor piano sonata
Trio: leggiermente e mormorando

CHOPIN: B minor Scherzo
Presto con fuoco

begun to earn more money, and alongside the details of his work the diary records an increased amount of entertainment and adds a stream of affectionate fussing about Max's first tooth and his other childish upsets. There was little time during the autumn for *Euryanthe*, since his assistant Franz Schubert was seriously ill and Morlacchi still unfit for much work after the strain of his five months' holiday in Italy.

Only two occasional cantatas intervened between the resumption of serious work on *Euryanthe* at the beginning of February. The first, Music and Choruses for *Den Sachsen-Sohn vermählet heute* (J.289), was written for the marriage of Prince Johann of Saxony to Princess Amalie Auguste of Bavaria. Commissioned at the same time as a cantata from Morlacchi, it uses a trite text by Ludwig Robert in which Muses and mythological heroes mingle with jolly Saxons to celebrate the occasion. Weber began work on it on 29th October and finished it on 13th November—a speed which is explained partly by the dullness of some of his music and partly by the re-use of earlier pieces. The overture comes from *Silvana*; No. 1 is a reworking of the Adagio of the Second Symphony; No. 2 uses parts of *Rübezahl* (some sections also turn up later in *Oberon*). Much the best number is the *Mädchen-Chor*, No. 4: Jähns's lament that Weber never rescued this charming piece from oblivion was perhaps the cue for Mahler when he made it the chorus in Act 3 in his version of *Die drei Pintos* (see Chapter 13). Weber was obliged to travel with Morlacchi and the whole choir to Freiberg for the official meeting of the happy pair; the bad weather upset Morlacchi's health again, and Weber had to rehearse both cantatas. The wedding took place on 21st November; his cantata was performed, without much success, on the 28th. A second so-called *Kleine Cantata*, *Wo nehm' ich Blumen her* (J.290), to a text by Theodor Hell for the birthday of Princess Therese, survives only in vocal parts (STB) and piano sketch; Weber supplied the piano part at the performance on 9th January.

Turning his attention once more to *Euryanthe*, Weber became increasingly alarmed over the poverty of the material Chezy was submitting. Various discussions were held with other writers, including Tieck; Weber seems to have been unnecessarily obstinate in rejecting their suggestions. News of the fiftieth Berlin performance of *Der Freischütz* coupled with a letter of congratulation and an honorarium of 100 thalers, served only to irritate him; he wrote an uncharacteristically angry letter to Brühl declining this meagre offer. Regrettably his other principal correspondence of these months has failed to come to light—an exchange of letters with Beethoven over the coming production of *Fidelio* with Wilhelmine Schröder making her début in the title role. There remains only a draft of Weber's first letter, out of four he wrote and three he received; it merely expresses his high regard for a masterpiece, 'every performance of which will be a festive day'. Later, acknowledging the receipt of 40 ducats from Könneritz, Beethoven spoke of 'my dear

friend Maria Weber'.[1] The performance on 29th April was a success, and
Schröder's début laid the foundations of her later fame in the part. Previously, on 10th March, Weber had enjoyed a personal success with a revival
of *Abu Hassan*: for his Fatime, Haase, he now wrote the aria 'Hier liegt,
welch martervolles Loos'. To his other tasks he added the promotion of
Benedict's interests, and was able to report to his pupil's father a success
with a court concert; the staging of an opera by one of his basses, Mayer,
which he supported in the face of complaints; and the exhausting routine of
work that should have fallen to his sick colleagues Morlacchi and Schubert.
Denied even the support of his leader, Polledro, who had been forced to
leave Dresden after a scandal, he began negotiations to have Gänsbacher
summoned to help him; but matters dragged on, and eventually Marschner
was appointed instead. The most cheering event of the spring was the visit
to Dresden in April of Ludwig of Bavaria (grandfather of Wagner's patron).
Losing patience with Rossini's *Riccardo e Zoraide*, he demanded, 'Give me
something by your young wizard Weber'; and at the hastily mounted performance of *Preciosa* startled the Dresden audience by leaning out of his box and
shouting 'Bravo!' There was also a performance of *Der Freischütz* with
Schröder as Agathe and her future brother-in-law, Emil Devrient, as Caspar
on 8th May before Weber felt able to leave on the 10th for his much desired
Hosterwitz and the chance to finish his opera.

He had the usual interruptions from visitors, who included Hummel and
P. A. Wolff, the latter a fellow-consumptive with whom he used to pace up
and down the garden discussing symptoms until silenced by Caroline; and
there were the routine tasks to be attended to in Dresden. But he was able to
work at *Euryanthe* for six or eight hours at a stretch on many days, though he
used to protest about the lack of a break: 'I wish I were a cobbler and had my
Sunday, and didn't know a thing about C major and C minor!' But by his
own description he was able to rest quickly and do with little sleep; he seems
to have had the consumptive's nervous energy, and his time was turned to
such good account that by 8th August the whole opera was sketched. On the
29th he noted in his diary, with his customary prayer of thanks, the completion of the entire opera. Only the overture remained to be written, in
Vienna.

[1] Letter of 17th July 1823: No. 1210 in Emily Anderson's edition, *The Letters of
Beethoven* (1961).

CHAPTER FIFTEEN

EURYANTHE

This music is as yet far too little known and recognized. It is heart's blood, the noblest he had; the opera cost him part of his life—truly. But it has also made him immortal.

ROBERT SCHUMANN: Theaterbüchlein (1847)

WEBER HAD first met Helmina von Chezy with Meyerbeer at Vogler's in 1813, when he expressed admiration of her songs. To her reproof that he had given no practical proof of this, he replied that he wanted something larger from her; but a firm approach did not come, she says, until, 'on a mild, golden October day of 1821 . . . whose sky was suffused with Italian warmth; I was lingering by the parapet as I crossed the bridge over the Elbe, contemplating the landscape, when turning round I saw Weber and his wife standing before me.'[1] Straightway he asked her to write him a libretto, overruling her protests that she knew nothing about the craft: she had no experience of drama, still less of opera, not having even seen one for years. However, delighted and flattered, she accepted the invitation. Weber brought a pile of librettos for her to study, recommending Jouy's book *La Vestale* as the best example for dramatic action and brevity of scenes, as well as for the type of song he wanted: he considered it a masterpiece, as opposed to Hoffmann's book for *Olympie*, whose 'rough, heavy verses' he mocked despite his admiration for Hoffmann in general. Feeling that a comedy would be best suited to current Viennese taste, Chezy at first suggested Calderón's *Méjor esta que estava*, playing in Vienna at the time; but as we have seen, Weber was anxious to match himself to a grand opera on a serious theme, and of her proffered alternatives, including *Magelone* and *Melusine*, he accepted *Euryanthe*.

Das Chez, as the exasperated Weber came to call her, was and is a figure more to be pitied than despised. Born Wilhelmine Christiane von Klencke in Berlin on 26th January 1783, known first as Minchen and later by her own wish as Helmina, she was married in her teens to a Prussian officer named

---

[1] Helmina von Chezy: *Carl Maria von Webers Euryanthe. Ein Beitrag zur Geschichte der deutschen Oper. NZfM*, Vol. 13, Nos. 1–6 and 9–11, July–August 1840. Writing nearly twenty years later, she presumably confused the date: Weber's approach must have come not in October but November, after Barbaia's letter. This account gives the full details of their collaboration through all its processes; it is also summarized, from a very different point of view, in MMW, Vol. 2, Ch. 23 and 24 *passim*.

Hastfer, from whom she fled to Paris in 1801 (her own parents had meanwhile also divorced). Here she set up with Friedrich and Dorothea Schlegel, and under their influence began devouring Romantic literature with a good deal more appetite than taste. Her second marriage, to the orientalist Antoine Léonard de Chézy[1] in 1805, proved no happier than the first, and in 1810 she returned to Germany with her two sons Wilhelm and Max, to whom she was devoted, moving restlessly from place to place and supplementing an allowance from her second husband with a small income from her writings. In 1817 she fetched up in Dresden, where she was cordially welcomed by Weber at Count Nostitz's and at the other literary meetings they both frequented. By now she was a highly eccentric figure, prematurely older than her thirty-four years, having put on weight and lost her looks following a heart attack, ludicrously dressed in clothes that no longer fitted her, given to untimely and protracted descents on all her friends, absurd, incompetent, lachrymose and pathetic. Max Maria and Benedict both heap bitter scorn upon her, and it is their accounts which have survived; but Weber himself always treated her with extraordinary patience, even when she tried him most sorely. She for her part always spoke and wrote loyally of him for the rest of her life.[2] She died in Geneva on 28th February 1856, quite blind.

The origin of the *Euryanthe* story she produced for him goes back at least to the first quarter of the thirteenth century. Its substance is common to a good many romances of the period: a husband boasts of his wife's fidelity, is challenged to a wager on it, comes to believe he has lost and plans a revenge upon her which she manages to elude; after various adventures the betrayer is discovered and punished, and the couple re-united. Certain points of detail also recur in these early tales. In the *Roman de la Violette* by Gerbert de Montreuil (*c.* 1220) the lady's false attendant enables the challenger to obtain alleged evidence of their intimacy by secretly observing her in her bath, when he sees:

> sur sa destre mamelote,
> Le semblant d'une violette.

In *Le Comte de Poitiers* the challenger is given tangible tokens with which to confront the husband, including a ring; similar features occur in other contemporary romances. Some of these points were used by Boccaccio in the story of *Bernabò da Genova e la moglie Zinevra*, the ninth Tale of the Second Day of the *Decameron* (1348–53). Here the challenger, Ambrogiuolo,

---

[1] She later always styled herself Helmina von Chezy, dropping the accent but retaining the French pronunciation.

[2] Though a contemporary account, borne out in her autobiography, *Unvergessenes*, Vol. 2, p. 230–1 (1858), suggests that she did blame Weber for the poor quality of the *Euryanthe* text. See Ludwig Schmidt: *Zeitgenössische Nachrichten über Carl Maria von Weber*, XVIII, June 1926. This includes the story that, finding a picture of Weber in a music shop maintaining its price of 4 thalers, a prospective purchaser exclaimed, 'So viel auch *nach der Oper?*'

FRIEDRICH KIND
Portrait by M. Knädig

P. A. WOLFF
Engraving by Schennis

HELMINA VON CHEZY
Anonymous sketch

J. R. PLANCHÉ
*Engraving by Onwhyn, after a
drawing by Briggs*

produces evidence of a mole with golden hairs growing beneath Zinevra's left breast, as well as a description of her bedroom. This was the version used by Shakespeare for *Cymbeline* (1609–10), in which Iachimo 'proves' Imogen's infidelity to Posthumus with first a description of her room (to which, like Ambrogiuolo, he has gained access in a trunk), following this up with a ring he claims she has given him and finally persuading Posthumus with evidence of:

> On her left breast
> A mole cinque-spotted, like the crimson drops
> In the bottom of a cowslip.

Other versions of the legend continued to circulate in Germany and Scandinavia, for instance in the late fifteenth-century *Historie von vier Kaufmännern* translated into English via Dutch as *Frederick of Jennen* (Antwerp 1518, London 1520); here the symbol of unfaithfulness is a black wart on the left arm. But Chezy's source was one of the earliest French romances, *L'Histoire du très-noble et chevalereux prince Gérard, comte de Nevers, et de la très-vertueuse et très chaste princesse Euriant de Savoye, sa mye.* A distorted version of this was published in Comte Louis de Tressan's famous *Bibliothèque universelle des romans* in 1780.[1] Chezy, however, went back to the MS in the Bibliothèque Nationale, and her translation was given to Dorothea Schlegel for use as *Geschichte der tugendsamen Euryanthe von Savoyen*, Part 2 of Friedrich Schlegel's *Sammlung romantischer Dichtungen des Mittelalters* (1804). Chezy also published it separately, under her own name and with a preface of her own, as *Euryanthe von Savoyen* (1823). Shorn of details and episodes irrelevant to our purpose, the original can be very briefly summarized as follows:

> In the year 1110, in the reign of King Louis the Fat, France has been laid low by wars and rebellions. The King encourages tournaments as a means of keeping alive an interest in fighting. Among those present at one such is Gérard de Nevers, a handsome nineteen-year-old knight. Encouraged to sing, he does so; but the Count Lysiardus de Forest challenges his devotion to his wife, Euryant, and wagers his lands against her fidelity. At Nevers, Euryant's false retainer, old Hondrée, bores a hole in the door of the bathroom and observes on Euryant's right breast a mole the shape and colour of a violet, which she has sworn only Gérard shall ever know of; Lysiardus, having also seen it, returns and produces this information to support his claim to have seduced her. Gérard sorrowfully takes Euryant away with him. In the desert, they meet a huge snake; when Euryant tries to sacrifice herself as a decoy to allow Gérard to escape, he relents in his purpose to kill her and abandons her

---

[1] Two stage versions followed this: *Gérard de Nevers et la belle Euriant*, 'scènes panto-mimes et chevaleresques en trois parties' by Cuvelier and Francony Cadet (Paris, Cirque Olympique, 11th February 1810): and *La Violette*, by Planard with music by Carafa and Leborne (Paris, Opéra-Comique, 7th October 1828).

instead. But she is rescued by a party of knights under the Count of Metz. Gérard returns miserably to his own home as a troubadour and learns of the treachery; after other adventures, including an amorous interlude with a girl named Eglantine, he re-encounters Lysiardus and defeats him. He takes pity and is about to bind his enemy's wounds when Lysiardus tries to stab him. Lysiardus is sent off to be tried and hanged, old Hondrée is condemned to be burnt, and Gérard and Euryant are united.

A marginal amount of historical accuracy lies behind this story. One of the first tasks of Louis's reign (1108–1137) was the subjugation of the robber barons, the most notorious of them being one Hugues du Puiset, whose name survives into the opera, attached to Eglantine; Louis was indeed a national hero, personally of immense courage, whose success in bringing peace to his country explains the rejoicing at the start of the opera.

Except in details such as the deletion of the mole on the breast and the bathroom scene, which would have been awkward to stage even if it could possibly have passed the censor, Chezy's first scenario keeps close to this: its outline runs as follows:

Act 1. Before the Court of France, Gerhard praises his wife Euryanthe and is challenged by Lysiart, who departs to prove her faithlessness. She receives him kindly, but is betrayed by her false friend Eglantine and made to seem to have revealed to Lysiart a family secret concerning a message written on a bloody dagger discovered by the family tomb. She is accused before the court and led away by the enraged Gerhard.

Act 2: Instead of murdering her in the desert, Gerhard abandons her as a merciful gesture to repay her self-sacrifice in attempting to decoy a lion away from him. The King and his hunting party find her, believe in her innocence, and take her with them. Gerhard returns to Nevers and learns of the treachery by overhearing a quarrel between Lysiart (now master of his castle) and Eglantine, whom Lysiart has promised to marry.

Act 3: At a tournament, an unknown knight defends the cause of Euryanthe. Lysiart, having silenced signs of remorse on Eglantine's part, attacks him and in the battle the knight's helmet is struck off, revealing Gerhard. Lysiart is killed, and all ends happily.

Both in outline and in much of the incident this was unacceptable to Weber: the atmosphere of chivalry was too artificial, the improbabilities of the lion in France and the bloody dagger bothered him, and in all the paraphernalia of tournaments and castles there were too many subsidiary roles, such as a small one for the Queen, and not enough motivation and characterization given to the main parts.

Moreover, he was anxious to introduce the supernatural element in which he felt at home, if possible replacing the episode of the dagger; and he wanted some disaster to lend strength to the dénouement. Chezy was, in fact, through inexperience keeping cautiously near the original, and she willingly agreed to new suggestions by Weber. These included the revelation of the important secret coming by way of a pair of dead lovers, the substitution of a poisoned ring for the dagger, and of an anonymous Monster for the lion, while Euryanthe was to seem to die by a fall from her horse so as to give tension to the dénouement; Weber was unsure as to how to dispose of the wicked pair. This is scarcely an improvement on Chezy's first attempt; and it must be held to Weber's account, and not hers, that it was he who insisted on the whole improbable episode of the ghostly lovers. For the rest, he advised her on the versification, 'I beg you—don't make the verses go at an operatic jog-trot, use all your fantasy, all your skill and don't spare me! Heap difficulty upon difficulty, make use of quantities one can be confused by, that will fire me, will give me wings! *Euryanthe* must be something new! must stand alone on its peak!'

Despite all the patience which Chezy gratefully says Weber praised in her, he seems to have recognised early on that she was ill equipped for the task, yet been either unable or unwilling to extricate himself from the collaboration—perhaps he simply felt that there was no one in Dresden who was any better suited to the work. Endless conferences took place, with advice sought from the highly practical Caroline, from the writer and translator of Petrarch, Carl Förster, and from Tieck, who strongly recommended a return to the simplicity of the plot used in *Cymbeline*. But Weber was not to be parted from his ghosts, and even conceived the plan of raising the curtain during the overture to show a *tableau vivant*, in Dresden style, depicting the interior of the family tomb—Euryanthe was to be discovered in prayer while the dead woman's ghost flitted overhead and Eglantine scowled upon the scene. When Tieck and other friends showed alarm at this notion, Weber grew angry and broke off discussions. Chezy had by now changed the name Gerhard, which Weber found unsuitable for singing, to Adolar, as well as Hondrée (Gundrieth in her translation) to Eglantine; she was also forced to drop the Queen, Lysiart's attempt (as in *Cymbeline*) to seduce Euryanthe, the final tournament and much else besides. Act 3 alone was rewritten eleven times, and still Weber was not satisfied: in a letter of 2nd February 1823 Carl Förster records being invited to make suggestions, especially about the ending: 'it was a great pleasure to hear him speak so perceptively about the piece and about how he approaches the composer's task.' Weber's MS alterations to Chezy's text show that the section from the Wedding March to the end is mostly his own work. With time pressing, a final compromise libretto was eventually agreed upon. (In the following summary, the identification of each set number is given at the end of the action it covers: there is no spoken dialogue, and often passages of recitative follow as well as introduce an aria without separate numbering.)

Act 1: In King Ludwig VI's palace, the chorus of ladies, nobles and knights sing to the joys of peace after victory, and of love. After a general dance, the King (bass) enquires why Adolar Count of Nevers and Rethel (ten.) is morose—to a jealous aside from Lysiart, Count of Forest and Beaujolais (bass). Adolar's thoughts are with Euryanthe in Nevers; the King offers to send for her, and invites Adolar to sing her praises (No. 1, Introduction: 'Dem Frieden Heil!'). Adolar obliges with a song about their pledging of love by the Loire (No. 2, Romanze: 'Unter blüh'nden Mandelbäumen'). He is crowned with a garland, and the chorus echoes his praise of her fidelity— all but Lysiart, who now casts doubts upon a woman's faith. Adolar is gradu- ally taunted into challenging him to a duel, but Lysiart instead issues a public challenge to a trial of Euryanthe's constancy (No. 3, Chor: 'Heil Euryanthe!'). In defiance of the King's advice, Adolar accepts the wager of Lysiart's estates against his own on the outcome (No. 4, Terzett mit Chor: 'Wohlan!').

Meanwhile, Euryanthe of Savoye (sop.) is alone at Nevers, finding only sadness in the peaceful sound of bells in the valley; even the stars seem to her less bright than Adolar's gaze (No. 5, Cavatina: 'Glöcklein im Thale').[1] Eglantine von Puiset (sop.) finds her; Euryanthe recounts how Adolar abduc- ted her from a convent and having taken her to Nevers has now gone off to fight. She has befriended Eglantine, whose family had been outlawed; but Eglantine has remained embittered and secretly hostile to Euryanthe. She now tries to discover a mysterious secret of Euryanthe, whom she has seen acting strangely by night, and protests that banishment would be preferable to Euryanthe's lack of trust (No. 6, Arie: 'O mein Leid'). Euryanthe is persuaded to explain that she has been praying for the peace of Adolar's sister Emma, whose ghost has recounted how when her lover Udo was killed in battle, she took poison from a ring; she is still separated from Udo, and can find no rest until the ring has been bathed in the tears of an innocent girl in extreme despair. Euryanthe is now horrified at having betrayed a secret with which she was solemnly charged by Adolar, but is reassured by Eglan- tine's assurances of good faith (No. 7, Duett: 'Unter ist mein Stern gegangen'). When Euryanthe has gone into the chapel, Eglantine gives vent to her jealous hatred; she plans to search Emma's sepulchre and offer proof of Euryanthe's betrayal to Adolar, whom she passionately and unrequitedly loves in secret. She is interrupted by the sound of Lysiart's trumpets as his retinue draws near (No. 8, Scene und Arie: 'Bethörte!'). Bertha (sop.), Rudolph (ten.) and the countryfolk lead in Lysiart and his men. The knights praise Euryanthe, who welcomes them and begs Lysiart to stay in her castle; he is filled with love for her, while Eglantine longs for help with her plan, the knights mutter of a conspiracy and the countryfolk renew their welcome (No. 9, Finale: 'Jubel- töne').

Act 2: Lysiart, alone, is prey to guilt and considers abandoning his evil plan to win Euryanthe; yet he cannot bear to give her up to his rival Adolar, whom he once more resolves to destroy. Eglantine now hurries out of Emma's tomb,

---

[1] Chezy took this from her *Der Enkelin der Karschin* (1812), where it appears as *Abend- dämmerung: Glocken im Thale*.

having removed the poisoned ring from the corpse's hand. Her jealous imprecations against Euryanthe are interrupted by Lysiart, who steps forward to offer help, freedom, his hand in marriage and the possession of Adolar's lands in return for an alliance (No. 10, Scene und Arie: 'Wo berg' ich mich'). They pledge their union and invoke the powers of night (No. 11, Duett: 'Komm denn').

In the King's hall, which is illuminated for a feast, Adolar stills his anxiety with the thought of Euryanthe's approach (No. 12, Arie: 'Wehen mir Lüfte Ruh?'). She rushes in ahead of her retinue, and they reaffirm their love (No. 13, Duett: 'Hin nimm die Seele mein'). The King and his nobles enter and welcome Euryanthe. Lysiart steps forward and claims Adolar's estates, producing Emma's ring as token of Euryanthe's love for him. Adolar is incredulous, but when Lysiart reveals knowledge of the guilty secret of Emma, she has to admit that she broke her oath of silence. The court is stunned at what they take to be a complete betrayal of Adolar, and Lysiart is awarded the estates his wager has won him. Adolar departs to wander in the desert, taking the anguished Euryanthe with him (No. 14, Finale: 'Leuchtend füllt die Königshallen').

Act 3. Between solitary rocks and cypresses, Adolar appears; he is dressed in black armour and descends slowly and morosely towards a fountain, followed by the half-fainting Euryanthe. She begs for a kindly word from him before he kills her; he reproaches her for her betrayal and the mockery she has made of their love, ignoring her protestations of innocence and faithfulness. Suddenly she sees a snake wriggling towards them and begs him to flee while she sacrifices herself as decoy; but he attacks it (No. 15, Recitativ und Duett: 'Hier weilest du?'). She invokes Heaven's aid for him; he is duly victorious, and in recompense for her self-sacrifice decides not to kill her but to abandon her to Heaven's protection (No. 16: 'Schirmende Engelschaar'). Alone, she resolves to pray for death and to hope that if ever Adolar returns and finds her grave, he will know she has been true. Upon her reverie steals the sound of horns (No. 17, Scene und Cavatine: 'So bin ich nun verlassen'). Huntsmen enter, praising the fresh morning and the joys of the chase. The King sees the dead snake and an unknown woman: they are all astonished to recognise Euryanthe (No. 18, Jägerchor: 'Die Thale dampfen'). She asks only for death, and when the King invites her to redeem her guilt she assures him that she has none, she is innocent. He is delighted, and when he learns of Eglantine's part in the plot, promises full restitution (No. 19, Duett mit Chor: 'Lasst mich hier'). She is transported with joy; but as she tries to rush away, she collapses, and fearing for her life, the King's men carry her off (No. 20, Arie mit Chor: 'Zu ihm! zu ihm!').

In an open space before the Castle of Nevers, Bertha, Rudolph and the countryfolk are decorating a lovers' cottage and singing a May Song. Adolar, his visor closed, approaches and sardonically pours scorn on lovers' vows, wishing only that his home may be his tomb. Recognizing him, the chorus assure him of Euryanthe's faithfulness, and Bertha tells how Lysiart is even now enthroning the treacherous Eglantine in Adolar's castle. He is stunned

(No. 21, Lied mit Chor: 'Der Mai'). They implore him to overthrow the traitors and swear their loyal support (No. 22, Solo mit Chor: 'Vernichte kühn das Werk'). A bridal march heralds Lysiart and the ashen Eglantine, who is troubled by visions of Emma's ghost but manages to master herself. Adolar, light dawning on him, intervenes; and when the knights go to obey Lysiart's order to seize him, they recognize him with joy. Lysiart is left fuming and Eglantine faints (No. 23, Hochzeitmarsch. Scene und Chor: 'Das Frevlerpaar!'). The knights threaten Lysiart, who is cursed by Adolar and the chorus (No. 24, Duett mit chor: 'Trotze nicht!'). The King appears and tells Adolar that Euryanthe's heart is broken. Eglantine bursts out into a rage of triumph over Euryanthe and contempt for Lysiart, who stabs her to death. He is disarmed; Adolar tries to intercede for him, claiming that he is himself Euryanthe's murderer. The huntsmen are heard rejoicing that Euryanthe has regained consciousness; the lovers are re-united, and Adolar declares that faithfulness has now expunged all crimes: Emma's troubled ghost may now find rest. All acclaim Adolar and Euryanthe (No. 25, Finale: 'Lasst ruh'n das Schwert!').

More abuse has been heaped on this libretto than on any other in the history of opera, the more so since it has been generally accepted that this was the rock upon which a potential masterpiece became wrecked. Even in its painfully achieved final form, the weaknesses are glaring: the subject is artificial, the language stilted, the plot riddled with holes of which none is more gaping than the failure of Euryanthe to clear up the whole misunderstanding in Act 2 when she is first accused by Lysiart. However, it could be argued that even a great plot may hinge on just such crucial suspensions of disbelief; a word in season from Desdemona would have exposed Iago at a very early stage. Moreover, it is perfectly possible that a character such as Euryanthe might be confused by Lysiart's accusations in support of a wager about which she knows nothing, and that in her guilty frame of mind after breaking her oath, she would assume that all the fuss concerned that alone. The point is not strictly relevant, for we cheerfully accept many more ridiculous contrivances in librettos for the sake of the music, and what really matters is how much the libretto means to its composer.

Whatever the difficulties he encountered in getting the libretto into some kind of workable shape, Weber was in no doubt that he wanted this subject. His attraction to the world of chivalry was that of the other Romantics of his time feeling themselves kin to the previous age of high Romanticism; all around him writers, including the author he had once attempted to recruit for his *Harmonische Verein*, Heinrich Zschokke, had succumbed to the incredible wave of enthusiasm for the *Waverley Novels* that was sweeping Europe (one of the early Scott operas was his pupil Marschner's *Die Templar und die Jüdin* (1829), which was much influenced by *Euryanthe*). Furthermore, he felt he recognized in the subject a breadth and nobility that were likely to match his ideas for the development of a grand romantic opera beyond the closed numbers and comparatively simple atmosphere of *Der Freischütz*. His interest in the subject was guided by two further factors that emerge from a study of the revisions he forced upon the labouring Chezy. Firstly, he saw in the opposed pairs of Adolar and Euryanthe, Lysiart and Eglantine, a novel kind of dramatic contrast based on the moral grounds he demanded, yet colourful and capable of being portrayed in music of fruitfully conflicting kinds. He was also attracted by the possibility of bringing into the drama the supernatural world with which he knew he had a special touch: and it was for this reason that he overruled the arguments of his friends and foisted upon the drama, in place of the censorable but more plausible evidence of the mole on the breast, the Gothick device of Emma's tomb and the restless ghost.

Weber was, in fact, once more laying down a structure that he considered would give the best opportunity to his talents—the composer's immemorial right. He had consolidated his gifts and brought them to a high pitch of mastery in *Der Freischütz*; now he was looking forward to a more ambitious genre of opera altogether, and a new sense of expansion marks his whole approach to the work. This can immediately be sensed in the harmonic field. Samiel's famous diminished sevenths had provided a clear but limiting harmonic antithesis to the more open style of the village life and Max's struggles to win Agathe; the opposition in *Euryanthe* was to depend upon a subtler conflict of harmonic styles. The essential harmonic pattern of the opera rests, then, principally upon the opposition of a simple diatonic manner for the world of chivalry and goodness to a highly developed chromaticism for the world of the supernatural and evil. There is accordingly a less sharply defined key system than in *Der Freischütz*, and the key-pattern that can be descried is always subject to the principal conflict.

In no other work does Weber take chromatic harmony to such extreme limits; indeed, it was not until Liszt and Wagner that certain passages of of *Euryanthe* were overtaken—principally, the ghost music of the overture, some of Eglantine's scenes and the extraordinary opening to Act 3 as the unhappy Adolar and Euryanthe pick their way through the desert, while bleakly shifting harmonies reflect, with true Romantic imagery, their misery against the desolation of the scene. The loosening of the closed forms also allowed him a much greater range of harmonic relationships. Though anchored to D minor, the opening of Act 3 in the desert has no key signature and ranges very wide indeed; the long recitatives have even greater fluency of movement, and there are also considerable stretches where a key signature seems irrelevant or is indeed discarded altogether—a very different matter from the discarding of key signatures in classical *recitativo secco*, for the recitatives of *Euryanthe* merge imperceptibly into symphonic developments and set arias. The reliance on the diminished seventh for sensation has lessened, and sevenths and ninths are used with an altogether new fluency to

open up the richest chromatic vein he had yet explored. The dissolution of
tonality is not merely adumbrated in *Euryanthe*; it is pursued an astonishingly long way.

Broadly, however, the opera is in Eb. This is the courtly tonality, in which
the overture opens and the last finale closes; it is that of the royal huntsmen.
Adolar's Romanze (No. 2) and prayer for help in Act 3 are in the dominant of
Eb, Bb; his Act 2 aria (No. 12) is in the sub-dominant, Ab. Towards the
flatter keys this side of the opera tends to gravitate, though Euryanthe
herself has some connexion with C major. Her Scene and Cavatine in Act 3
as she is deserted (No. 17) is in G minor, and the horror of the accusation in
Act 2 drives her, with powerful effect, down to Db. The villains, on the other
hand, tend towards the sharper keys. Eglantine rages against Euryanthe in
Act 1 (No. 8) in E major, having first 'concealed' her feelings when talking
to Euryanthe by assuming E minor. Her great Act 2 duet with Lysiart is as
sharp as B major. Outside these contrasts stand the countryfolk's May
Song (A major) and Wedding March (D major), whose fairly sharp keys are
presumably dictated by their remoteness from the aristocratic key of Eb.
There is further a tendency for individual Acts to centre round certain keys.
From the original Eb, Act 1 is pulled towards G major and its dominant D
(in which it ends); Act 2 is pulled towards C and its subdominant F (it ends
in F minor). Thus from the original Eb there is Weber's favourite modulation of a third,[1] first upwards, then downwards. But it must be emphasized
that these are no more than tendencies, with exceptions: the central harmonic tension of the work is not one of tonality, but is braced by the opposition of diatonic and chromatic.

Clearly a dramatic harmonic basis such as this, which Weber at last felt
technically ready to control, confers a more expressive unity on the opera
than was achieved by the *Freischütz* key-structure, and at the same time
opens up far wider possibilities; it matches the nature of a work that makes
an important move in the direction of Wagnerian music drama. With the
domination of closed numbers gone, or at any rate weakened, Weber was also
able to take the logical next step and strengthen the unity by increased use of
Leitmotiv. In *Freischütz* this was circumscribed; the freedom of form in
Euryanthe opens the way to the use of musical motives not as simple references or even half-concealed colouring to a situation, but as a formulation of
character which would be adaptable to different situations. It would also
provide a method of giving formal coherence in and between movements
that were no longer set arias. Two of the principal motives in *Euryanthe* are
fairly primitive in application. It is in the nature of what it says that Adolar's
declaration of faith should be more or less immutable:

---

[1] This *Terzverwandschaft*, or relationship of keys by thirds, had interested Haydn
towards the end of his career, and it was subsequently to absorb Beethoven.

Ex. 66

Much the same is true of the theme of the lovers' union:

Ex. 67

With the ghosts' music, however, there is a subtler method at work; for its harmonic colouring is so individual that it can seep like a wraith into the texture to suggest the forlorn tragedy beyond the grave, and the influence this exerts over the living (Ex. 68, p. 280).

The handling of Eglantine is worthy of the mature Wagner, for though her immediate descendant is Ortrud, the use of her *Leitmotiv* looks forwards to the techniques Wagner was to develop throughout *The Ring*. On its first appearance, this figure memorably suggests the false friend, shifty and insinuating (note the close spacing of the diminished seventh with the middle notes low in the violas' darkest register) (Ex. 69, p. 281).

The semi-quaver groups can be modified to assume a diatonic innocence when Eglantine wishes, while retaining their unmistakable shape; and throughout the scene in which she tries to wheedle the secret out of Euryanthe, the figure is varied with great skill to suggest her various approaches, cajoling, reproachful, affronted. The real chance comes when Eglantine, left alone (No. 8), allows her hatred for Euryanthe to break into the open; and a complete scena (the division into Scene und Arie is practically meaningless) unfolds with the semiquaver figure as the basis for much of the invention, combined very effectively as she reveals her hopeless love for Adolar with a yearning cello figure seething restlessly below her concoction of the plan to overthrow Euryanthe. That Weber did not pursue this identification through-out the opera is due partly to his association of the motive with her deceitful-ness, so that once teamed with Lysiart she is acting more openly, partly to the fact that he had not yet achieved enough independence from closed numbers to allow him to place his full trust in the power of *Leitmotiv*.

Nevertheless, although the main weight of the structure has not yet fully passed from set arias on to the recitatives, the distinction between the two is far from obvious. The breakdown can be seen beginning in Act 1. Adolar's Romanze (No. 2) leads directly into a chorus whose formal nature is disturbed by Lysiart's intervention: the loose structure that ensues is a dramatic illustration of order being shattered, and not until Adolar manages to assert, 'Ich bau' auf Gott und meine Euryanth'' does virtue, and the courtly world, regain its balance and the scene end on a sturdy chorus and the re-emphasis of Eb. More importantly, in the long run, Weber is enabled to develop a style of heightened dramatic declamation that he takes up again when in turn Euryanthe's Cavatine (No. 5) is followed by the intervention of Eglantine. The whole of Act 2, divided into the Lysiart-Eglantine scene at Nevers and

Ex. 68

the scene in the King's castle, is a masterly dual piece of continuous composition. Weber's old talent for relating contrasted numbers so as to build up a larger structure lies behind the method; but though there may perhaps not be the fluency of movement between narrative and moments of heightened expression which he could later have achieved, there is a flair for containing the expression in a free-ranging yet disciplined melodic declamation that worthily anticipates Wagner's *unendliche Melodie*.

This increased emphasis on unity imposes further demands upon Weber. The chorus has a structurally more crucial role than in *Der Freischütz*: even the May Chorus and the Huntsmen's Chorus play a more dramatic part than their equivalents in the previous opera, for though the Huntsmen once again stand for the restoration of a happy normality to a figure who has lost it, they are the actual means of bringing this about and not merely a symbol. The major function of the chorus is to take part in the emotions of the characters, to share or oppose them, and to assist in moving the drama forward. The development of *Leitmotiv*, coupled with the weakening of the set aria, also moves the burden of expression further away from the singers and on to the orchestra. Weber was naturally well equipped to meet this demand. After the

Ex. 69

primary colours of *Der Freischütz* we find here an increased subtlety of orchestration, and if in this as in other matters something is lost in vernal freshness, there is a gain in richness and depth. This is particularly noticeable in the string writing, where Weber places less reliance on his gift for bringing out new character in individual instruments and scores with heightened feeling for concerted string ensemble. Even here the particular characteristics of the different instruments are magically used: the ghost music of the overture, for eight violins over tremolo violas, is an outstanding instance; there is the extraordinary string storm that boils in furious unison demi-semiquavers beneath Lysiart's dedication to revenge in No. 10 (the same figure which Weber had employed in his *Leyer und Schwerdt* song *Gebet während der Schlacht*); the weird opening to Act 3 as violins and then full strings weave chromatically through throbbing woodwind and horns; the sinister use of violins over a held string chord for Eglantine's *Leitmotiv*; and the tender opening of Euryanthe's Cavatina (No. 5) on two solo cellos over a bass counterpoint. The same is true of the woodwind writing, which without any yielding in understanding of an instrument's qualities manages to make richer use of the ensemble: perhaps the most striking example is the opening of Adolar's 'Wehen mir Lüfte' (No. 12) when woodwind sing their apprehensive song first unaccompanied and then with clarinets and bassoons over a sawing viola: the colour is somewhat Berliozian, and must also surely have

Ex. 70

been in Liszt's mind when he composed the *Gretchen* movement of his *Faust Symphony*. It was Liszt who wrote of *Euryanthe*, 'we find in Weber a marvellous divination of the future shaping of the drama; and the endeavour to unite with opera the whole wealth of instrumental development' (Ex. 70, opposite and below).

Such instances could be multiplied, and the subtlety and care with which Weber writes is underlined by the Wedding March for the evil pair, when the apparent jubilation is relentlessly exposed by the harsh, thick doublings as

LISZT: *Eine Faust-Sinfonie*

much as by the chromatic inflections. This is a world apart from the bright
textures and sharp rhythms with which Weber characterizes the court.

Melodically, too, Weber was required by the new demands to extend his
style from the folk-based tunes that had characterized *Freischütz*. The larger
subject, the opportunity for depicting subtler characters, the looser forms all
impelled him towards a freer manner and a closer understanding of character
rather than type. With Adolar, there is some advance in warmth and range of
feeling over the simple Max: however, he remains a troubadour, bold,
virtuous and amorous, the polarities of his character charted by the bluffness
of 'Ich bau' auf Gott' and the tender grace of 'O Seligkeit, dich fass' ich
kaum' (No. 12):

Ex. 71

Euryanthe is a character of greater interest; and though Weber, in
common with most composers (indeed most artists of any kind), found it
hard to portray goodness as vividly as evil, he does develop her character
with the course of events. Her beautiful opening Cavatina (No. 5) casts her
in much the same mould as Agathe, but her experiences in the desert bring
out more subtle qualities: the broken phrases of her second Cavatina (No.
17), which remain halting and listless even when she is recognized by the
King, are a true image of her distress, and transform naturally into the
excitable broken leaps of her joy at the thought of seeing Adolar once more.
This fragmentation of her melody vividly suggests a character near breaking
point, and to anyone who listens as well as looks the ensuing collapse should
come as no surprise.

Nevertheless, greater interest resides in the evil pair. If Adolar bequeaths
some of his characteristics to Lohengrin (and to Tannhäuser) and Euryanthe
establishes the model of the virtuous heroine that was repeated in Elsa, the
descendants of Lysiart and Eglantine are Telramund and Ortrud. The whole
of the Lysiart-Eglantine scene is worth the closest comparison with the great
duet that opens Act 2 of *Lohengrin*: one example alone, as each couple invokes
the powers of darkness and takes an oath, will suffice to show how precisely
Wagner was influenced (Ex. 72, opposite and p. 286).

Like Telramund, Lysiart is a villain on a grand scale, made the more
Satanic by his recognition of virtue and conscious falling away from it. He

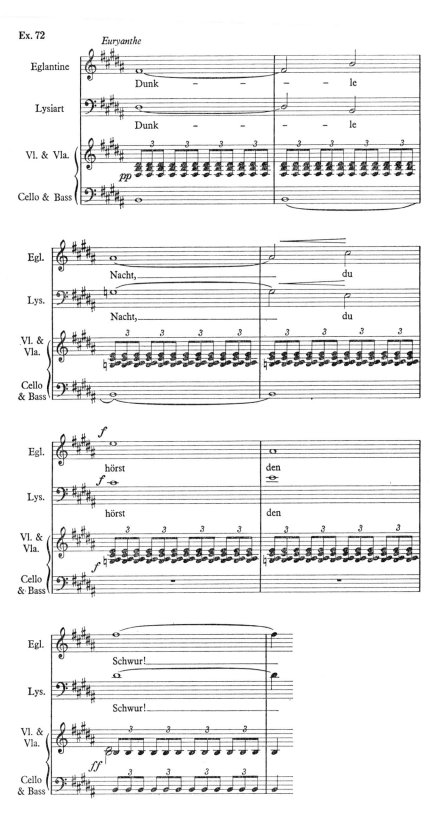

opens Act 2 with huge accented dotted-note figures that leap across two and
a half octaves in a fine image of jealous rage; but his G major Andante is a
genuine, and curiously touching, acknowledgement of Euryanthe's goodness
and his remoteness from it. Yet when braced to his resolve, he remains true
to it; and it is Eglantine who gives way at the climax and is murdered by him.
At the start, he is more than he realises under her influence; for like Ortrud,
she is totally corrupt, possessed by evil and preying on weakness.

This superior forcefulness of the evil pair would make the outcome of the
opera seem contrived were it not that Weber has the ability to characterize
the 'good' side of opera not only through the virtuous pair. The vividness of
his invention even in the simplest, most diatonic music is a unifying force
in its own right, and gives all the choruses, dances and marches by knights,
peasants and huntsmen a mediaeval freshness of atmosphere, a natural
colour and sharpness to which Adolar and Euryanthe are kin and their
adversaries foreign. This much is carried over from *Der Freischütz* without
any recourse to mock-mediaevalism. Other influences are less easy to chart,

for *Euryanthe* is a work that (apart from the general debts in Weber's operatic style already discussed) has few antecedents. Possibly he knew Méhul's *Ariodant*, in which there is something of the same scope of plot and character much more crudely deployed, as well as a mixture of slow and fast sections coupled with a suggestion of *Leitmotiv*; the similarities in recitative technique with *Idomeneo*, that other great pre-Wagnerian masterpiece, are likely to be coincidental. But the influence *Euryanthe* had on succeeding works is immense. The immediate beneficiary was Weber's follower Marschner. *Der Freischütz* leaves its marks upon *Hans Heiling* in details such as the ubiquitous diminished sevenths, the folk manner of Konrad's song and the Wedding Scene, but the deeper implications derive from *Euryanthe*—the fears and doubts in Heiling's love song for Anna, the drawing of a sinister baritone in firmer lines than the tenor, the *Durchkomponierung* of scenes such as that of Anna lost in the wood. Again, if in *Der Vampyr* we scent Agathe in Emmy's first aria and Max in Aubry, as well as the Wolf's Glen in the flute shrieks and groaning chromatic scales of the opening melodrama outside the Vampyr's cave, there are suggestions that the example of Eglantine and Lysiart has not been lost. *Der Templar und die Jüdin* is a grand opera very much in *Euryanthe* vein: there is the contrast between a diatonic manner to depict chivalry and chromaticism for the darker elements, coupled with a more consciously elevated manner and (though Marschner's melodic invention is much weaker) a liking for achieving effects in the orchestra and even purely by way of orchestration. Both *Hans Heiling* and *Der Vampyr* treat a theme that was to obsess many of the Romantics as well as Wagner in *Lohengrin* and *Der fliegende Holländer*, the incompatibility of the human and spirit worlds. Emmy's mother may be Agathe; her daughter is Senta. Yet Marschner lacked the gifts to be more than a token link between Weber and Wagner: his horrors fail to evoke the genuine shiver of conviction Weber gave them, and suggest more the hollow *Schauerromantik* of the lesser lights of the contemporary drama; and though he shares with Weber a genuine feeling for nature and countryfolk, what was real and instinctive with Weber soon becomes cliché when Marschner lacks the inventive matter to fill out the manner. Wagner, who wrote the words and music for an Allegro to Aubry's aria in *Der Vampyr* and composed *Die Feen* rather under the work's influence, was very guarded in his admiration for Marschner, but gladly acknowledged his debts to Weber (not in full, but perhaps Wagner was constitutionally incapable of settling debts in full). Not only *Lohengrin* but passages and much of the vocal style of *Tannhäuser* derive from Euryanthe's flexible use of recitative, arioso and aria; the Act 3 prelude of *Lohengrin* is possibly influenced by the opening of Weber's overture, the desolate opening of Act 3 of *Tristan* by the opening of Weber's Act 3 and perhaps the sound of the horns of the royal hunt by that in *Euryanthe*. Tovey goes so far as to call *Euryanthe* 'both a more mature work of art and a more advanced development of Wagnerian music-drama than *Lohengrin*'[1]; certainly one must agree that although Wagner had incomparably the larger mind and that nothing in *Euryanthe* matches the Grail Prelude, the general level of invention is consistently higher than in *Lohengrin*. *Euryanthe* makes the development of Wagnerian music-drama inevitable; as in the case of his last piano sonata, it is a transitional work, moving forward from the success consolidated in *Der Freischütz* into a phase that he never lived to explore. Instead of being the first of his middle period operas, with *Freischütz* the triumph of his youth, it was the last but one.

As was his custom, Weber wrote the brilliant overture last. It is not so closely connected to the drama as in the case of *Der Freischütz*: instead of paraphrasing the dramatic action in sonata form, it takes two of Adolar's themes, 'Ich bau' auf Gott und meine Euryanth' ' and 'O Seligkeit' as first and second subjects, and after the insertion of the ghost music pursues a fugue based on an inversion of a dotted-note figure that is in turn derived from 'Ich bau' auf Gott'. In Berlin in 1825 he also added a Pas de Cinq to go in before the May Song in No. 21: some of this is music taken from No. 6 ('Licht der Weisheit') in the music he wrote for Eduard Gehe's drama *Heinrich IV* in 1818 (J.237), and from No. 4 of *L'Accoglienza* (J.221), re-used once before as an insert for Spontini's *Olimpie* (J.305). It may also be noted that No. 9, the Finale to Act 1, uses music from the Cantata *Du bekränzend* (J.283) (at the Allegretto) and the *Marcia Vivace* (J.288) (at the opening Vivace).

Already for the first performance Weber was required to make cuts—a very difficult matter with an organically unified opera, as he told Brühl on 28th January 1824.[2] However, his own shortenings are acceptable, for they do not alter the sequence and balance of the numbers or affect the characterization. Other cuts followed in subsequent productions, less happily: for instance, Eglantine's 'O mein Leid' was dropped, thus removing much of the claim she has upon Euryanthe's sympathies.

But the systematic mutilation of *Euryanthe* was really inaugurated by Conradin Kreutzer. Weber had cut 172 bars; Kreutzer's removal of 352 bars not only drops some fine music (especially in Nos. 10 and 12) but further weakens the characterization of Eglantine. Kreutzer alleged that Weber had accepted these in the interests of shortening a work that at its première had lasted from 7.00 until 10.45 (until 10.00 Weber maintained); but though he marked in a piano score a reference to 'the excellent Viennese *Beschneidung* according to the judgement of Herr Kapellmeister Conradin Kreutzer', his diary refers to the piano score 'as it is *zersetzt* [disintegrated] for Vienna'.

Unquestionably *Euryanthe* presents problems; though in almost every case

---

[1] D. F. Tovey: *Essays in Musical Analysis*, Vol. 4, No. 154: note on *Euryanthe* overture.

[2] The original Schlesinger score, and some others following it, give these cuts at the end.

the surgery committed on the ailing patient has been more destructive than the disease. Its faults are chronic, but by no means unendurable. Of the many attempts to 'save' the work, most operate, however well-meaningly, on a basic misunderstanding of Weber's structure. With Castil-Blaze's efforts for Paris, there is not even well-meaning. For the Odéon on 14th January 1826 he scored, unaided, parts of the music from Weber's piano score as *La Forêt de Senart, ou La Partie de Chasse de Henri IV*, a so-called *Opéra-comique en trois actes*, based on a comedy by Collé, with *paroles ajustées sur la musique de Mozart, Beethoven, Weber, Rossini, Meyerbeer, etc. [sic]*. This included four sections of *Euryanthe* and two of *Freischütz*. Castil-Blaze's version of *Euryanthe*, in something nearer Weber's original form, was given without success at the Opéra in 1831; and revived at the Théâtre-Lyrique on 1st September 1857, with a new translation by A. de Leuven and Vernoy de St. Georges that returned to the device of the mole on the breast, while turning Eglantine into a gipsy, Sarah, renaming Adolar as Odoar and Lysiart as Reynold and introducing two comic squires. Dialogue replaced the recitative, there were other alterations, and Berlioz's *Invitation to the Dance* orchestration and parts of *Preciosa* were inserted.

A more serious attempt to clear up some of the awkwardnesses in the plot was made by Mahler while Director of the Vienna Hofoper. His version, produced on 19th January 1904, dispenses with the ghosts by causing Emma to die honourably from the ring, which is then given to Euryanthe by Adolar as a love token and stolen by Eglantine. However, together with the improbable ghosts has to go some excellent music. Mahler also dispensed with the snake, though he retained Euryanthe's swoon at the moment of her rescue.

Hermann Stephani's version (Dresden, Hoftheater, Easter Saturday 1911) suggests as a reason for Euryanthe's unnecessary silence about her innocence, the need to suffer to expiate her indiscretion and so give Emma rest; but his revisions involve barbarous cuts, so that Nos. 15, 16 and 17, including the marvellous opening to Act 3 and Euryanthe's second Cavatina, have to go and the Act opens on the Huntsmen's Chorus. He also makes a number of puzzling musical alterations.

An attempt at an altogether new text was made by Hans Joachim Moser, who managed to fit the music to a *Märchen* by Moritz von Schwind he found in the Weimar Museum called *Die sieben Raben und der getreuen Schwester*. *Die sieben Raben* was performed in Berlin on 5th March 1915; but it cannot be said to be a version of *Euryanthe*. The most successful version was made by Rolf Lauckner, with the musical help of Donald Tovey. Their alterations included the disappearance of Emma and the snake, while the story of the ghosts was rewritten to concern the purification with innocent tears of a belt used as a murder weapon by Udo. The compromise is not entirely successful —it keeps much of the improbability that is the chief stumbling block and makes some questionable alterations, as well as cutting some important

10

music—but it does follow Weber's opera loyally and attempt to present something as near the original as is consistent with dramatic plausibility.

However, this has not exhausted the attempts at devising a more stage-worthy *Euryanthe*. A version by Franz Benecke manages to keep the music unaltered; but the same cannot be said for the version made for Stuttgart in 1954 by Kurt Honolka. Reducing the duration to an hour and three-quarters, he has altered the ghost episode back to the textual original of the birthmark, of which Lysiart obtains evidence by being admitted to her room when she is under the influence of a sleeping draught (to the ghosts' music) administered by Eglantine (rechristened Claudia). But the cuts mean dispensing with some of the finest music in the score, again including the opening to Act 3, and the chopping about of the music involves various other musical and dramatic solecisms, to say nothing of a final chorus newly composed on themes from the overture.

Another version, for the Philopera Circle by Franz Manton and produced at St. Pancras Town Hall on 1st July 1962, made a number of drastic cuts, including in Nos. 8, 12, 13 and 17, reshuffled the music and among its revisions required Euryanthe to sing some of Adolar's music. The dénouement was given a new twist by making Eglantine accompany the grief-stricken Euryanthe into the desert, then abandon her; and at the end allowing the King to pretend that Euryanthe was dead as a ruse to trap Eglantine into betraying the plot.

What is to be done? All the revised versions, even the most faithful, ignore the fact that for better or worse—and we have to concede that it was for worse—Weber set his music to the text provided by Helmina von Chezy, and to none other. To alter it is to alter a conception that was carried through with extraordinary vision and detail. Whatever the weaknesses of the libretto, the dramatic flow of the music it prompted is carefully controlled and well-balanced; one need only observe the well-judged disposition of the cheerful pieces. When so many equally feeble librettos are accepted, it is disastrous that a work of the scale and mastery of *Euryanthe* should be allowed to languish. A really intelligent, wholehearted production of the original *in toto* would demonstrate that, as Beethoven said when asked to suggest revisions, it is too late now to revise the work; that as it stands, with all its weaknesses, it is a key work in the history of opera and a flawed masterpiece in its own right.

CHAPTER SIXTEEN

DRESDEN-4: 1823-1826

Unter is mein Stern gegangen
Bange Ahnung sagt es laut.
HELMINA VON CHEZY: *Euryanthe*

THE FIRST symptoms of Weber's fatal illness had appeared as early as 1812. In the January of that year he complains in his diary of sharp pains and what he calls 'rheumatism' in his chest. The trouble recurred in the summer, when he also noted that his life-long lameness was worse. From then on there are regular references in the diary to illness, apart from those concerning more severe collapses such as that in Prague in 1813. In 1817 he found his health deteriorating further; he suffered from stomach trouble and piles, which suggest a tubercular infection of the bowels, and a sore throat that would not clear up for five weeks. He amused himself by planning a Hoffmannesque tale of a musician whose sinister attacks by disease make him forget his art. 1819 found him still worse, in January often 'very weak' or 'very ill and exhausted' with recurrent fevers; and these or similar comments occur with increasing frequency. He was unwell on the journey to Vienna in 1822; 1823, the year of *Euryanthe*, seems to have been a comparatively dormant phase of the disease before its final stages.

Weber's concern about his health fills the diaries and there are suggestions that, heroically as he overcame severe pain and weakness, he at first rather enjoyed the macabre pleasure of discussing symptoms with fellow invalids. Max Maria records that his father placed an exaggerated trust in doctors, regarding their least word as oracular and confusing his courses of treatment by changing them according to the latest advice. In times when medicine was at a comparatively primitive stage, with no cure known for tuberculosis (it had not even been discovered to be infectious), the foolishness of this needs no underlining. In 1819 he was treated by Drs. Bienitz and Hedenus, the latter evidently a kindly man but a physician of the old school with somewhat erratic diagnostic powers: he decided the seat of Weber's illness was abdominal, and it was left to the younger Dr. Weigel to realise that the main trouble was in the throat and chest. Contemporary descriptions tend to fasten on the magnetic personality and the charm that dominated the weakness; but Weber's sense of drama would perhaps have been equally gratified with the effect his actual sickliness made on the nine-year-old Wagner: 'His fine, narrow face with its lively yet often heavily veiled eyes made a powerful impression on me; while his pronounced limp, which I often observed as he passed our window on his way home from exhausting rehearsals, impressed on my imagination the picture of the great musician as an exceptional superhuman being.'[1] Psychological factors, linked to the superstitious fear that he was beset by an 'evil star', influenced his attitude towards his disease, whose progress was hastened by the crippling overwork and the strain of long, irregular hours and journeys in appalling conditions to which he had been subjected ever since infancy. During the Berlin success of *Der Freischütz* he seems to have been in excellent health and spirits; yet on the return to Dresden he notes that he is 'very tired and ill' (6th July 1821), and the rejection of *Die drei Pintos* coincided with his first haemorrhage. Though normally an amiable and highly sociable man, goodnatured to a fault in giving his time to unworthy people and causes, he grew increasingly irritable as his hopes for establishing German opera as a going concern in Dresden gradually filtered away and as the dragging disease wore him lower and lower. By the completion of *Euryanthe* he evidently sensed that he was near the end of his reserves; he lacked the strength to build on that new achievement, and there seemed only darkness ahead.

In a mood of deep pessimism he said goodbye to Caroline on 16th September and set off for Vienna with Julius Benedict. Not even the sale of *Euryanthe* to Holbein, the Prague theatre director, for ten ducats more than he had asked, could dispel the feeling as he entered Vienna that both he and his opera were mortally sick. The success of *Der Freischütz* was showing signs of rebounding against him, for not only had it set uncomfortable standards but various imitations had by now sated the Viennese with its effects. Moreover, the Italian company assembled by Barbaia, with Michele Carafa conducting and Rossini himself supervising, had been delighting the city since the early part of the year, not with grandiose Spontinian spectacles but with Rossini's *Barbiere di Siviglia*, *Otello*, *Gazza Ladra*, *Cenerentola* and *Donna del Lago*, Cimarosa's *Matrimonio Segreto* and other lighthearted Italian works: the singers included Barbaia's ex-mistress and Rossini's new wife, Isabella Colbran; his famous Semiramide, Joséphine Fodor-Mainvielle; the tenors Giovanni Davide and Domenico Donzelli; and the great Lablache himself as principal bass. 'A pair of artists such as Fodor and Lablache have never come my way,' Weber wrote to Caroline after *Matrimonio Segreto* on the 20th. 'I was completely bowled over, and Fodor sang an inserted aria so beautifully that I was convinced that if only she would sing Euryanthe, one would go mad.' Against all his prejudices Weber was conquered by the charm and skill of Rossini's music, growing angry with the poor showing German opera was putting up against such rivalry—apart from Beethoven and Schubert, the opposition was in the hands of Kreutzer, Weigl and Schuppanzigh. Weber even (for which he mocked himself the next day) stormed out of the theatre

[1] Richard Wagner: *Mein Leben* (1911).

because he had been so forcibly impressed by the Dandini-Magnifico duet in Act 2 of *Cenerentola*. He wrote almost daily to Caroline of his doings—of the children in whom, as a new father, he took especial interest, of the difficulties with casting *Euryanthe*. He had originally wanted Caroline Ungher, but the popularity of Henriette Sontag caused him to waver; and the morning after her triumph in the title role of *La Donna del Lago*—thanks largely, she acknowledged, to advice from Fodor-Mainvielle, she had matured greatly since Weber had seen her Prague—he called on her with the score of *Euryanthe* and persuaded her to accept the principal role. He had meanwhile given the part of Eglantine to Therese Grünbaum, fending off her suggestion that the opera be re-named accordingly. Anton Haitzinger was cast as Adolar, Anton Forti as Lysiart. Gradually his spirits revived, not least with the discovery that Vienna held more of his partisans than he had originally supposed, and he was reported to look ten years younger: 'I cough a bit, but no more than I do at home after I've been talking.'

An unsuspected body of support was now discovered in the members of a peculiar society named, after one of Oehlenschläger's dramas, *Ludlams Höhle*. Half secret society for artists and intellectuals (numbering Grillparzer and Moscheles among its members, as well as Haitzinger and Forti), half *Stammtisch* at Heidvogel's inn in the Graben, its rites were buffoonish and its significance negligible. However, one of the club choruses, *Schwarz ist rot und rot ist schwarz* aroused the suspicions of the police that reference was being made to banned political colours; and when the Ludlamites explained that they had merely followed their tradition by electing their stupidest member, a drunken red-faced ex-actor named Schwarz, to the office of president, the society was promptly banned for satirizing his Imperial Majesty. Before this, however, Weber had been inducted and solemnly passed from 'shadow' to 'body' (or full member) with the name of Agathus the Mark-Hitter: Benedict became Maledünntus, or Wagner der Weber-junge (a heavy reference to the follower of the great Faust of music).[1] After some initial bemusement at their antics, and discomfort at spending his time coughing in a cellar swirling with smoke, Weber became an enthusiastic member—the more so when he realised that here were potential allies in his coming enterprise.

Further signs that he could expect a good deal of sympathy for *Euryanthe* came from conversations in the music publisher's S. A. Steiner; and it was in this shop that Beethoven one day spotted Benedict, demanded to know if he were Weber's pupil, and suggested that they pay him a visit in the company of his friend (and Steiner's successor) Tobias Haslinger. Duly on 5th October the three of them rose at six and drove the twenty miles to Baden

---

[1] MMW, Vol. II, pp. 404–8. But Benedict (*op. cit.*, p. 98) records that their full election did not take place until after the opera's première, when Weber was named Euryanthus the Mark-Hitter.

through heavy rain, where Benedict remarked upon the notorious chaos of Beethoven's rooms—

> everything in the most appalling disorder—music, money, clothing on the floor, the bed unmade, broken coffee-cups upon the table, the open pianoforte with scarcely any strings left and thickly covered with dust, while he himself was wrapped in a shabby old dressing-gown.[1]

To Beethoven's tale of woe about his treatment at the hands of the public, the theatres, the Italians and his ungrateful nephew, Weber suggested visiting Germany and England, where he was better appreciated: but pointing to his ear Beethoven cried, 'Too late!', and bore Weber off to a meal at a hotel. Weber's diary notes:

> We lunched together, very gay and happy. This rough, repulsive man paid me his attentions, and served me at table as carefully as if I had been his lady. In brief, this day will always be memorable to me, as it will to all who were there. It gave me real pride to be given all this friendly attention by this great spirit.

Beethoven succeeded in bringing the conversation round to *Euryanthe*, demanding, 'What's the libretto like?' Weber hastened to answer, 'Very tolerable! full of good situations', but Beethoven had caught sight of Haslinger shaking his head, and laughed, 'Always the old story! German poets can't put a good text together!' 'And *Fidelio*?' retorted Weber. 'That's a French original,' replied Beethoven, 'translated first into Italian and then into German'. 'And what librettos do you think are the best?' '*La Vestale* and *Les Deux Journées*!' replied Beethoven without pausing for thought. After a long conversation they rose to part, and Beethoven repeatedly embraced Weber, his own huge fist enveloping Weber's thin hand. His last words were, 'Success to the new opera! I'll come to the première if I can!'[2]

The *Euryanthe* rehearsals got off to a bad start with the *Leseprobe* on 3rd October. Although Weber declaimed the text so dramatically that Gottdank, the stage manager, goodhumouredly offered him a job on the spot, the cast were baffled by the obscurities and illogicalities in the plot, and bombarded him with questions about Emma and Udo's part in it, and Euryanthe's failure to accuse Lysiart to his face in Act 2. Sharply reminded of the weaknesses in the story to which he had committed himself, Weber unhappily tried to revert to his plan of a tableau in the overture; but the idea was defeated by the theatrical management supported by Chezy. However, once the musical rehearsals had begun the singers were caught up in the fascination of the new and difficult music. To the management's astonishment, the

---

[1] Benedict: *op. cit.*, p. 87.

[2] This description of their meeting is in MMW, Vol. II, pp. 510–12. Max Maria based his account on Weber's diaries and Benedict's independent report (Benedict: *op. cit.*, p. 87–8).

chorus instead of disappearing as soon as possible asked only for a brief break before tackling their parts again; when one rehearsal went on until half past three, Grünbaum merely observed that her children must be getting rather hungry, though Sontag did make a number of complaints to Chezy (who had known her mother).[1] Weber's almost daily letters to Caroline report ever-increasing enthusiasm from the cast, who had been moved to tears, and his own pleasure at the way they were mastering the music.

Outside the theatre, matters were less encouraging. Gottdank was complaining about 'this difficult, learned music which is so hard to understand'; and Schubert, who had attended some of the rehearsals, objected, 'there are clumsy masses which Weber cannot control. He should have left things alone.' However, as his own operas show, Schubert's dramatic sense was not his strongest point; and it did not save him from in turn falling victim to Chezy, since his commission for *Rosamunde* cannot have come until after October.[2] Having moved to nearby Baden with her family during the summer, Chezy now proceeded to attack Weber with demands for more money on the grounds that the alterations to the text had occasioned much extra work and that a fairer arrangement, given the coming productions in other cities, would be a percentage of royalties. She further threatened that if he did not pay 600 thalers she would stop the performance. However grotesque a nuisance Chezy made herself in Vienna with complaints about her monstrous treatment, there were plenty who recognized the injustice whereby a librettist could be bought outright for a small sum. Even Max Maria admits that the chief factor in Weber's agreeing to allow her a percentage on future performances was his fear of public opinion; and to keep her quiet he made her a down payment of 50 ducats, emphasizing that this was not her due but a gift (to Caroline he declared that it was also tribute to his 'evil star').

His restored spirits were dampened again by the penultimate dress rehearsal, which lasted from ten in the morning until 2 o'clock. Even his most loyal supporters among the invited audience were somewhat dashed by a work lasting four hours; and Weber himself, sitting down gloomily to lunch after it was over, observed, 'I'm afraid my *Euryanthe* will become *Ennuyante*.' A Viennese wit declared, 'Since Weber writes for eternity, his opera has to last an eternity.' But the singers and the orchestra, who had pleased him with their playing of the overture he completed on the 19th, remained loyal to the work; and the final dress rehearsal on the 24th went excellently and delighted the audience, so Weber wrote to Caroline two hours before the première on the 25th, adding 'My star has had its ration, so *ich baue auf Gott und meine Euryanthe*'.

The Kärntnertor Theatre was packed for the première on the evening of

[1] Wilhelm Chezy: *Erinnerungen aus meinen Leben* (1863).
[2] Otto Erich Deutsch: *Schubert: a documentary biography*, p. 293 (1946). Deutsch also thinks it possible that Weber warned Schubert not to set a libretto by Chezy.

the 25th; of the musical and literary lights of Vienna, the notable absentee was Beethoven, who sent a note excusing himself. Benedict has left a very full account of the occasion and describes the incident just before the overture:

> Out of the surging waves of the pit, swaying to and fro, arose, on the top of the last bench, the figure of a by no means prepossessing lady, past the meridian of life, in a shabby dress, an old worn-out hat and a shawl that had seen better days. Her attempts to gain in a rational way the front seat allotted her having been frustrated, the gangways being impassable, she tried to find her way *over* the crowd, exclaiming loudly, 'Make room, make room for me, I say! I tell you I am the poetess!' This, accompanied by mocking shouts of laughter, was taken up by the whole pit and echoed by the boxes, 'Room for the poetess! room for the poetess!' and did not cease till Frau Helmina von Chezy was squeezed into her seat, after having been literally passed over the heads of the people.[1]

The merriment was stilled by Weber's entry. The overture, Benedict reports, went less well than at the dress rehearsal owing to nerves affecting the violins' intonation; but the first act was well received, increasingly so until the storm of applause at the curtain caused Weber to shake his head ominously and remark, 'They have fired off their powder too soon.' He was right: although some of the succeeding numbers were well received, the plot began to confuse the audience and the Act 2 curtain fell, says Benedict, 'amidst much applause, accompanied, however, by some unmistakable signs of disapproval.' But at the final curtain Weber was recalled alone, after a bow with all the principals, and Benedict happily records 'an unceasing torrent of applause'. Weber went on to a triumphant reception with the members of *Ludlams Höhle*, where he was fêted until the small hours. His last act of the day, at a quarter to two, was to write to Caroline with the news of his success.

He continued the letter next morning with a detailed description of the evening's events, underlining how well the work had been received; a letter to Lichtenstein on 13th November also emphasizes the success. Gottdank, who knew his Viennese public, observed that the applause was impressive but did not come from the heart. It seems likely that in his anxiety to persuade himself of the success of *Euryanthe*, Weber was fastening upon signs of approval and dismissing as stupid or malicious any reservations. The latter were not so easily ignored as he hoped. Although the *AMZ* placed the work above *Medea* and *Fidelio*, claiming that time was needed to understand it, and there were voices such as Griesinger's in the loyal Dresden *Abendzeitung* declaring that 'the day of the new dramatic music has dawned', others were more hostile. Even Grillparzer, a Ludlamite, complained about 'no trace of melody . . . no invention . . . this opera can only please idiots, dolts, or footpads and assassins.' On the whole the literary world, while

---

[1] Benedict: *op. cit.*, p. 91.

deploring the text, approved of the new development in opera which *Euryanthe* represented: musicians were more reserved. Schubert was candid to the point of upsetting Weber in preferring *Der Freischütz*, privately denouncing the work's formlessness and lack of melody, the evidence that no learning could be acquired at the feet of a charlatan (Vogler) and the fact that 'whenever a scrap of tune appears, it is crushed like a mouse in a trap by the weighty orchestration.' The discussions in Steiner's after the second performance were interrupted by the entrance of Beethoven. 'Now how did the new opera go?' he demanded of Haslinger. 'Outstanding! a great success!' wrote Haslinger in Beethoven's conversation book. 'I'm delighted, I'm delighted!' replied Beethoven, 'thus the German wins over sing-song!' After asking about Sontag, he smiled and told Benedict, 'Tell Herr von Weber, I would have come, but what for?—for a long time now . . .', and he pointed to his ears and left the shop.[1]

Weber conducted the second and third performances, handing over to Conradin Kreutzer for the fourth; and after an audience with the Emperor on 1st November he left Vienna on the 5th. Benedict stayed behind to keep an eye on the subsequent performances, but had not the heart to report what he found. By the eighth performance the theatre was half empty; Kreutzer's cuts made no difference, and the artists began to lose interest and give slovenly performances; after the 20th performance it was withdrawn. Weber's subsequent letters to Gottfried Weber and Danzi show that he had somewhat modified his expectations, feeling that his friends' raptures had aroused false hopes of another *Freischütz*. He travelled first to Prague, spending the two-day journey, says Max Maria, slumped silently in the corner of his carriage. Here the fiftieth performance of *Freischütz* had been delayed for him to conduct; but though cheered by the enthusiasm he found, he hurried on after the performance, reaching home in Dresden on the afternoon of the 10th. When he entered his own theatre again, he was given a formal reception by Hellwig, the stage manager, with choruses sung in his honour; and this was capped by a royal command for the production of *Euryanthe*.

But the year ended in disappointment. With Morlacchi once more on leave and his assistant Franz Schubert once more ill, Weber made another application to have Gänsbacher appointed to help him. He was astonished to have the request granted, within a week, on 29th November. He wrote to Gänsbacher on the 1st enclosing funds for the journey, arranged him a room in the *Goldene Engel*, set Caroline to work organizing food and wine and was delighted to find his health picking up in anticipation of working with a congenial colleague. But only a few days previously Gänsbacher, unable to wait any longer for news from Dresden, had accepted the post of *Kapellmeister* at St. Stephen's in Vienna in place of Josef Preindl, who had died on

[1] MMW, Vol. II, p. 534.

26th October. When Benedict returned to Dresden, he was alarmed by the change in Weber:

> He seemed to have grown older by ten years in those few weeks; his former strength of mind, his confidence, his love for the art had all forsaken him. Sunken eyes, general apathy, and a dry, hectic cough bespoke clearly the precarious condition of his health. He attended his official duties as before with the most scrupulous punctuality, but his creative powers were at a complete standstill.[1]

Benedict was not exaggerating. Between finishing the overture on 19th October 1823 and beginning *Oberon* on 29th January 1825, Weber wrote nothing at all apart from a single song—the pretty little French romance *Elle était simple* (J.292) written to console the author of the poem, Ferdinand de Cussy, who had unsuccessfully conveyed invitations to work in Paris. He had become the musician of his unwritten story, driven by a mortal disease to forget his art. Listlessly he went about his duties, his enthusiasm and appetite for work gone, returning only fitfully. The production of *Euryanthe* had been postponed because Wilhelmine Schröder-Devrient was expecting a child: this was duly christened on 9th March with Caroline as godmother; by the 16th Schröder-Devrient was at the first rehearsal. Preparations went well; there were eleven rehearsals, and after only a fortnight Weber was able to bow to his company, sweeping off his skull-cap, and declare, 'Now ladies and gentlemen, the opera is all ready.' The performance on 31st March was the triumph he hoped for. Yet this too, was mitigated by the eventual failure of long, complicated and acrimonious negotiations between Weber, Brühl and Spontini over the Berlin première; while reports came in of the failure of the work at its productions at Cassel, Frankfurt (8th March) and Prague (12th March).

These strains took further toll upon Weber's health. His diary several times records periods of ill-health during February and March; his breath became shorter, his cough more painful, he was forced to give up his daily walk, and his fits of shivering came on so acutely at the receipt of any letter that Caroline was obliged to accompany the postman's arrival with sedatives. He was in no state to compose, but he managed to keep up an interest in the affairs of other composers. Carl Reissiger, later Weber's successor at Dresden, had attracted some attention with his *Didone Abbandonata* on 31st January, thanks in part to Weber's help; and he was pleased to see Meyerbeer's *Margherita d'Anjou* well received by the Italians at its Dresden production on 20th March, though to Gottfried Weber he deplored his old friend's Italianization. He gave great encouragement to the Princess Amalie, who was writing a Stabat Mater; and roused himself to conduct a performance of Haydn's *Seasons* on 6th June. 'It went excellently, I could even say perfectly,'

---

[1] Benedict: *op. cit.*, p. 101.

he wrote to Lichtenstein on the 7th, 'and I had the marvellous feeling of being able to express myself with my orchestra as completely as if I were sitting at my piano alone and playing what I liked. These are the rewarding moments for the superhuman load that bears on me.' Wilhelm Müller, who was there, noted that, 'In conducting Weber became so moved and excited that he stood as if transfigured and often seemed to be making music with his whole face.'[1] He spent most of his early summer quietly at Hosterwitz, playing with his children and his animals in the sun, or wandering slowly in the fields with Caroline, who was once more pregnant. When asked what he was working at he would merely reply that he was lazing. He made a small cart to which he harnessed the dog so that it could pull along Max with the cat and the monkey.

He did, however, allow himself to be persuaded to contribute to a concert in honour of the centenary of Klopstock's birth at Quedlinburg on 2nd July, on condition that he be allowed to choose his own programme. Together with the soprano Funk and the flautist Anton Fürstenau, he left Dresden on the 27th, arriving on the 30th. His own concert on the 2nd consisted on the setting of the Lord's prayer by Johann Naumann, Friedrich Schneider's cantata *Den Fürsten des Lebens* and the third part of Handel's *Messiah*. The latter may have been partly in tribute to Klopstock's enormous Christian epic, *Der Messias*, but it was also a work that Weber had long loved; and though he held that a man's emotions should be kept firmly in control, as Funk began 'I know that my Redeemer liveth' he was unable to prevent himself from dropping his baton, burying his face in his hands on his desk and bursting into tears. When the orchestra, who thought he was ill, made a movement to go to his aid, he recovered himself, but he was left too exhausted to play himself next day as arranged; and despite the greatest respect and affection shown him on all sides, he remained sunken in gloom and longing for home.

After only two days in Dresden, he reluctantly set off again on the 8th for a cure in Marienbad, where his diary records that he took twenty-eight mud and shower baths, but still continued to suffer from bad nights with pain and agues. Back in Dresden again, he set about narrowing the range of his activities first by dismissing Benedict, for whom he had secured a conducting post at the Kärntnertor Theatre in Vienna; he wrote a cordial letter to Benedict's father and another somewhat in Lord Chesterfield vein to his pupil[2] accompanying it with a generous testimonial. His antipathy to work grew to a positive disgust: presentiments of death began to haunt him, and he set about trying to scrape together money with a greed quite foreign to his normal, cheerfully improvident nature.

Meanwhile, great interest had been developing in Weber across the

[1] Wilhelm Müller: *Tagebuch und Briefe*, ed. Allen and Hatfield (1903).
[2] Kaiser 154.

Channel. Attracted by the tales of the success of *Der Freischütz*, an unscrupulous playwright, composer, arranger and impresario named Barham Livius had visited Weber in Dresden at the end of 1822, bought copies of *Der Freischütz* and *Abu Hassan* and apparently prepared a version of the former for the London stage. However, no fewer than five other versions were rushed on to the stage by shrewd managers before his.[1] The first was an anonymous piece under the title of *The Fatal Marksman; or the Demon of the Black Forest* (Royal Coburg Theatre, predecessor of the Old Vic, 23rd February 1824). This may have been no more than a melodramatic spectacle; but the next, *Der Freischütz; or, the Seventh Bullet*, was a genuine performance of the opera (English Opera House, 23rd July 1824) arranged by William Hawes in a translation by W. McGregor Logan. Among the singers were John Braham, Mary Anne Paton and Catherine Stephens. This stimulated, as well as a version of *Preciosa* (English Opera House, 26th August 1824), a version of the opera by J. H. Amherst, simply entitled *Der Freischütz* (Royal Amphitheatre, 30th August 1824), which was followed within a week by a preposterous melodrama, using of Weber's music only the Bridesmaids' and Huntsmen's Choruses, by Edward Fitzball entitled *Der Freischütz; or the Demon of the Wolf's Glen, and the Seven Charmed Bullets* (Surrey Theatre, 6th September 1824). In the middle of its run an anonymous burlesque *Der Freischütz* appeared, (Olympic Theatre, 4th October 1824). On 14th October, Charles Kemble, manager of Covent Garden, mounted Livius's version (accepting a certain amount of help from him in the production) as *Der Freischütz; or the Black Huntsman of Bohemia*. It seems certain that Livius's text was revised or partly rewritten by his friend J. R. Planché. One more version of the long-suffering work followed that year, in the edition by Henry Bishop (*Der Freischütz*: Drury Lane, 10th November 1824); and there was the final accolade of the travesty by 'Septimus Globus' mentioned in Chapter 11 (never acted).

Kemble may seem to have been surprisingly late in the field; in fact, he had sensed more shrewdly than his opportunist rivals the growing wave of enthusiasm for Weber and acted accordingly. After Weber returned from his cure at Marienbad he received a letter from Kemble on 18th August inviting him to write a new opera for Covent Garden and to come himself for May, June and July to conduct performances also of *Der Freischütz* and *Preciosa*.[2] Similar offers had been coming in from Paris since June. Weber hesitated. Now, wrecked in health and his hopes in ruins, he suddenly

---

[1] For further details see Percival R. Kirby: *Weber's Operas in London*, 1824–1826, *MQ* , July 1946.

[2] A letter from Weber to Lichtenstein on 6th September mentions an earlier proposal for him to come as Director for the next season, from October to July 1825, and write two operas. No details survive, nor of the London offer to write an opera which he mentions to Lichtenstein on 18th December 1822.

found himself an international figure. His trough of apathy, and the presentiment that he had not long to live, made him unwilling to bother any further with the struggle to succeed; yet he needed to scrape together as much as possible to provide for his family if he did die. His friends, among them Moscheles, then passing through Dresden, urged him to decide for London. He consulted Dr. Hedenus in confidence, and was told that if he immediately went to rest in Italy he could expect five or six years; if he went to London it would be months or even weeks. Weber calmly pointed out that rest would earn nothing for his family. Moved chiefly by his sympathy for England and his respect for Kemble's theatrical connexions, he wrote on 21st August accepting, but pointing out that he could not finish the opera before Easter 1825 at the earliest. On 15th September a delighted reply from Kemble invited him to choose a German subject, perhaps *Faust* or *Oberon*. Weber fastened with growing enthusiasm on the latter, partly out of the feeling that having forestalled Spohr with *Freischütz*, he should concede *Faust*, and on 7th October wrote to Kemble asking him to send the libretto as soon as possible. He also asked for full details about singers, their compasses and styles, personal appearance and acting talent; but proposed only rather vague financial terms. This modest, even casual mode of business—in sharp contrast to Rossini's insistence on £2,500 for conducting three operas, plus £50 for an appearance and other benefits on a princely scale—led Kemble to offer him only £500 and his expenses. Weber refused, preferring to let matters rest until they could meet, and trusting in any case to extra pickings in musical London from the notoriously wealthy milords. The autumn wore on without word from Kemble. Könneritz had been replaced on 11th September as director of the theatre by the less sympathetic Wolf von Lüttichau; Weber's appeal to P. A. Wolff to join him as producer, so as to strengthen his hand, was courteously refused; Morlacchi gained new prestige with two recent recruits to his company, Pallazesi and Buonfigli, in a brilliant performance of Rossini's *Zelmira* on 13th November, whereas the public received Schröder-Devrient in Spohr's *Jessonda* coolly. News came in December of Castil-Blaze's piracy and perversion of *Freischütz* as *Robin des Bois*. On top of these upsets, there was the worrying silence from England. As Weber told Lichtenstein on 9th December, with Caroline in a depression, himself ill and seeing no hope of improvement, debts mounting and winter upon him, the added frustration of not knowing the outcome of his negotiations was almost the last straw. It was getting too late, in any case, for an opera to be written by March. However, he began to learn English, feeling that he could hardly set the language or hope to understand the English themselves and their tastes without a proper working knowledge of it. He set to work systematically with early morning lessons under an Englishman named Carey on 20th October, filling note-books with exercises ranging from practice in the English written alphabet (which he wrote with a neatness very different from his German script scrawl) to advanced exercises. He had 153 lessons, and the gift he had once shown in mastering Czech stood him in good stead: even when not guided by Carey, his letters are reasonably accurate and indeed stylish when corresponding over quite complicated matters. One of the few mistakes he made in English prosody with *Oberon* was to set the italicized word in 'A *lonely* Arab maid' as a trisyllable: although it survives thus into printed copies, this was corrected by another hand in his conducting score.[1]

His letters to Lichtenstein show some recovery. He reports determination to finish *Die drei Pintos* that winter, evidently under urging from his friend to try and return to composition. At last on 30th December, he received from London the first act of *Oberon*. Though pleased with Planché's verses, he was troubled at not being able to see the whole work at once, even in outline, and wrote to Kemble requesting postponement until the following season. Despite the hopelessness of circumstances, he had regained his spirits sufficiently to contemplate work, to write more cheerful letters, and to caricature his own horrors by appearing at a masquerade at Count Kalkreuth's in a costume covered with painted noses, whispering to the guests, 'I've got Nositis! A terrible disease! All the noses I get grow on my body. Get away from me, it's catching . . .'

The year 1825 opened with the birth of a child to Caroline on 6th January. Weber had hoped for a daughter but was thankful enough to have a healthy second son, whom he christened Alexander Heinrich Victor Maria.[2] In the theatre he was depressed to find Morlacchi's *Tebaldo ed Isolina* better received than Cherubini's *Faniska*; but his mind was more vividly occupied with the material for Acts 2 and 3 of *Oberon* that arrived from Planché on 18th January and 1st February.[3] His English had advanced to such a degree that he was able to assure his librettist on 6th January, 'I thank you obligingly for your goodness of having translated the verses in French but it was not so necessary, because I am tho yet a weak however a diligent student of the English language.' He wrote almost as if to an old friend, suggesting that their collaboration encouraged this and would benefit from it. His chief anxiety, apart from specific requests and suggestions, was over the nature of the work. 'The cut of an English Opera is certainly very different from a German one', he wrote on 6th January; and again, having begun the music on 23rd January, on 19th February, 'The intermixing of so many principal actors who do not sing, the omission of the music in the most important

---

[1] BM Add MS 27,747.

[2] Alexander von Weber showed much promise as an artist, but died of tuberculosis in Dresden on 31st October 1844.

[3] The only piece of *Oberon* Weber wrote before seeing the whole text was Huon's 'From Boyhood trained' (Act 1), sketched on 27th January. It is not true, as has been suggested, that he worked without knowledge of plot or situation.

moments—all these things deprive our *Oberon* the title of an Opera, and will make him unfit for all other Theatres in Europe; which is a very bad thing for me, but—*passons la dessus.*' Weber was led by Planché into accepting that English taste could take nothing but ballad opera larded with sensational effects; there was an all too substantial element of truth here, as the English versions of *Der Freischütz* suffice to show, but Weber privately intended to rewrite *Oberon* so as to incorporate recitatives and give it a more cohesive dramatic form for the German stage.

He had meanwhile been approached with another commission from Britain, this time to join Pleyel, Kozeluch, Joseph Haydn, Beethoven and Hummel in contributing arrangements of Scottish folk songs to the collection planned by the Edinburgh publisher and folklorist George Thomson. The accompaniment was to be for flute, violin, cello and piano. On 24th February Weber told Lichtenstein that he was proud to follow Haydn in this work; and in all he set twelve between 10th February and 26th June 1825, telling Thomson on 30th June with some pride (and in English) that he hadn't needed to avail himself of the editorial permission to alter tunes when necessary. All the same, Thomson returned two of them with requests for modifications to the accompaniments. Weber duly sent them on 18th September with a somewhat cool covering letter in English: 'I have the honour to send you herewith the two Ritornelles, agreeably I hope to your wishes. If I have not been capable to satisfy you entirely, it depends upon my unfittingness to compose in conformity with commands. I pray, to let me know in what time the Scottish airs will appear, and to send me one copy of them. I thank you heartily for your good wishes respecting my health, which I find much better after the use of the Bath of Ems.'[1] The alterations are mostly slight simplifications, especially to the harmony; in general Weber has set the tunes clearly and with charm. They were published, posthumously, in their original form and with a dedication to their German translators; when they appeared in Thomson's *Melodies of Scotland* (1831–8) there were substantial alterations from what Weber had written.

As spring came on, the Webers took a new country house at Cosels Garten in the suburb of Neustadt—Hosterwitz was too far for him to manage—and here he spent the time spared from his official duties entirely with his family, gardening a little, pistol-shooting, making Max a suit of armour and a toy theatre. He sat for what has become the best known of all his portraits to Ferdinand Schimon, a singer turned painter, and for a wax relief to Krüger, engraver of the Dresden royal mint, who was to strike a medal in his honour. He had to decline the invitation to conduct *Euryanthe* at Leipzig, though he sent a careful list of metronome markings to his substitute, Aloys Präger,

---

[1] BM Add MS 35, 265, f. 153; the receipt for 40 ducats in Weber's MS is f. 155 of the same number. A fair copy MS of the songs, including the revised versions, is BM Add MS 35, 271.

emphasizing (as did Beethoven in his turn) that metronome marks were nothing without the spirit of the music: 'The beat (the tempo) must not be a tyrannically restrictive or impulsive mill-hammer, but must be to the piece of music what the pulse is to the life of a man. There is no slow tempo in which there are not places needing a faster motion so as to prevent a feeling of dragging. There is no Presto which does not equally demand more relaxed playing in certain places so as not to remove the means of expression through over-enthusiasm.' He even recommends altering his notes if the singer cannot manage them without detriment to the expression.[1] To an anonymous enthusiast who had come to Dresden that year to hear *Euryanthe* and stood in a thunderstorm outside Weber's house before being invited in, he remarked, 'In it I followed the wishes of the *savants*, who blamed me for thinking too much of popular taste in *Der Freischütz*. My God, I was not thinking of the crowd or the musicologists; I was thinking only of the poem which had my sympathies.' He gave his visitor dinner, played him parts of *Oberon*, and spoke with enthusiasm of the musicality of the English people.[2]

After further bickerings over the money for *Oberon*, Weber gave in to his doctors and agreed to go for another cure, this time to Ems. In Weimar, where he stayed with the Hummels, he met Goethe's son and yielded to persuasion to pay a call on the great man. The visit was not a success: Goethe kept him waiting in an anteroom, twice sending out to enquire what the man's name was, and when he eventually penetrated to the presence Weber was waved to a chair, questioned briefly about acquaintances at Dresden, and then summarily dismissed. Weber was so angry that he became ill two hours later, had to send for a doctor, and after a feverish night spent two days in bed. Recovering, he pressed on through Gotha (where he was delighted to find the Varnhagens), Frankfurt and Wiesbaden, arriving in Ems on 15th July.

In Wiesbaden he had been touched to find his table companion struck dumb to encounter the author of *Freischütz*; in Ems he was similarly fêted, removed from his original cheap room to the best in the hotel, invited to balls, excursions and parties. He responded with enthusiasm, but the round was exhausting, and he was homesick for the family he felt he had not long to enjoy. At Ems he was visited by Kemble in company with Sir George Smart, who was in Germany on his way to Baden to ascertain from Beethoven tempos of his symphonies. From Coblenz, on 10th August, Smart and Kemble set out for Ems, walking for about three and a half hours through woods and valleys in the rain. They found Weber shaving, and at first distant to Kemble owing to the non-payment of some *Freischütz* royalties; but when Kemble explained that he had sent the money by Barham Livius (who never paid it), Weber softened and having showed them 'an extra-

[1] Written 6th, 8th and 9th March, first published *AMZ*, 1848, No. 8 (Kaiser 151).
[2] *Une visite à Weber en 1825*, trans. Duesberg, in *Les Modes Parisiens*, 1854.

SIR GEORGE SMART

Portrait by William Bradley

ordinary, vile, confidential letter from Livius', produced some madeira to cheer them after their wet walk. Kemble paid him £30 for the *Preciosa* score and after lunch, for which Weber insisted on paying, they returned for coffee and to discuss the proposal for £500 for *Oberon*. Weber lent them his carriage to take them back to Coblenz; he appeared, said Smart, 'a *bon enfant* and behaved with gentlemanly unaffected kindness, but he is rather lame and out of health.'[1] Max Maria denies that any agreement was in fact reached, his father being evidently sufficiently reassured by the two men's 'ruhiges bestimmtes, echt britisch klares Wesen'.

Apart from a little waltz for the Crown Princess Elisabeth of Prussia (not preserved, though his diary for 17th August mentions it) and an extemporization to P. A. Wolff's recitation of Goethe's *Braut von Korinth*, Weber wrote no music at Ems, concentrating on his cure and enjoying himself. He was cheered to learn that *Euryanthe* would be done at Berlin after all; and leaving Ems on 20th August he came, after a special performance of *Euryanthe* at Frankfurt, to Dresden once more on the 31st.

Smart, who had meanwhile been hearing reports of Weber's death, in Vienna and Prague, arrived in Dresden on 27th September and went immediately to the theatre for a *Freischütz* conducted by Weber; 'who', Smart's diary notes drily, 'consequently was not dead'. He admired the performance, with reservations; *Euryanthe*, on the 29th, he thought ideally well done, though like most contemporaries he felt it was a piece that needed several hearings before it could be understood: 'It contains science in abundance and modulations in all directions, the audience should be professors of the first rank.' Smart stayed until 6th October, spending a good deal of time with Weber and his wife, who had moved back into Dresden for the winter at the end of September.

Whether to soften Spontini's opposition or simply out of good nature, Weber now proposed *Olympie* to celebrate the coming marriage of Prince Max with the Princess Luisa of Lucca; he even contributed, since Morlacchi was busy with a cantata, *La Lite sopita*, for the occasion, some music and recitative to be sung by the goddess Diana in honour of the royal pair (*Doch welche Töne*: J.305). The performance, on 12th November, was coolly received, though a worse fate met Morlacchi's cantata: a false fire alarm in the theatre just as the performance began caused a panic which was partly brought under control by the King remaining stoically in his box. However, the principal tenor, Buonfigli, had vanished into the night and could not be found, so that the programme had to be cut. Weber had resumed work on *Oberon* on 19th September, and was delighted to find ideas flowing. He was also able to add some information to the researches into the authorship of Mozart's Requiem by Gottfried Weber; a score belonging to the dead singer Mariottini contained various amendments, together with a note that

[1] *Leaves from the Journals of Sir George Smart*, ed. H. B. and C. L. E. Cox, p. 72 (1907).

no transcriptions had been made from the Offertorium, Sanctus and Agnus Dei, since Mariottini believed them to be by another hand. Act 1 of *Oberon* was finished on 18th November, Act 2 up to the finale on 27th November and on 3rd December he was able to tell Planché that two acts were virtually completed. On the 5th he went to Berlin, where he stayed once more in the Beers' house (with Heinrich Beer, the father of the family having meanwhile died). He began attending rehearsals on the 8th, but his voice had grown so weak that he had to use an interpreter to explain his wishes to the orchestra; and though so exhausted that every effort left him bathed in perspiration, he managed to attend evening rehearsals and work with individual singers. On the 18th he finished the *pas de cinq* requested by Brühl and the dancer Hoguet to please the ballet-loving King; this was inserted in No. 21, the May Song. During the rehearsals Lüttichau turned up from Dresden, and was astonished to find his local *Kapellmeister* treated with such respect; as they left the stage door with Lichtenstein after the second dress rehearsal, a waiting crowd cheered the composer, at which Lüttichau turned and exclaimed 'Weber, are you really a famous man then?'

Weber had hoped to spend Christmas at home. It was a time he particularly enjoyed with his family; but the performance was not due until 23rd December and all he could do was to write saying that he would be thinking of them, adding 'If I can be with you for the New Year, I'll be there for the whole year.' He knew this was only clinging to a superstitious hope: when Holtei asked after his health, he snapped, 'How am I? Excellent! I've only got consumption; but that doesn't matter a bit, my dear fellow.' To Gubitz, who doubted if he could survive the journey to London, he answered sadly, 'My dear friend, I shall earn a good deal of money in England, I owe that to my family, but I know very well—I'm going to London to die. Be silent; I know it!' The performance of *Euryanthe* on the 23rd was a great success. Weber was called before the curtain after Act 1, and later he was given a reception at Jagor's restaurant where, at Lichtenstein's request, Zelter took the chair (concealing this from Goethe when he wrote describing the occasion). Brühl persuaded him to wait in Berlin until the dues of 800 thalers could be agreed with the authorities, and triumphantly brought the money to the shivering composer in bed. After conducting a second performance on the 28th, Weber left Berlin early on the 29th for home.

He spent January working on Act 3 of *Oberon* (beginning on the 10th), tidying up his affairs and preparing for the journey. He made sure that Caroline was present at all consultations with lawyers and concluded a hasty agreement with the Königstadt Theatre in Berlin for *Oberon* (thus naturally offending Brühl), also attempting to secure some kind of copyright for his music in Germany with a round-letter to theatres.[1] Caroline, terrified, worked on his friends to dissuade him from going. But to Böttiger, who tried

[1] Kaiser 156.

to suggest how important it was for all of them, musicians, friends and family alike, that he should take care of himself and stay at home, he merely replied, 'Böttiger, it's all one! Whether I go or not, in a year I'm a dead man. But if I go, my children will eat when their father's dead, and if I stay they'll starve. What would you do in my place?' To his fellow-Ludlamite Schwarz, who came to see him, he confessed sadly, 'I'd just like to get home again, Schwarz, to see Lina, Max and Lexel, then in God's name let His will be done—but to die there—that would be hard.' He felt compelled to turn down Kemble's offer to conduct all the oratorios at Covent Garden during Lent, though he agreed to take on four; and he gratefully accepted Smart's invitation to come and stay in his house until he could fix himself up with lodgings. Written on 4th January, this letter did not reach Smart until the 26th, who the next day sent a long and very considerate reply giving Weber all details he could possibly need to help him get from Dover to London, promising him a piano in his room and every attention.[1] Hopes of persuading Gottfried Weber to accompany him were disappointed, but he was glad to accept an offer from Anton Fürstenau (Bärmann also offered, but in thanking him Weber tactfully pointed out that the chance of engagements would be of great benefit to the comparatively unknown young flautist). Caroline took some comfort from the fact that he would be well looked after. From Könneritz he bought a travelling carriage. He bade an emotional farewell to his company and paid a formal visit to take leave of the King. Caroline spent the last night sitting up watching over him; and early on the morning of 16th February Fürstenau called for him in the new carriage. The children were still asleep; he kissed them goodbye, embraced Caroline, stepped into the carriage and was wrapped in a rug. The door was slammed. Caroline ran back to her room and sank to her knees crying, 'I have heard the lid close upon his coffin!'

---

[1] The correspondence, printed in H. B. and C. L. E. Cox: *op. cit.*, p. 240–5, is in BM Add MS 41771.

CHAPTER SEVENTEEN

OBERON

Noch einmal sattelt mir den Hippogryphen, Musen,
Zum Ritt ins alte romantische Land!

C. M. WIELAND: *Oberon*

SHAKESPEARE HAS bequeathed us the image of Oberon as King in a vaguely Elizabethan fairy court, lordly and capricious, vindictive towards his Queen but more or less benevolent towards the lovers who stray across his path. The malice in his character is the principal relic of quite different origins that go back into mediaeval lore. His name is a version of Auberon, from Alberon, which in turn is equated with Albrich and later Alberich. Though the latter, through the *Nibelungenlied* and Wagner, has become completely identified with evil, this is really in his embodiment as Schwarzalberich (Wotan is Lichtalberich); the name derives from the Old High German and Middle High German *alp* or *alb*=elf, pl. *elber*, and the Gothic *reiks*=ruler. In Merovingian legend he is a magician who wins for his eldest son the hand of a princess of Constantinople; and in the mediaeval German poem *Ortnit* the hero is also aided in his wooing by his father Alberich, the king of the dwarfs. In *Huon de Bordeaux* Oberon is a hump-backed dwarf, only three feet high with an angelic face; he tells Huon that he is the son of the Lady of the Hidden Island (Cephalonia) and Julius Caesar.

Les prouesses et faitz du noble Huon de bordeaux, per de France, duc de Guyenne, as one edition entitles it, was one of the *chansons de geste* in the cycle known as the *Geste du Roi*. This was composed in the first half of the thirteenth century, possibly by a *jongleur* from Saint-Omer who took Auberon from Germanic legend, and adding other elements from other legends put together a story which in its earliest extant form runs to over 10,000 lines. It was subsequently turned into prose, and survived as a popular country tale up to the twentieth century.

Comte Amaury, having borne false witness against Huon and Gerard, young sons of Duke Seuin (Seguin) of Bordeaux, conspires with Charlemagne's son Charlot to ambush them on their way to Paris. Gerard is wounded, and in revenge Huon slays Charlot without realising who he is. When the truth emerges in Paris, Huon submits himself to judgement and a tournament with Amaury, which he wins. But Charlemagne (who is presented throughout as in his second childhood and whose judgement is sharply questioned by the court) sides with Amaury and banishes Huon, charging him to go to Babylon to the table of Admiral Gaudisse, cut off the head of the greatest lord there, kiss three times Gaudisse's daughter Esclarmonde, demand tribute and bring a handful of his beard and four of his back teeth. In Huon's absence, Gerard oppresses his subjects. On the way Huon meets an old French hermit, Gerasmes, who warns him against passing through the wood where dwells 'un Roy Oberon le fayé; il n' a que trois pieds de hauteur: il est tout bossu, mais il a un visage angélique'. Huon and Gerasmes leave together and meet Oberon; he carries a magic horn, made in Cephalonia by four fairies, that can cure sickness, sate hunger and thirst, cheer misery and summon any man from afar. Oberon stops them escaping by making them dance to the horn; Huon accepts his offer of assistance, and is given the horn with which, when in great need only, he can summon Oberon to his aid. After various adventures, including killing a giant and taking his ring as passport, he comes to Babylon. But having meanwhile broken faith with Oberon he blows his horn in vain when challenged, though the court fall to dancing helplessly. He cuts off a Paynim King's head; the Admiral sees the ring and allows him to kiss Esclarmonde, but has him seized when he finds out how it was obtained. After many complications, Esclarmonde contrives his escape; he kills the Admiral and takes his beard and teeth, which he hides in Gerasmes's side. They set out for home. But Huon breaks faith with Oberon again by making love to Esclarmonde, and is immediately shipwrecked. Pirate Paynims beat Huon and seize Esclarmonde. After further adventures they are united and married in Rome. Huon is now betrayed by his brother Gerard, who steals the beard and teeth so that Huon cannot prove the success of his mission to Charlemagne. Oberon causes the horn, which Huon has forfeited, to be returned; Huon summons him and is saved, Oberon proclaiming that he has stood by Huon by reason of his constancy.

In 866 Charles l'Enfant, one of the sons of Charles the Bald, was killed in circumstances similar to Charlot's murder by a certain Aubouin; there was also a Count Seguin of Bordeaux under Louis the Pious in 839. These, and possibly other minor details of fact, were gathered into the romance of *Huon*, which like most similar tales became a receptacle for various incidents drawn from different legends as time went by. It achieved great popularity in England by way of the translation of John Bourchier, Lord Berners, in about 1540; and it is the prime source of C. M. Wieland's *romantisches Helden-gedicht*, *Oberon* (1780).

Wieland made a number of important alterations and additions to the material of the original tale. He cut out many of the superficialities and irrelevancies which were put in simply as makeweight diversion, both before and after the main action, dropping the treachery of Gerard, the beheading of the heroine's father and the placing of the beard and teeth in Gerasmes's side. The latter is transformed into Scherasmin, still an old man but made into a faithful squire, brave but cunning, and with a penchant for story-telling. Oberon is 'ein Knäbchen, schön'; his horn sets all men (including the reluct-and Scherasmin) dancing when blown softly, and summons Oberon when

blown loudly; he also gives Huon a cup that will fill with wine when an honest
man drinks from it but will burn the lips of a villain. It is with their arrival
in Baghdad (which, as in many romances, is interchangeable with Babylon as
a vaguely remote oriental city) that the course of the plot takes some different
turns, most importantly with the belated introduction of the Oberon-
Titania quarrel.

> Huon and Scherasmin learn that the Sultan's daughter Rezia is due to be
> married to her cousin Prince Babekan, but is distracted by a dream she has
> told her nurse Fatme of a dwarf accompanied by a handsome young knight.
> Oberon helps Huon to perform his mission and delivers him and Rezia, with
> Scherasmin and Fatme, to the coast of Askalon with instructions to take ship
> for Rome and get married, meanwhile remaining 'as brother and sister' on
> pain of his displeasure. On the voyage Rezia is baptized a Christian as Amanda.
> Seeing Huon grow more and more passionate, the anxious Scherasmin tries to
> distract him with the story of January and May. This concerns the argument
> of Oberon and Titania over a case of human infidelity and Oberon's refusal to
> consort with Titania until a pair of faithful human lovers be found. Separating
> from Scherasmin at Lepanto, Huon takes ship and seduces Rezia; immedia-
> tely a fearful storm arises and the lovers, now deprived of Oberon's horn, are
> cast into the sea and thrown up on a desert island. Rezia is befriended by
> Titania and with her help delivered of a child, Huonnet. Fatme has mean-
> while been sold as a slave in Tunis to the King's gardener, and here Scherasmin
> finds her on his search for Huon. Rezia is carried off by pirates, who leave
> Huon tied up, and is sold to the King of Tunis. Titania cheers Rezia with a
> promise that all shall be well; Oberon releases Huon and transports him to the
> gardener's at Tunis, where he disguises himself in the hope of rescuing Rezia.
> Searching for her in the harem, he is discovered by Queen Almansaris, who
> tries to win him as her consort in compensation for the Sultan having fallen
> in love with a newcomer, Zoradine (really Rezia). Fatme advises Huon to
> send a message to Rezia by way of the symbols in a bunch of flowers. But this
> is intercepted and misunderstood by the Queen, who makes an assignment
> that Huon supposes to come from Rezia. When they meet, he is cold, and one
> of her attempts to seduce him is interrupted by Almansor; Huon is accused
> by the jealous Queen of assaulting her, and is sentenced to be burned alive.
> Rezia fails to persuade the Sultan to release Huon, and decides to die with
> him rather than become Queen. As the pyre is being lit, thunder is heard, the
> lovers' bonds fall away and a horn is seen hanging round Huon's neck. Huon
> blows it and sets all Tunis dancing; they are transported to the realm of the
> reconciled Oberon and Titania and thence, with Scherasmin and Fatme, to
> Paris where Huon is at last received into the favour of Charlemagne.

Wieland based his poem on the prose version of *Huon de Bordeaux*
published, like the *Euryanthe* source, in Comte Louis de Tressan's *Bibliothèque universelle des romans*, in April 1778, at the same time importing other
elements. In the introduction to the last edition of his *Oberon* (1796) he
points out that the two main trends of the plot are the love story of Huon and

Rezia and the reconciliation of Oberon with Titania; and most of his new characterization of *Oberon* derives from Shakespeare's *A Midsummer Night's Dream*. Instead of the quarrel over the Indian boy, however, he ingeniously imports the tale of January and May (in his sixth *Gesang*) from the satire of that name by Pope, whose source was in Chaucer's *Merchant's Tale* (in neither are Oberon and Titania mentioned by name, Chaucer calling them Pluto and Proserpina, Pope 'the monarch of the fairies and his bride'). The episode of the banishment of Huon and Rezia to the desert island (seventh and eighth *Gesang*) is thought possibly to have come from Johann Georg Schnabel's *Die Insel Felsenburg* (1731–43), the longest and most popular of the *Robinsonaden*. Wieland's poem suggests that reconciliation is possible only by the realization of a moral ideal, the fidelity to death, if need be, of a human couple—the stirrings of the Romantic preoccupation with the Redemption through Love motive.

Oberon was the last major work of Wieland's long and full life, and its somewhat self-conscious Romanticism is exemplified in the famous opening lines:

> Noch einmal sattelt mir den Hippogryphen, Musen,
> Zum Ritt ins alte romantische Land!

Yet it is told with a freshness and humour that enliven the Romantic convention, as if Wieland was prepared to adopt this manner of speech only half-seriously; the effect is not unlike that of the non-satirical portions of Byron's *Don Juan*. The poem was immensely popular among Wieland's contemporaries, winning from Goethe the opinion that, 'So long as poetry remains poetry, gold gold, and crystal crystal, his *Oberon* will be loved and admired as a masterpiece of poetic art.' Curiously, the first librettist to take it up for an opera was neither German, nor even a Romantic, the Dane Jens Baggesen whose feuds against Romanticism were directed especially at Weber's friend Oehlenschläger. His three-act *Holger Danske* was set as an opera by Friedrich Kunzen (1761–1817) and produced in Copenhagen on 31st March 1789. It is quite a fresh and attractive piece, written in separate numbers and in its treatment of the hero Holger Danske (=Huon) and Rezia being saved from the stake suggesting an early Rescue Opera. Although dramatically lame, with too many sylphs' choruses slowing up the action, it includes some excellent numbers (notably an aria for the sleeping Rezia) and was successful enough to become accepted as a Danish national opera. It anticipates Weber only in coincidences such as the use of the diminished seventh when Scherasmin exclaims in the wood, 'How horrible! how still!', and in opening on the magic horn (Ex. 73, p. 312).

The same year saw the production at the Theater an der Wien on 7th November of *Oberon, König der Elfen* by an Austrian composer of Moravian origin, Paul Wranitzký (Pavel Vranický) (1761–1820), described both as an operetta and a *Romantisch Komisch Oper*. The text seems to have been based on Wieland and also on Fredericke Seyler's libretto *Huon und Amande*, and written by the same Carl Giesecke who claimed a hand in Mozart's *Magic Flute*. It is a more stageworthy piece than *Holger Danske*, and was indeed very successful until Weber's *Oberon* and even had revivals subsequently. The layout is similar to that of Kunzen's opera, with Act 1 proposing the trial, Act 2 finding Hyon [*sic*] in Baghdad, Act 3 describing the rescue from burning in Tunis. A further *Oberon* opera, *Huon und Amande* by Carl Hanke (1754–1835), who was cantor at Flensburg and later music director at Hamburg, seems to be lost.[1]

Wieland's poem had reached England in 1781, in a translation by James Six; but the first published version seems to have been that by William Sotheby (2 vols., 1798), a wealthy amateur who was a friend of Scott, Wordsworth and many other of the English Romantics and who adopted some of their mannerisms with none of their genius in his translations from German, Latin and Greek. What is, in Wieland, somewhat scented but perfectly acceptable for its period, becomes artificial in Sotheby, as can be seen in the comparison of one stanza, Scherasmin's reminiscence of his childhood in France.

WIELAND:

Du kleiner Ort, wo ich das erste Licht gesogen,
Den ersten Schmerz, die erste Lust empfand,
Sei immerhin unscheinbar, unbekannt,
Mein Herz bleibt ewig doch vor allen dir gewogen,
Fühlt überall nach dir sich heimlich hingezogen,

Ex. 73

[1] The *Oberon* mounted at Drury Lane on 28th March 1826 as rival attraction to Covent Garden's *Oberon* can hardly be included in a list of operas. Assembled with music by Cherubini (the *Lodoïska* overture), Winter (parts of *Das unterbrochene Opferfest*) and Mozart, it used the Huon and Amanda story chiefly as a basis for stage and costume effects, which Weber admired while deploring everything else.

Fühlt selbst im Paradies sich doch aus dir verbannt;
O möchte wenigstens mich nicht die Ahnung trügen,
Bei meinen Vätern einst in deinem Schoss zu liegen!

SOTHEBY:
Thou little spot! where first I sucked the light,
Thou witness of my earliest smile and tear!
Lov'd haunt! tho' distant far, how fair appear,
Thy scenes in daydreams floating on my sight!
Where'er I wander, my returning mind,
Still feels itself to thee in secret join'd!
Feels without thee e'en Paradise unblest—
Oh! be the brooding true that swells my breast!
O lay me in thy lap amid my sires reclin'd!

This was the version known to Planché, the librettist of what he and Weber entitled in full *Oberon: or the Elf King's Oath* (J.306). Born in 1796 of Huguenot descent, James Robinson Planché had had an early success with a play for Drury Lane and went on to prove his facility by turning out ten pieces for the Adelphi in 1820-1. Later he was to publish a *History of British Costume*, arrange the armour in the Tower of London and become a senior member of the College of Arms, interests that first showed themselves in the dresses he designed for Charles Kemble's revival of *King John* at Covent Garden in 1823—apparently the first occasion on which a historical drama had been dressed in period costume. Presumably it was this knowledge of chivalry, coupled with his facility, that led Kemble to choose him as Weber's librettist. His text, which he described with more accuracy than was perhaps intended as 'the fragile threads on which a great composer has ventured to string his valuable pearls,' does make several intelligent improvements, chiefly by basing the motivation of the whole plot on Oberon's 'fatal vow', in cutting the island idyll and in developing the subsidiary pair of lovers. It can be summarised as follows:

Act 1: In Oberon's bower, a group of fairies is singing over their sleeping King (No. 1, Introduction; 'Light as fairy foot can fall'). Puck (sop.) chases them away, explaining that Oberon and Titania have separated over whether men and women are more inconstant, and will not meet until they find a constant couple. Oberon (mezzo) wakes and repents his vow (No. 2, Aria: 'Fatal vow!'). Puck reports that Charlemagne, as punishment for killing his son Scharlot, has sent Huon of Bordeaux to Baghdad to kill the man on the Caliph's left hand and kiss his daughter in betrothal. He takes Oberon to where Huon and his young squire Sherasmin are sleeping. Oberon causes there to appear to Huon a vision of 'the interior of a Persian kiosk' in which is seated Reiza[1] (sop.) and urges Huon to come and rescue her (No. 3, Vision: 'O why art thou sleeping'). Sherasmin (bar.) wakes Huon (ten.) and they are given by Oberon a magic horn that brings aid or sets men dancing, and a golden cup that fills

---

[1] Planché spells her name thus.

with wine of its own accord—much to Sherasmin's mingled alarm and delight. Oberon warns that if impure lips touch the cup, it will burn like molten lead. Fairies appear, and Oberon promises Huon his aid, transferring him to the banks of the Tigris outside Baghdad before vanishing (No. 4, Ensemble: 'Honour and joy'). They hear cries and see Prince Babekan (speaker) being attacked by a lion; they rescue him. But when he tries to drink from the cup they offer, it burns him; enraged, he attacks Huon and Sherasmin with the aid of his retainers, but is routed. In her cottage Namouna (speaker), grandmother of Reiza's attendant, Fatima, welcomes Huon and Sherasmin and tells them that tomorrow Reiza is to marry Babekan against her will, but has had the vision of herself as a hind rescued from the pursuing Babekan by a strange knight she has now sworn to marry. Looking more closely at Huon and growing suspicious at his resemblance to Reiza's description, she hurries off to the palace. Huon reflects that to his devotion to honour in battle has now been added the emotion of love (for the première Planché and Weber inserted, for John Braham, the aria 'Ah! 'tis a glorious sight to see' (No. 23) to replace the original No. 5, 'From Boyhood trained'). In the harem in Baghdad, Reiza is telling Fatima (sop.) she would die before submitting to her betrothed, Prince Babekan, but in any case feels her rescuer to be near. Fatima goes in answer to a knock. In the Finale (No. 6: 'Haste, gallant knight'), Reiza urges speed upon the unknown knight; Fatima returns with news that a knight has indeed appeared swearing to rescue Reiza; the harem guard is heard approaching, chanting that the faithful are now called to prayer and rest, leaving Reiza excitedly awaiting her deliverance.

Act 2: In the banqueting hall of the palace, a chorus is praising the Caliph Haroun Alraschid (speaker) and cursing infidels (No. 7, Chor: 'Glory to the Caliph!'). The Caliph silences them and tells Babekan that the hour has come for his marriage to Reiza. But as she is brought forth (No. 8), Huon and Sherasmin rush in with drawn swords. Reiza flies to the arms of Huon, who kisses her. The Caliph bids his slaves kill Huon; Babekan claims that right but is cut down by Huon. The slaves rush at Huon, who sounds the horn and freezes them to the spot, thus allowing him to escape with Reiza while Sherasmin seizes Fatima (No. 9a). In the palace gardens, the Saracen guards are routed; Oberon appears, expresses satisfaction with Huon, learns that Reiza is willing to follow him, and conjures up before them the port of Ascalon and a ship that will take them to Greece (Melodrama: No. 9b and 9c). Huon and Reiza leave while Sherasmin woos Fatima, who declares she is only a simple Arab girl inexperienced in love but willing to accept Sherasmin if he truly wants her (No. 10, Ariette: 'A lonely Arab maid'). Huon urges them to hurry, and all four express their pleasure at leaving together and their high hopes for the future (No. 11, Quartett: 'Over the dark blue waters'). Standing on some rocks, Puck (sop.) summon spirits to wreck Huon's ship; they declare this to be simple (No. 12, Solo and Chor: 'Spirits of air and earth and sea!'). In a cave on the shore where they have been wrecked Huon tries to revive Reiza (again at Braham's request, Planché and Weber here later inserted the Preghiera, 'Ruler of this awful hour', No. 12a). She revives and the waves wash up the magic cup, whose wine refreshes her. Huon leaves her to look for help. She is overawed by the majesty and power of the sea, in calm and storm, morning light and sunset; she notices a boat and waves her veil to attract attention (No. 13, Scene und Arie: 'Ocean! thou mighty monster'). But out of the boat leap Abdallah (speaker) and his fellow pirates; they seize her, overpower Huon when he returns but accept Reiza's pleas for his life and leave him tied up. As they leave, Oberon appears in a car drawn by swans, and summons Puck (No. 14), who is told to take Huon in seven days' time to Tunis and lay him at the door of Ibrahim the gardener; meanwhile an arbour encircles Huon, and as the moon rises mermaids are heard singing of their delight in rocking on the surface of the sea; the earth spirits dance with the mermaids, delighting in the beauty of the night (No. 15, Finale: 'Oh! 'tis pleasant').

Act 3: Out of Ibrahim's house in Tunis comes Fatima, bewailing the fate that has delivered her there from the shipwreck as a slave and has separated her from Reiza. But she has had a dream prophesying good fortune, a vision of her father's tent and a song about a girl who escaped with her lover (No. 16, Lied: 'O Araby!'). Sherasmin comes to ask if she has seen their master, who has gone to the town; he is more cheerful because happy to be married to Fatima and together they sing of their very different childhoods: now they are slaves, but slaves together (No. 17, Duett: 'On the banks of sweet Garonne'). Puck causes Huon to appear; as the surprised Sherasmin is telling him that they are in the garden of the Emir, Fatima discovers that a ship has just arrived bearing, for the Emir, a beautiful lady answering Reiza's description. But Sherasmin is worried that the horn has gone, and suggests that Huon disguise himself (No. 18, Terzettino: 'And must I then dissemble?'). In the harem, the Emir Almanzor (speaker) makes Reiza welcome, though she remains sad (No. 19, Cavatine: 'Mourn thou, poor heart') and resists his advances. Almanzor's wife Roshana (speaker) enters to Almanzor's embarassment, and is dismissed, to her fury. In Almanzor's garden, Fatima is delighted to have arranged for Huon to enter the gardener's service. Huon is surprised to have had a bouquet flung at him, but Fatima explains the meanings of the flowers in it; the message of Reiza's faithfulness and her plan for their escape revive his hopes completely (No. 20, Rondo: 'I revel in hope and joy'). Huon is led by Nadina, a harem slave, to Roshana's apartment; she promises him the throne of Tunis if he will kill Almanzor and marry her. He refuses, and she summons her female slaves to aid her persuasion (No. 21, Chor und Ballet: 'For thee hath beauty').[1] He still refuses and tries to escape; Almanzor returns and Roshana pretends that Huon has broken in and attacked her; he is led away to die, though Almanzor does not believe her and has her, too, seized and removed to be killed. In Ibrahim's garden Sherasmin is anxiously waiting; when he angrily declares Oberon to be a treacherous spirit, he is pricked by a rose-bush, and discovers, hanging there, the magic horn. Fatima comes to say that all is lost and Huon is to be burned alive. Sherasmin sounds the horn, which makes Fatima laugh helplessly, and they set off to the

[1] Originally for mixed voices, altered for SSA by Weber in London.

rescue. In the court, Reiza implores mercy for Huon, but when she declares she is his wife and refuses to give him up for Almanzor, she is condemned to die with him. Huon is brought in to go to the stake. But in the Finale (No. 22: 'Hark! What notes are swelling!') as the pyre is about to be lit, the horn sounds and all the slaves begin to dance. Huon, Reiza, Sherasmin and Fatima give thanks; another, stronger blast causes the pyre to vanish, Almanzor and the slaves to flee, Oberon and Titania to appear in the clouds. Oberon tells Huon and Reiza that their trials are over and that he will take them to Charlemagne's court; the magic ends, he tells them, and he is indebted to them for their proof of faithfulness. In Charlemagne's palace Huon kneels and reports that he has truly performed his task. The chorus joins in praise of Huon and Reiza.

In his autobiography, Planché attempts to justify what he realized was an unsatisfactory text for an opera. Part of the blame he lays on the audience: 'Ballads, duets, choruses, and glees, provided they occupied no more than the fewest number of minutes possible, were all that the playgoing public of that day would endure. A dramatic situation in music was "caviare to the general", and inevitably received with cries of "Cut it short!" from the gallery and obstinate coughing or other significant signs of impatience from the pit.'[1] Contemporary accounts bear out the melancholy fact that Planché knew the English musical stage at this low ebb of its history only too well, its pre-occupation with sensational stage effects (advertised with loving detail on posters of the period), with ballad-like numbers, with extra diversions in the evening's programme, with picturesque subjects and favourite singers, its total rejection of anything approaching music-drama as Weber was trying to develop it.[2] No wonder, in such conditions, that there did not exist artists who could have understood and performed the work the composer might have made out of *Oberon*; Planché states that 'None of our actors could sing and but one singer could act—Madame Vestris—who made a charming Fatima', and in apportioning the blame for the wrecking of Weber's last opera, we should not forget Kemble.

As regards the versification of the individual numbers, Planché was pre-pared to throw Sotheby overboard. He ingeniously turns Sherasmin's reminiscence into a duet with Fatima, contrasting their different back-grounds, and writes a verse perfectly acceptable as material for the comic squire that Sherasmin has now become:

> On the banks of sweet Garonne,
> I was born one fine spring morning,
> Soon as I could run alone,
> Kicks, and cuffs, and tumbles scorning,

[1] J. R. Planché: *Recollections and Reflections*, Vol. I, p. 80 (1872).
[2] But Fanny Kemble: *Record of Girlhood*, p. 163 (1878) suggests that though *Oberon* is a finer work than *Freischütz*, the English public would have taken better to *Euryanthe* or *Preciosa*.

Shirking labour, loving fun,
Swigging wine, and hating water,
Fighting ev'ry neighbour's son,
And kissing ev'ry neighbour's daughter.
O how fast the days have flown
On the banks of sweet Garonne.[1]

Unfortunately, when he came to deal with the main characters and plot, Planché was visited by ambitions. His dialogue retains most of Sotheby's artificiality, with inversions, puns, obscure references and constant use of the second person singular. Too much of the sentimental-heroic atmosphere and too little of the substance is retained, so that the characters are reduced to mere stuffed costumes. Worse, Planché's knowledge of his customers' devotion to spectacular scenes and transformations led him to load the work with them—there are no fewer than eight scenes in Act 3 alone. No wonder the bemused Weber wrote to him on 19th February 1825 protesting about the number of non-singing actors and the omission of music at the most important moments, which seemed to him so much against the nature of opera. But as can be seen by comparing the libretto with the sources, Planché was chiefly concerned to transform a romantic tale into the format that would be acceptable to his audiences, and everything could be sacrificed to their desire for picturesqueness, spectacle, and simple numbers for favourite singers: it did not matter that the story was left with various loose ends and absurdities, that no situation or character is properly developed, that the motive for some incidents (such as the shipwreck) has become obscure; while the many characters who put in a brief appearance and the number of scenes in different places, so far from confusing the dramatic issue, seemed nothing but a recommendation to the expert pantomime writer which Planché became. He must, however, be defended on the charge that he allowed Huon and Reiza to be rescued from every danger by supernatural aid: he himself indignantly retorted that their ordeals were 'among the severest known to humanity—shipwreck on a desolate island—separation—slavery—temptation in its most alluring forms, and the imminent danger of death in the most fearful manner', all when 'utterly hopeless of fairy aid.' It is their constancy, not Huon's knighthood, which is under trial.

Receiving the text at first piecemeal, Weber cannot immediately have realised the real nature of the work to which he was committing himself. His first letter to Planché[2] cordially accepts Act 1, praising the verses and asking

[1] This is the version in the original published libretto (Hunt and Clarke, 1826). Various alterations were made to all the verses during the setting of the text and preparation of the work, and Planché himself made subsequent revisions.

[2] Weber's letters of 6th January and 19th February 1825 are in MMW, Vol. II, pp. 588–90. These two (the former without the PS urging the need to see the whole text as soon as possible) and a third of 3rd December 1825 are also in Planché: *op. cit.*, Vol. I, pp. 75–9.

only that the role of the chorus in the finale should be made subordinate to
Reiza's excited hopes; the result is one of his best strokes, as the harem guard
paces steadily across the scene and into the night while Reiza's ecstatic
coloratura swoops and plunges over their plodding little tune. The letter of
19th February remains complimentary while objecting to the nature of the
work as a whole and making specific requests: an Act 2 duet and a chorus for
the pirates were dropped, Weber wishing to spend the time gained on a love
duet. He regretted that it was dramatically impossible to insert this at the
moment of the lovers' meeting, and decided that the right place would be in
the scene on the seashore. He also asked for 'a *mad* aria for Sherasmin, when
he discovers the horn, in which Fatima's lamentations unite and close the
scene with a beautiful contrast' (Act 3: nothing came of this). Gently he
reminded Planché that, 'The composer looks more for the expressions of
feelings than the figurative; the former he may repeat and develope [*sic*] in all
their graduations, but verses like—

> Like the spot the tulip weareth
> Deep within its dewy urn

or in Huon's song—

> Like hopes that deceive us,
> Or false friends who leave us
> Soon as descendeth prosperity's sun,

must be said only *once*'. If that, one is tempted to add: the sibilants alone
try the most expert singer. On 3rd December 1825 he suggests omitting 'O
Araby' unless Planché objects, in which case he will write it in England; and
reports that he now feels the love duet sent by Planché must be omitted
after all as it will not be effective in the planned position.

By now, of course, it was too late to withdraw from a venture about which
Weber had been developing doubts, even if his own situation had made such a
move possible. In the early stages the idea must have seemed attractive
enough, while the then primitive stage of his English would not have allowed
him to be sure enough of the gaucheness of Planché's style to protest; moreover, it has to be allowed that a composer who accepted Helmina von Chezy's
verses in his own language showed an exaggerated degree of tolerance. Only
when he was irrevocably committed did he begin to realize the nature of the
piece; and resolving to rewrite the work as an opera with recitatives for
Germany when he returned home, he set about making the best of a bad job.

Having accepted Planché's farrago, Weber's problem was to justify it
musically and to confer some measure of unified character upon it. There was
no clear antithesis between darkness and light as in *Der Freischütz* which
might suggest a comparable use of key patterns. Nor was there a practical
method of contrasting the chivalric element with the supernatural as in
Euryanthe by way of different harmonic references, since in *Oberon* the

supernatural was closely involved with the hero in a rapid succession of adventures. *Oberon* is a D major opera, but with a harmonic ground plan free from associations such as those of its two predecessors. Weber immediately recognized that there were three worlds here, the chivalric, the oriental and the enchanted; and the small space in which he was obliged to work led him to a new concentration and distillation of style so that each world can be conjured up in sometimes only a few bars of memorably vivid invention, embodied in perhaps only a few instruments. Planché's devotion to 'the figurative' and his reluctance to weary an audience (or to overtax his own talent) with a developed character or situation further impelled Weber to refine and concentrate his manner. His understanding of the maximum effect to be drawn from instruments was never more needed, nor more beautifully expressed; and more than in *Der Freischütz* or *Euryanthe*, he shows how closely orchestration may be connected to the new harmonic effects after which he was reaching. Nevertheless, he felt obliged to cast about for some other way of connecting the disjointed scenes, and the natural, flexible method was *Leitmotiv*. Perhaps he remembered that he had once praised Hoffmann's *Undine* and its device whereby 'a few melodies thread themselves quietly through the whole fabric and give it inner cohesion.' Searching through the Dresden library, he turned up two books which provided him with a clue. In Vol. 1 of Carsten Niebuhr's *Reisebeschreibung nach Arabien* (1774) he found a picture (Tab. xxvi) of various Arabian instruments, including a *seméndsje*, a kind of narrow 2-stringed or 3-stringed fiddle with a coconut resonator and beside it a fragment of music. Niebuhr comments, 'This is the usual instrument of fiddlers that go round with Egyptian dancers, and the notes are the tune of a song which the dancers sing to the *seméndsje* and often repeat.'

Ex. 74

In Vol. 1 of La Borde's *Essai sur la Musique* Weber further found an example of a *danse turque*.[1]

Ex. 75

[1] This is also quoted, with slight differences in bars 7 and 8, in Sir William Jones: *On the Musical Modes of the Hindus* (written 1784, publ. 1799).

From this the seed of *Oberon* was to grow—or rather, towards it, for it is not until the Finale of Act 1 that Weber quotes the first of these nor until the Finale of Act 3 that he uses the second, slightly revised as follows:

Ex. 76

The essential feature common to both tunes, the rise and fall of a third, provided him with the famous horn call that opens the overture—the superiority of this haunting sound over Kunzen's similar attempt is the measure of Weber's instrumental genius—and also a wealth of other references to suggest the constant working of the fairy world in Huon's affairs. Obviously so simple a figure could be found many times over on every page of every piece of diatonic music; but the following examples are unmistakably deliberate invocations of the horn call as token of Oberon's precipitation of the events and his magic hand in them; there are arguably others where at least a half-reference is intended (Ex. 77, opposite and p. 322).

With this device, his most systematic use of *Leitmotiv*, Weber seems to have felt that he had hit upon the right method of drawing together the disparate strands of the work. And in a sense *Oberon* with all its faults also draws together everything that had gone before in Weber's operas—the chivalric world of *Euryanthe* and *Silvana*, the supernatural in *Der Freischütz* and *Rübezahl*, the oriental in *Abu Hassan*, perhaps most of all the intense nature feeling of *Freischütz*, *Silvana* and *Euryanthe*. In the absence of any very subtle characters, it is upon such atmospheres and upon mood pictures within them that Weber is forced to rely. He was even prepared to take the scenic devices and transformations into his music: there is the fascinating change that comes over the music as Oberon conjures up Baghdad, and 'Ocean! thou mighty monster' itself is very much composed with an eye to visual effects—the storm clearing to reveal the glory of the setting sun. He later came to admire the Covent Garden effects enormously. Yet though there are few ensembles, the form in which development of character or situation can be best played out, and few large arias, *Oberon* is in many ways a transitional work towards Wagner. This shows not least in the manner in which a character is coloured by way of his relationship with the natural world and the elements.

STAGE DESIGNS BY GRIEVE FOR *OBERON*

Above: Act 1, scene 1: Vision from Oberon's bower of the banks of the Tigris, with the city of Baghdad in the distance.

Below: Act 2, scene 1: The Caliph's harem, 'with vestibule and terrace overlooking the Tigris'.

These models, designed for the Covent Garden revival on 13th March 1843, are possibly based on the originals.

For one who had only ventured on the sea very briefly, during his trip to Denmark in 1821, Weber shows an uncanny feeling for the element he doubtless felt to be particularly apt for treatment in an opera for Englishmen. The storm conjured up by Puck's spirits heaves and slaps with a surge entirely different from that in the Wolf's Glen; and the whole of the end of Act 2, beginning with the lulling of the Mermaid's Song—surely the most beautiful piece in the whole of Romantic opera—is a ravishing tone-picture of a warm nocturnal seascape with Weberian fairies quivering in the air above the

Ex. 77

Overture, opening

No. 1, "Light as fairy foot can fall", opening.

Andante quasi Allegretto: *sempre tutto ppposs.*

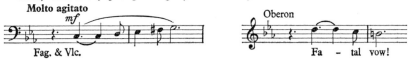

No. 2, "Fatal vow", opening bass figure, and vocal entry.

No. 3, "O why art thou sleeping", introduction

No. 6, "Haste, gallant knight".

No. 7, "Glory to the Caliph", opening.

Fag., Vlc., Db.

No. 11, "Spirits of air".

Presto agitato (the spirits appear)

No. 14, "O, 'tis pleasant", opening, with ostinato acct. figure continuing on horn.

Andante con moto

Vl. con sord. & Vl. solo

No. 17, "On the banks of sweet Garonne".

Andante grazioso

Sherasmin

On the | banks — of sweet Ga -ron - ne

Str.

No. 19, "Mourn thou, poor heart": figure between 1st and 2nd strain, and similarly at end.

Andantino

gently rocking sea creatures. In 'Ocean! thou mighty monster' the portrait of the sea becomes so full as to lift the whole scena above the normal scale of the opera's numbers, and even to suggest a rather different character (and singer) for Reiza. There is a Wagnerian expansiveness in the opening apostrophe; the rushing semi-quavers and furious tremolos, taken up from Puck's storm, were to suggest much in *Der fliegende Holländer* to Wagner, who must also have remembered the trumpet in his Sword motive and especially Weber's sun bursting forth when he came to awaken Brünnhilde to the sun at the top of the mountain in *Siegfried* (Ex. 78, below).

The unifying force here is not the horn motive but the arpeggio of the common chord, one effectively suited to the suggestion of the ocean's

Ex. 78

WEBER: *Oberon* No. 13, "Ocean! thou mighty monster".

WAGNER: *Siegfried*, Brünnhilde's awakening.

Ex. 79

breadth and majesty. The opening recitative makes this clear at the words 'round about the world'. A figure at 'and fling'st thy folds' is taken up for the first *allegro*, with its tune dashing up and down the arpeggio like the slapping of the waves. The calm *maestoso* when the sun appears makes greater use of repeated notes—a simple, graphic image for a level sea—with the arpeggios then returning. And the final presto hurls them up and down with precipitous joy at Reiza's sight of the boat she thinks brings rescue.

Obviously a work cast in this manner will tend to lean less upon vocal melody than upon the orchestra for its character; and orchestrally *Oberon* is Weber's masterpiece. The first aria, Oberon's 'Fatal vow', is Wagnerian not only in its restless urgency of movement but in the manner in which the vocal line seems to grow out of the orchestra rather than impose a certain kind of accompaniment on it: this might almost be the Flying Dutchman himself, in the 6/8 section of 'Die Frist ist um' (Ex. 79, opposite).

However, neither this magnificent aria nor Reiza's great scena are characteristic of *Oberon* as a whole. It is upon the shorter numbers and upon the exquisite colour with which Weber 'fixes' them like photographs in the listener's mind that the work depends—the high clarinet and bassoon figure framed by horn and in turn framing Reiza's guitar song 'O, why art thou sleeping';[1] Oberon's unfolding of Baghdad before Huon's astonished gaze, the air seeming to clear and to breathe a milder, mysterious warmth (bassoon and strings alone); the contrast of *Euryanthe*-like chivalrous tones in 'From boyhood trained' with Reiza's gentle, syncopated woodwind figure in the following 'Haste, gallant knight' and her appearance before the court; the oboe, clarinet, bassoon and solo violin as Puck's spirits prepare to dance; the swirling flutes and clarinets as Oberon appears in his car drawn by swans; the soft movement of the sea in the Mermaids' Song through which the horn gently and steadily calls; the rapt effect of Huon's *Preghiera* over divided violas and cellos. Any number of other strokes could be singled out whereby Weber fastens upon an extraordinary, unprecedented yet ideal texture for the situation. Berlioz, who passionately admired the score and was indeed profoundly influenced by it, points out the remarkable use in the overture of violas and cellos above two clarinets in their lowest register, which he finds *neuf et saissisant*:[2] and the whole of *Oberon* might be taken as a primer of how to score for woodwind. The oriental atmosphere is suggested with the greatest delicacy—a hint of triangle as Reiza is brought in, to remind us that her beauty is exotic—where a lesser composer might load the work with crude mock-Orientalisms. It is the poetic sensation of the exotic in which the Romantic composer interests himself, not its mimicry, as when, in another effect admired by Berlioz, he omits the tonic E from the final

[1] Weber's conducting score (BM Add MS 27,746) shows that for the première this was given with off-stage harp.

[2] Hector Berlioz: *Grand Traité d'Instrumentation*, p. 49 (1843).

chord of the Mermaids' Song, creating a strange effect of dramatic suspense.[1] Nowhere is this more apparent than in the overture, Weber's last orchestral work and perhaps the purest distillation of his peculiar genius for instrumental poetry. The three notes of Oberon's horn are themselves evocation, not imitation: Tovey wrote, 'When it sounds, we see and hear as if space were annihilated; and everything becomes exquisitely clear and tiny, because its immense remoteness is that of our own inmost soul.'[2] The little flickering, falling chromatic phrase for the fairies and the soft fanfare taken from the final triumphal march are pictured as if seen very far off in the recesses of the imagination; and it is this frontispiece, so to speak, to Wieland's *alte romantische Land* which opens the way to the brilliant incidents of the story. Weber, with the greatest virtuosity he had yet shown in his overtures, brings into a sonata movement the final theme for 'On board then!' in 'Over the dark blue waters' and Huon's 'A milder light' in 'From boyhood trained', together with Puck's 'Whether ye be in the cavern dark' from his 'Spirits of air' and Reiza's ecstatic 'My husband, my love' as, in 'Ocean! thou mighty monster', she believes rescue to be at hand.

The whole nature of *Oberon*, then, both in its subject and in the method of treating it which Weber was led to adopt, is orchestral rather than vocal; yet the freshness and charm of his melodies is if anything at its peak in the disjointed numbers which comprise it. There is a wistful, intense lyricism about this swan-song opera, written in haste to provide for his family by an exhausted musician with death at his elbow; and it is this quality which transcends the music's obvious unevenesses. Some of these arise from Weber's unhappiness about the nature of the work. The contrast between formal song, such as Reiza's Cavatina, and the numbers that attempt to extend into something larger and more continuous is not on the whole very convincingly managed, and in the circumstances hardly could have been. Nevertheless, the melody pitched between formal tune and accompanied recitative has greater fluency and grace than in *Euryanthe*; it is in touches such as these, as well as in larger matters, that the poignancy of Weber's failure to write the operas he had in him becomes so painful. Other weaknesses spring from the sheer pace at which he was forced to work, especially near the end. The perfunctory close to the Act 3 finale is a concoction of the final chords of *Peter Schmoll* and the March from Weber's music to Eduard Gehe's tragedy *Heinrich IV* (J.237) (from No. 5 of this incidental music he also took a brief insert to accompany Oberon's conjuring up of the port of Ascalon). No. 21, immediately preceding this finale, was taken from No. 6 of *L'Accoglienza* (J.221), originally a chorus of Tuscans singing 'De mirti e d'uli'; and No. 3 of the same work provided material for Reiza's cabaletta over the Arab theme in the finale of Act 1. Weber's old friend Alexander von Dusch suggested to Jähns in 1860 that

[1] Hector Berlioz: *Oberon*, in *A Travers Chants* (1862).
[2] D. F. Tovey: *Essays in Musical Analysis*, Vol. 4, note on *Oberon* overture, p. 59.

one of the original ideas for *Oberon* went back to their time together in Schloss Neuburg in 1810: 'It is still vivid in my mind how late one evening Carl Maria sang me the melody of an Elf Chorus that was in his mind, and I am certain something of it must have found its way into *Oberon*.' Another friend, G. Roth, recalled an episode from the period of the work's composition, the summer of 1824. Approaching Hosterwitz at noonday through the still countryside, Weber became aware of the humming and whirring of insects all around them, and seizing Roth's arm he put his finger to his mouth and whispered, '*Oberon*!' The incident is not too fanciful bearing in mind Weber's ability to let natural scenes transmute themselves into musical ideas as he travelled about (see Chapter 6) and the similar stories of incidents that started in his mind ideas for *Der Freischütz*; presumably in both these instances the product was the chorus, No. 1, 'Light as fairy foot can fall'.

It is not only the suggestions of *Leitmotiv* which remind us of Weber's respect for Hoffmann's *Undine* and its treatment of a water-fairy: the storm, and particularly the spirits' music preceding it and again at the end of Act 2, recall *Undine*, as do the attempts to link the music with dialogue. But just as it was *Der Freischütz* which gave the most complete expression to the darkest forest spirits in German legend, so it is *Oberon* which fixed for years to come the style for depicting the fairy world. The example fell on fertile ground with one of Weber's greatest admirers, the boy Mendelssohn, whose *Midsummer Night's Dream* overture was written two months after Weber's death, on 6th August 1826; coincidentally (since *Oberon* did not reach Germany until that December) its coda uses the phrase Weber set in his Mermaids' Song to the words 'And the last faint light of the sun has fled'. It colours operas by Nicolai, Lortzing and Marschner (in particular *Hans Heiling*) to say nothing of the whole of the fairy element in Sullivan's *Iolanthe*, which is based on *Oberon* from the soft rising notes and answering sevenths which open the overture to the final chorus and its obvious lifting of Sherasmin and Fatima's 'Let's be merry' in 'On the banks of sweet Garonne'. The influence on Wagner was rather subtler but no less pervasive: the style of declamatory melody here and in *Euryanthe* clearly suggests his own *unendliche Melodie*, and as well as drawing much in his orchestral style from the work—particularly 'Fatal vow!', the revelation of Baghdad and 'Ocean! thou mighty monster'—he was surely remembering Roshana's flower maidens tempting Huon when he came to write a not dissimilar lilt for his own in *Parsifal*.

However fruitful the influence of *Oberon* on other composers' operas and however high its standing, it has like all Weber's operas except *Der Freischütz* become better known by repute than in performance. Undeniably there are good reasons for this; and Planché cannot for once be blamed for the creation of casting difficulties over Reiza, who is required to sing music that encompasses both the tender Agathe-like Cavatine 'Mourn thou, poor heart' and a scena, 'Ocean! thou mighty monster', which demands the voice of a Brünnhilde. Yet *Oberon* is too beautiful an opera to be consigned to the reference shelf, and like *Euryanthe* it has been the victim of many well-meaning attempts to give it a new lease of life. In this case, however, some kind of revision is necessary, particularly when the composer's wishes are known to have lain in the direction of rewriting it with recitatives. Not the most devoted lover of the period can now swallow whole the entertainment as Planché devised it: at best, one can accept it with good humour for the sake of hearing exactly how Weber dealt with the situation. In 1860 Benedict himself contributed recitatives and added sections from other works for a famous revival at Her Majesty's on 3rd July in Italian (trans. S. M.Maggioni) with Therese Tietjens as Reiza and Marietta Alboni as Fatima: this gave singing roles to Babekan (with the duet 'Trotze nicht' from *Euryanthe* now as a duet with Huon) and to Roshana (with Eglantine's 'O mein Leid'); he further added from *Euryanthe* the duet 'Hin nimm' as the missing love duet for Huon and Reiza. Previously, however, there had been the German première at Leipzig on 23rd December 1826 in the standard translation by Theodor Hell that all too faithfully matches the quality of the original; and there was also an attempt at revising text and music by K. Meisl and Franz Gläser in Vienna on 25th March 1827. Castil-Blaze tackled the work after his own fashion as *Huon de Bordeaux* for Toulouse in May 1846; but the first serious attempt at keeping to the original score while clearing up the awkwardnesses was made by Theodor Gassmann, who for a production at Hamburg in 1866 shortened the dialogue, cut out some of the spoken episodes and speaking roles and reduced the original sixteen scene changes to eight. This was followed by the most ambitious of all attempts to compose the spoken dialogue as recitative, made by Franz Grandauer with music by Franz Wüllner for the Vienna production in 1881. The orchestration intelligently matches Weber's and the recitatives are certainly ingenious, becoming rather more in certain passages such as the development of Puck's theme *pp* in violins as he works a transformation. But by keeping strictly to *Oberon* material Wüllner imposes an impossible discipline on himself; though he approaches the task ambitiously he relies rather heavy-handedly on the device of the rising notes of the horn-call, and as well as producing some uncharacteristic music he weakens a crucial amount of the effect of Weber's numbers by anticipating their music.

Other arrangers also felt that this version was too clumsy. The so-called Wiesbaden Version (1900) by Georg von Hülsen, J. Schlar and Joseph von Lauff makes revisions in the text and adds melodramas. Felix Weingartner (1914) reduced the scene changes of Act 3 to four, shortened the dialogue and added some music of his own composition to make a Terzett with Namouna in Act 1, a recitative for Roshana (who is built up into something of an

Eglantine anti-heroine figure) and a quartet in Almanzor's garden. Artur Bodansky (1918) also tried to reduce the number of scene changes, but he eliminated Roshana altogether, making the Caliph and Charlemagne basses and Babekan, Almanzor and Abdallah baritones. His cuts were not always wise—they included 'A lonely Arab maid'—and his fifteen recitatives were simple to the point of barrenness. Other attempts follow fairly regularly. In 1953 there was published one by Karlheinz Gutheim and Wilhelm Reinking which made a new translation from Planché and simply presented as clean a text as possible in the context of *Singspiel*. Horst Seeger's version (Leipzig, 1966) rearranges and alters the course of events so as to make the adventures more the subject of the contest between Oberon and Titania, who steps into Roshana's shoes and even takes over Reiza's 'Haste gallant knight'. Seeger retains the separation of the numbers and rejects recitative but recasts the story so as to clear up various points, to reduce the scene changes and generally to bring the piece closer to the atmosphere of Romantic *Singspiel*; but he breaks up and distributes the Act 1 and 3 finales, and in general creates an effect of scrappiness.

Probably the most successful compromise solution was Mahler's (eventually produced at Cologne, 10th April 1913). Based on sketches he left, a text was prepared by Gustav Brecher, with a scenic layout devised by Alfred Roller to include three scenes in Act 1, five in Act 2 and five in Act 3. Mahler's contribution rests on the insertion of seven pieces, mostly melodramas, to maintain a sense of musical continuity without destroying the essential nature of the work. After No. 2 ('Fatal oath') he uses as No. 2a a pair of phrases taken from the melodrama with which Weber accompanies the conjuring up of the port of Ascalon. Another melodrama (No. 3a, after 'O, why art thou sleeping') accompanying Oberon's promise of help uses the first twenty-two bars of the overture very effectively. The melodrama No. 8a accompanies Huon's meeting with Reiza and blowing of the horn in the Caliph's palace, and uses forty-three bars from the overture as it leads into the second subject (i.e. 'A milder light'). No. 13a comes (more questionably) after 'Ocean! thou mighty monster' and is an aria for Oberon, a shortened version of his original No. 2 ('Fatal vow') in which, as the pirates bear Reiza off, he expresses sympathy for the lovers in their trials but bids them hold fast. Then, as Oberon raises the arbour over Huon, Mahler repeats a shortened version of the music of No. 1 ('Light as fairy foot can fall'), in G instead of F. Lastly, after 'On the banks of sweet Garonne' Mahler inserts the music of the Allegro of the overture (in A instead of D), somewhat altered, as Puck reveals that Huon is in Tunis.

CHAPTER EIGHTEEN

LONDON: 1826

There is no such thing as a natural death: nothing that happens to a man is ever natural, since his presence calls the world into question. All men must die; but for every man his death is an accident and even if he knows it and consents to it, an unjustifiable violation.

SIMONE DE BEAUVOIR: *A Very Easy Death*
(trans. Patrick O'Brien)

FROM OSCHATZ, the first posting station on the road to Paris, Weber sent back his horses and his old coachman Johann. The parting from this last link with Dresden upset him so much that he had to hurry back into the carriage to avoid people's eyes, so he wrote to Caroline from Leipzig, that night, reassuring her that Fürstenau was 'coddling me like a woman in labour' and that he was very comfortable and much enjoying the fine weather as they journeyed towards France.[1] After a stop on 19th and 20th February in Frankfurt, where Gottfried Weber and Hoffmann turned up and took him to a performance of *Judas Maccabaeus*, they set off again and spending a night each in Mainz, Kaiserslautern and St. Avold, they reached Verdun on the 23rd. Weber was delighted with his first sight of a large open French fireplace and with the chance, in Epernay on the 24th, of drinking his family's health in champagne. On the 25th they entered Paris,[2] the only casualties on what he emphasized to Caroline was a very comfortable journey being 'one button off my trousers and one broken window. The former still awaits my technical skill.'

Partly in order to spare himself, perhaps partly so as to avoid a confrontation over the treatment of his works by Castil-Blaze, Weber had decided to remain incognito in Paris. On the morning after his arrival he immediately broke his resolve and set out to pay calls on Paer, Auber, Catel, Desaugiers *fils*, Berton and Cherubini. Rossini had asked the publisher Schlesinger to warn him of Weber's arrival so that he could pay his respects; but Weber determined to get the courtesy in first and turned up unannounced at Rossini's. Shocked at finding him so pale and wasted, coughing so much

---

[1] Letter of 16th February 1826. The fifty-three letters of Weber's journey to London were collected and published by his grandson Carl von Weber in *Reise-Briefe von Carl Maria von Weber* (1886).

[2] For the fullest account of Weber's stay in Paris, see Adolphe Jullien: *Weber à Paris en 1826* (1877).

NEVER ACTED.

Theatre Royal, Covent-Garden,

Tomorrow, WEDNESDAY, April 12, 1826,

Will be performed *(for the first time)* a Grand Romantic and Fairy OPERA, in three acts, (Founded on WIELAND's celebrated Poem) entitled

OBERON:

OR,

THE ELF-KING's OATH.

With entirely new Music, Scenery, Machinery, Dresses and Decorations.

The OVERTURE and the whole of the MUSIC composed by

CARL MARIA VON WEBER,

Who will preside that Evening in the Orchestra.

The CHORUS (under the direction of Mr. WATSON,) has been greatly augmented.
The DANCES composed by Mr. AUSTIN.
The Scenes painted by Mess. Grieve, Pugh, T. and W. Grieve, Luppino, and assistants.
The Machinery by Mr. E. SAUL. The Properties by Mess. BRADWELL,
The Dresses by Mr PALMER, Miss EGAN, and assistants.

Fairies.

Oberon, *King of the Fairies,* Mr. C. BLAND; Puck, Miss H. CAWSE,
Titania, *Queen of the Fairies,* Miss SMITH.

Franks.

Charlemagne, *King of the Franks,* Mr. AUSTIN,
Sir Huon, of Bourdeaux, *Duke of Guienne,............*Mr. BRAHAM,
Sherasmin, *his Squire,..............*Mr. FAWCETT.

Arabians.

Haroun-Al-Rashchid, *Caliph of Bagdad,* Mr. CHAPMAN,
Baba-khan, *a Saracenic Prince,* Mr. BAKER, Hassan, *Master of a Vessel,* Mr. J. ISAACS,
Hamet, Mr. EVANS, Amrou, Mr. ATKINS,
Reiza, *Daughter of the Caliph,..........*Miss PATON,
Fatima, Madame VESTRIS,
Namouna, *Fatima's Grandmother,* . Mrs. DAVENPORT.

Tunisians.

Almansor, *Emir of Tunis,......*Mr. COOPER,
Abdallah, *a Corsair,* Mr. HORREBOW, Slave, Mr. TINNEY,
Roshana, *Wife of Almansor,..........*Miss LACY;
Nadina, *a female Slave,* Mrs. WILSON.
Officers, Soldiers, Slaves, &c. of the different Courts,——Fairies, Sprites, &c.

Order of the Scenery :

OBERON'S BOWER,

With the VISION. Painted by Mr. Grieve.
Distant View of Bagdad, and the adjacent Country on the Banks of the Tigris,
By Sunset. Grieve
INTERIOR of NAMOUNA's COTTAGE, T. Grieve
VESTIBULE and TERRACE in the HAREM of the CALIPH, overlooking the Tigris. W. Grieve
GRAND BANQUETTING CHAMBER of HAROUN. T. Grieve
GARDENS of the PALACE. Pugh
PORT OF ASCALON. T.Grieve
RAVINE amongst the ROCKS of a DESOLATE ISLAND,
The Haunt of the Spirits of the Storm. Pugh

Perforated Cavern on the Beach,

With the OCEAN—in a STORM—a CALM—by SUNSET—
Twilight—Starlight—and Moonlight. T. Grieve
Exterior of Gardener's House in the Pleasure Grounds of the Emir of Tunis. Grieve
Hall and Gallery in Almansor's Palace. W. Grieve
MYRTLE GROVE in the GARDENS of the EMIR. Pugh
GOLDEN SALOON in the KIOSK of ROSHANA. W. Grieve.
The Palace and Gardens, by Moonlight. Grieve.
COURT of the HAREM. Pugh.
HALL of ARMS in the Palace of Charlemagne. Grieve & Luppino

☞ *Books of the Songs to be had in the Theatre, price 10d.*

To which will be added (23d time) a NEW PIECE, in one act, called

THE SCAPE-GOAT.

Old Eustace, Mr. BLANCHARD, Charles, Mr. COOPER,
Ignatius Polyglot, Mr. W. FARREN, Robin, Mr. MEADOWS,
Molly Maggs, Miss JONES, Harriet, Miss A. JONES.

W. REYNOLDS, Printer, 9. Denmark-Court, Strand

PLAYBILL FOR THE FIRST PERFORMANCE OF *OBERON*

and exhausted by the effort of climbing the stairs, Rossini tried to dissuade him from the London trip. Having failed, he promised to produce letters of introduction (including one to George IV), and waved aside apologies for newspaper attacks in Vienna on the grounds that he could not read German.[1] Finally he embraced his guest and saw him off standing bare-headed in the street. After dining well in a new restaurant, Weber went to the Théâtre Feydeau to see Auber's *Emma*, which he admired, and then on to a concert by the twenty-four-year old violinist, Charles Bériot. On all sides he was greeted with a volume of affection and respect that began to exhaust him. Two visits from his revered Cherubini greatly touched him; but the swarm of lesser artists who collected made him wish he had not abandoned his incognito, and he did not even greatly enjoy a dinner arranged by Schlesinger at which Pasta sang for him. One composer he would surely have been delighted to meet was his great admirer, Berlioz, who spent the day of the revival of Spontini's *Olympie*, 27th February, vainly pursuing him about Paris—an irony characteristic of them both:

> How much I wanted to see him! How my heart beat as I followed him on the evening when, already suffering and just before his departure for England, he wanted to see the revival of *Olympie*! My chase was in vain. In the morning Lesueur had said to me, 'I've just had a visit from Weber. Five minutes ago you could have heard me playing him whole scenes out of our French scores on the piano; he knew them all.' Going into a music shop several hours later: 'If you knew who was sitting there just now!' 'Well, who?' 'Weber!'; arriving at the Opéra and hearing the crowd repeat, 'Weber has just crossed the foyer, he's gone into the auditorium, he's in the first row of boxes'—I despaired at never being able to find him. But it was all useless; no-one could point him out to me. Like the opposite of Shakespeare's ghosts, he was visible to everyone but remained invisible to one man alone. Too obscure to dare to write to him and without friends in a position to introduce me, I didn't succeed in seeing him.[2]

Weber praised the performance of *Olympie* and admired the whole atmosphere of show in the Opéra; but it was Boïeldieu's *La Dame Blanche* at the Théâtre Feydeau on the following night that really impressed him, and as well as asking Caroline to recommend it to Theodor Hell he himself wrote to Hell urging him to translate 'the best comic opera since *Figaro*' and to get Marschner to put it straight into the Dresden repertory. He spent one of his five days in Paris with Antoine Gros, then painting the dome of the Panthéon

---

[1] Rossini claimed that his only German phrase was, 'ich bin zufrieden' (which got him arrested when a Viennese policeman asked him his name). However, the details of this meeting should be treated with caution, resting as they do solely on Rossini's account to Wagner in 1860 (see Edmond Michotte: *Souvenirs personelles. La Visite de R. Wagner à Rossini*, p. 21–4 (1906)). There are no traces of published attacks on Rossini by Weber in Vienna, though he was of course an outspoken adversary.

[2] Hector Berlioz: *Mémoires* (1870).

and receiving visitors only at the top of his 100-foot scaffolding so as not to waste time. On 1st March he visited the Conservatoire, where Fétis was giving a composition class. As Weber appeared, Fétis was explaining the difference between the ancient modes of plainchant and modern tonality; Weber insisted that the lesson should not be interrupted and afterwards walked down the road with him, explaining his own theories, which Fétis found as vague as those of Vogler.

Weber had not really intended to stay so long in Paris. Although he had a letter of introduction from King Friedrich to the Duke of Orleans, he was planning to use this on a longer visit on the way home; but a loose iron tyre on his carriage compelled him to wait until a dilatory smith could mend it on 1st March. At 5 o'clock on the morning of the 2nd, a cold, damp day, Weber and Fürstenau got up and half an hour later were on their way. Travelling by way of Amiens and Montreuil, whose inns and cooking earned high praise from Weber, they reached Calais on the 3rd. The strain of Paris and the journey, through very wet weather, caused him to have a seizure shortly before they arrived; but he insisted on boarding the English steamboat *Fury* as arranged at 9 o'clock the next morning, and setting off at 10 they reached Dover three hours later. Writing to Caroline, he concealed his seizure and made light of the rough crossing and his seasickness, stressing how much he had enjoyed the foaming sea and the first glimpse of England's white cliffs. At Dover he was waiting with the rest of the passengers when he heard his name called and the chief customs officer appeared, waived all formalities and welcomed him personally ashore. The next morning at 8 o'clock they took the express coach, drawn by four horses Weber thought would not have shamed a prince's stables, and sped towards London through a spring countryside that enchanted him:

> The meadows covered with the most beautiful green, the gardens filled with blossoming flowers, all the buildings of an elegance and neatness contrasting unbelievably with the filth of France. The big rivers dotted with ships of all sizes (including the largest English ship of the line, with 148 guns), the pretty cottages, busy streets—in short, a truly unique journey.

Pausing for a brief meal in Rochester, they reached London at about five o'clock. Smart met them, a cab was summoned, and with their belongings piled high all around them, they accompanied Smart to his house in Great Portland Street.[1]

Here Weber was installed on the second floor with an excellent piano in his room and even a bath available in the house, protected from visitors and solicitously looked after by a couple named Hall who had been with Smart for sixteen years; Fürstenau was lodged nearby with a German locksmith,

---

[1] Smart's house, then No. 91, was renumbered No. 103 in the middle of the nineteenth century.

Heinke, at a pound a week. Even allowing for his anxiety to set Caroline's mind at rest in his letters, he seems to have been comfortable and happy to be settled in England: 'the whole English way of life is very sympathetic to my nature, and my little bit of English is incredibly useful to me when I go out.' His chief worry was over some bank collapses in Germany; for himself he evidently felt secure enough to admit to Caroline his seizure in Calais, especially since his cough was temporarily gone. Mostly he rested, though he dined at the Kembles. His hostess he described as 'a plump, cosy woman of the greatest friendliness'; their daughter Fanny in turn calls him 'very ugly . . . with high cheekbones, long hooked nose and spectacles', adding, 'his hollow, sallow, sickly face bore an expression of habitual suffering and ill-health.' But she also observed, 'He has the air and manner of a well-born and well-bred man of the world, a gentle voice, and a slow utterance in English, which he spoke but indifferently and with a strong accent; he generally conversed with my father and mother in French.' Despite these criticisms, she managed to develop a romantic passion for him and was already wearing his picture in a miniature round her neck when they met.[1] Soon afterwards he also dined with a music-seller, whose handsomely appointed house caused him to remark softly, 'I see it is better to sell music than to write it.'[2] As well as the £500 for composing *Oberon*, he was to receive £225 from Kemble for conducting four oratorio concerts; there was also the chance of a Benefit and other concerts.

Already on the 6th he had made his first visit to Covent Garden, which he found 'a beautifully decorated, not too large house.' He was more interested in the theatre than the work they went to hear, *Rob Roy*, and as he stepped up to the rail to examine the stage he was startled to hear cries of 'Weber! Weber's here!' Amid cheers, the *Freischütz* overture was called for and played amid cheers: 'Could one expect or hope for more enthusiasm, more affection? Are these the *cold* English welcoming me?' He went on to express high hopes for *Oberon*: 'Miss [Mary Anne] Paton is a singer of the very first rank and will sing Reiza divinely. Braham the same, though in another style. There are other very good tenors, and I can't understand what it is people have to say against English singing. The singers show good Italian training, fine voices and expression. The orchestra is not outstanding, but quite all right . . . the chorus very good.'

The next day he took a piano rehearsal for the first of what eventually proved to be five Oratorio Concerts, or 'Grand Performances of Antient and Modern Music', at Covent Garden and that evening went with Moscheles to Morlacchi's *Tebaldo e Isolina* (with Giovanni Battista Velluti), escaping after an act and getting to bed by ten o'clock. After working on the finale of *Oberon* the following morning, he took the last rehearsal for his concert with the

---

[1] Fanny Kemble: *Record of a Girlhood*, pp. 154, 158 (1878).
[2] *The Literary Gazette*, No. 491, p. 380, 17th June 1826.

very enthusiastic orchestra from 11 to 3. The house was in formal dress in the evening and rose as one man when Smart led Weber in; the applause was overwhelming, and only after a quarter of an hour was Weber able to begin the selection from *Der Freischütz*. It was a heartwarming start to his visit; he was given another tremendous reception afterwards and received in aristocratic boxes. When his state of health was perceived (he had coughed badly during the concert), Great Portland Street was besieged with jellies, lozenges and cough-cures. 'Tell Lüttichau the whole world honours me except my King!' he had previously written to Caroline.

Oberon rehearsals began on the 9th. Although Weber kept up a stream of cheerful comment about the singers to Caroline, the truth was not so encouraging. As Planché had said, only Lucia Elizabeth Vestris was completely adequate; Chorley declared that she possessed 'one of the most luscious of low voices, great personal beauty, an almost faultless figure, which she adorned with consummate art, and no common stage address.'[1] Mary Anne Paton (Reiza) indeed had a superb voice and a strikingly good figure, but her technique was imperfect and her acting, Planché observed, was 'destitute of histrionic ability';[2] Kemble more simply described it as 'like an inspired idiot', and she maddened Weber with her stupidity in rehearsal.[3] Towards the end of March her child died and rehearsals had to be postponed; when she returned she seems to have been unable to concentrate, for once she apologized to Weber, 'I know not how it is—I never can do this as it should be', to which he replied characteristically, 'The reason is because you do not know the words.'[4] When he reproved her, 'My dear lady, why give yourself so much trouble?' she assured him she was only too willing to oblige and was confused to be answered, 'But I have not wish you to sing so much more notes than I have written'.[5] The situation over Sherasmin was so hopeless that John Fawcett, the stage manager, acted the part while a bass, Isaacs, was brought in to help out in the quartet (later the whole part was taken over, successfully, by Duruset). Two sopranos, Miss Love and Miss Hammersley, declined the part of the Mermaid because of difficulty in hearing the orchestra from the back of the stage; eventually Weber declared 'Little Goward will sing it.' But Mary Anne Goward, a twenty-year-old pupil of Smart's sister-in-law who had sung Aennchen in the Lyceum *Freischütz* the year before, encountered the same difficulty. Fawcett snapped, 'That must come out! it won't go'; at which, 'Weber, who was standing in the pit, leaning on the back of the orchestra, so feeble that he could scarcely

---

[1] Henry Chorley: *Thirty Years' Musical Recollections* (1862).

[2] Planché: *op. cit.*, p. 82.

[3] Fanny Kemble: *op. cit.*, p. 160–2.

[4] *The Literary Gazette*, No. 491, p. 380, 17th June 1826.

[5] John Edmund Cox: *Musical Recollections of the Last Half Century*, Vol. I, p. 138 (1872).

stand without support, shouted, 'Wherefore shall it not go?' and leaping over the partition like a boy, snatched the baton from the conductor, and saved from excision one of the most delicious *morceaux* in the opera.'[1] He praised her, she later recalled, as 'the most natural singer I ever heard'; she in turn remembered him as 'the most perfect gentleman I ever met, such beautiful hands, and his sad face and fragile appearance excited much sympathy among all of us on the stage.'[2] The minor singers were on the whole satisfactory: Planché thought Smart's pupil Harriet Cawse 'an arch and melodious Puck' and Charles Bland 'happily gifted with a voice which enabled him to execute at least respectably the airs assigned to the King of the Fairies', though Benedict found the latter 'a bad actor with an offensive voice.'

With the role of Huon the situation was still more tricky. By universal consent John Braham was a superb singer, especially in Handel—Weber himself called him the greatest in Europe—but his taste was decidedly faulty and as an actor he left a great deal to be desired. Sir Walter Scott declared, 'Braham was a beast of an actor, but an angel of a singer'; asked to comment on this remark years later, Mary Anne Goward replied that when Braham had nothing to do on the stage he was bad, but when he had something dramatic in his part he could give quite good effect to it.[3] He was always inclined to force his voice and to introduce the florid decorations he could manage so well in order to play to the gallery, where he was a firm favourite; but by 1838 his voice is said to have suffered and become lower, a process which may have been setting in by 1826 (when he was already forty-nine) and accounted for his objecting to the original No. 5 of *Oberon*, 'From boyhood trained', with its repeated top B's. He insisted on a replacement, and getting a new verse from Planché, Weber with an ill grace wrote for him 'O, tis a glorious sight to see' on 5th and 6th April, bringing it downstairs declaring, 'I hope this will please Mr. Braham.'[4] Though it has the merit, from Braham's point of view, of going no higher than A (and that only twice), it is a perfunctory piece of empty heroics. 'What is to be done?' Weber lamented to Caroline. 'Braham knows his public, and is their idol . . . And I liked the first aria so much. For Germany I'll leave everything as it is.'

During the sixteen rehearsals of *Oberon* Weber was also busy with his concert engagements and with the social round out of which he hoped to scrape more guineas. The second Oratorio Concert on 10th March included Handel's *Acis and Galatea* as well as excerpts from *Der Freischütz* (Overture,

[1] Planché: *op. cit.*, p. 81.

[2] Andrew de Ternant: *Weber's English 'Mermaid'*, in *The Chesterian*, June 1926. Mary Anne Goward lived to be ninety-four, dying in 1899. At her funeral one of the mourners, William Ganz, dropped a small wreath of sea-weed on her coffin exclaiming, 'Farewell, sweet Mermaid, your name will live forever in the annals of Romantic opera!'

[3] J. Mewburn Levien: *The Singing of John Braham* (1945).

[4] H. B. and C. L. E. Cox: *op. cit.*, p. 248.

Laughing Chorus, Bridesmaids' Chorus and Huntsmen's Chorus); at the third the real success, more than Locke's *Macbeth* music and even twelve *Freischütz* numbers, was the *Jubel* overture. After Fawcett's Benefit on 18th March, Weber was too weak to comply with all the demands for encores: going on to dinner with an M.P., he was seized with a spasm and a fit of blood-spitting in the carriage, and eventually had to be carried up the stairs by Smart and Mori. Once at the table he recovered sufficiently to conceal his weakness and join animatedly in the conversation. This concert had brought together most of his *Oberon* singers; and Weber himself conducted the overture to *Der Freischütz*, a work that by now he had grown to detest. Not the first composer nor the last to prefer a neglected work to a popular one, he was irked by the failure of *Euryanthe* to achieve its rival's success, particularly when the latter had produced so little money. When someone boasted that he had done much to introduce *Freischütz* to England, Weber retorted, 'You'd have done better to let it alone; you'd have spared me much annoyance. So far I've had nothing else from it.' At a party at Coutts's on the 19th he was lying exhausted on a sofa after accompanying singers and improvising on *God save the King* when Lady Guilford asked him for the *Freischütz* overture. He replied curtly, 'That's not piano music, Madam'. When she showed him the cover of his own piano arrangement of it, he heaved himself up remarking, 'You're quite right to remind me of that mistake; I'll play it to punish myself.' Later he told Smart, 'She has taught me a lesson. I will never again arrange overtures for the pianoforte.' The project of giving *Freischütz* at Covent Garden only filled him with horror.

Accounts of how Weber was treated during his stay in London differ, and this remained a subject of some bitterness for many years afterwards. Smart, of course, did everything he could to tend a man who was obviously at the very limit of his endurance, and in the acrimonious exchanges that began after Weber's death, Fürstenau was at pains to correct the impression growing in Germany that Kemble had treated Weber ungenerously. A tactless letter from Böttiger, in which Caroline had no part and of which she disapproved, was met with a full explanation from Fürstenau that not only had Smart put himself out to lavish every care on the sick composer, but that Kemble was considered to have made a contract disadvantageous to himself. Fürstenau further defends the management of Covent Garden, whose efforts Weber greatly appreciated, and suggests that a good deal more might have been done, if only in the way of attending his concerts, by the Germans living in London to whom they had been recommended. The feeling that Kemble was in some way guilty of sharp practice seems to have arisen from Weber letting it be known that he was going to England to make a lot of money, coupled with the fact that, as Fürstenau wrote, 'People in Germany think London is paved with gold. I was once of the same opinion myself, and

WEBER IN LONDON

CONDUCTING *DER FREISCHÜTZ* AT COVENT GARDEN
Engraving by J. Hayter

a person must have been here in order to judge.'[1] Nevertheless, although Fürstenau goes out of his way to praise the care and generosity shown by the English to Weber, the conditions of London musical society were not best arranged to flatter the visitor. At a Philharmonic concert in the Argyle Rooms on 13th March he was warmly received when symphonies by Beethoven and Haydn were played in his honour; but on 3rd April he was engaged himself to conduct, for the sum of £15, and though the performance of his *Freischütz* and *Euryanthe* delighted him, as had the playing at the previous concert, six hundred people could not be found to fill the hall and the applause struck him as tepid. He left over-excited and shivering; the blood-spitting was growing worse and more frequent, and his breath was shorter.

Max Maria bitterly contrasts the enthusiasm shown to Weber by the general public with the aloofness of the aristocracy, whom he declares totally given over to the Rossini fashion. It is true that Weber was not taken up in the manner that Rossini had been, nor so well paid; but rather than discrimination against a German artist, this was the failure of an enfeebled and comparatively undomineering man to overcome, as the charming and courtly Rossini had, the long-enduring tendency of London's great houses to treat a musician as on the same social and artistic level as a children's conjuror. Weber had never lacked in social graces nor in respect for princes, and he was indeed well received by the Duke of Clarence, and by the Duchess of Kent, whom he accompanied in some of his own songs and in whose house he met her six-year-old daughter Princess Victoria. But these visits meant giving up professional appearances at other houses, where his treatment was different. He described to Caroline a visit to the Marquis of Hertford's:

> At about half past ten I went to Lord Hertford's. God! What a crowd of people. A magnificent hall, 500–600 people there, all superbly turned out. Almost the whole Italian opera company, also Velluti, the famous Puzzi,[2] and a bass player, the equally famous Dragonetti. Finales were sung and so on, but nobody listened. The shouting and clapping of the throng of people was appalling. There was an attempt to get a little quiet while I played, and about 100 people gathered interestedly about me. What they heard, God alone knows, because I didn't hear much. I thought busily of my thirty guineas and so kept my patience. Eventually at 2 o'clock everyone went in to supper, and I excused myself.

Nevertheless, he enjoyed the luxury of the aristocratic houses, the thickness of the carpets beneath his swollen feet, the asparagus, the flowers on all sides. Though he found he had to buy another pair of shoes for going out in the evening, and he did not share the English taste for thick soup, on the whole

[1] The full correspondence is in H. B. and C. L. E. Cox: *op. cit.*, pp. 253–61.

[2] Giovanni Puzzi (1792–1876), one of the greatest horn players of his day, had settled in London in 1817.

he took cordially to the food. He greatly enjoyed the good quality of the meat and game, and particularly relished the oysters, though he repeats the ancient charge against English cooking: 'the number of dishes is not great, and though it may have been by chance, everywhere I came across the same food with the identical sauce.' Possibly his efforts to keep earning hastened the end; and all his private concerts brought him only £90.

There remained several pieces to be written for *Oberon*. On 23rd March he had completed the Rondo No. 20, 'I revel in hope and joy' for Braham. A somewhat empty, flashy piece suggesting that he had by now got the measure of Braham's gifts, it does not go above G except in a final optional cadenza, with which Braham would doubtless have done as he pleased. Reiza's 'Mourn thou, poor heart' followed on the 26th, Fatima's 'O Araby' on the 29th—two of the most touching pieces in the whole opera—and having rearranged the Chorus No. 21 'For thee hath beauty' for SSA and, on 6th April, unwillingly satisfied Braham's demand for the Aria 'Ah, 'tis a glorious sight to see' to replace 'From boyhood trained' he supposed that only the Overture now remained to be written. On Sunday 9th April, three days before the première, he was able to record its completion, and with it, 'Die ganze Oper Gott sei Dank!' But Braham had not finished with him, and asked for another aria to show off a different side of his voice. Weber complied with the traditional Italian device of a *Preghiera*—surely Braham's suggestion —and on 11th April, the eve of the first performance, produced the beautiful 'Ruler of this awful hour'.[1]

By the beginning of April he had sunk even lower physically, with severe chest constriction, fever and diarrhoea, and was consumed with homesickness. His face drained of colour, his hands shook so violently that he could hardly feed himself and could only manage a glass if it were half filled, his feet were so swollen that he could not get into his smart shoes and stockings in order to attend receptions. His letters to Caroline attempt to put a bold face on things and describe an astonishing amount of activity, but the note of longing to be home always wells through to reveal the misery and anxiety beneath the assurances that he is well. He does go so far as to admit that the 10th was 'rather a hard day'. In the morning he sketched the *Preghiera* for Braham and at 11 o'clock went to a dress rehearsal that lasted until a quarter to five, going on to dinner with a General Murray before conducting his *Ruler of the Spirits* overture and *Athalia* scena (Paton) at an Academy concert. The following day saw the final rehearsal. Not until after telling Caroline of the success of the première did he admit all had not gone well; a piece of scenery fell on Mary Anne Paton's head and the rehearsal had to finish

---

[1] The original MS of *Oberon*, less Braham's two extra arias, was given to the Tsar Alexander II in 1855 by Max Maria, and is now in the Leningrad Public Library. The fair copy from which Weber conducted the first performances, with a number of cues and other markings (not of significance) in his own MS, is BM Add MS 27,746-8.

JOHN BRAHAM AS SIR HUON OF BORDEAUX
IN *OBERON*

without her big aria, though it ended in general applause and hopes for a great success. The scenery and costumes he was delighted with: he compared the former—substantial rocks and a clever sea effect for the Mermaid's Song—very favourably with what was available at Dresden; and Planché's knowledge of costumes had ensured that the detailed directions given in the libretto had been faithfully carried out. Weber told Caroline that the production was supposed to have cost £7,000.

For some weeks the first twelve performances of *Oberon* had been sold out. As Weber drove up to the opera house on the evening of the 12th, a loud voice shouted into the auditorium, 'Weber is arriving!' and the ensuing silence caused the alarmed composer to imagine the house to be half empty. But no sooner had he appeared than the audience rose to him, shouting and cheering, waving hats and handkerchieves, while the orchestra tapped their violins with their bows (a custom unfamiliar to him and one whose sound seems to have bewildered him). The overture was encored, as were all the individual numbers, some twice. Cawse and Bland disappointed; but Paton had recovered sufficiently from her troubles to give a fine account of 'Ocean! thou mighty monster'; Braham was the anticipated success as Huon; and Vestris, by all accounts a charming Fatima, burst into such natural peals of laughter in the last act at the prompting of the magic horn that the entire house was infected and echoed her merriment.[1] Much of the applause was clearly directed at the scenery—especially the effect in Act 2 of the setting sun reflected in the water—but there was no counter-demonstration from rival factions and at curtain-fall the repeated shouts of Weber's name made it clear where most credit was being given. After a delay, Weber appeared on the stage himself—an unprecedented action which displeased some of the newspapers, though they were careful to praise his modest manner of accepting the honour.[2] He was delighted with the way everything had gone; the only reproach he is recorded as making was a gentle one to Mary Anne Goward: 'My little girl, you sang that very nicely; but what for did you put in that tone?' A report in *John Bull* suggests that Weber's old fire at checking these unwanted appoggiaturas had somewhat abated, though he allowed nothing to escape him. Back at Smart's before midnight, he found time to write a brief note of his triumph to Caroline before falling asleep.

Not unexpectedly, a reaction set in next morning. When Fürstenau came into his room with some medicine, Weber said with a weak smile, 'Off with you! all this messing about with medicine is no more use, I am a shattered machine. God, if only it would hold together until I'd embraced Lina and the boys again!' Yet he wrote to Caroline the same morning that though he was

[1] *The Literary Gazette*, No. 482, p. 236–8, 15th April 1826.
[2] e.g. *The Harmonicon* No. xli, p. 108, May 1826. Both journals carried somewhat reserved reviews, praising details though feeling the music's originality meant that appreciation of it would only come slowly.

very tired, he was well—only depressed that he must wait another month before leaving for home. From now on the gap widens between what he tells Caroline and what he writes in his diary. He reproaches her gently for not writing more, but his reports on his health are carefully framed to give a convincing picture of perfectly bearable illness: he never allows her to glimpse the suffering recorded in the diary, and only in the cries of longing to be home, to see Hosterwitz again and its sunshine, and to hug his boys (have they forgotten him?) does he reveal the depths of his misery and fright. On the 17th he wrote that he was sleeping well, and if the days were not good enough to praise, they were not bad enough to grumble over; the diary for previous day records that he was very shocked by the amount of blood he had brought up. The continued exertion of conducting at Covent Garden and the bad weather dragged him ever lower: 'this is a day on which to shoot oneself', he wrote home on the 18th, 'such a dark yellow fog that one can hardly exist in the room without a light. The sun has no rays and is like a red point in the sky; it's absolutely terrible.' It was the coldest spring anyone could remember, and he laments that the climate does not match England's other beauties. On the 21st he writes that he has conducted eight performances of *Oberon*, each time to a full house (the twelfth and last was on the 25th); for the next four days the diary notes that he is unwell, and though grateful to be able to consult Dr. P. M. Kind (a nephew of the *Freischütz* librettist), reluctant to submit to the recommended inhalations of prussic acid (whose purpose is now medically obscure). Again on the 28th he reassures Caroline about his cough and his general health; again the diary betrays him—for the 27th, 'At 10 o'clock so ill, such constriction!! O God!' He dragged himself out on the 29th to the first performance of Bishop's *Aladdin*, another attempt by the Drury Lane management after their unsuccessful *Oberon* to provide a counter-attraction to Covent Garden's. Hardly had he entered his box when the house rose to him in homage, which touched him deeply; and when what he noted, among much other feeble music, as a pretty Huntsmen's Chorus came along, the stalls replied by whistling his own to him. He continued to fulfil engagements, dining and playing at private houses and at Benefits for singers. May came, with snow and the same east wind that had been harassing him; and the diary's record of fever, pain and breathlessness grows steadily worse.

For the annual Festival of the Royal Society of Musicians on 13th May he had been invited to contribute a piece (as before him had Haydn, Winter and Spohr). Not wishing to disappoint, he reworked the March (J.13) of his early Six Easy Pieces for wind band and for choir and orchestra (J.307). To weak to score it, he had to dictate the instrumentation and even the second and third parts of the March to Fürstenau. He was too ill to attend the concert; though when at last the weather improved on the following day he was able to enjoy a day's outing to Greenwich with Smart and Fürstenau; and

on the 17th Smart took him on the hills to the north of London for the air and
for a meal at 'Hamsted'. At Braham's Benefit next night the hall was invaded
by a gang of roughs, come to hear Braham sing sailor's songs to the gallery,
who shouted and stamped while Weber conducted his *Ruler of the Spirits*
overture. 'Could no-one see that Weber himself was conducting?' demanded
Moscheles. 'I'm sure I don't know, but the screams and hubbub in the
gallery while the overture was being played, without a note being heard from
beginning to end, made my blood boil.'[1] They reduced Mary Anne Paton to
silence by laughing during her performance; when she resumed, a voice from
the gallery bawled, 'Joe, I hope you're cool and comfortable', to which a deep
answer came from the stalls, 'Yes!' In the ensuing noise Paton cried 'I
cannot sing!' and fled in tears, leaving Weber outraged and miserable. His
diary notes that he had spent the day in pain and hardly able to get his breath;
yet he was well enough the next day to go with Göschen (a young German
friend), Fürstenau and Dr. Kind to Richmond. Weber was much moved by
the green of the woods and by the flowers in the sunny spring weather, and
enjoyed a brief outing on the river. His health continued up and down until
the 26th, the day of his own concert. For the popular soprano Catherine
Stephens he had agreed to write a new song. By her own choice, this was to
the words, 'From Chindara's warbling fount I come', from Thomas Moore's
Lalla Rookh. The effort of writing was so great that he was twice forced to
give up, and in the end only completed the vocal line (J.308); at the concert
he accompanied her himself, and Moscheles, who was present, later wrote
down what he remembered as the piano part to Weber's last composition. A
note by Smart records:

> Composed expressly for W. Ward Esq., M.P. for London. By the late C. M.
> von Weber in Sir George Smart's house, in which C. M. von Weber died—
> this Song was the last of his compositions, of which *the Voice part only* was
> found among his papers after his death. The first and last sym[s] and the
> Pianoforte Accompaniment were added by Mr. Moscheles; it was sung by
> Miss Stephens at C. M. von Weber's Concert on May 26th 1826 accompanied
> by himself. C. M. von Weber received 25 guineas from W. Ward Esq. for
> *the Copyright of this Song*, which he gave to Miss Stephens (now the Dowager
> Countess of Essex, No. 9 Belgrave Square, London).[2]

It is a simple, charming tune that betrays very little weakness of invention.
He also arranged his *Jubel-Cantate* as *The Festival of Peace*. Maria Caradori-
Allan, Harriet Cawse, Braham and Henry Phillips were the singers; Weber
took the rehearsals, hunched in a great chair and hardly able to speak above a
whisper until the chorus embarked upon a prayer *fortissimo* and he interrupted, 'Stop! stop! not like that! would you bellow like that in the presence of

---

[1] Moscheles: *op. cit.* Certain details of this concert vary in his account.

[2] *Weberiana*, Classe III, Bd 4, No. 77. Jähns's correspondence with Lady Essex failed
to obtain the MS from her.

the Almighty?' Many other distinguished musicians contributed to the concert, the second half of which was a full concert in itself: *Oberon* overture; Scena ed Aria from *Atalia*, 'Misere me!' (J.121); an extemporization by Moscheles; 'From Chindara's warbling fount'; a new fantasia with variations on an *Oberon* theme played by Fürstenau; 'Durch die Wälder'; *Euryanthe* overture.[1] The tenor Pierre Begrez was having his own Benefit at the house of the Duke of St. Albans and the Oaks were being run at Epsom—more than enough to keep the Argyle Rooms half-empty. Bitterly disappointed at the failure of this last effort to scrape together money, he was helped out of the hall by Fürstenau and collapsed on a sofa. His friends gathered round and tried to cheer him, but all he replied, holding Göschen by the hand, was 'What do you say to that? That's Weber in London!' Back at Smart's a mustard plaster was applied to his chest; weak and frightened, he was put to bed at 1 o'clock.

A London amateur musician who met him during these weeks has left an account of such occasions:

> I had seen him, whilst conducting his music, throwing his whole heart and soul into the work, imparting a stimulus to principals, band, and chorus such as they had never experienced before, and manifesting an energy that would have wearied a man in rude health . . . But on passing to his private room— where the *entrée* had been most kindly accorded me both by Sir George Smart and himself—as I then saw him panting for breath, torn to pieces by a hacking consumptive cough, and reeking with cold perspiration, all the delight I had experienced vanished. How gratefully would he recognize with a weary smile any slight attempt to minister some small relief to the excruciating agony of the half-suffocation against which he struggled with all the determination of his energetic spirit! How kindly, too, would he press my shoulder as he leaned upon it whilst tottering to the stage-door to be driven to his home! How, with all the good breeding of a thorough gentleman, he tried to keep up a conversation with numerous indiscriminating persons, who, without apparently the slightest cognisance of the pain they were inflicting, crowded upon and about him; and how wearily he sank back in his carriage, and sighed as if his spirit would escape thereby, when he had got quit of them—are incidents that could not fail to make an indelible impression . . .[2]

On the morning of the 27th he felt a little better; he notes in his diary that he slept well and had a bearable day, apart from an attack of breathlessness. Sunday 28th May found him exhausted and stunned. Thoughts of home by now entirely obsessed him. As, with the consumptive's flashes of nervous energy, he had been able to rouse himself to bursts of activity even when completely limp with fatigue, so now he seemed to be sustaining himself during these days by sheer determination to survive until he could get home.

[1] Concert announcement in BM Add MS 41,778.
[2] J. E. Cox: *Musical Recollections of the Last Half-Century*, p. 132 (872).

Fürstenau nobly cancelled his Benefit (he had not done well in London, having played badly through illness at a concert on 1st May, and was far from being a wealthy man). On the 29th they formed their new plan, and the next day Weber added a postcript to a letter already begun. He could no longer conceal the weakness that made his hand shake as he wrote, but goes on to emphasize his impatience at the thought of coming home, adding that Caroline should now receive his most solemn command to write in answer to *poste restante* Frankfurt: he was coming straight home on the 12th, and not, as originally planned, by Paris. He had to confess that though the concert was an artistic success, the receipts had been poor. And at last he admits, 'I can't walk or speak. I shan't be able to deal with any business for years, so—better come straight home. From Calais via Brussels, Cologne, Coblenz, up the Rhine to Frankfurt; what a beautiful journey! As I must now travel slowly and rest for half the day, this will take us at least a fortnight . . .' The same day the diary records that he was very ill, with hardly any breath and an alarming fever. His last appearance was at Mary Anne Paton's Benefit that evening; he noted that the *Freischütz* overture went well, but that the rest was beyond him. They reached Great Portland Street at 10 o'clock, Weber breathless and obliged to lean on Fürstenau, and fixed the day of departure for the following Tuesday, 6th June. Weber spent a good night, 'but the same breathlessness. The whole day indoors . . . very bad'. On 1st June: 'Very ill. Hardly any breath. Midday with Smart. In the evening, Kind, Stumpf, Fürstenau to tea. *The bloodspitting serious*'. His friends saw how painfully each breath came, and Dr. Kind told them he thought the end could not be far off. Fürstenau wanted to sit up with him, but Weber, ever scrupulous about his privacy, refused, insisting 'I'm not so ill as you make me out!' He would not even allow Smart's servant, Lucy Hall, to sleep in the anteroom. Kind applied another plaster to relieve his breathing; he noted next morning that he had slept well, and wrote to Caroline saying that the plaster had helped him greatly and that he hoped soon to be with them all again: he ends, 'think cheerfully of your above all loving Carl.' He was urged to put the journey off until he had gained some strength, but the suggestion of delay only irritated him: 'I must get back to my own ones! To see them just once more, and then let God's will be done!' His friends did not see how he could possibly manage the journey; he could not stand without pain, his diarrhoea no longer yielded to remedies, yet he was determined to go and only with difficulty could they persuade him to see his doctors on the 3rd: 'I am going to travel, do what you like.' Moscheles made one of his regular calls on the 3rd, and again on the 4th when Göschen also came with Kind. Weber offered to take a message to Göschen's father in Germany, and to the suggestion that he was leaving behind many friends and admirers shook his head, saying 'There's a big difference!' He dined in his room with Smart, drinking two or three glasses of port (Smart had gone to some expense to get hock for him, but Weber suggested that he would prefer port to a wine that was better in his own country). He spent the rest of the evening lying on a sofa and talking of nothing but the journey. They persuaded him to go to bed at 10 o'clock, but he firmly declined Fürstenau's renewed offer to sleep in his room; he yielded, however, to their pressure to leave his door unlocked that night. Fürstenau and Smart helped him upstairs, and he held his hand out to Smart, who thought him rather better and was going out to a musical party at the Coutts's saying, 'God reward you for all your love!' Fürstenau helped him to undress and attended to the plaster on his chest. Weber wound up his watch, and as Fürstenau left, said, 'Now let me sleep.' His friends sat together discussing how to stop him attempting the journey home, and left at about midnight. As Fürstenau went, he noticed that the light in Weber's room was out.[1]

Across Great Portland Street lived Weber's friend the harp-maker Stumpff, who was in the habit of calling across to him in the morning. Getting no answer on the morning of Monday 5th June, Stumpff enquired with the servants. Lucy Hall said she had tried Weber's door earlier, but found it locked after all and was worried at not getting the usual answer from him. She woke Smart. He sent immediately to Heinke, who arrived with the alarmed, half-dressed Fürstenau and carrying his locksmith's tools. Moscheles was also sent for.[2] At about ten to seven the door was forced. The bed-curtains were torn back. Weber was lying still, with his head resting on his left hand and a calm expression on his face.

A doctor was hastily summoned to open a vein, but hardly had he raised Weber's hand than he let it fall, saying 'It is all useless; the man has been dead these five or six hours.' All his effects were in order, his clothes neatly arranged in the drawers for packing for the journey and his papers in readiness.[3] Moscheles found a small laundry list by the bed, and kept it in his pocket book ever afterwards as a memento. Smart took possession of the will, which caused him a good deal of trouble and expense to execute. An account in Weber's hand recorded total payments in England of £1071. 1. 0d; but Smart, supposing that some must have been sent on to Germany, could only find £782. 6. 0d. in the room; this, with Weber's effects, he later gave to Fürstenau. In the afternoon a post-mortem was held, and a medical certificate issued:

[1] MMW, Vol. II, p. 704. By Fürstenau's own account, Göschen and Kind had left at 10, and he himself stayed until 11.30. Quoted in Adolph Kohut: *Weber–Gedenkbuch* (1887).
[2] By his own account in his diary (*op. cit.*), Moscheles was present as the door was forced; Smart and Max Maria say he was not sent for until later.
[3] The effects (listed in BM Add MS 41,778, ff.45 and 46) included an opera glass given him by Stumpff, a gold ring, and a diamond brooch, a German lottery ticket, a watch, a case of razors, spectacles, a pair of dress shoe buckles, the silver cup presented by Hawes and four parcels of music and papers; the clothes included several suits and coats and thirty-one shirts.

On examining the body of C. M. von Weber we found an ulcer on the left side of the larynx, the lungs almost universally diseased, filled with tubercles, of which many were in a state of suppuration with two vomicae one of them about the size of a common egg, the other smaller. The which was a quite sufficient cause of his death.

F. Jencken, M.D. Chas. F. Forbes, M.D. P.M. Kind, M.D. Wm. Robinson, Surgeon

91 Great Portland Street
5th of June, 5 o'clock[1]

Dr. Forbes also wrote privately to Smart that evening:

My dear Sir,
The appearances which presented themselves on examining the body of Carl Maria von Weber were as follows. An ulcer in the larynx, left side, the lungs full of tubercles large and small, many of them in a state of suppuration—two vomicae in the left lung—the one about the size of a hen's egg the other rather smaller—on the upper surface of the left lung were two bladder like appearances which I at first took for Hydatids—the one as large as a walnut, the other rather larger than a hazel nut. They arose from a rupture of the air cells of the lungs; the investing membrane became consequently distended with air. This appearance is frequently seen in the lungs of a broken-winded horse.

Believe me, my dear sir,
Yours faithfully,
Chas. F. Forbes.

Monday evening, June 5, 1826[2]

The body was embalmed and put into a lead coffin, which was sealed. The news of his death spread rapidly, and musical London united in sorrow. The Philharmonic Concerts opened their next programme on 12th June with the Dead March from *Saul*, and a Benefit was arranged for Weber's family on 17th June (Kemble refused to accept the fact that he was legally absolved from this). But though Drury Lane closed its doors that night so as not to provide a rival attraction, the house was only two-thirds full. Max Maria attributes this to the news of war from Greece, but has some bitter things to say against the German community in London, who stayed away. A plan to give Mozart's Requiem in aid of a memorial to Weber foundered: the Roman Catholic Bishop refused to give his consent for admission to be charged to the Catholic Chapel in Moorfields, where the coffin was to be lodged, and the Dean and Chapter of St. Paul's would not tolerate a Catholic Requiem in the Cathedral; accordingly no money could be taken. At about half past nine on 21st June the funeral procession started from Great Portland Street; it consisted of sixteen mourning coaches and four private carriages, and the

---

[1] Two copies of this death certificate, together with all the papers relating to Weber's London concerts, death and funeral are in BM Add MS 41,778.

[2] BM Add MS 41,771. A vomica is an ulcerous cavity or abcess in the lungs; a hydatid is a watery tumour.

hearse, drawn by six black horses, carried the coffin to which a Latin inscription had been affixed. All the leading singers in London, headed by Lablache, offered their services for the occasion; and as the Requiem finished, twelve musicians carried the coffin into the vault to the strains of the Dead March from *Saul*.[1] Braham also made a musical tribute of his own with a song *The Death of Weber*, to words by Planché and based on *Freischütz* melodies—a tasteless affair matching trite sentiments to highly inappropriate music.

Fürstenau remained in London until the middle of August tidying up affairs, having written meanwhile not directly to Caroline but to her closest friend, Charlotte von Hanmann. Caroline and the boys were at Hosterwitz, and Fraülein von Hanmann stopped her carriage on the way at the house of Roth, the clarinettist, to ask him to come and help her break the news. But Caroline happened to be looking out of the window, and seeing her friend make an unexpected stop she leapt to her own conclusions. She ran across to the house and found her two friends standing in the garden in tears. Max, then four, followed her: 'Almost forty years have passed since then, but in his ears there still shrills the cry with which his mother clutched at him as she rose from where she had fainted on the grass and bent her tear-stained, childlike face over him.'[2]

Deeply shocked, Caroline was for a time listless and unable to think of the future, and fell prey to well-meaning advice from all sides; but Meyerbeer and Lichtenstein were particularly kind and helpful, and before long she set about putting her affairs in order. Although she complained about the Dresden court, her pension of 150 thalers was doubled, and as a shrewd business woman she managed to dispose of the copyrights of her husband's scores quite well. Benefits were held all over Europe, and enough came in to support the family in possibly greater material comfort than they had known during Weber's lifetime. In 1841 Caroline was able to inform the Prussian minister that she could meet the fees for Max attending the University of Berlin.

Some fourteen years after Weber's death, a Frenchman in London tried to locate his coffin in Moorfields. In the end, helped by two choirboys and the verger, he discovered it and began agitating for something to be done to remove it from the enormous pile of accumulating coffins, the older of which were thrown out as the new ones came in.[3] An article appeared in the magazine *Europa*; a committee was formed at Dresden urging the return of the remains to German soil. There were objections, particularly from the Saxon court, who solemnly suggested that the precedent of returning all dead

---

[1] For the fullest account of the funeral, see *The Quarterly Magazine and Review*, No. viii, p. 121–130 (1826).

[2] MMW, Vol. II, p. 710–11.

[3] Anon: *Gazette Musicale de Paris*, 21st January 1841.

Kapellmeisters to Dresden might prove an awkward one. At last, in 1844, Weber's successor Richard Wagner busied himself with trying to arrange matters. Meyerbeer made over the proceeds of a Berlin production of *Euryanthe* to the committee; and in London Benedict and Max Maria, then studying there, did what they could to assist. On 25th October 1844 the English ship *John Bull* carrying Weber's coffin docked at Hamburg. Ships from all over the world dipped their colours in tribute, and the Funeral March from the *Eroica Symphony* was played as the body transferred to a small boat for its journey up the Elbe. But the river froze at Wittenberge and the boat stuck. The coffin was transferred to a train and, reaching Dresden on 14th December, was ferried across the river to the dense crowds waiting on the other side. It was growing dark, and the procession moved slowly off to the Catholic cemetery accompanied by funeral music arranged from the Overture and the Cavatina from *Euryanthe* for wind instruments by Wagner, who conducted. The next day the coffin was interred. There were speeches, a performance of a chorus by Wagner, *An Weber's Grabe*, and a poem by Theodor Hell. Wagner himself made a speech during which, affected by the sound of his own words and the circle of listeners, he fell silent as if in a trance, feeling himself outside himself and observing the entire scene as if detached from it. 'In my youth,' he wrote later in *Mein Leben*, 'I had learned to love music by way of my admiration of Weber's genius; and the news of his death came as a terrible blow to me. To have come in contact with him again, so to speak, and after so many years by this second funeral, was an event that stirred me to the very depths of my being.'

LIST OF WORKS

OPERAS

Das Waldmädchen (J. Anh 1). Romantic-comic opera in 2 acts. Text by Carl von Steinsberg. Comp. 1800. Only fragments extant. Prod. Freiberg (Saxony), 24th November 1800, by Steinsberg's company.

Peter Schmoll und seine Nachbarn (J.8). Opera in 2 acts. Text by Joseph Türk, after the novel by Carl Gottlob Cramer. Comp. 1801–2: music complete, dialogue lost. Prod. Augsburg, ? March 1803.

Rübezahl (J.44–6). Opera in 2 acts. Text by Johann Gottlieb Rhode, after the folk legend. Comp. 1804: fragments, unprod.

Silvana (J.87). Romantic opera in 3 acts. Text by Franz Carl Hiemer, after the text for *Das Waldmädchen*. Comp. 1808–10. Prod. Frankfurt-am-Main, 16th September 1810, cond. Weber; London, Surrey Theatre, 2nd Sept. 1828 (trans. C. A. Somerset).

Silvana (mime and speaker)	Caroline Brandt
Mechtilde (sop.)	Margarethe Lang
Clara (sop.)	Isermann
Rudolph (ten.)	Mohrhardt
Albert (ten.)	Hill
Adelhart (bs.)	Berthold
Krips (bs.)	Lux
Fust (bs.)	Leissring
Kurt (bs.)	Krönner
A Herald	
Chorus	

Abu Hassan (J.106). *Singspiel* in 1 act. Text by Franz Carl Hiemer, after *The 1001 Nights*. Comp. 1810–11. Prod. Munich, Hofbühne, 4th June 1811, cond. Weber; London, Drury Lane, 4th April 1825, trans. W. Dimond with music adapted by T. S. Cooke; New York, 5th Nov. 1827, London version.

Fatime (sop.)	Josepha Flerx-Lang
Abu Hassan (ten.)	Georg Mittermaier
Omar (bs.)	Joseph Muck
Chorus	

Der Freischütz (J.277). Romantic opera in 3 acts. Text by Friedrich Kind, after Apel and Laun's *Gespensterbuch*. Comp. 1817–21. Prod. Berlin, Schauspielhaus, 18th June 1821, cond. Weber; London, English Opera House (Lyceum), 22nd

July 1824, trans. W. McGregor Logan with music adapted by William Hawes; New York, 2nd Mar. 1825, probably the Covent Garden version. There is also an earlier adaptation as *The Wild Huntsman* by Washington Irving, 1823–4, publ. Boston Bibliophile Society 1924.

Agathe (sop.)	Caroline Seidler
Max (ten.)	Carl Stümer
Aennchen (sop.)	Johanna Eunicke
Caspar (bs.)	Heinrich Blume
Cuno (bs.)	Wauer
Ottokar (bar.)	Rebenstein
Kilian (bar.)	Wiedemann
Samiel (speaker)	Hillebrand
A Hermit (bs.)	Gern
First Bridesmaid (sop.)	Henriette Reinwald
Chorus	

Euryanthe (J.291). Grand heroic-romantic opera in 3 acts. Text by Helmina von Chezy, after a French romance. Comp. 1822–3. Prod. Vienna, Kärntnertor, 25th Oct. 1823, cond. Weber; London, Covent Garden, 29th June 1833; New York, Met., 23rd Dec. 1887, with Lilli Lehmann.

Euryanthe (sop.)	Henriette Sontag
Adolar (ten.)	Anton Haitzinger
Eglantine (sop.)	Therese Grünbaum
Lysiart (bs.)	Anton Forti
King Ludwig (bs.)	Seipelt
Bertha (sop.)	Teimer
Rudolph (ten.)	Rauscher
Chorus	

Oberon (J.306). Romantic opera in 3 acts. Text by J. R. Planché, after Wieland's poem in Sotheby's translation. Comp. 1825–6. Prod. London, Covent Garden, 12th April 1826, cond. Weber; Leipzig, 23rd Dec. 1826; New York, 9th Oct. 1828.

Reiza (sop.)	Mary Anne Paton
Huon (ten.)	John Braham
Fatima (sop.)	Lucia Elizabeth Vestris
Sherasmin (ten.)	John Fawcett
Oberon (ten.)	Charles Bland
Puck (con.)	Harriet Cawse
Mermaid (sop.)	Mary Anne Goward
Chorus	

Die drei Pintos (J.Anh.5). Comic opera in 3 acts. Text by Theodor Hell, after the *Novelle* by Carl Seidel. Comp. begun 1820, unfinished: text revised by Carl Weber and Gustav Mahler, music completed, chosen from Weber's works and scored by Mahler. Prod. Leipzig, Neues Stadt-Theater, 20th January 1888, cond. Mahler; London, John Lewis Theatre, 10th Apr. 1962.

Clarissa (sop.)	Baumann
Gaston (ten.)	Hedmont
Gomez (ten.)	Hübner
Laura (mezzo)	Artner
Pinto (bs.)	Grengg
Ambrosio (bar.)	Schelper
Pantaleone (bs.)	Köhler
Landlord (bs.)	Proft
Inez (sop.)	Rothhauser
Majordomo (ten.)	Tietz

Chorus

THEATRE MUSIC

Overture and 6 numbers, in Schiller's translation of Gozzi's comedy *Turandotte* (Op. 37: J.75). 1809.

Rondo alla polacca for tenor 'Was ich da thu' ', in Haydn pasticcio *Der Freybrief* (J.77). 1809.

Duet for soprano and tenor, 'Dich an dies Herz', in Haydn pasticcio *Der Freybrief* (J.78). 1809.

Four songs for voice and guitar, 'Über die Berge', 'Rase, Sturmwind, blase', 'Lass mich schlummern', 'Umringt vom mutherfüllten Heere' (No. 4 with male chorus), in Kotzebue's drama *Der arme Minnesinger* (in Op. 25: J.110–113). 1811.

Scena ed aria for soprano, 'Ah, se Edmondo', in Méhul's opera *Héléna* (Op. 52: J.178). 1815.

Two songs for baritone and for soprano and bass, 'Mein Weib ist capores' and 'Frau Lieserl juhe!', in Fischer's *Singspiel, Der travestirte Aeneas* (J.183–4). 1815.

Deutscher (J.185). See Orchestral Works.

Two songs for baritone and for tenor, 'Wer stets' and 'Wie wir voll Glut', in Gubitz's 'patriotic *Festspiel*', *Lieb' und Versohnen* (J.186–7). 1815.

Ballade for voice and harp, 'Was stürmet', in Reinbeck's tragedy *Gordon und Montrose* (Op. 47, No. 3: J.189). 1815.

Ariette for soprano (text missing), in Huber's drama *Das Sternenmädchen im Maidlinger Wald* (J.194). 1816.

Romance for voice and guitar, 'Ein König einst gefangen sass', in Castelli's drama *Diana von Poitiers* (J.195). 1816.

10 numbers and 1 song for unaccompanied mezzo-soprano, 'Lasst den Knaben', in Müllner's tragedy *König Yngurd* (J.214). 1817.

Solo for 2 guitars, in Moreto's comedy *Donna Diana* (in J.220). 1817.

Song for solos and chorus, 'Hold ist der Cyanenkranz', in Kind's festival play *Der Weinberg an der Elbe* (J.222). 1817.

Romance for voice and guitar, 'Leis weht es', in Kind's drama *Das Nachtlager von Granada* (J.223). 1818.

Two-part song for tenor and bass, 'Sei gegrüsst, Frau Sonne, mir', in Holbein's 'romantic *Spektakel-Lustspiel' Die drei Wahrzeichen* (J.225). 1818.

Dance and song, for tenor and chorus, with Andantino, 'In Provence', in Hell's
  drama *Das Haus Anglade* (J.227). 1818. (Dance and song possibly spurious).
8 numbers in Gehe's tragedy *Heinrich IV, König von Frankreich* (J.237). 1818.
Scene and aria for soprano, 'Was sag ich?', in Cherubini's opera *Lodoïska* (Op. 56:
  J.239). 1818.
Chorus for SSB, 'Heil dir, Sappho!' in Grillparzer's tradegy *Sappho* (J.240). 1818.
Song for voice and piano or guitar, 'Ein Mädchen ging', in Kind's drama *Der
  Abend am Waldbrunnen* (Op. 71, No. 2: J.243). 1818.
4 vocal numbers, march and melodrama, in Rublack's drama *Lieb' um Liebe*
  (J.246). 1818.
Agnus Dei for SSA and wind instruments, in Blankensee's tragedy *Carlo* (J.273).
  1820.
4 harp numbers, in Houwald's tragedy *Der Leuchtthurm* (J.276). 1820.
Overture and 11 numbers, in Wolff's drama *Preciosa* (J.279). 1820.
  1. Overture.
  2. Gipsy March, Chorus 'Heil Preciosa!'.
  3. Melodrama.
  4. Ballo.
  5. Melodrama.
  6. Gipsy Chorus, 'Im Wald'.
  7. Preciosa's Song, 'Einsam bin ich'.
  8. Off-stage music.
  9. Gipsy Chorus, 'Die Sonn' erwacht!'.
  10. Ballo.
  11. Gipsy March.
  12. Chorus and Ballet, 'Es blinken so lustig', and Melodrama.
Song for SSA and SSA chorus and guitar, 'Sagt, woher', in Shakespeare's drama
  The Merchant of Venice (J. 280). 1821.
1 instrumental number (from First Symphony's Adagio) and 5 choruses, in Robert's
  festival play *Den Sachsen-Sohn* (J.289). 1822.
Music and recitative for bass and soprano, 'Doch welche Töne', in Spontini's opera
  Olympie (J.305). 1825.
                (See also under Arrangements).

CONCERT ARIAS

Recitative and Rondo for soprano and orchestra, 'Il momento s'avvicina' (Op. 16:
  J.93). 1810.
Scena ed Aria d'Atalia for soprano and orchestra, 'Misera me!' (Op. 50: J.121).
  1811.
Scena ed Aria for tenor, chorus and orchestra, 'Qual altro attendi' (J. 126). 1811.
Scena ed Aria d'Ines de Castro for tenor, choruses and orchestra (1st. Op. 53:
  J.142). 1812.
Scena ed Aria d'Ines de Castro for soprano and orchestra, 'Non paventar' (Op.51:
  J.181). 1815.

CHURCH MUSIC

Mass in E♭ ('Jugendmesse'), for SATB soloists, SATB choir and orchestra. 1802.

Mass in E♭ ('Missa Sancta No. 1'), for SATB soloists, SATB choir and orchestra (J.224). 1818.

Offertory, for soprano, chorus and orchestra, 'Gloria et honore', for Missa Sancta No. 1 (J.226). 1818.

Offertory, for soprano, chorus and orchestra, 'In die solemnitatis', for Missa Sancta No. 2 (J.250). 1818.

Mass in G ('Missa Sancta No. 2'), for SATB soloists, SATB choir and orchestra (Op. 76: J.251). 1819.

Agnus Dei (see Theatre Music).

CANTATAS

Der Erste Ton (Rochlitz), for reciter and orchestra with final SATB chorus (Op. 14: J.58). 1808.

Hymn, *In seiner Ordnung schafft der Herr* (Rochlitz), for SATB soloists, SATB chorus and orchestra (Op. 36: J.154). 1812.

Kampf und Sieg (Wohlbrück), for SATB soloists, SATB chorus and orchestra (Op. 44: J.190). 1815.

L'Accoglienza (Celani), for SSSTBB soloists, SATB chorus and orchestra (J.221). 1817.

Natur und Liebe. See Unaccompanied Choral Works and Partsongs.

Jubel-Cantate (Kind), for SATB soloists, SATB chorus and orchestra (Op.58: J.244). 1818.

Du, bekränzend uns're Laren (Kind), for SSTB soloists, SATB chorus, piano and flute (J.283). 1821.

Kleine Cantate. See Accompanied Choral Works and Partsongs.

ACCOMPANIED CHORAL WORKS AND PARTSONGS

An die Hoffnung: 'Hoffnungsstrahl' (anon.), for 3 voices and ad. lib. piano. 1802.

Grablied: 'Leis wandeln wir' (anon.), for voice, TTB and 9 wind instruments (J.37). 1803.

Die Lethe des Lebens: 'Wenn, Brüder' (Baggesen), for bass, SATB choir and piano (Op. 66, No. 5: J.66). 1809.

Trauer-Musik: 'Hörst du der Klage' (anon.), for SATB choir, baritone and 10 wind instruments (J.116). 1811.

'Lenz erwacht' (anon.), for SSTTBB (choir and solo) and piano (J.131). 1812.

An eine Freundin: 'Zur Freude' (Voigt), for voice, TTB and piano (Op. 23, No. 6: J.133). 1812.

Schwäbisches Tanzlied: 'Geiger und Pfeiffer' (Sauter), for voice, TTB and piano (J.135). 1812.

'Heisse, stille Liebe schwebet' (anon.), for voice, TTB and piano (Op. 23, No.5: J.136). 1812.

Kriegs-Eid: 'Wir stehn vor Gott' (Collin), for unison male voices and 7 instruments (J.139). 1812.

Lebenslied am Geburtstage: 'Freunde, dass Glut' (Gubitz), for 4 male voices and piano (2nd Op. 53, No. 1: J.165). 1814.

Leyer und Schwerdt, Vol. 2, No. 4: 'Männer und Buben'. See Unaccompanied Choral Works.

Zwei Kränze zum Annen-Tage: 'Flüstert lieblich' (Kind), for male voices and piano (2nd Op. 53, No. 3: J.218). 1817.

'Schöne Ahnung ist erglommen' (Kind), also 'Schmückt das Haus' (Illaire), also 'Singet dem Gesang zu Ehren' and other texts, for 4 male voices and piano (2nd Op. 53, No. 2: J.228). 1818.

Natur und Liebe: 'Beglückt, beglückt' (Kind), for SSTTBB and piano (Op. 61: J.241). 1818.

'Deo Rosa' (Hell), for 4 male voices and piano (unfinished—J.Anh.3). 1821.

Kleine Cantate: 'Wo nehm' ich Blumen her' (Hell), for STB and piano (J.290). 1823.

Reiterlied II: 'Hinaus!' (Reiniger), for 4 male voices and piano (J.293). 1825.

Schützenweihe: Hörnerschall! Überfall!' (Oertel), for 4 male voices and piano (J.294). 1825.

UNACCOMPANIED CHORAL WORKS, PARTSONGS AND CANONS

Canon: 'Mädchen, ach' (Breiting), for 3 voices (Op. 13, No. 6: J.35). 1802.

Canon: 'Wenn du in den Armen der Liebe', for 3 voices. 1802.

'Ein Gärtchen und ein Häuschen drin' (anon.), for voice, T & B (J.36). 1803.

Chorlied (text missing), for SATB (J.69). 1809.

Canon: 'Die Sonata soll ich spielen' (composer), for 3 voices (J.89). 1810.

Canon: 'Canons zu zwey sind nicht drey' (anon.), for 3 voices (J.90). 1810.

Canon: 'Leck' mich im Angesicht' (anon.), for 3 voices (J.95). 1810.

Das Turnierbankett: 'Füllet die Humpen' (Bornemann), for 2 male voice choirs with TTB solo (Op. 68, No. 1: J.132). 1812.

Canon: 'Zu dem Reich der Töne schweben' (Gubitz), for 4 voices (J.164). 1814.

Canon: 'Scheiden und leiden ist einerlei' (anon.), for 4 voices (J.167). 1814.

Canon: 'Leise kömt der Mond' (anon.), for 4 voices (Hirschberg 33). 1814.

Leyer und Schwerdt, Vol. 2 (Körner), for 4 male voices (Op. 42). 1814.

    1. *Reiterlied I:* 'Frisch auf' (J.172).

    2. *Lützow's wilde Jagd:* 'Was glänzt' (J.168).

    3. *Gebet vor der Schlacht:* 'Hör' uns, Allmächtiger!' (J.173).

    4. *Männer und Buben:* 'Das Volk steht auf', with piano (J.170).

    5. *Trinklied vor der Schlacht:* 'Schlacht, du brichst an!' (J.171).

    6. *Schwertlied:* 'Du Schwert an meiner Linken' (J.169).

Dreistimmige Burleske on Mozart's *Zauberflöte:* 'Drei Knäbchen' (composer), for TTB (J.180). 1815.

Canon: 'Weil Maria Töne hext' (Gubitz), for 3 voices (J.193). 1816.

'Ei, ei, ei' (trad.), for TTB (Op. 64, No. 7: J.249). 1818.

Gute Nacht: 'Bald heisst es wieder' (Kannegiesser), for 4 male voices (Op. 68, No. 5: J.261). 1819.

Freiheitslied: 'Ein Kind ist uns geboren!' (Kannegiesser), for 4 male voices (Op. 68, No. 3: J.262). 1819.

Ermunterung: 'Ja, freue dich' (Kannegiesser), for 4 male voices (Op. 68, No. 2: J.262). 1819.

Doppel-Canon (without text) for 4 voices (J.272). 1819.

Husarenlied: 'Husaren sind gar wack're Truppen' (Thale), for 4 male voices (Op. 68, No. 6: J.284). 1821.

12

Schlummerlied: 'Sohn der Ruhe' (Castelli), for 4 male voices (Op. 68, No. 4: J.285). 1822.

SOLO SONGS
(with piano accompaniment unless otherwise stated)

Die Kerze: 'Ungern flieht das süsse Leben' (Matthison) (J.27). 1802.

'Umsonst entsagt' ich' (anon.) (Op. 71, No. 4: J.28). 1802.

'Entfliehet schnell von mir' (Seida) (J.38). 1803.

'Ich sah sie hingesunken' (Swoboda) (J.41). 1804.

Wiedersehn: 'Jüngst sass ich am Grabe' (Wallner) (Op. 30, No. 1: J.42). 1804.

'Ich denke dein' (Matthison) (Op. 66, No. 3: J.48). 1806.

Liebeszauber: 'Mädel, schau mir in's Gesicht' (Bürger), with guitar (Op. 13, No. 3: J.52). 1807.

Er an Sie: 'Ein Echo kenn' ich' (Lehr) (Op. 15, No. 6: J.57). 1808.

Meine Farben: 'Wollt ihr sie kennen?' (Lehr) (Op. 23, No. 1: J.62). 1808.

Klage: 'Ein steter Kampf' (Müchler) (Op. 15, No. 2: J.63). 1808.

Serenade: 'Horch, leise horch!' (Baggesen) (J.65). 1809.

Das Röschen: 'Ich sah ein Röschen (Müchler) (Op. 15, No. 5: J.67). 1809.

'Was zieht zu deinem Zauberkreise' (Müchler) (Op. 15, No. 4: J.68). 1809.

Rhapsodie (or *Die Blume*): 'Traurig, einsam' (Haug) (Op. 23, No. 2: J.70). 1809.

Romanze (*Die Ruinen*): 'Süsse Ahnung' (Reinbeck) (J.71). 1809.

'Sanftes Licht, weiche nicht' (Reinbeck), with guitar (Op. 13, No. 4: J.72). 1809.

'Meine Lieder, meine Sänge' (Löwenstein-Wertheim) (Op. 15, No. 1: J.73). 1809.

Der kleine Fritz an seine jungen Freunde: 'Ach, wenn ich nur' (trad.) (Op. 15, No. 3: J.74). 1809.

Trinklied: 'Weil es also Gott gefügt' (Lehr) (J.80). 1809.

Canzonetta: 'Sicchè t'inganni', with piano or harp (anon.) (J.88). 1810.

Die Schäferstunde (or *Damon und Chloe*): 'Endlich hatte Damon sie gefunden' (Hiemer), with guitar (Op. 13, No. 1: J.91). 1810.

Das neue Lied: 'Ein neues Lied!' (Herder) (J.92). 1810.

Wiegenlied: 'Schlaf, Herzenssöhnchen' (Hiemer), with guitar (Op. 13, No. 2: J.96). 1810.

Die Zeit: 'Es sitzt die Zeit' (Stoll), with guitar (Op. 13, No. 5: J.97). 1810.

Des Künstlers Abschied: 'Auf die stürm'sche See hinaus' (Dusch), with guitar or piano (Op. 71, No. 6: J.105). 1810.

Canzonetta: 'Ah, dove siete' (anon.), with guitar or piano (Op. 29, No. 1: J.108). 1811.

'Maienblümlein, so schön' (Eckschläger) (Op. 23, No.3: J.117). 1811.

Canzonetta: 'Ch'io mai vi possa' (anon.), with guitar or piano (Op. 29, No. 3: J.120). 1811.

Canzonetta: 'Ninfe se liete' (anon.), with guitar or piano (Op. 29, No. 2: J.124). 1811.

Romanze (*Wiedersehn*): 'Um Rettung' (Duke August of Gotha) (J.129). 1812.

Sonett: 'Du liebes, holdes, himmelsüsses Wesen' (Streckfuss) (Op. 23, No. 4: J.130). 1812.

Lebensansicht: 'Frei und froh' (anon.) (Op. 66, No. 5: J.134). 1812.

Bettlerlied: 'I und mein junges Weib' (trad.), with guitar or piano (Op. 25, No. 4: J.137). 1812.

Liebe-Glühen: 'In der Berge Riesenchatten' (Gubitz), with guitar or piano (Op. 25, No. 1: J.140). 1812.

'Sind es Schmerzen' (Tieck) (Op. 30, No. 6: J.156). 1813.

Unbefangenheit: 'Frage mich immer' (anon.) (Op. 30, No. 3: J.157). 1813.

Reigen: 'Sagt mir an' (Voss) (Op. 30, No. 5: J.159). 1813.

Minnelied: 'Der Holdseligen' (Voss) (Op. 30, No. 4: J.160). 1813.

'Es stürmt auf der Flur' (Rochlitz) (Op. 30, No. 2: J.161). 1814.

Gebet um die Geliebte: 'Alles in mir glühet' (Gubitz) (Op. 47, No. 6: J.166). 1814.

Leyer und Schwerdt, Vol. 1 (Körner) (Op. 41: J.174–7). 1814.

  1. *Gebet während der Schlacht:* 'Vater, ich rufe dich!'

  2. *Abschied vom Leben:* 'Die Wunde brennt'.

  3. *Trost:* 'Herz, lass dich nicht zerspalten'.

  4. *Mein Vaterland:* 'Was ist des Sängers Vaterland?'

Der Jüngling und die Spröde: 'Weile, Kind' (Gubitz) (Op. 47, No. 4: J.192). 1816.

Mein Verlangen: 'Ach, wär' ich doch' (Förster) (Op. 47, No. 5: J.196). 1816.

Die gefangenen Sänger: 'Vöglein, einsam' (Schenkendorf) (Op. 47, No. 1: J.197). 1816.

Die freien Sänger: 'Vöglein hüpfet' (Förster) (Op. 47, No. 2: J. 198). 1816.

Die Temperamente beim Verluste der Geliebten (Gubitz) (Op. 46: J.200–3). 1816.

  1. *Der Leichtmüthige:* 'Lust entfloh'.

  2. *Der Schwermüthige:* 'Sel'ge Zeiten'.

  3. *Der Liebewüthige:* 'Verrathen!'

  4. *Der Gleichmüthige:* 'Nun, ich bin befreit!'.

Leyer und Schwerdt, Vol. 3 (Körner) (Op. 43: J.205). 1816.

  Bei der Musik des Prinzen Louis Ferdinand von Preussen: 'Düst're Harmonieen hör' ich klingen'.

Alte Weiber: ' 's is nichts mit den alten Weibern' (Nicolai) (Op. 54, No. 5: J.211). 1817.

Liebeslied: 'Ich hab' mir eins erwählet' (trad.) (Op. 54, No. 3: J.212). 1817.

Wunsch und Entsagung: 'Wenn ich die Blümlein schau' ' (Op. 66, No. 4: J.213). 1817.

Das Veilchen im Thale: 'Ein Veilchen blüht' (Kind) (Op. 66, No. 1: J.217). 1817.

Lied der Hirtin: 'Wenn die Maien' (Kind) (Op. 71, No. 5: J.229). 1818.

Gelahrtheit: 'Ich empfinde fast' (Opitz) (Op. 64, No. 4: J.230). 1818.

Volkslied: 'Weine, weine' (trad.) (Op. 54, No. 7: J.231). 1818.

Die fromme Magd: 'Ein' fromme Magd' (Ringwald) (Op. 54, No. 1: J.232). 1818.

Volkslied: 'Wenn ich ein Vöglein wär' ' (trad.) (Op. 54, No. 6: J.233). 1818.

Volkslied: 'Mein Schatzerl is hübsch' (trad.) (Op. 64, No. 1: J.234). 1818.

Heimlicher Liebe Pein: 'Mein Schatz' (trad.) (Op. 64, No. 3: J.235). 1818.

'Rosen im Haare' (Breuer, after Hafiz) (Op. 66, No. 2: J.238). 1818.

Abendsegen: 'Der Tag hat seinen Schmuck' (trad.) (Op. 64, No. 5: J.255). 1819.

Triolett: 'Keine Lust' (Förster) (Op. 71, No. 1: J.256). 1819.

Liebesgruss aus der Ferne: 'Sind wir gescheiden' (trad.) (Op. 64, No. 6: J.257). 1819.

Volkslied: 'Herzchen, mein Schätzchen' (trad.) (Op. 64, No. 8: J.258). 1819.

Das Mädchen an das erste Schneeglöckchen: 'Was bricht hervor' (Gerstenbergk) (Op. 71, No. 3: J.267). 1819.

Sehnsucht (Weihnachtslied): 'Judäa, hochgelobtes Land' (Kannegiesser) (Op. 80, No. 2: J.269). 1819.

Elfenlied: 'Ich tummle mich (Kannegiesser) (Op. 80, No. 3: J.270). 1819.

Schmerz: 'Herz, mein Herz' (Blankensee) (Op. 80, No. 4: J.274). 1820.

An Sie: 'Das war ein recht abscheuliches Gesicht' (Wargentin) (Op. 80, No. 5; J.275). 1820.

Der Sänger und der Maler: 'Ei, wenn ich doch ein Maler wär' ' (anon.) (Op. 80, No. 6: J.278). 1820.

Lied von Clotilde: 'Wenn Kindlein' (Clotilde von Nostitz) (Op. 80, No. 1: J.281). 1821.

Das Licht im Thale: 'Der Gaishirt steht' (Kind) (J.286). 1822.

Romance: 'Elle était simple et gentilette' (Cussy) (J.292). 1824.

Gesang der Nurmahal aus 'Lalla Rookh': 'From Chindara's warbling fount I come' (Moore), piano part reconstructed by Moscheles (J.308). 1826.

VOCAL DUETS WITH PIANO

'Se il mio ben' (anon.), for AA, orig. with instrumental acct. (Op. 31, No. 3: J.107). 1811.

'Mille volte' (anon.), for SS (Op. 31, No. 1: J.123). 1811.

'Va, ti consola' (anon.), for SS (Op. 31, No. 2: J.125). 1811.

Abschied: 'O Berlin, ich muss dich lassen' (trad.), for 2 voices (Op. 54, No. 4: J.208). 1817.

Quodlibet: 'So geht es in Schnützelputz-Häusel' (trad.), for 2 voices (Op. 54, No. 2: J.209). 1817.

Mailied: 'Tra, ri, ro!' (trad.), for 2 voices (Op. 64, No. 2: J.210). 1817.

SOLO INSTRUMENTS AND ORCHESTRA

Romanza Siciliana, for flute (J.47). 1805.

Six Variations on 'A Schüsserl und a Reind'rl', for viola (J.49). 1806.

Grand Pot-Pourri, for cello (Op. 20: J.64). 1808.

Andante and Rondo Ungarese, for viola (J.79, rev. as J.158). 1809.

Variations, for cello (J.94). 1810.

Piano Concerto No. 1 in C (Op. 11: J.98). 1810.

Clarinet Concertino (Op. 26: J.109). 1811.

Clarinet Concerto No. 1 in F minor (Op. 73: J.114). 1811.

Adagio and Rondo, for harmonichord (J.115). 1811.

Clarinet Concerto No. 2 in E♭ (Op. 74: J.118). 1811.

Bassoon Concerto in F (Op. 75: J.127). 1811, rev. 1822.

Piano Concerto No. 2 in E♭ (Op. 32: J.155). 1812.

Andante and Rondo Ungarese, for bassoon (Op. 35: J.158, rev. of J.79). 1813.

Horn Concertino (Op. 45: J.188). 1815.

Konzertstück, for piano (Op. 79: J.282). 1821.

ORCHESTRAL WORKS

Symphony No. 1 in C (Op. 19: J.50). 1807.

Symphony No. 2 in C (J.51). 1807.

Grande Ouverture à plusieurs instruments (Op. 8: J.54).[1] 1807.
Overture: *Der Beherrscher der Geister* (Op. 27: J.122).[2] 1811.
Deutscher (J.185).[3] 1815.
Tedesco (J.191). 1816.
Jubel-Ouvertüre (Op. 59: J.245). 1818.

MUSIC FOR WIND INSTRUMENTS

Tusch, for 20 trumpets (J.47a). 1806.
Waltz, for fl, 2 cl, 2 hn, tpt, 2 fag (J.149). 1812.
Marcia vivace, for 10 trumpets (J.288). 1822.
March, for wind band (J.307).[4] 1826.

CHAMBER MUSIC

Quartet for piano and strings (J.76). 1809.
Quintet for clarinet and strings (Op.34: J.182). 1815.
Trio for flute, cello and piano (Op. 63: J.259). 1819.

SOLO INSTRUMENTS AND PIANO

Nine variations on a Norwegian air, for violin and piano (Op. 22: J.61). 1808.
Six Progressive Sonatas, for piano and violin (J.99–104). 1810.
Seven variations on a theme from *Silvana*, for clarinet and piano (Op. 33: J.128). 1811.
Grand Duo Concertant, for piano and clarinet (Op. 48: J.204). 1816.
Divertimento assai facile, for guitar and piano (Op. 38: J.207). 1816.

PIANO SOLO

Six variations on an original theme (Op. 2: J.7). 1800.
Twelve Allemandes (Op. 4: J.15–26). 1801.
Six Ecossaises (J.29–34). 1802.
Eight variations on a theme from Vogler's *Castor et Pollux* (Op. 5: J.40). 1804.
Six variations on a theme from Vogler's *Samori*, with violin and cello ad. lib. (Op. 6: J.43). 1804.
Seven variations on Bianchi's 'Vien quà, Dorina bella' (Op. 7: J.53). 1807.
Seven variations on an original theme (Op. 9: J.55). 1808.
Momento capriccioso (Op. 12: J.56). 1808.
Grande Polonaise (Op. 21: J.59). 1808.
Piano Sonata No. 1 in C (Op. 24: J.138). 1812.
Seven variations on a theme from Méhul's *Joseph* (Op. 28: J.141). 1812.
Six Favourite Waltzes of the Queen of France, Marie Louise (J.143–8). 1812.
Variations on a Russian theme ('Schöne Minka') (Op. 40: J.179). 1815.
Piano Sonata No. 2 in A♭ (Op. 39: J.199). 1816.

[1] Revision of *Peter Schmoll* overture (J.8, 1801).

[2] Revision of lost *Rübezahl* overture (1805).

[3] Arrangement of song in *Der travestirte Aeneas* (J.184, 1815).

[4] Also arr. for SATTB chorus and orchestra. Revision of No. 5 of *Six Petites Pièces Faciles* (J.13, 1801).

Piano Sonata No. 3 in D minor (Op. 49: J.206). 1816.
Seven variations on a gipsy song (Op. 55: J.219). 1817.
Rondo Brillante ('La Gaité') (Op. 62: J.252). 1819.
Aufforderung zum Tanze (Op. 65: J.260). 1819.
Polacca Brillante ('L'Hilarité') (Op. 72: J.268). 1819.
Piano Sonata No. 4 in E minor (Op. 70: J.287). 1822.

PIANO DUET

Six Petites Pièces Faciles (Op. 3: J.9–14). 1801.
Six Pieces (Op. 10: J.81–6). 1809.
Eight Pieces (Op. 60: J.236, 242, 248, 253, 254, 264, 265, 266). 1819.

MISCELLANEOUS

Six Fughettas (Op. 1: J.1–6). 1798.
[*Strafpredigt über die französiche Musik*]: 'Französ'sche Musika' (? composer:
musical comment in a letter), unacc. 1801.
[*Komisches musikalisches Sendschreiben*]: 'Theuerster Herr Kapellmeister' (com-
poser: musical greeting to Danzi), for voice with figured bass (J.60). 1808.
Unaccompanied melody, for clarinet (J.119). 1811.
Canon: 'Prost Neujahr!' (? composer: burlesque musical greeting in a letter to
Gänsbacher), for 34 voices and 74 F♯ trumpets (*sic*) (Hirschberg 29). 1811.
Four Solfeggi, for voice (J.Anh.67–70). 1818.
Music and Song, 'Du hohe Rautenzweig', for prologue by Theodor Hell on the
marriage of Prince Friedrich August and the Grand Duchess Caroline (J.271).
(See also Arrangements, 1819.)
Fragment of an unknown work, melody only (J.Anh.4). 1823.
[*Vatergruss*]: 'Du gute, gute Mäzze' (composer: greeting to his son Max Maria
in a letter to Caroline) (Hirschberg 68). 1823.

ARRANGEMENTS

Piano score of Vogler's opera *Samori* (J.39). 1803.
Instrumentation (for wind instruments) of four songs by Duke August of Gotha
(J.150–3). 1812.
 1. 'Ihr kleinen Vögelein'.
 2. 'Lebe wohl, mein süsses Leben'.
 3. 'Die verliebte Schäferin'.
 4. 'Beim kindlichen Strahl'.
Arrangement and orchestration of Weigl's Duet, 'Ein jeder Geck', in Fischer's
Singspiel, *Die Verwandlungen* (*oder Der travestirte Aeneas*), for 2 sopranos and
orchestra (J.162). 1814.
Arrangement and orchestration of anonymous Ariette, 'Ihr holden Blumen', in
Fischer's *Singspiel, Die Verwandlungen,* for soprano and orchestra (J.163). 1814.
Orchestration of Paer's Recitative and Cavatine, 'Von dir entfernt', in Méhul's
Héléna, for soprano and orchestra (J.215). 1817.
Orchestration of Nasolini's Recitative and Duet, 'Ja, liebe', in Méhul's *Héléna,* for
soprano, tenor and orchestra (J.216). 1817.

Melody of 'God Save the King'.
  1. 'Den König segne Gott' (anon.), for TTBB (J.247). ?1818.
  2. 'Heil dir im Siegekranz' (anon.), for TTBB (Hirschberg 56). ?1818.
  3. 'Du hoher Rautenzweig' (anon.), for SATB and 6 wind (J.271). 1819.
  (See also Miscellaneous, and in *Jubel-Ouvertüre*.)

Ten Scottish National Songs, for voice with preludes and accompaniments for
  flute, violin, cello and piano (J.295–304). 1825.
  1. 'The soothing shades of gloaming' (Pringle).
  2. *The Troubadour:* 'Glowing with love' (Scott).
  3. 'O poortith cauld' (Burns).
  4. *Bonny Dundee:* 'True-hearted was he' (Burns).
  5. 'Yes, thou may'st walk' (Richardson).
  6. 'A soldier am I' (Smyth).
  7. 'John Anderson, my jo' (Burns).
  8. 'O my luve's like the red, red rose' (Burns).
  9. 'Robin is my joy, my dear' (Vedder).
  10. 'Whar hae ye been a' day' (Machnell).

BIBLIOGRAPHY

The most complete list of writings on Weber runs to nearly 100 pages; this is Hans Dünnebeil: *Schriftum über Carl Maria von Weber* (4th edn., 1957). There is also a very full and detailed bibliography in Lucy and Richard Poate Stebbins: *Enchanted Wanderer* (1940); this includes a number of references not in Dünnebeil, and the two lists should be used in conjunction with each other. Rather than summarize the very large number of critical studies etc. listed in these bibliographies, I have concentrated here on some notes on the sources.

The principal source material for the life of Weber consists of his diary, his letters and his miscellaneous writings. Weber kept a diary from 26th February 1810 until 3rd June 1826. It comprises an extremely detailed record of his day to day life, his actions and thoughts, notes on the progress of works, even his petty cash accounts. The diary eventually filled seven volumes, written in the spidery hand whose deciphering is sometimes a problem even to experts, and against Weber's wishes was preserved intact by Caroline Weber after his death. It has been transcribed by Franz Zapf, of the Hosterwitz *Weber-Gedenkstätte*, though at the time of writing (1967) it still awaits publication in more than scattered excerpts. The annotated register of Prague productions has also survived, and is in the Library of the Rudolfinum, Prague.

No substantial general collection has yet been made of Weber's voluminous, vivid and highly informative correspondence. The principal special collections are as follows.

Reise-Briefe von CMvW an seine Gattin Carolina (ed. Carl von Weber, 1886).
Covers the 1823 visit to Vienna and the London visit.
Briefe von CMvW an Hinrich Lichtenstein (ed. Ernst Rudorff, 1900).
Briefe von CMvW an der Grafen Carl von Brühl (ed. Georg Kaiser, 1911).
77 bisher ungedruckte Briefe CMvWs (ed. Leopold Hirschberg, 1926).

Weber's other writings were first assembled by Theodor Hell in *Hinterlassene Schriften von CMvW* (3 vols., 1828). However, the most comprehensive and practical edition, fully annotated, is Georg Kaiser: *Sämtliche Schriften von CMvW* (1908).

The standard thematic catalogue of Weber's music is F. W. Jähns: *CMvW in seinen Werken. Chronologisch-thematisches Verzeichniss seiner sämmtlichen Compositionen* (1871). Based on the example of Köchel's Mozart catalogue, this adds much personal comment to very full factual details. There is a useful little summarized catalogue by Hans Dünnebeil: *CMvW. Verzeichnis seiner Compositionen* (1947), and by the same author a comparative chronological table of Weber's life and contemporary events, *CMvW: Leben und Werken dargestellt in chronologischer Tafel* (1953). Jähns also collected a very large amount of MSS, printed scores, documents, books, letters, pictures, playbills, mementoes and other relevant material, and drew up an elaborate catalogue, *Weberiana*. All this material, with other items subsequently added, is lodged in the special *Weber-Gedächtniszimmer* in the State Library, Berlin. Some personal belongings, pictures and other material are kept in the *Weber-Gedenkstätte* in the composer's former country house at Hosterwitz, outside Dresden.

Almost all Weber's music has at some time been in print. Two collections of unusual material are of special note. Leopold Hirschberg: *Reliquienschrein des Meisters CMvW* (1926) prints 73 rare pieces—all that at the time remained unpublished except for the *Jugendmesse*, *Peter Schmoll* and *L'Accoglienza*. In the same anniversary year of Weber's death, 1926, a complete edition was begun, *CMvW: Musikalische Werke. Erste Kritische Gesamtausgabe*. Under Hans Joachim Moser, this was planned with a group of editors that included Strauss and Pfitzner as well as leading musicologists, but never progressed beyond two volumes devoted to the youthful operas.

Upon the original source material, as well as his family information, Weber's son Max Maria von Weber based a preliminary study of his father's life that led to *CMvW. Ein Lebensbild* (3 vols., 1864–6: Vol. 3 is a collection of Weber's writings). Though in various respects inaccurate and forgivably biassed, it remains an indispensable and highly readable source. The English version by J. Palgrave Simpson: *CMvW. The Life of an Artist* (2 vols., 1865) is abbreviated, distorted and very inaccurate.

Some of the more important first-hand accounts of Weber are included in the following works by his contemporaries:

Julius Benedict	*CMvW* (1881).
Helmina von Chezy	*Unvergessenes* (1858).
Wilhelm von Chezy	*Erinnerungen aus meinem Leben* (1863–4).
C. L. Costenoble	*Tagebücher* (1912).
August Schmidt	*Denksteine* (1848). The section on Gänsbacher includes most of his unpublished autobiography.
Eduard Genast	*Erinnerungen eines alten Schauspielers*, ed. R. Kohlrausch (n.d.).
F. W. Gubitz	*Bilder aus Romantik und Biedermeier. Erlebnisse*, ed. P. Frederick (1922).
Heinrich Heine	Sämtliche Werke, ed. Gerich, Vol. 2 (1925).
Fanny Kemble	*Record of a Girlhood* (1878).
J. C. Lobe	'Gespräche mit Weber': an essay frequently reprinted, most accessibly in *Consonanzen und Dissonanzen* (1869).
Felix Moscheles	*Life of Moscheles by his wife*, ed. A. D. Coleridge (1873).
J. R. Planché	*Recollections and Reflections*, Vol. 1 (1872).
George Smart	*Leaves from the Journals of Sir George Smart*, ed. H. B. and C. L. E. Cox (1907).
Louis Spohr	*Selbstbiographie* (1860–1; trans. 1865 and 1878).
Richard Wagner	*Mein Leben* (1911; trans. 1911).

A number of other references will be found as footnotes to the main part of the present book, where mention is also made of some of the most useful critical studies dealing with special aspects of Weber's life and work. Two essential studies of Weber's work as an opera director must be added to the exhaustive lists compiled by Dünnebeil and Stebbins. Zdeněk Němec: *Weberova Pražska Léta* (*Weber's Prague Years*) documents the relevant period thoroughly and includes the only publication of the complete Prague opera register; this section, although translated into Czech, is usable by those with even a minimal knowledge of the language. Wolfgang Becker: *Die deutsche Oper in Dresden unter der Leitung von CMvW, 1817–1826* (1962) documents this period thoroughly and critically.

The best general critical studies of Weber are as follows (all are in German except for Spitta (English) and Coeuroy (French)).

André Coeuroy   *Weber* (1925).

Erwin Kroll   *CMvW* (1934). The best general study, well illustrated.

Hans Schnoor   *Weber auf dem Welttheater* (1943). Concentrates on *Der Freischütz* and its later career.

Hans Schnoor   *Weber. Gestalt und Schöpfung* (1953). Concentrates on Weber in Dresden.

Karl Laux   *CMvW* (1965). A useful short paperback study for a projected longer work.

Philipp Spitta   Weber entry in the first four editions of *Grove's Dictionary*; the 5th abbreviates this.

INDEX

Weber's works are indexed under the entry for Weber himself